Post-Anarchism

T0317507

POST-ANARCHISM

A Reader

Edited by
Duane Rousselle and Süreyyya Evren

Fernwood Publishing
HALIFAX & WINNIPEG
www.fernwoodpublishing.ca

First published 2011 by Pluto Press
345 Archway Road, London N6 5AA
www.plutobooks.com

Published in Canada by Fernwood Publishing
32 Oceanvista Lane, Black Point, Nova Scotia, B0J 1B0
and 748 Broadway Avenue, Winnipeg, MB R3G 0X3
www.fernwoodpublishing.ca

Fernwood Publishing Company Limited gratefully acknowledges the financial support of the
Government of Canada through the Canada Book Fund, the Canada Council for the Arts, the
Nova Scotia Department of Tourism and Culture and the Province of Manitoba, through the
Book Publishing Tax Credit, for our publishing program.

Library and Archives Canada Cataloguing in Publication
Post anarchism : a reader / Duane Rouselle, Süreyyya Evren
Includes bibliographical references and index
ISBN 978–1–55266–433–9

1. Anarchism. I. Rouselle, Duane, 1982–   II. Evren, Süreyyya, 1972–
HX833.P68 2010   335'.83   C2010–907567–6

Copyright © Duane Rousselle and Süreyyya Evren 2011

British Library Cataloguing in Publication Data
A catalogue record for this book is available from the British Library

ISBN   978 0 7453 3087 7   Hardback
ISBN   978 0 7453 3086 0   Paperback (Pluto Press)
ISBN   978 1-55266 433 9   Paperback (Fernwood)

Library of Congress Cataloging in Publication Data applied for

10   9   8   7   6   5   4   3   2   1

Designed and produced for Pluto Press by
Chase Publishing Services Ltd, 33 Livonia Road, Sidmouth, EX10 9JB, England
Typeset from disk by Stanford DTP Services, Northampton, England
Printed and bound by CPI Group (UK) Ltd, Croydon, CR0 4YY

Contents

Preface

Post-anarchism has been of considerable importance in the discussions of radical intellectuals across the globe in the last decade. In its most popular form, it demonstrates a desire to blend the most promising aspects of traditional anarchist theory (centrally, the attitude of hostility in the face of representation) with developments in post-structuralist and postmodern thought. However, since its inception, it has also posed a broader challenge to the reification of anarchist theory. It might be argued, as Lewis Call suggests in this book, that today 'a kind of post-anarchist moment has arrived'; whether or not this moment marks the final becomings of a vanishing philosophical mediator whereby what used to be explicitly regarded as 'post-anarchism' has simply become 'anarchism' (post-anarchism without its defining critique against 'traditional anarchism') is a matter for future investigation. However, I remain convinced that post-anarchism is the radical contemporary equivalent of the traditional anarchist discourse which, without proper force and direction, remains as impotent or as strong as traditional anarchism ever has been. In this sense, I would suggest that post-anarchism is simply another word to describe a paradigm shift that erupted at the broader level of anarchist philosophy and which has yet to be fully developed on the streets.

Post-anarchism decentralizes the political movement, motions toward tactical rather than strategic action, brings anarchist thought into touch with a range of influences (in this sense post-anarchism reflects a 'cultural studies' approach) and provides the foundation for a thousand lines of flight; post-anarchism brings traditional anarchism into new relationships with the outside world. I believe that it is only those anarchists who speak within the broader trend of post-anarchism, a trend which is situated uniquely in the present context, who are capable of grappling with today's issues. Today's anarchists may not be post-structuralist but they surely embody the element of post-structuralism's critique and the presumption of its focus in various ways. The book that you are holding aims to demonstrate this point.

The post-anarchists have been under attack. The brunt of this attack emerges from other anarchists who argue that the post-anarchists have too hastily declared a new tradition for themselves through highly selective and reductive readings of the traditional literature. This is the critique of the post-anarchist reduction of traditional anarchist literature. A second and emerging critique is that the post-anarchists have given up on the notion of 'class' and have retreated into obscure and intoxicating academic diatribes against a tradition built of discursive straw. In any case, it is without any question that post-anarchism has proved itself worth a second look: if one considers oneself a radical today, one will have to exercise extreme caution to avoid the force and influence of the post-anarchists. One need not be a post-anarchist to appreciate what post-anarchism has to offer and the condition it seeks to explain; it is in this spirit of exploration and possibility that I offer, with Süreyyya Evren, *Post-Anarchism: A Reader*. And for making these essays accessible to the wider public and to an anarchist-sympathetic readership, we make absolutely no apologies.

Our aim in this book is to offer readers the most comprehensive and up-to-date collection of post-anarchist material at an affordable price and in an accessible way in order to re-stimulate debates about its importance as a general movement of thought. My hope is that this book will help to resolve lingering tensions about the discourse through which post-anarchists are often accused of speaking (what Lacan has called the 'discourse of the university'). Likewise, many anarchist academics are suspicious of the prefix 'post-'. The range of perspectives brought together in this volume demonstrates that there is diversity within post-anarchism and that critics should be made aware of their own reduction of the 'post-anarchist' body of thought.

What will surely be regarded as an academic pursuit by practising anarchists, and what will no doubt be regarded as an anarchist pursuit by thinking academics, has ostensibly been resolved into a mutual rejection of sorts. Here, one should be careful to distinguish academic writing from academic patronage (writing from the academy should in all cases be distinguished from writing *for* the academy) – a conflation that is very often assumed rather than argued convincingly. My best advice is to take what one finds useful in the post-anarchist literature and to dispose of what one finds to be in the service of the 'university'; here, we can only offer the tools and it is your job to build your own shelter.

Duane Rousselle

Acknowledgements

Duane Rousselle: I would like to thank Jason Adams for his invaluable assistance in providing the needed infrastructure and motivation for this project; Aragorn! for his friendship and support in pursuing this and other projects; Süreyyya Evren for partaking in long late-night discussions about post-anarchism and for his support and effort during the tiresome editing process; Uri Gordon, Saul Newman and Stevphen Shukaitis for offering advice and direction; Richard J.F. Day, who rescued me from three narrowly avoided disasters; Mohammed Jean-Veneuse for teaching me the value and meaning of friendship; the Department of Sociology at the University of New Brunswick for their kind donation of $50 toward reprint/permissions costs for this book; the Faculty of Arts at the University of New Brunswick for their kind donation of $150 toward reprint/permissions costs for this book; Pluto Press (especially David Castle and Will Viney), who have been supportive and more than a pleasure to work with; all contributors for believing in the project and making this book happen, especially those who worked with me to produce original material; and, lastly, but surely not least, Joady Jardine, my dancing star, for her endless encouragement and inspiration.

Süreyyya Evren: I would like to thank my post-anarchist comrades in Turkey, especially Erden Kosova and Bülent Usta, who have been with me for the last 15 years, helping to transform my post-anarchist politics into a general approach to culture; all the world post-anarchists I have met in person; Jason Adams, Saul Newman and Lewis Call for their commitment to post-anarchist philosophy despite the rise of debates; and Duane Rousselle for never giving up with this project. I would also like to thank Ruth Kinna and Dave Berry from Loughborough University for making it possible for me to work on all of these subjects within an embracing academic environment and for always being there whenever I needed advice; my 'anti-post-anarchist' comrade Alex Pritchard for always keeping the anarchist collective spirit up; and Matt Wilson, the anti-taboo anarchist in Loughborough, for all of his support and friendship. Lastly, to everyone waiting for the party we will have in my home when the book hits the shelves: my little ones, Yaz and Ada, and my dear Neval ...

Introduction
How New Anarchism Changed the World (of Opposition) after Seattle and Gave Birth to Post-Anarchism

Süreyyya Evren

Anarchism is widely accepted as 'the' movement behind the main organizational principles of the radical social movements in the twenty-first century. The rise of the 'anti-globalization' movement has been linked to a general resurgence of anarchism. This movement was colourful, energetic, creative, effective and 'new'. And credit for most of this creative energy went to anarchism (Graeber, 2002: 1). Anarchism appeared to be taking back its name as a political philosophy and movement from the connotations and metaphors of chaos and violence. The mainstream media strategy of focusing exclusively on the black bloc tactic, unfortunately, only reproduced these connotations[1], but it also helped to attract more attention toward the political thinkers and activists who understood what all this fuss was about. In turn, more scholarly and political works on anarchism and the new 'movement' emerged.

We generally use quotation marks when referring to the 'anti-globalization movement' because there is no one single author of the movement who would give it an official name; also, the activists and groups involved did not reach a consensus in naming the movement. It has been referred to as the Global Justice Movement, the Movement of Movements, the Movement, the Alter-Globalization Movement, the Radical Social Change Movement, Contemporary Radical Activism, the Anti-Capitalist Movement, the Anti-Corporate Movement, the Global Anti-Capitalist Protest Movement, the Counter-Globalization Movement, the Anti-Corporate-Globalization Movement, the Grassroots Globalization Movement. The discontent most of the activists felt with the term 'anti-globalization' was first of all grounded on the fact that it was coined by the 'enemy' (a 'Wall Street term' or a term coined by the corporate media) to label the activists as outmoded, blind, self-referential youngsters spitting against the wind (the unstoppable globalization) for no valid reason other than the joy of damaging property. And activists also objected to the term because they were not opposed to globalization per se (cf. Conway, 2003).

On the other hand, the left has historically found strategic value in the recuperation of pejorative labels. As Kropotkin points out, the term anarchism itself is a close example of this trend. Kropotkin was hearing critiques concerning the connotations of anarchy as, in common language, 'disorder' and 'chaos', and he was instructed that it was not a very wise idea to use the term 'anarchism' for a political philosophy and movement (Kropotkin, n.d.: 1). In this short essay, which was first published in *Le revolte* on 1 October 1881, Kropotkin embraced the term 'anarchy'. He made reference to the 'beggars' of Brabant who didn't make up their own name (referring to the Dutch Sea beggars: Dutch rebels against the Spanish regime in the late sixteenth century) and the 'Sans-culottes' of 1793, referring to the French revolution:

> It was the enemies of the popular revolution who coined this name; but it too summed up a whole idea – that of the rebellion of the people, dressed in rage, tired of poverty, opposed to all those royalists, the so-called patriots and Jacobins, the well-dressed and the smart, those who, despite their pompous speeches and the homage paid to them by bourgeois historians, were the real enemies of the people, profoundly despising them for their poverty, for their libertarian and egalitarian spirit, and for their revolutionary enthusiasm.

Borrowing the same spirit, here, we prefer to use the term 'anti-globalization movement'. Still, we should keep in mind that the term is used in a way that implies a resentment of global capitalism or the global neo-liberalist agenda.

The relationship between anarchism and the anti-globalization movement has been mutual; on the one hand, anarchism was the defining orientation of prominent activist networks and it was the 'principal point of reference for radical social change movements' (Gordon, 2007: 29). Thus anarchism was providing the anti-globalization movement with organization principles that were tested well in advance. And on the other hand, the 'anarchistic' rise of anti-globalization, the popularity it gained and the major role it played in the first years of twenty-first-century radical politics, through an open embracing of anarchistic notions and the massive incorporation of anarchist activists within the wider movement, was 'widely regarded as a sign of anarchism's revival' (Kinna, 2007: 67); as Gordon puts it, 'the past ten years have seen the full-blown revival of anarchism, as a global social movement and coherent set of political discourses, on a scale and to levels of unity and diversity unseen since the 1930s' (2007: 29). A tradition that has been 'hitherto mostly dismissed' required a respectful engagement with it (Graeber, 2002: 1). Simply put, the anti-globalization movement brought anarchism back to the table. In Todd May's words: 'Anarchism is back on the scene' (May, 2009: 1).

The dominant position Marxism previously occupied as 'the' left political philosophy and movement was openly questioned and becoming unstable – indeed, Marxism was challenged by the anti-globalization movement beyond the confines of the variant employed within the USSR. Anarchism, as a form of political theory and practice, has been unseating Marxism to a large extent. There were forms of anarchist resistance and organization appearing everywhere in society: 'from anti-capitalist social centres and eco-feminist communities to raucous street parties and blockades of international summits, anarchist forms of resistance and organizing have been at the heart of the "alternative globalization" movement' (Gordon, 2007: 29). Anarchism was 'the heart of the movement', 'its soul; the source of most of what [was] new and hopeful about it' (Graeber, 2002: 1):

> The model for the kind of political and social autonomy that the anti-capitalist movement aspires to is an anarchist one, and the soul of the anti-capitalist movement is anarchist; its non-authoritarian make-up, its disavowal of traditional parties of the left, and its commitment to direct action are firmly in the spirit of libertarian socialism. (Sheehan, 2003: 12)

So, at first, it was anarchists and the principles of traditional anarchism that served as the organizing principle of the new and emergent anti-globalization movement. In turn, the emergent movement served both as a global platform for testing anarchist principles in the new conditions of world politics, and as an Archimedes' lever that largely displaced Marxism and brought anarchism to the attention of activists and academics worldwide, making anarchism recognized again.[2] It led to an 'almost unparalleled opportunity to extend the influence of their (anarchists') ideas' (Kinna, 2005: 155); and at the level of theory, it not only gave rise to anarchist-influenced research but it also fostered a specifically 'contemporary' anarchist theory. It was a new opportunity for anarchists to rethink anarchistic social theory. We witnessed growing numbers of scholarly publications and events on anarchism (Purkis and Bowen, 2004; Cohn, 2006a; Moore and Sunshine, 2004; Day, 2005; Kissack, 2008; Anderson, 2005; Antliff, 2007).

But this empowered, updated 'contemporary' anarchism was not a reincarnation of nineteenth-century anarchism from the days of the First International or the 1934 Spanish anarchist revolution. Rather, this was something 'new': there was a consensus that this was an anarchism re-emerging – it was, certainly, 'a kind of anarchism'. But which kind?

Soon after David Graeber's article 'The New Anarchists' was published in one of the most prominent Marxist-oriented journals, *New Left Review*, the term had become widely accepted.[3] For example, Sean Sheehan began his introductory book *Anarchism* (Sheehan, 2003) with a chapter titled 'Global Anarchism: The New Anarchism'. A book which was supposed to cover anarchism as a political philosophy and movement began with detailed accounts of the 'Battle of Seattle', the legendary protest against the World Trade Organization (WTO) in November 1999 (Sheehan, 2003: 7–23). And of course, when the term was used among activist circles, it was not necessarily a reference to David Graeber's use of it in his *New Left Review* article. The expression 'new anarchists' enjoyed a 'wider usage within contemporary anarchist scenes' (Gee, 2003: 3).

The main 'newness' of the 'new anarchism' was basically its spectrum of references. All the anarchistic principles employed were defined as a consequence of actual activist experiences. There was no intention to describe the movement as an application of an anarchist theory (which is itself a fundamental anarchistic attitude). For Graeber, the anti-globalization movement is about creating new forms of organization. It is not lacking in ideology. Those new forms of organization are its ideology. It is about creating and enacting horizontal networks instead of top-down structures like states, parties or corporations; networks based on principles of decentralized, non-hierarchical consensus democracy. (Graeber, 2002: 70)

Nevertheless, Uri Gordon offers an analysis of 'present-day anarchist ideology from a movement-driven approach' (Gordon, 2007: 29). It is no surprise that in the ideological core of contemporary anarchism[4] he finds an 'open-ended, experimental approach to revolutionary visions and strategies' (Gordon, 2007: 29).

This open-endedness gave 'new anarchism' an additional elusiveness which later contributed to its rupture from 'classical anarchism'. 'Classical anarchism' is another controversial term and it is positioned as a fixed ideology that is represented through the work of a select band of nineteenth-century anarchist writers; even these writers' thoughts are reduced to certain clusters of ideas that only help to confirm prejudices about the 'classical anarchists'. The discussions surrounding the ideas concerning the 'new' versus 'classical' anarchism were even understood as a part of the 'conceptual and material evidence' of 'a paradigm shift within anarchism' (Purkis and Bowen, 2004: 5).

In many cases, this was translated into a debate formulated as 'post-' versus 'classical' anarchism. Mostly, this contemporary need to reposition anarchism fostered all the new studies and discussions on post-anarchism. Post-anarchism was largely understood in the framework of 'new'/'post-' versus 'classical' anarchism. There was a 'close fit between' the 'new' anarchism's 'system of coordination' and the way 'post-anarchism' refers to post-structuralism 'on how to build a left that embodies its own values'. '[A] left whose values are immanent is a left that thrives without authority and repression, and rids itself of both inward- and outward-directed ressentiment' (Kang, 2005: 90). Part 2 of our book, 'Post-Anarchism Hits the Streets', explores 'on the ground' post-anarchist practice. Tadzio Mueller's contribution is especially crucial here because it illustrates the problems and possibilities within the everyday politics of the movement. Richard Day's contribution is exemplary in exploring the political logic of what he calls the 'newest' social movements and in discussing the largely declining role of the logic of hegemony for today's (after the year 2000) activism. Jason Adams, a seminal figure in the short history of post-anarchism, takes the hegemony debate further in his chapter 'The Constellation of Opposition', and pinpoints Seattle (N30) as a decisive event in the development of contemporary practices of resistance.

Post-anarchism's relationship to the anti-globalization movements is also confirmed by two of the most prominent writers associated with post-anarchism in the English-speaking world, Saul Newman and Todd May. During interviews conducted by the Turkish post-anarchist magazine *Siyahi*, both agreed that the 'post-Seattle anti-globalization movements' 'absolutely' and 'certainly' had parallel motives with post-structuralist anarchy/post-anarchism. May lists 'similar ideas informing both movements': 'irreducible struggles, local politics and alliances, an ethical orientation, a resistance to essentialist thinking'.[5] Newman goes even further, and while emphasizing the parallel motives between the anti-globalization movement and post-anarchism, he draws upon his definition of post-anarchism:

> Post-anarchism is a political logic that seeks to combine the egalitarian and emancipative aspects of classical anarchism, with an acknowledgement that radical political struggles today are contingent, pluralistic, open to different identities and perspectives, and are over different issues – not just economic ones. (Newman, 2004)

Here Newman defines post-anarchism as an attempt to combine insights from classical anarchism with new anarchist epistemologies. But on the other hand it is possible to argue that post-anarchism is actually an attempt to create the theoretical equivalent of the anti-globalization movements. The rise of debates on post-anarchism is directly linked to the post-Seattle spirit of the anti-globalization movements. Theoretical attempts to marry post-structuralism/postmodernism and anarchism in various ways were suddenly embraced by activist-oriented scholars worldwide. Not because similarities between certain aspects of classical anarchist thought and post-structuralist theories created excitement, but because post-structuralism was so related to the rhizomatic character of the new anarchism that is shaking the foundations of the globe. If its 'form of organization' was the real ideology of the new global movement, then it was extremely likely that scholars would begin to link the features of this ideology to post-structuralist theory, and thus understand the practices of the 'movement' as rooted in a post-structuralist perspective. However, the turning of post-anarchism into an 'ism' – a current among the family of various anarchisms – owes much to the web site and email list created by Jason Adams.

Adams started the email listserv as a Yahoo! Group on 9 October 2002. He made an informative web page dedicated to the subject on February of 2003 and then changed his email listserv service provider to the Spoon Collective. The tone of the email exchanges at that time reflected a certain youthful excitement.[6] Adams himself was an activist–academician who had spent the entire year organizing the WTO protests in Seattle, where he was living at the time. He also played an important role by organizing the N30 International Day of Action Committee which set up the primary web site and international email listserv that was used to promote coordinated action against the WTO worldwide. The WTO protests were the real turning point for him; it was during this time that he began to move towards embracing 'post-anarchism'. In his essay 'Post-Anarchism in a Nutshell',[7] he gave a short description of post-anarchism and outlined what it was all about and what constituted its theoretical lineage (Adams, 2003). Adams understands post-structuralism as a radically anti-authoritarian theory that emerged from the anarchistic movements of May 1968 and which developed over three decades, finally emerging in the form of an explicit body of thought: 'post-anarchism'. This in turn informed and extended the theory and practice of one of its primary roots (traditional anarchism).

This positioning of post-structuralism is not as peripheral as it would first seem. Julian Bourg, for example, sees an ethical turn through the legacy of May 1968. Depicting May 1968 as the 'implicit ethics of liberation', he saw a continuity of ethical debates that began with May 1968 and continued into the 1970s with 'French theory' (Bourg, 2007: 7):

> The ethics of liberation [...] emerged in those social spaces where class-based revolutionary – and even reformist – politics were judged insufficient. For example, the popular statement 'the personal is political' was in essence eminently ethical; 1968 itself implied an ethics, the ethics of liberation, with both critical and affirmative sides. (Ibid.: 6)

What Bourg calls 'an ethics of liberation' has always been the primary concern of anarchists in revolutionary/political action and theory. That's why prefigurative politics have been one of the touchstones of anarchism. According to Bourg, the activists of May 1968 were arguing that freedom was not free enough, equality was not equitable enough and imagination was not imaginative enough (ibid.: 7). The connection suggested by Bourg is about the historical roots of ethical concerns within 'French thought' that goes back to the social movements and activism of May 1968. Bourg argues that Deleuze and Guattari's *Anti-Oedipus* brought to the fore the ethical antinomian spirit of 1968 and concretized a broader cultural ambience of post-1968 antinomianism (ibid.: 106–7). When Bourg lists the values of the May 1968 movement, anyone familiar with anti-globalization movements, anarchism and French theory, would easily see parallels: 'imagination, human interest, communication, conviviality, expression, enjoyment, freedom, spontaneity, solidarity, de-alienation, speaking out, dialogue, non-utility, utopia, dreams, fantasies, community, association, antiauthoritarianism, self-management, direct democracy, equality, self-representation, fraternity and self-defence' (Bourg, 2007: 7).

Douglas Kellner also sees this connection as an obvious one:

> Thus, in place of the revolutionary rupture in the historical continuum that 1968 had tried to produce, nascent postmodern theory in France postulated an epochal [...] break with modern politics and modernity, accompanied by models of new postmodern theory and politics. Hence, the postmodern turn in France in the 1970s is intimately connected to the experiences of May 1968. The passionate intensity and spirit of critique in many versions of French postmodern theory is a continuation of the spirit of 1968. [...] Indeed, Baudrillard, Lyotard, Virilio, Derrida, Castoriadis, Foucault, Deleuze, Guattari and other French theorists associated with postmodern theory were all participants in May 1968. They shared its revolutionary [...] and radical aspirations, and they attempted to develop new modes

of radical thought that carried on in a different historical conjuncture the radicalism of the 1960s. (Kellner, 2001: xviii)

Kellner's interpretation of the general flow of May 1968 in terms of 'postmodern theory', Bourg's emphasis on post-structuralist works as concretized forms of the spirit of 1968 and Adams' way of locating post-anarchism as post-structuralism finally coming back to its roots (i.e. the spirit of May 1968 found in contemporary anti-capitalist movements which are equally anti-author-itarian) show a fruitful 'family tree' for post-anarchism. Instead of taking post-structuralism as a separate body of thought apart from activism in general and specifically apart from anarchism as something that can be or should be rethought in combination with activism/anarchism, here in Adams' approach we see a historical tracing of post-structuralism following the contexts in which it was created. And he finally depicts post-structuralism as a continuation and theoretical equivalent of anarchistic activism since the 1960s.

Todd May wrote his *The Political Philosophy of the Poststructuralist Anarchism* in 1994, well before the Battle of Seattle – 'five days that shook the world', as the title of one collection has it (Cockburn and St. Clair, 2000). Andrew Koch's early article 'Poststructuralism and the Epistemological Basis of Anarchism' was also one of the first attempts at a scholarly marriage of post-structuralism and anarchism. Part 1 of our book, 'When Anarchism Met Post-Structuralism', is a collection of some of the main pieces which should be regarded as the first attempts to think anarchism together with post-structur-alism; this phase of post-anarchism was concerned primarily with exploring the possibilities for a convergence. Koch's chapter and May's book were not embraced with great enthusiasm when they were first published; similarly, Hakim Bey's 'Post-Anarchism Anarchy' was not thought to be among this frame of thinking in the 1990s. They were, rather, discoveries of the post-anarchism that emerged after Seattle. One of the first scholarly attempts to formulate a 'post-anarchist' body of thought, in the mid 1990s, came from Saul Newman, who continued to work on the politics of post-anarchism, took part in debates, clarified and defended his own approach to post-anarchism quite extensively, and was therefore seen as the representative of a theoretically distinguished domain of political theory. Thus, his chapter, 'Post-Anarchism and Radical Politics Today', is an important formulation of this standpoint.

Nevertheless, this also made Newman a victim of rather harsh criticism from anarchist circles for undermining the fathers of anarchism. But it was Andrew Koch who ought to be held 'responsible' for starting the stream of post-anarchist reductions of the classical anarchist tradition. He argued that the eighteenth- and nineteenth-century anarchists' attacks on the state were based on a 'rational' representation of human nature (Koch, 1993: 328); this claim played an important role in categorizing classical anarchism as essentialist – anarchist responses to prominent post-anarchists of the English-speaking world frequently responded to this claim by demonstrating that there were different understandings of human nature in the traditional texts. However, Koch, with the help of the post-structuralist literature, was aiming to 'assist in the construction of an epistemologically grounded defence of anarchism' (ibid.: 328): he argued that post-structuralism conveys a logic of opposition by demonstrating how political oppression is linked to the larger cultural processes of knowledge production and cultural representation. He thereby defended uniqueness and diversity, demonstrating that post-structuralism stands against any totalizing conception of being (ibid.: 348).

Koch was offering post-structuralism as a new opportunity, as a new toolbox, to reformulate the claims of anarchism in a way that would rescue it from its rational conceptualization of human nature. This 'good intention' was not appreciated by all anarchists though. Benjamin Franks, for example, pointed out that Newman's (actually it was Koch's as well) '"salvaging" of anarchism was not only unnecessary but also potentially misleading', for it was based on a misrepresentation of anarchism (Franks, 2007: 135). It was commonly agreed that whilst seeking to correct the faulty epistemological and teleological bias of traditional theory, post-anarchists remained wedded to a conception of the anarchist past which was itself faulty (Antliff, 2007; Kinna, 2007; Cohn and Wilbur, 2003). Part 3 of our book, 'Classical Anarchism Reloaded', presents the most important examples of this criticism.

When the idea of a rupture from classical anarchism to a new anarchism/post-anarchism became one of the central issues in anarchist debates during the 2000s, George Crowder's book *Classical Anarchism* became popular again after a decade (Crowder, 1991). Crowder had evaluated classical anarchism from a liberal perspective and he used the term 'classical anarchism' to describe four prominent figures of anarchist thought: Godwin, Proudhon, Bakunin and Kropotkin. We shall see that positioning anarchism as a political philosophy represented by a select few thinkers from the classical epoch, a trend started by Eltzbacher (1975), created many problems for post-anarchism theory later on.

In a review of Crowder's book *Classical Anarchism*, Sharif Gemie criticized this reductionism of anarchist theory (Gemie, 1993). Gemie argued that Crowder's selection of anarchist thinkers was suspect and he asked why Max Stirner was omitted, for example, when William Godwin was included.[8] And, more remarkably, Gemie continued by asking why propagandists of greater importance, such as Jean Grave or even Octave Mirbeau, were not included (Gemie, 1993: 90). This leads to some key questions: Who (what) represents anarchism? What are the politics behind the history-writing processes regarding anarchism? Why is it that thinking of Mirbeau as one of the key classical anarchist figures is, even today, such a marginalized position to take?

As mentioned above, post-anarchism became a worldwide phenomenon in the 2000s. Saul Newman's work was translated into Turkish, Spanish, Italian, German, Portuguese and Serbo-Croat. More importantly, new texts were written in various languages. We witnessed a growing interest in rereading anarchism through postmodern/post-structuralist lenses, namely through/with Foucault, Deleuze, Lyotard, Derrida, Lacan, Nietzsche, Baudrillard and others. There was once again a problem of naming this current: Todd May's expression 'post-structuralist anarchism' depicted a marriage of post-structuralism and anarchism (May, 1994).

The problem with 'post-structuralist anarchism' is that it represents an intersection of anarchism with a limited range of thinkers who are generally referred to as 'post-structuralist'. May would find no problem with this; he even excludes some post-structuralist thinkers (such as Derrida and Baudrillard) because he believes that their work is not appropriate for any political project. For May, Derrida 'remains without a clearly articulated philosophy' and Baudrillard's 'thought tends toward the reductionist and comprehensive rather than the multiple and local'; thus he reserves the term 'post-structuralist' for the works of Foucault, Deleuze and Lyotard (May, 1994: 12).

This understanding eliminates possible fields of research on different intersections between different anarchisms and thinkers like Bakhtin, who are not directly post-structuralist but had a huge influence on post-structuralism. When the term 'post-structuralist anarchism' is preferred, there is no way to think anarchism through hypertext or Cixous or Irigaray or art works or facts from political life or, perhaps most importantly, everyday life. It limits the scope to just some of the possible philosophical works. So, 'postmodern anarchism' in this sense sounds more open and effective.

The term 'postmodern' is much more flexible. For example, the postmodern matrix of Lewis Call reaches and combines Marcel Mauss, Saussure, Durkheim and Freud on the one hand and cyberpunk, Chomsky and Butler on the other. Using 'postmodern anarchism' also enabled Call to extend his work across cultural studies and dedicate a chapter to cyberpunk (Call, 2002). Call depicts postmodern anarchism as an anarchism that seeks to undermine the very theoretical foundations of the capitalist economic order and all associated politics – by using Nietzsche's anarchy of becoming, Foucault's anti-humanist micropolitics, Debord's critique of the spectacle, Baudrillard's theory of simulation, Lyotard's 'incredulity toward metanarratives' and Deleuze's rhizomatic nomad thinking; and to show that contemporary popular culture does indeed exhibit a very serious concern for profoundly new forms of radical politics, in this regard he incorporates the cyberpunk fiction of William Gibson and Bruce Sterling (Call, 2002: 118–19).

Saul Newman used the term 'post-anarchism', which directly brought to mind 'post-Marxism', especially considering that the introduction to *From Bakunin to Lacan* was written by Ernesto Laclau. Benjamin Franks worked on this affinity more than any other reviewer of the tradition (Franks, 2007: 131–4).

Comparing these three expressions, it can be seen that Call's suggestion of postmodern anarchism was mostly denied by the wider milieu because of the negative connotations that today come with the term 'postmodern'. Nowadays, 'postmodern' is not a respected term for an area for scholarly work, and also for many activists it is symptomatic of post-USSR neoliberal world capitalism. Besides, some well-known anarchist writers of the twentieth century, namely Murray Bookchin, Noam Chomsky and John Zerzan, articulated ruthless criticisms against 'postmodern thinkers' and that left an anti-postmodern impulse within anarchism (Bookchin, 1995; Chomsky,

2006; Zerzan, 2002). It is common within anarchist circles to come across anti-postmodern sensibilities, sensibilities which react to Foucault as if he were a petty-bourgeois nihilist, who, having deconstructed everything ends up with nothing to hold on to (Mueller, 2003: 34). And as Tadzio Mueller nicely put it, this criticism is nothing but the theoretical equivalent of the familiar branding of anarchists as brainless 'rent-a-mob' types with no positive proposals (ibid.: 34–5).

Todd May's post-structuralist anarchism, along with Koch's project of utilizing post-structuralism for solving some epistemological problems of anarchism, is in fact in harmony with Newman's project of combining those two bodies. But there is a slight difference; May is predominantly working on the politics of post-structuralism, while gaining some insights from anarchism to create a more effective post-structuralist politics, whereas Newman, as seen in his book *From Bakunin to Lacan* and in interviews, comes from within the anarchist tradition and tries to gain some insights from post-structuralism to create a more effective anarchist politics. But post-anarchism is better understood as an anarchist theory first and foremost rather than a post-structuralist theory. At the end of the day, it is an anarchism, it is not a new kind of post-structuralism. Newman even describes it as a combination and composition of classical anarchism and contemporary anarchism, which means that post-structuralist qualities are being framed through the lenses of contemporary anarchism. However, the prefix 'post-' irritated some anarchists, who thought that the term suggested that the prefix also applied to its new object as well, implying that anarchism, at least as thought and practised, was somehow obsolete (Cohn and Wilbur, 2003).

So, could it really be possible to surpass 'classical' anarchism? But what is that anarchism which is subject to attempts to surpass it? And if someone claims that anarchism is outmoded isn't that also a claim to define what anarchism is (and vice versa)? What do we mean when we say 'anarchism'? How was this knowledge shaped?

We can roughly define the main periods of anarchism since the nineteenth century: the first period ends in 1939 with the defeat in Spain, the second period begins with and embraces the movements from the 1960s and the third period runs together with the anti-globalization movements. Post-anarchism studies mainly belong to this third period, which is also sometimes referred to as the third wave of anarchism (Adams, 2003; see also Aragorn! 2006, who refers to it as 'Second Wave Anarchy'). But one of the additional features of this 'third wave' was its reflexive ability to open anarchist history to new evaluations, rereadings and re-conceptualizations.

There is a certain need to question given histories of anarchism, to show their contingency and 'take them apart'. There are no given truths on anarchism. The positions and discourses of those who wrote anarchist histories determine the main elements of anarchism as we know it today. Studying the histories of anarchism leads one to consider history's nature as a form of knowledge and to question how knowledge on anarchism was arrived at. There was an 'anarchist canon' which existed before the post-anarchist attempts at 'saving' it. And it seems like an important task to decode the biases affecting information on what is anarchism, what represents anarchism, and the anarchist canon. How do exclusions work within knowledge production processes on anarchism? What are the structural assumptions behind the canonization of anarchism?

Most of the known works on post-anarchism in English, which were fundamentally disapproved of by anarchists for misrepresenting anarchism, were in fact taking the given histories about anarchism for granted. Clichéd notions of classical anarchism were not some invention of post-anarchists keen on building straw-person arguments from reductions in the traditional canon and discourse. Instead of accusing some post-anarchists for employing problematic conceptions on anarchism, I would like to ask where those conceptions actually came from in the first place.

Todd May mainly compares the writings of Deleuze, Foucault and Lyotard with the writings of Kropotkin and Bakunin, with a little reference to Emma Goldman, Colin Ward and Bookchin. Saul Newman adds Lacan, Stirner and Derrida to the picture, especially underlining Lacan and Stirner. Lewis Call broadens this a little and describes a postmodern matrix of writers from Nietzsche to Baudrillard, comparing their work with more or less the same anarchist classical thinkers and partly with Chomsky and Bookchin. Lewis Call, Saul Newman and Todd May all refer to anarchism as a thought that can be grasped by summarizing the views of a few Western thinkers.

This is in contradiction with the anarchist understanding of theory and practice, in which there is no hierarchy between the form and content. As a current example, when David Graeber wrote about the 'new anarchism' that can be seen in anti-globalization movements, he insisted that the ideology of the new movement is the form of its organization and organizational principles (Graeber, 2002). This is a quite typical stance of anarchism. Although Call, May and Newman become part of a project which combines anarchist theory with theories critical of modernity, their approach to anarchist history is not really shaped with these same concerns. First of all, ignoring Graeber's position (and the position of contemporary anarchisms) but more importantly ignoring Kropotkin's notion of the 'anarchist principle', they give priority to selected anarchist texts (without questioning or explaining the selection criteria) and they understand anarchist practices/experiences as simple applications of these theories, whereas anarchist history has always been against this hierarchy of theory over practice.

And then, as a continuation of this logic, these writers gave priority to Western modern anarchist thinkers ('dead white males', as Mueller puts it), implying that the texts and actions of non-Western and/or non-Modernist anarchists were just applications (if not imitations) of modern Western anarchism. And that would mean that the truth of Western anarchism is the as-yet-hidden-truth[9] of non-Western anarchism(s) whereas the truth of written anarchism is the as-yet-hidden-truth (and *telos*) of anarchist practice. As a result, many post-anarchist works also fail to detect Eurocentric assumptions in the formation of the canon of classical modern anarchism. Jason Adams has given some examples of how we can detect Eurocentric elements in writing the history of anarchism (Adams, 2003).[10]

Taking into account all of the missing pieces, and the missing communication between post-anarchist works in different languages, we tend to see that today's post-anarchism is in an introductory period. For example, all these post-anarchist works operate with an excuse; they behave as if a justification were needed for bringing anarchist and post-structuralist philosophy into a dialogue with one another. They explain their motivation for constituting post-anarchism as a distinct area of specialization by resorting to their belief that their area of study is thought to be irrelevant to both academic and anarchist circles. Legitimization of a need to identify with a post-structuralist/ postmodern anarchism is felt to be required before the research is further conducted. This apologetic attitude is seen in May, Call, Newman and Day, but not in Jason Adams.[11] And they all legitimize post-anarchism by first trying to show that Marxist theory has collapsed or failed or it was too problematic to rely on. This means Marxist theory was presupposed as the norm, the ground for comparison. Adams begins from anarchism instead of ending with it; he starts at 1968 and advances toward the present.

Call refers to the collapse of Marxism and attempts to locate proofs that Marxism's revolutionary project has failed. If a worldly defeat proves that the ideology was wrong then how do we defend anarchism? If anarchist revolutionaries have heretofore won nowhere, how is it that they will win today? How does anarchism prove that it can transform the world while it hasn't transformed any country or region for a sufficient period of time? These questions naturally follow from the logical structure of Marxism. They (Call, May, Day and Newman) all in some way see the collapse of the Soviet Union as indicating the end of Marxism, which hardly seems fair. Why is Marxism judged as an unsuccessful experiment while anarchism is judged only by its potential and its theories? It is conceivable that the same judgment could be applied to anarchism; but that would force anarchists to admit that anarchism was more or less defeated after the Spanish revolution.

As someone working on post-anarchism as well, Adams showed in his early article 'Non-Western Anarchisms' that one has to critically investigate the history of anarchism as well. Before comparing classical anarchism with post-structuralist philosophy and before making a genealogy of affinity in the realm of 'classical anarchism' (that's the term Richard Day deploys in *Gramsci is Dead*)[12] one must first endeavour to make a genealogy of the anarchist 'canon'.

The main problem so far of the post-anarchist literature[13] referred to above is that it has not undertaken a new reading of the anarchist canon; the post-anarchists did not investigate classical anarchism from their post-structuralist perspectives, but instead compared post-structuralist theory with what was readily available in a classical anarchism written mostly from a modernist perspective. Many problems are rooted in this choice I believe.

Trying to find where the problems emerge (as in the search for origins) is similar to asking why it is so easy for many to rely on the assumption that anarchism is based on an idea of a good human essence.[14] Todd May, for example, does not even feel a need to cite any references when he describes the traditional anarchist reliance on an essentially 'good' human nature: 'anarchists have a two-part distinction: power (bad) vs. human nature (good)' (May, 2000).

If we go back and have a look at David Morland's book on anarchist understandings of human nature, *Demanding the Impossible: Human Nature and Politics in Nineteenth-Century Social Anarchism*, we see that even the 'usual suspects' (Proudhon, Bakunin and Kropotkin) do not have such an understanding of human nature (Morland, 1997). Then where does this cliché come from? (It is interesting that Dave Morland shows that part of this cliché comes from basic texts on political theory – books that anarchists or left intelligentsia would normally never read, but academicians working on related areas would: for example, Ian Adams' *Political Ideology Today*, or Andrew Heywood's *Political Ideologies: An Introduction*).

Jesse Cohn made a supporting point when he wrote about the relations between anarchism and Nietzsche:

> For Proudhon, 'the living man is a group' 'not an origin, a source, but a resultant'.[15] Kropotkin, too, speaks of the subject as a 'resultant' the shifting product of 'a multitude of separate faculties, autonomous tendencies, equal among themselves, performing their functions independently [...] without being subordinated to a central organ 'the soul'.[16] For Bakunin, this multitude is a microcosm of the wider social field, always 'in a sort of conspiracy against [itself]' or '[in] revolt against [itself]'.[17] (Cohn, 2006b)

Also, in a 1989 article titled 'Human Nature and Anarchism', Peter Marshall notes that 'while classic anarchist thinkers, such as William Godwin, Max Stirner and Peter Kropotkin, share common assumptions about the possibility of a free society, they do not have a common view of human nature [...] and their views of human nature are not so naïve or optimistic as is usually alleged' (Marshall, 1989: 128). Marshall also deals with this subject in his well-known book *Demanding the Impossible* (Marshall, 1993). There he notes that some anarchists

> insist that 'human nature' does not exist as a fixed essence. [...] and the aim is not therefore to liberate some 'essential self' by throwing off the burden of government and the State, but to develop the self in creative and voluntary relations with others. (Marshall, 1993: 642–3)

As we mentioned above, there is a discussion on the understanding of human nature in anarchism and particularly classical anarchism, and a tendency to reduce anarchism to a few classical writers. However, there are differences in the list of the canonic classical anarchist thinkers as well. For example Colin Ward thought that it was customary to relate the anarchist tradition to four major thinkers and writers: Godwin, Proudhon, Bakunin, Kropotkin

(Ward, 2004: 3). Also, in the introduction to his book on anarchism, Alan Ritter wrote: 'The arguments treated in this book as representing the gist of anarchism are drawn from the four authors – Godwin, Proudhon, Bakunin and Kropotkin – whose contributions to anarchist theory are universally regarded as most seminal' (Ritter, 1980: 5). But, on the other hand, for Irving Horowitz the classical anarchists were Bakunin, Malatesta, Sorel and Kropotkin (Horowitz, 1964: 17). Or, for Henri Arvon, the theoreticians of anarchism were William Godwin, Max Stirner, Proudhon, Bakunin and Tolstoy (Arvon, 2007). As a very early attempt to reduce anarchism to just a few thinkers, Paul Eltzbacher's list of seven prominent anarchists, first published in 1900 in German, included Proudhon, Godwin, Stirner, Bakunin, Kropotkin, Tucker and Tolstoy (Eltzbacher, 1975; Kinna, 2005: 10). And as one of the contemporary scholars working on the intersections between anarchism and post-structuralist theory, Daniel Colson takes Stirner, Proudhon and Bakunin as the main theorists, precursors or founders of anarchism (Colson, 2004: 14). For Colson, Kropotkin, together with Reclus and Guillaume, is one of the 'anarchist intellectuals who came after [them]', (Colson, 2004: 14). Nevertheless, Colson's contribution to the debates on post-anarchism/ classical anarchism mostly relate to the way he understands the libertarian workers' movement (instead of a few key theorists) as compared with post-structuralist theory.

Colson first lists various interpretations of Nietzsche (from the extreme-right interpretation to the Christian reading) and thus depicts an 'explicitly anarchist reading [...] a reading we might qualify as "libertarian" and linked to the renewal of libertarian ideas during the last thirty years, though external to the anarchist movement per se. Foucault and Deleuze are its best-known French representatives.' Here Colson categorizes Foucault and Deleuze as the prominent figures during the last 30 years in a renewal of libertarian ideas external to the anarchist movement. Those ideas, and the anarchist movement in the same period, together constitute the libertarian tradition of the era. Once again, the relation between post-structuralism and anarchism is shown not as a relation to be constructed or invented but as a relation that is already there.

Considering the significance of Nietzsche for post-structuralist theory (Schrift, 1995: 7), it is particularly important to consider the way Colson links Nietzsche to anarchism through a libertarian ('post-structuralist') interpreta-tion of Nietzsche. He compares this libertarian Nietzsche with the libertarian workers' movement, revealing direct links between the libertarian thought of the last 30 years and the libertarian workers' movement of the past (Colson, 2004: 16–25). The way Colson celebrates the syndicalism (and direct action) of anarchism through Nietzsche is similar to the celebration of the anti-globalization movements today. Thus Colson, along with Adams, represents another but apparently a less dominant current within post-anarchism, which takes political struggles like the libertarian workers' movement as something that represents what ('classical'/'historical') anarchism *is*.

Part 4 of the book, 'Lines of Flight', marks the theoretical strength of post-anarchism when used in cultural studies. Sometimes as a method, sometimes as just an inspiring perspective, post-anarchism highlights and seeks to describe the theoretical revitalization of the libertarian tradition. Reconsidering Emma Goldman's place in anarchist history from a post-anarchist approach, as Hilton Bertalan does, or exploring anarchism in popular culture and science fiction through a TV serial like 'Buffy the Vampire Slayer', are both attempts to change the limits and dynamics of the anarchist canon (a project Lewis Call develops through his studies on popular-culture elements of a wide range covering 'V for Vendetta', cyberpunk novels and 'Battlestar Galactica') and to use post-anarchism as a theoretical tool, adding a libertarian touch to cultural studies. Jamie Heckert deepens this use of post-anarchism, dwelling on gender relations and their role in the new anarchist politics. Nathan Jun uses post-anarchism to help us in theoretical debates about post-structuralist philosophy. And Michael Truscello opens us up to post-anarchist studies of technology.

Generally speaking, post-anarchism is a new and developing current in the world radical political scene, and also in cultural studies. In this reader, we aim to present the major reference points so far, the key theories articulated and the discussions surrounding these theories, and to provide the reader with some insight into these emerging fields of debate.

NOTES

1. See Tony Blair's depiction of the movement of anarchists as a 'travelling circus' that 'goes from summit to summit with the sole purpose of causing as much mayhem as possible.' See 'Blair: Anarchists will not stop us', BBC News, 16 June 2001. <http://news.bbc.co.uk/1/hi/uk_politics/1392004.stm>

2. Teoman Gee, an anarchist activist and writer from the United States, explains:

   [For] [t]he first ten years of my involvement in anarchist politics (from 1989 to 1999) being an anarchist was an oddity, and the scene pretty much resembled a social ghetto that was often enough only subject to ridicule and despised, even amongst non-anarchist political radicals. At best, we were seen as incurable idealists, chasing dreams of a just society made for fairy-tales much rather than the real world. [...] One often didn't dare declare oneself an anarchist in radical networks geared towards single-issue political activism, just to avoid the danger of not being taken seriously. [...] What does seem essential is to recall the isolated and disregarded socio-political space we found ourselves in as anarchists for almost all of the 1980s and 1990s. [...] This has changed drastically since November 1999, especially in the US. It's common now to read about anarchists in the media, to introduce oneself as an anarchist, to refer to your neighbor as an anarchist. Anarchists finally seem to have recognition. (*New Anarchism: Some Thoughts*, Teoman Gee, Alpine Anarchist Productions, 2003, pp.5–6.)

3. On the other hand, Graeber rejects the 'honour' of being the person who first coined the term. He even denies that he has ever used it:

   I never used the expression 'new anarchist' myself. It's in the title of the *New Left Review* piece, but the magazine makes up the title, not the author. I didn't object to it but I would never use it as a title in that way. Insofar as I've ever consciously designated myself a particular type of anarchist it's 'small a' – which is above all the kind that doesn't go in for particular sub-identities. (Personal email, 17 November 2007)

   Ironically he is sometimes introduced as: 'anthropologist, "new anarchist" theorist and activist, David Graeber' (cf. <http://www.glovesoff.org/features/gjamerica_4.html>). Actually, the first version of Graeber's article was first published as 'The Globalization Movement: Some Points of Clarification' in *Items and Issues* 2(3) (Fall 2001), the newsletter of the *Social Science Research Council* (see <http://publications.ssrc.org/items/ItemsWinerter20012.3-4. pdf>). The article displayed an early and strong attempt to conceptualize the ideology of the new movement as a set of anarchistic organizational principles. It was so 'new' that as I was trying to translate the piece into Turkish (it was later published in *Varlık*, December 2001, no. 1131, pp.45–9) I couldn't understand some key terms and asked the author their meanings. These terms were 'break-outs', 'fishbowls', 'blocking concerns', 'vibes-watchers', 'facilitation tools' and 'spokes-councils' – a collection of technical terms used within the movement for direct democracy which were mentioned by Graeber himself on purpose simply to show that such a technical language existed. Detailed explanations of those terms can be found in the longer *New Left Review* version of the article.

4. Tadzio Mueller goes further and claims that

> if anarchism is anything today, then it is not a set of dogmas and principles, but a set of practices and actions within which certain principles manifest themselves. [...] Anarchism is not primarily about what is written but what is done. (Mueller, 2003: 27)

So here Mueller first denies the superior position of theory over practice and then suggests that it is practice/experience that is in the superior position.

5. Interview with Todd May (May, 2004). Also in the interview (with Rebecca deWitt), May says: 'As an activist, I find myself in accordance with the recent demonstrations intended to eliminate the WTO.' (May, 2000).

6. See the full archive of the post-anarchism email listserv from the Spoon Collective at <http://www.driftline.org/cgi-bin/archive/archive.cgi?list=spoon-archives/postanarchism.archive>. But the tone of excitement can perhaps be better traced to the Yahoo! Group archives, which is open to members only: <http://groups.yahoo.com/group/postanarchism>.

7. This oft-cited essay was also published with the title 'Postanarchism in a Bombshell' in *Aporia Journal*. See <http://aporiajournal.tripod.com/postanarchism.htm>.

8. A few years later, Saul Newman heard this call, dismissed Godwin and used Stirner on a large scale; but Newman did not adopt Stirner as one of the leading classical anarchists but as a precursor of post-structuralism (Newman, 2001). Although *From Bakunin to Lacan* was first published in 2001, Newman's book was based on his Ph.D. thesis completed in 1994–98.

9. I am borrowing the phrase from Agnes Heller and Ferenc Feher. See Agnes Heller and Ferenc Feher, *Postmodern Political Condition* (Cambridge: Polity Press, 1988), p.2.

10. Adams' *Non-Western Anarchisms* and Sharif Gemie's *Third World Anarchism* have both been translated into Turkish and more importantly they have been perceived as crucial anarchist texts, whereas they are not much appreciated in Western anarchist circles; this is itself a sign of different priorities concerning this issue among anarchist circles worldwide. Additionally, Aragorn! in his essay 'Toward a Non-European Anarchism, or Why a Movement Is the Last Thing that People of Color Need', suggests the terms 'non-European anarchism' and 'extra-European anarchism'. <http://theanarchistlibrary. org/HTML/Aragorn___Toward_a_non_European_Anarchism_or_Why_a_movement_is_ the_last_thing_that_people_of_color_need.html>.

11. 'Postanarchism in a Nutshell', Jason Adams, <http://theanarchistlibrary.org/HTML/Jason_ Adams_Postanarchism_in_a_Nutshell.html>. Here Adams starts by looking at possible roots to the current post-anarchist tendency without any discussion on why Marxism has failed.

12. Especially see Chapter 4 ('Utopian Socialism Then …') in Richard J.F. Day, *Gramsci Is Dead: Anarchist Currents in the Newest Social Movements* (London: Pluto Press, 2005). Another problem with *Gramsci Is Dead* is that Day understands genealogy as simply tracing back the history of something (in this case 'logic of affinity'). That is clearly not genealogy in the Nietzschean/Foucauldian sense – this is simply family tree. Genealogy requires that we ask questions about the birth of something; a genealogy of affinity in the Nietzschean/

Foucauldian sense would begin by asking – Who first wrote about affinity? Where did this affinity came from and how? What were the forces and struggles? How did it develop? Etc.

13. There is a certain language gap that makes it difficult to refer to 'post-anarchist literature' in the world. In the English-speaking world, usually there is no concern about this, and without a doubt, writers refer to 'post-anarchists' or 'post-anarchist writers' instead of saying 'English-speaking post-anarchists' or 'post-anarchist literature in English', and thus ignore contributions made in other languages such as French, German or Turkish. Jürgen Mumken and his friends in Germany issued numerous post-anarchist publications and set up a web site for post-anarchist archives, www.postanarchismus.net (this is the latest of a series of web sites dedicated to post-anarchism; Jason Adams's Postanarchism Clearing House was the first, started in February 2002, followed by www.postanarki.net in December 2003, which was prepared by the post-anarchist magazine *Siyahi* and included articles in Turkish and English, and the blog pages of Siyahi Interlocal, which was a joint project of Adams and *Siyahi* to make an international post-anarchist magazine in English – a project that has only recently come to fruition. Web pages in Spanish are following; these can be traced through the Spanish Wikipedia at es.wikipedia.org/wiki/Postanarquismo. Two original books have been published in Germany by the same group of writers, and several books on post-anarchism saw the light in Turkish (in accordance with the 'as-yet-hidden-truth' concept, these books are never mentioned when writers give a picture of 'post-anarchism so far'). So in this introduction, when not mentioned otherwise, by 'post-anarchists' I mainly mean writers who have made book-length contributions to the field in English – Todd May (*Political Philosophy of the Poststructuralist Anarchism*), Saul Newman (*From Bakunin to Lacan: Anti-Authoritarianism and the Dislocation of Power*), Lewis Call (*Postmodern Anarchism*) and Richard Day (*Gramsci Is Dead: Anarchist Currents in the Newest Social Movements*). It is also important to keep in mind that we do not have one homogeneous universal post-anarchism. In particular, political cultures give birth to different anarchisms and different post-anarchisms. For example, the post-anarchism developed in the Turkish context reflects much greater concern about the historiography of anarchism, in opposition to the assumption in many canonic approaches that exhibit anarchist practices as mere applications of anarchist theory. English-speaking post-anarchists never discuss Emma Goldman when they discuss the problems of classical anarchism – simply because, very strangely, she has been dropped from the representative canon. Her very early attempts at a Nietzschean anarchism are thus left in the shade. The difference is, if you take her as a part of the core, you have to accept that there are many post-1968 themes represented in the classical anarchist literature. But if she is out of the core, than hers is merely a unique case of a propagandist feminist anarchist (immigrant) – it is without any representative value. Thus, Hilton Bertalan's article on Emma Goldman in Part 4 of our book is a highly significant intervention.

14. However, when Mueller rejects the claim that all anarchists believe in such an essentialist understanding of power vs. human nature, he also points out that there are anarchists today among activist circles who really think this way. Mueller posits the situation as two struggling camps within anarchism (Mueller 2003: 31).

15. Proudhon, Oeuvres 12.64, 8.3.409, translated by Jesse Cohn.

16. Kropotkin, *Kropotkin's Revolutionary Pamphlets*, 119–20.

17. Bakunin (1972: 239).

REFERENCES

Adams, I. (1993). *Political Ideology Today*. Manchester: Manchester University Press.

Adams, Jason (2003). 'Postanarchism in a Nutshell'. Retrieved 2 March 2006 from <http://info. interactivist.net/article.pl?sid=03/11/11/1642242&mode=nested&tid=9>.

Anderson, Benedict (2005). *Under Three Flags: Anarchism and the Anti-Colonial Imagination*. London & New York: Verso.

Antliff, Alan (2007). *Anarchy and Art: From the Paris Commune to the Fall of the Berlin Wall.* Vancouver, BC: Arsenal Pulp Press.

Aragorn! (2006). *Second Wave Anarchy.* Pistols Drawn. See <http://littleblackcart.com/index. php?main_page=product_book_info&products_id=45>

Arvon, H. (2007). *Anarşizm.* İstanbul: İletişim.

Bakunin, Mikhail (1972). *Bakunin on Anarchy: Selected Works by the Activist–Founder of World Anarchism* (Sam Dolgoff, ed. and trans.). New York: Alfred A. Knopf.

Bookchin, Murray (1995). *Social Anarchism or Lifestyle Anarchism: The Unbridgeable Chasm.* Edinburgh: AK Press.

Bourg, J. (2007). *From Revolution to Ethics: May 1968 and Contemporary French Thought.* McGill–Queen's University Press.

Call, Lewis (2002). *Postmodern Anarchism.* Lanham: Lexington Books.

Chomsky, Noam (2006). *Chomsky on Anarchism* (Barry Pateman, ed.). AK Press.

Cockburn, A. and St. Clair, J. (2000). *Five Days That Shook the World: The Battle for Seattle and Beyond.* London: Verso.

Cohn, J. (2006a). *Anarchism and the Crisis of Representation: Hermeneutics, Aesthetics, Politics.* Selingsgrove: Susquehanna University Press.

—— (2006b). On Anarchism and Nietzsche. *Siyahi* 7 (Spring). Istanbul.

—— and Wilbur, S. (2003). 'What's Wrong with Postanarchism?' Institute for Anarchist Studies web site. Publication date 31August 2003. <http://theanarchistlibrary.org/HTML/Jesse_Cohn_ and_Shawn_Wilbur__What_s_Wrong_With_Postanarchism_.html>.

Colson, D. (2004). 'Nietzsche and the Libertarian Worker's Movement'. In *I Am Not a Man, I Am Dynamite! Friedrich Nietzsche and the Anarchist Tradition* (J. Moore and S. Sunshine, eds). Brooklyn: Autonomedia.

Conway, J. (2003). 'Civil Resistance and the "Diversity of Tactics" in the Anti-Globalization Movement: Problems of Violence, Silence, and Solidarity in Activist Politics', *Osgoode Hall Law Journal* 41(2&3): 505–30.

Crowder, G. (1991). *Classical Anarchism: The Political Thought of Godwin, Proudhon, Bakunin and Kropotkin.* Oxford: Clarendon Press.

Day, Richard (2005). *Gramsci Is Dead: Anarchist Currents in the Newest Social Movements.* London and Ann Arbor: Pluto Press.

Eltzbacher, P. (1975). *Anarchism: Exponents of the Anarchist Philosophy.* London: Freedom Press.

Franks, Benjamin (2007). 'Postanarchism: A Critical Assessment'. *Journal of Political Ideologies* 12(2): 127–45.

Gee, T. (2003). *New Anarchism: Some Thoughts.* Alpine Anarchist Productions.

Gemie, S. (1993). 'Review of George Crowder, *Classical Anarchism, The Political Thought of Godwin, Proudhon, Bakunin and Kropotkin*'. Oxford, Clarendon Press, 1991. *European History Quarterly* 23(1): 90–1.

Gordon, U. (2007). 'Anarchism Reloaded'. *Journal of Political Ideologies* 12: 29–48.

Graeber, D. (2002). 'The New Anarchists'. *New Left Review* 13.

Heywood, A. (2003). *Political Ideologies: An Introduction.* Palgrave Macmillan.

Horowitz, I. (1964). *The Anarchists.* New York: Dell.

Kang, K.M. (2005). *Agonistic Democracy: The Decentred 'I' of the 1990s.* Unpublished thesis for the degree of doctor of philosophy. Australia: University of Sydney.

Kellner, D. (2001). 'Foreword'. In *When Poetry Ruled the Streets: The French May Events of 1968* (A. Feenberg and J. Freeman, eds). New York: State University of New York Press.

Kinna, R. (2005). *Anarchism: A Beginner's Guide.* Oxford: Oneworld.

—— (2007). 'Fields of Vision: Kropotkin and Revolutionary Change'. *SubStance* 36(2): 67–86.

Kissack, T. (2008). *Free Comrades: Anarchism and Homosexuality in the United States 1895–1917.* Edinburgh: AK Press.

Koch, A.M. (1993). 'Poststructuralism and the Epistemological Basis of Anarchism'. *Philosophy of the Social Sciences* 23: 327–51.

Kropotkin, P. (n.d.). *On Order.* Pirate Press: Sheffield.

Marshall, P. (1993). *Demanding the Impossible: A History of Anarchism.* London: Fontana.

—— (1989). 'Human Nature and Anarchism'. In *For Anarchism, History, Theory and Practice* (D. Goodway, ed.). London and New York: Routledge.

May, T. (2009). 'Introduction'. In *New Perspectives on Anarchism* (Nathan J. Jun and Shane Wahl, eds). Plymouth: Lexington Books

—— (2004). 'Interview with Todd May'. *Siyahi* 1 (November–December). Istanbul.

—— (2000). 'Interview with Todd May', by Rebecca deWitt. *Perspectives on Anarchist Theory* 4(2) (Fall).

—— (1994). *The Political Philosophy of Poststructuralist Anarchism*. Pennsylvania: Pennsylvania State University Press.

Moore, J. and Sunshine, S. (2004). *I Am Not a Man, I Am Dynamite! Friedrich Nietzsche and the Anarchist Tradition*. New York: Autonomedia.

Morland, D. (1997). *Demanding the Impossible? Human Nature and Politics in Nineteenth-Century Social Anarchism*. London and Washington: Cassell.

Mueller, T. (2003). 'Empowering Anarchy: Power, Hegemony, and Anarchist Strategy'. *Anarchist Studies* 11(2): 26–53.

Newman, S. (2004). 'Interview with Saul Newman', by Süreyyya Evren, Kursad Kiziltug, Erden Kosova. *Siyahi* 1 (November–December). Istanbul.

Purkis, J., and Bowen, J. (2004). *Changing Anarchism: Anarchist Theory and Practice in a Global Age*. Manchester: Manchester University Press.

Schrift, A. (1995). *Nietzsche's French Legacy: A Genealogy of Poststructuralism*. New York and London: Routledge.

Sheehan, S. (2003). *Anarchism*. London: Reaktion.

Ritter, A. (1980). *Anarchism: A Theoretical Analysis*. Cambridge: Cambridge University Press.

Ward, Colin (2004). *Anarchism: A Very Short Introduction*. Oxford: Oxford University Press.

Zerzan, John (2002). *Running on Emptiness: The Pathology of Civilization*. Los Angeles: Feral House.

Part 1
When Anarchism Met Post-Structuralism

1
Post-Structuralism and the Epistemological Basis of Anarchism[1]

Andrew M. Koch

The problem of defining the 'proper' relationship between the individual and the larger community is as old as civilization. Classical and modern political theories have traditionally addressed this problem by grounding descriptive and prescriptive political formulations in conceptions of human nature or human essence. Questions regarding the aggressiveness, avarice and rationality of the individual have provided the underlying dynamic for the debate regarding the necessity and form of external institutions. In the classical and modern periods, the conflict over how to represent the character of the individual culminated in a variety of competing political formulations. If human beings are self-serving and aggressive, then the strong coercive state becomes necessary. If the individual is shaped by the social body, then community practice becomes the essence and the teleology of human endeavours. If human beings are rational, to the extent that they can formulate a structure for controlling their aggressiveness, conflicts can be mediated. 'Authority' becomes a substitute for force, and participation and consent provide the legitimacy for collective decisions.

Within this general framework the writings of classical anarchism can also be examined. The eighteenth- and nineteenth-century anarchists' attacks on the state were based on a 'rational' representation of human nature. Reason, compassion, and gregariousness are essential to this view of anarchism. Not only is the state, as a coercive institution, fundamentally in conflict with this view of human nature, but the rigid monolithic character of its structure inhibits both the spontaneous character of association and the expression of genuine human kindness. And, although the foci of the classical anarchists differ and their prescriptions vary, the general ontological character of their argument is similar.

This chapter explores the origins and evolution of another perspective within the archaeology of ideas. As an epistemological problem, the relationship between the individual and the collective takes on a fundamentally different character. The major question is no longer one of representation but of validity: by what measure can any ontological characterization of *essence* or *nature* be justified? Is there any validity to the representation of human nature that underlies state practices?

The chapter attempts to demonstrate how the general critique of Enlightenment epistemology, beginning in the nineteenth century and continuing today in the work of the post-structuralists, may be recast to assist in the construction of an epistemologically grounded defence of anarchism. After briefly outlining the ontological justification for anarchism found in the works of Godwin, Kropotkin and Proudhon, the focus shifts to epistemological issues. First, the general questions raised by Max Stirner's defence of anarchism in *The Ego and His Own* are examined. Then, Nietzsche's critique of Enlightenment epistemology is surveyed for the questions it raises about truth, knowledge and method. Finally, the epistemological questions raised by the twentieth-century movement known as post-structuralism are explored for their relevance in reformulating the support for the objectives of anarchism.

Post-structuralism challenges the idea that it is possible to create a stable ontological foundation for the creation of universal statements about human nature. In the relationship between theory and practice, these foundational claims have been used to legitimate the exercise of power. Without the ability to fix human identity, the political prescriptions that rely on such claims are open to question. This creates the basis for a different approach to the formulation of anarchist politics, what has come to be termed *post-anarchism*.

The chapter concludes by rejecting the claim that post-structuralism cannot create a rationale for resistance to the state. Post-structuralism confronts the state by undercutting the foundational premises that support it. Rejecting the modernist epistemology and the universalist ontology, the post-structuralist's argument asserts a plurality of contexts for the generation of discourse. The recognition of plurality becomes the basis for resistance to that which would impose universals. In political terms, *that* resistance is directed against the state.

ONTOLOGICAL JUSTIFICATIONS FOR ANARCHISM

The central feature of an ontological defence of anarchism is the representation of human nature. One of the most clearly elaborated ontological defences of anarchism can be found in William Godwin's *Enquiry Concerning Political Justice* (1971). Godwin's argument is that human beings are perfectible, not because each is able to reach a final condition, but because each is capable of continually improving (ibid.: 144). The perfectibility of human nature is associated with the question of truth and justice, which is, in turn, generated by the power of reason.

Godwin asserts a set of propositions regarding the character of human nature and then draws logical inferences from those assertions. Godwin believed that all human beings are equal in that they have an innate ability to reason (ibid.: 231). The problem in society, then, is not to find the perfect person to rule but to cultivate sufficiently the reasoning capacities of all individuals. Once we have sufficient confidence in our own reasoning abilities, our acceptance of rule by others will be shaken. Confidence in others is the offspring of our own ignorance (ibid.: 247).

Godwin's characterization of human nature, government and power are linked to a transcendental notion of truth. *Truth* and *justice* have an abstract condition of existence in which the world has only imperfect manifestations: 'Truth is omnipotent' (ibid.: 143). Vices and moral weakness are founded on ignorance (ibid.: 143). Truth will be victorious not only over 'ignorance' but also over sophistry (ibid.: 140). For this victory to occur, however, the truth must be communicated (ibid.: 140). Man's perfectibility is advanced as he uncovers the truths of his existence and communicates them to others. Governments, which have become the foundations of inequality, exist because of ignorance. As ignorance declines, so will the basis of government (ibid.: 248).

The same strategy for the justification of anarchism is found in the work of Peter Kropotkin (1987). Kropotkin bases his analysis of mankind on a conception of universal animal nature. In contrast to Darwin, Kropotkin asserted that human survival has been enhanced by cooperation, not competition. Most animal species that have survived use 'mutual aid' as a tool for survival. From this naturalistic observation, Kropotkin suggested that the history of the human species also shows the tendency toward cooperation. In the modern age, however, this natural condition has been mitigated by social conditions. Since the sixteenth century, with the emergence of the centralized nation state and the economic logic of capitalism, the institutions that supported mutual aid among the human species have been in retreat (ibid.: 203, 208).

To Kropotkin, 'progress' is measured according to those institutions that extend the natural condition of mutual aid (1987: 180). Modern institutions, however, corrupt the individual. The undesirable traits in human beings will be eliminated by disposing of the institutions that promote such characteristics (ibid.: 83). Kropotkin acknowledged that this will not be easy to achieve because the law serves the ruling class (Kropotkin cited in Gould and Truitt, 1973: 450–1).

Pierre Joseph Proudhon presented a similar ontological justification for anarchism. In *What Is Property?* Proudhon argued that the idea of property was not natural to the human condition (1966: 251). The system of property leads to inequality that can only be maintained by force. Proudhon was, however, equally critical of state communism. Communism oppresses the various faculties of individuals (ibid.: 261). In place of either of these systems, Proudhon proposed a form of social organization he called *liberty*. For Proudhon, liberty is the condition in which mankind is capable of exercising rationality in the organization of society (ibid.: 283). Liberty brings the body of scientific knowledge to bear on political questions. Political truths exist and can be understood by rational scientific inquiry (ibid.: 276). To the extent that a society is enlightened, the need for oppressive state authority diminishes. Ultimately, human reason will replace the oppressive state.

The sample of writers is clearly not an exhaustive list of anarchists in the nineteenth century. It is, however, a representative sample of a particular approach to anarchism in which several recurring themes emerge. Although the characterization of the human being differs slightly among the authors, they share a common concern for the delineation of the human character in order to proceed in their critique of the contemporary order. Although the representational character of this methodology is my primary interest, it should also be noted that the content of that representation is similar in the authors mentioned. The human being is seen as a rational, cognitive and compassionate creature. Corruption takes place within social institutions and is not an essential part of human nature. As reason takes mankind toward the truth, rational individuals lose their need for the state.

ORIGINS OF AN EPISTEMOLOGICAL DEFENCE OF ANARCHISM

In contrast to an ontological defence of anarchism, an epistemologically based theory of anarchism questions the processes out of which a 'characterization' of the individual occurs. If the validity of any representation can be questioned, then the political structures that rest on that representational foundation must also be suspect. If the conditions for the existence of the truth claims embraced by the political order are demonstrated to be suspect, and if the representations by which the character of the state is propagated and legitimated are open to interpretation, doubt, or shown to be grounded in fiction, then the authority of the state may be legitimately questioned.

The elements for an epistemologically based critique of the state can be traced back to the nineteenth century in the writings of Max Stirner and Friedrich Nietzsche. In the contemporary world, the same challenges to the Enlightenment view of knowledge, and ultimately to the state, can be found in the writings of the post-structuralists.

The Nineteenth-Century Attack on Representation

Max Stirner's *The Ego and His Own* (1973) is a subjectivist's defence against the power of the state. What is unique about the work, especially in relation to other nineteenth-century anarchist thought, is the method Stirner employs for his defence of egoism. Stirner's main task is not to construct an alternative view of human nature but to suggest that the systems of thought that have been employed in the Western philosophic and political tradition are based on an error. The error is that they construct a fixed idea of the human being and then seek to construct man in the image of that idea. Thoughts and conceptions, themselves, become the chains that enslave us. We are prisoners of our conceptions (ibid.: 63).

Stirner traces the emergence of the Idea in the history of Western thought. Ancient man was concerned with the world, and the world was its own truth. The mind was to be used as a weapon, a means against nature (ibid.: 17). But the world is in a constant state of change. Therefore, truth is a fleeting moment. This was an unsettling position for modern man.

Stirner identified the transformation to the modern age with the emergence of spiritualism and the creation of static concepts. Specifically, he argued that the modern age emerged with the decline of ancient civilization and the rise of Christianity. Asserting that the modern age is characterized by the notion of the Idea, or Concept, Stirner suggested a natural affinity between the spiritualism of modern philosophy and the spiritualism of Christian thought. Whether in spiritual or secular matters, both convey the same 'foolishness' of the fixed idea (ibid.: 44).

Stirner claimed that the individual loses uniqueness in the face of the generalized and fixed concept of 'Man'. This claim is especially relevant in the area of politics. Stirner surveyed what he considered to be three types of liberal thought: political, social and humane. Each ultimately rests on the creation of an image to which the individual must conform. Political liberalism is possible only through the creation of the idea of citizenship. It transforms individual into citizen in the image of the state (ibid.: 107). Social liberalism robs people of their property in the name of community (ibid.: 117–18). However, humane liberalism, because of its subtlety, is the most insidious because it removes the uniqueness of human beings and turns the real living ego, man, into the generalized concept, Man (ibid.: 128). The individual is lost to the Concept. Servitude continues, but in the name of humanity rather than God, King or country. Stirner rejected all three of these liberal formulations and sought to find the place for man that has been lost in the modern age.

Stirner opposes the attempt to formulate a notion of human 'essence' (ibid.: 81), yet his alternative is clearly not wholly successful. He is aware of the problem but lacks the linguistic tools to escape it. He, therefore, lapses into his own characterization of the human subject at various points throughout the work. This leaves the work as a whole unable to remove the notion of the historical subject, even within a general attack on its characterization.

The significance of the work is clearly in its reformulation of the methodological problems; Stirner's position is an early formulation of the attack on representation. This is reflected in his condemnation of 'concepts', 'principles' and 'standpoints' that are used as weapons against individuals (ibid.: 63). More generally, Stirner's attack has the character of a universal condemnation of 'ontological culture'. The culture of 'being' and the representations of that being are characterized as suspect at best and dangerous at worst. Rather than focusing on a competing model of human nature, Stirner was concerned with showing the linkage between ideas and the context in which they are generated. This method is similar to that labelled 'genealogy' by Nietzsche and the post-structuralists.

Nietzsche, Genealogy and the Problem of Language

In the latter half of the nineteenth century, Friedrich Nietzsche created a language with which to analyse the presuppositions that underlie the Enlightenment view of knowledge. Nietzsche denied the validity of Kant's assertion that there is a transcendental reality of which our knowledge is limited. In denying the existence of a transcendental realm of *things in themselves*, Nietzsche is raising doubts about the foundation on which the entire Enlightenment enterprise has been built. The magnitude of this assertion cannot be over-emphasized.

Whether one subscribes to the Platonic notion of the forms, adheres to the Kantian notion of a thing in itself, or defends the Hegelian totalizing teleology of world history, to Nietzsche these are nothing more than fictions. Each of these systems of thought suggests that there is a substratum to reality in which the true causal dynamic of world events resides. Thus what has passed in history as epistemology has been little more than metaphysics (Nietzsche, 1957). Science also rests on presuppositions, the truth of which cannot be proved. For Nietzsche, the world is neither true nor real, but living (Deleuze, 1983: 184).

Nietzsche will not deny that these fictions have served a utility function in human history. At the beginning of *The Use and Abuse of History* (1957), Nietzsche suggests that the drawing of a line to establish a specific horizon, distinguishing the knowable and the unknowable, the visible and the invisible, allows for the generation and reproduction of knowledge and culture (ibid.: 7). Within the metaphysics of culture, falsity and narrowness are virtues when compared to the intellectual paralysis generated by ever-shifting horizons (ibid.: 8).

At this point an epistemological paradox around the idea of exclusion appears. To generate knowledge, particularly of history and culture, one must continually limit the universe of one's objects, closing the system. One must draw a boundary around that which is relevant. But to do so removes the phenomenon from the context of its occurrence. This process negates the possibility of truth. Therefore, history never contains truth; it is the past transformed to resemble the present (ibid.: 15).

Cultural and historical analyses create fiction. This is logically true, regardless of the utility of the proposition. Because the past is continually reconfigured to resemble the present, any notion of an ahistorical universal is absurd. The historical character of truth is also reinforced in a second way. Because truth does not and cannot exist apart from those who possess it, and because those beings are historical entities, truth is a historical phenomenon (Strong, 1988: 44).

If universal truth is denied, then the domain of intellectual inquiry is transformed. The quest for knowledge is not satisfied by representations. There is no longer the possibility of stating truth about human beings or nature. Representations of being, truth and the real are only fictions (Nietzsche, 1967: 266). If this is accepted, then there remains a twofold intellectual task. The first is to unmask the existing structure of culture so as to reveal its metaphysical illusions (genealogy). The second task is to return to the individual a conception of life stripped of its illusion. This is represented by the 'will to power'. These ideas are clearly related. If the will to power is in part the will to truth, which Nietzsche suggests it is, and if the ideal of truth does not reside in true reality, it must be contained in the medium of truth, language. Language contains the concepts that characterize the world. The genealogical method explores the process by which facts acquire their status from the utility function they serve in the language of history.

Nietzsche's genealogical exploration is concerned with the way in which the facts of the contemporary world have been created. Of particular interest is the creation of morality. To this point in history, claimed Nietzsche (1956), the intrinsic worth of values had been taken for granted; they must be called into question: 'We need to know the conditions from which those values have sprung and how they have developed and changed: morality as a consequence, symptom, mask' (ibid.: 155).

Questioning the origin and status of values suggests the link between language, knowledge and power that will be an essential component of the post-structuralist claims. Language expresses a set of conceptualizations about the world. And, because the person who makes a statement using the concepts contained in language is not making an objectively true statement, the world of appearance is a creation of those who speak and give the world its image (Nietzsche cited in Kaufman, 1968).

Thus Nietzsche asks 'Who speaks?' when moral positions are asserted. In exploring the genealogy of the concept *good*, Nietzsche claimed that its genesis was in the utility it served for the nobles (ibid.: 160). As the concept of good, originally associated with the actions of the nobility, is adopted by the lower strata, the concept loses its necessary connection to the existence of an aristocracy. Yet the association of good with nobles remains ingrained in the language.

The problem created by this representation of moral virtue is that it generates a 'fixed' characterization of human nature. This is true whether the characterization of human nature is *good* or *bad*. In fact, Nietzsche claims that the characterizations of good and bad are dependent on each other, suggesting that no knowledge at all is conveyed by their usage. However, the result of this characterization is a fixed, ahistorical notion of morality that can be applied to individuals. Society becomes immersed in the process of sorting the good from the bad and of assigning responsibility based on that characterization.

By denying the possibility of a moral representation of human nature, Nietzsche brings into question the process that has dominated the political experience of the Western world. If morality has its basis in interest rather than truth, the foundations that underlie political assertions of right and justice are also obliterated. Claims of the state have their genesis in the interests of those who created the language of justice in the same way that the interests of the commercial classes and the royal dynasties created the concept of nationalism (Nietzsche cited in Kaufmann, 1968: 61).

If politics cannot be organized around truth because it lacks transcendental grounding, and politics cannot be organized around justice because its representation reflects the interests of those who define it, then politics is reduced to the expression of power. The state is organized immorality (Nietzsche, 1967: 382). It represents the 'idolatry of the superfluous' (Nietzsche cited in Kaufmann, 1968: 162). The morality of the state is the instinct of the herd, with the force of numbers legitimating its actions.

Nietzsche asked, 'Under what conditions did man construct the value judgments "good" and "evil"?' (Nietzsche, 1956: 151). By replacing the transcendental claims of morality with the genealogical enterprise, Nietzsche suggested a method for the critique of all universal claims to knowledge in the West. Nietzsche contextualized all claims, whether in the discourse on physical nature or moral propositions. Both convey the tools of a species seeking a conceptual ordering of the world to enhance survival.

Thus, while Nietzsche rejected the ontological claims that provided the foundation for much of nineteenth-century anarchism, he made a monumental contribution to the development of post-anarchism. Nietzsche also introduced a question which would open a new avenue of inquiry for twentieth century post-structuralism. Under what conditions does contingent knowledge take on the character of a fact?

POST-STRUCTURALISM AND THE CRITIQUE OF ENLIGHTENMENT EPISTEMOLOGY

Inspired by Nietzsche and linguistic philosophy, the movement of post-structuralism in the late twentieth century continues to challenge the Enlightenment epistemology. The works of Jacques Derrida, Michel Foucault and Jean-François Lyotard, as three of the most notable members of the post-structuralist movement, all signify a break with what they perceive to be an epistemology based on the fixed idea. These authors and other post-structuralists reflect a shift away from the ontological character of the human discourse that dominated the eighteenth and nineteenth centuries.

In analysing the problems with Enlightenment epistemology, the common features of the post-structural position emerge. Reacting specifically to the structuralism of Saussure and Lévi-Strauss, the post-structural criticism is a comprehensive critique of the idea of representation. Linked to the questioning of the status of representation and to the rejection of a fixed conception of human nature is the denial of the 'grand narratives' that underlie mass politics.

In the attack on representation, there is an implicit negation of any fixed content for subjectivity in social and historical discourse. The post-structuralists reject what they consider the ontological character of modern individualism which has provided the foundation for nineteenth- and twentieth-century liberal ideology. They also reject the teleological character of twentieth-century Marxism.

The post-structuralists challenge the idea that truth and knowledge are simply the result of a linear accumulation of facts about objects in the world. Science, economics, culture and politics change as the language, concepts and ideas regarding what is acceptable as truth change. Thus the linear view of knowledge is replaced with a conceptualization of knowledge that is contingent on a plurality of internally consistent *episteme*. It is this idea that raises questions about the foundational basis of the modern state.

Representation, Language and Truth

Of central concern to the post-structuralists is the contrast between the modern and postmodern understanding of knowledge. At the centre of this debate is the status of representation. Representation signifies a process by which experience is turned into the signs of experience, which can then be ordered for recovery and use. Whether ordered from appearance (classical episteme) or according to function (modern episteme), the epistemological problem remains. The epistemology of representation requires a closed system. This is the only way that the identities of the signified can remain stable (Laclau cited in Ross, 1988: 73).

The attack on representation is an attack on the idea of a closed system (Arac, 1986: xxii). The argument centres on the claim that a closed system always omits an element contained in the object that it seeks to describe. In addition, the idea of representation fixes the meaning of the sign outside its context, making communication through the use of signs almost meaningless (Derrida, 1982b: 299–301). The post-structuralist critique of representation links the process of concept formation to the production and reproduction of language (Benhabib, 1987: 106–9). The attack on representation results in the conclusion that the communication of intended meaning is always inhibited because the meaning of the sign can never be clearly communicated.

In place of the idea of representation, post-structuralism uses the model of grammar as the framework for statements (Foucault, 1973: 237). The paradigm of language replaces the paradigm of consciousness (Benhabib, 1987: 110). The model of grammar for the context of knowledge formation has several important features. First, grammar contains its own internal laws governing discourse, regardless of the content of the message. The rules governing the truth claims of the message are then internal to the system of language itself and do not require the construction of an external system of verification. Second, because the verification of signs and symbols occurs internationally, there is no possibility of a metalanguage that links the various languages. (This is the focus of Lyotard's 1984 argument in *The Postmodern Condition*.) Third, because each language has different symbolic referents, statements must be context specific. This makes the communication across different systems of language difficult, if not impossible. Finally, with the plurality of possible grammatical systems, and the context-specific nature of their claims, irreconcilable tension must exist among heteromorphous language systems.

This assertion clearly distinguishes the position of the post-structuralists from the critical theory of Jürgen Habermas. Habermas argues that it is possible to transcend the subject-centred reason in the formulation of rules governing discourse (1990: 341). It is possible, therefore, to deduce an ideal speech situation in which discourse occurs that is free from the influence of institutionalized power. But if the post-structuralists are correct, what would such a speech situation produce? Despite his denial, Habermas must assume a form of Kantian universalism if the outcome of ideal speech is to be meaningful. This denies the heteromorphous nature of systems of grammar and the context-specific use of the sign. To the post-structuralists, the ideal speech situation will produce skewed languages speaking at one another – neither truth nor consensus.

In linking the production of truth to the production of heteromorphous languages, the post-structuralist renews the Nietzschean idea of genealogy as the method of inquiry for social practice. The Nietzschean question 'who speaks?' in the realm of discourse suggests that the conditions that gave rise to an assertion of truth are the proper focus of investigation. This concentration provides the basis for an analysis that is not dependent on the idea of a transcendent subject (Foucault, 1980). The real question is not what something is in itself. There is no such metalanguage that can support the idea of essence. Genealogical analysis focuses on the context that makes a statement of 'this is' possible. In describing the application of this method to the study of the prison, Foucault states that he studies the practice of imprisonment to understand the 'moral technology' in which the practice becomes accepted as natural (1981: 4–5). Thus there is a direct connection between the accepted practice and the production of truth that supports that practice.

The important questions for the post-structuralists pertain to the assumptions and complex social relations in which language is produced, reproduced and validated. The task of post-structural analysis is not to replace one set of axiomatic structures with another but to provide a reading of scientific, cultural and social texts such that the contradictions, assumptions and *a prioris* are made explicit (Aronowitz cited in Ross, 1988: 55). Only in this way can the connections among language, the production of truth, and the institutions of power be made apparent.

EPISTEMOLOGICAL RELATIVISM AND THE CRITIQUE OF POWER

The post-structuralists are concerned with the epistemological status of discourse, and, as they clearly indicate, their position has political implications. The political side of their epistemological critique links the context in which the political statements are formulated to the institutions that generate the rules and procedures for institutional discourse. As Foucault asserted, all institutions of power have a mechanism for generating and controlling discourse (1980: 93). Thus, discourse not only generates legitimating discourse for that institution but also controls the right to speak within the institutional framework (Foucault, 1977: 214). The political–epistemological link, therefore, connects the production of knowledge with the production of power. By examining the process in which what is called knowledge comes to be labelled as such, and by claiming that the label of knowledge is tied to a specific historical context for the production of knowledge, the post-structuralists seek to undermine the foundations from which the dominant political ideologies of the twentieth century have drawn their legitimacy. If the concepts under which action is coordinated are fictions, then the legitimacy of those actions is open to question.

Post-structural analysis of the political environment substitutes a focus on epistemology for the modernist focus on ontology. The concern changes from 'what is human nature?' to 'how have we come to this belief about human nature?' This epistemological focus decentres the understanding of politics because it suggests heteromorphous arenas for the production of truth. Languages emerge in a plurality of episteme. A plurality of languages requires the decentring of politics.

If post-structuralism counters the universal claims of the modernist epistemology and replaces them with a notion of plurality and contingency, then it can challenge the content of the dominant ideology without the substitution of one popular truth for another (Ross, 1988: ix). Where no *a priori* exists regarding the subject, there can be no universal regarding politics. The post-structuralists argue that the human discourses need to give up universals (Mouff cited in Ross, 1988: 34).

If truth is relative to the construction of a language in which taxonomies, concepts and facts are used to judge and regulate activity, then truth is not something to be discovered but something that is produced. The post-structuralists claim that the creation of knowledge needs to be understood as a process in which contingent value is replicated within a closed epistemological system. For this reason, there is a link between the social, economic, scientific and political discourses within any society: 'In any given culture and at any given moment, there is always only one episteme that defines the conditions of possibility of all knowledge, whether expressed in a theory or silently invested in a practice' (Foucault, 1973: 168). Each episteme supports a different form of domination. In any given period, then, the system in which knowledge is produced and reinforced maintains the political order.

The post-structuralists oppose the tyranny of globalizing discourse on any level (Foucault, 1980: 80, 83). The methodologies suggested by Derrida, Foucault and Lyotard (deconstruction, genealogy and paralogy, respectively) are all designed to decentre the production of language and truth to more accurately reflect the contingent and relative character of knowledge. Society contains a plurality of heteromorphous languages. Genealogical analysis reveals that history has been a struggle among these languages (Foucault, 1980: 83).

At this point, the attack of the post-structuralists appears entirely negative in character. There is no possibility of truth; there are only contingent truths. There are no legitimating foundations for politics. There are only power struggles in which the power is masked, effectively or ineffectively, in the production of legitimating discourse through self-replicating institutions of power. The existing political order is generated from a language of representation that is context specific and insupportable in its universalism.

Post-Structuralism, the State and Anarchist Theory

Several aspects of the post-structuralists' position have particular importance for an epistemological formulation of anarchism. The attempt to fix human nature or to create any idea of human essence is clearly rejected. The idea that legitimacy can be grounded in process is also suspect (cf. Derrida, 1982a: 304). The post-structuralist position also eliminates any idea of historical inevitability or teleology. History is the discourse of the present projected onto the past.

In general, post-structuralism provides the tools for a systematic deconstruction of the claims to legitimacy of any institutional authority. If truth determines how we live, and the production of truth is relative to a particular episteme and the corresponding constellation of power, then how we live is ultimately determined by power, not truth in either the Platonic or the Kantian sense. Dismantling the myths on which politics is based demonstrates the prejudices of existing practice. Removing the possibility that the state can be based on truth reveals the existing structures of power in social relations.

However, despite this stance regarding the institutions of power, Jürgen Habermas (cited in Foster, 1983), Stephen White (1988: 190), Stanley Aronowitz (cited in Ross, 1988: 48) and others argue that in denying the possibility of authoritative values the post-structuralists' position lacks the ability to provide a normative defence of the individual. They argue that although the post-structuralists' focus on the historical and epistemological contingencies in which power arose may provide descriptive statements, this position is not sufficient to make a choice regarding the existing relations of power. For this reason, Habermas identifies post-structuralism as a neoconservative attack on the foundations of modernism. The post-structuralists, he claims, are not able to make any determinations of what is just and unjust.

But to Foucault and the other post-structuralists, the claims of critics such as Habermas, White and Aronowitz are based on an ontology and universalism that are characteristic of modernism. The modernist critics of post-structuralism support their critique of power with an ontology of the subject that is then contrasted with what they consider the prevailing ideology. The content of concepts such as just and unjust are tied to the ontological strategy that underlies modernist politics. Whereas it is accurate to say that Foucault suggested that the study of social interaction should reveal the structures of power that lead to representations of just and unjust, it is equally true that he concluded his analysis by saying that the real target is power and the legitimating mechanism that serves power (1977: 211).

The political question that emerges from the post-structuralists' strategy concerns what remains after the epistemological critique of power. Is there any type of politics that *can* be defended? It is into this space that the epistemological foundation of anarchism emerges.

THE EPISTEMOLOGICAL BASIS OF ANARCHISM

The central problem for anarchist theory, in the light of the post-structuralist critique of power and knowledge, is to build a non-representational basis for anarchism. A new theory of anarchism cannot be based on the ontological assumptions contained within the classical anarchist literature. The characterization of human beings as benevolent or rational cannot be sustained with any more certainty than the claims that human beings are selfish and irrational. Anarchism must find its grounding outside any fixed structure.

There are three paths that can be taken in reconstructing a justification for anarchism in the aftermath of post-structural theory. The first focuses on the contingent nature of knowledge. Anarchy is the real, empirical character of society without its facade. The second argument suggests that anarchism is the only possible normative position toward the state given the plurality of validating episteme. If there is no condition under which a particular normative condition can be validated, then the plurality represented by the anarchist position is unassailable. The third possibility suggests moving the political context away from the notion of representation and toward a non-ontological conception of individuality. The first two suggestions are essentially negative in character. The third offers the possibility for a positive political critique from within the general framework of the post-structuralist epistemology.

The Empirical Assertion of Anarchy

The assertion that there is no foundation for truth means that a claim 'to know' is contingent on its respective episteme. All statements must reflect the context in which discourse is generated. Discourse is a mediated process of conceptualization relative to the constrictions of language.

Experience cannot be recaptured by language. The closed grammatical and semantic system used for discourse must, by its nature, omit elements of experience. Any attempt to categorize or reformulate experience creates fiction. A reconstituted experience takes the forms, categories and concepts created in a historical and collectively grounded context. Reflection on experience is, therefore, historical context reflecting back on itself.

If discourse is relative to the governing episteme, and if all claims to truth are subject to those same constraints, then the ability to formulate a universally valid, rational or normative discourse would be impossible. If that is the case, the discourse that has come to rationalize the existence and functioning of the state within the modernist episteme is valid only within the closed and constrained sets of assumptions and concepts that constitute its context. Given that meaning in discourse is generated by metaphorical reference to individuated experience and that those individuated metaphorical references are plural, the communication of intended meaning is impossible. Within this epistemological framework, the idea that consensus can be achieved in political discourse through the imposition of a structural context, whether democratic or otherwise, is reduced to nonsense. Taken together – the relativity of both ontology and epistemology, the plurality of language systems, and the impossibility of communicating intended meaning – the potential to reach consensus without either deception or force becomes impossible. The true character of the society is revealed as anarchy, the realization of which is prevented by the various fictions used to legitimize state power. The anarchistic nature of existing society remains an undercurrent to the surface relation of power.

The post-structuralist critique of Enlightenment epistemology, therefore, suggests the deconstruction of the state's normative and rational facade. The state is revealed as a set of power relations. Stripped of the illusions that reinforce the dominant ideology, force appears as the real component of social and political relations. Without ideological justification to support the institutional structure, social relations are naturally anarchistic. Anarchy is the true, empirical, character of society.

The Normative Defence of Anarchism

Given the heteromorphous nature of possible attitudes, rules and prescriptions, consensus is not logically possible. Consensus can only be reached using a totalizing conception of society. But given the plurality of experiences, interests, languages and epistemological contexts, such universalism can only take the character of totalitarian politics.

If the validity of norms, values and morals resides in popular will, as opposed to transcendental notions of truth and justice, then dominant norms become both ontologically and epistemologically indefensible. The defence of norms, values and morals takes the form of force disguised as ontological necessity. This condition cannot be mitigated by majoritarian forms of democratic practice.

If knowledge, as the construction of truth, cannot be externally validated, and epistemological and ontological plurality is the background for political reality, then anarchism becomes the only defensible normative position. Anarchism denies the state's claims to have the legitimate right to determine what is sacred and profane. Anarchism represents the condition in which the optimal state of external plurality can exist.

The normative character of anarchism comes from the negative character of its assertion. If the actions of states are based on a positive claim about the character of the individual, and if that characterization, along with the very idea of characterization, is rejected, then state actions are reduced to actions of collective force. Within this perspective, the burden of proof has been reversed. It is not resistance to the state that needs to be justified but the positive actions of the state against individuals. Opposition to the state fills the only remaining normative space once the basis for state action has been denied.

Anarchism and Non-Reflexive Individualism

If a positive basis for anarchism is to be constructed within the post-structuralist epistemological critique, the issue of subjectivity must be addressed. Is it possible to construct a theory of anarchism without the reintroduction of the representative subject as historical actor? This can be achieved, I argue, on the basis of non-ontological assertions regarding the individual within the post-structural epistemology. This, of course, means that the content of subjectivity must be eliminated. The movement of the post-structuralists toward language philosophy offers one possibility.

The political argument revolves around the conditions that are necessary for discourse, political or otherwise. Discourse is metaphorical in character. Signs and symbols are transmitted between a sender and a receiver. These two poles are the necessary conditions for discourse. (Jean Baudrillard has used the metaphor of a 'living satellite' to describe each participant in discourse; Baudrillard cited in Foster, 1983: 127.) Given the post-structuralists' arguments regarding the contingency and plurality of language systems, this assertion can provide an epistemologically grounded defence of the most radical form of individualism.

Post-structuralism argues that there is a social component to discourse. Discourse is produced in a context in which the episteme underlying the production of statements is validated and reinforced in the process of generating truth claims. The context in which knowledge is produced influences the measure of what qualifies as knowledge as well as establishing the semantic limits for discourse. The assertion that there is a role for both knowledge context, as epistemological milieu, and subjective experience, as the origin of content, suggests both the contingent character of knowledge and the uniqueness of knowledge to each discursive pole.

If the context for discursive statements is both culturally specific and experientially unique, then a double problem for the communication of meaning emerges. On the collective level, each culture will generate a unique set of metaphors with which to construct meanings. There is no linguistic means to impose a universal set of signs and meanings. In addition, on the individual level it must also be concluded that each sensing organism has a unique experiential context from which to generate statements. The metaphors of any culture cannot close the gap between the uniqueness of experience and the standardization necessary for discourse.

The relative nature of both epistemological context, as historical milieu, and experience, as a field of sensation unique to each discursive pole, denies not only the ability to form epistemologically sound universals but also demonstrates the fallacy of the claim that moving towards consensual politics will by necessity lead to humanitarian political practice. Therefore, to the post-structuralists, the ideal speech situation discussed by Habermas will provide a condition for the discovery of the majority interest, but it will not, by necessity, limit majoritarianism. There is no implicit plurality of legitimate meanings to compete with the majority.

To the post-structuralists, the impossibility of communicating perfect meaning in political discourse suggests the impossibility of creating consensual politics. This is the case because both the descriptive and prescriptive statements that form the foundation for consensual politics are reducible to subjectivist claims. The truth value of any such assertions has been dissolved by the post-structuralist critique. The plurality of languages and the individuated nature of sensory experience suggest that each denotative and prescriptive statement must be unique to each individual. Consensual politics is reduced to an expression of power, the ability for one set of metaphors to impose itself onto the discursive system to impose its validating conditions for truth.

By suggesting the epistemological conditions in which discourse occurs, the post-structuralists have generated a claim for a non-reflexive, non-onto-logical individualism. This individualism is non-reflexive in the sense that the individual is not turned back on itself to create a justification or definition of *uniqueness*, *worth* and *value*. Worth does not require a definitional content. This is the case because individual worth is not defined internally, as a representation of some norm or specific character trait. Individuation is imposed externally by conditions necessary for discourse. Discourse requires a sender and a receiver. Each participant reflects, as discourse, the unique experience of that being. The value of discourse is all that must be assumed.

Any assertion of common biological composition among each receiver–sender is mitigated by the uniqueness of the experience that provides the context for discourse. The problem of representation is avoided by the denial of any notion of essence in the discussion of the individual. The only assertion is empirical, not ontological. Individuals are biologically separated. Because the environment is infinitely complex, the formation of reflexive content is infinitely pluralistic. Anarchism is the only justifiable political stance because it defends the pluralism that results from individuated meaning in discourse. By logical extension, the individuals who generate that plurality have legitimate claims against the state, which by its nature engages in either totalitarian universalism or consensual majoritarianism. By exploring the necessary conditions for discourse, and in examining the nature of that discourse, post-structuralism suggests an epistemologically based theory of anarchism.

CONCLUSION

In the nineteenth century, the challenge to the fixed idea and the 'tyranny of structure' raised questions about the epistemological character of modernity. In the twentieth century, building on Nietzsche, linguistic theory and aesthetics, the philosophic movement known as post-structuralism has raised questions about the universalism contained within the modernist tradition. To the post-structuralists, modernity accomplished the subjugation of individuals through the use of an epistemology that prioritizes thought and its residue, the concept, over what is immediate and sensual. From the assumption of a transcendent unity of thought, whether as the 'doctrine of the forms' or as things in themselves, the idea of political unity rests its foundation on this epistemological doctrine.

The post-structuralists' view that the content of subjectivity is relative and contingent on the discourse that determined the acceptability of statements as true or untrue questions the assumptions on which the modern nation state is built. In this view, the state acts to impose its definition of subjectivity on human beings. The deconstructionist strategy used by the post-structuralists makes possible a critique of all forms of institutional power by challenging the category of subjectivity that makes collective political action possible.

Post-structuralism has provided the analytic tools to clarify what Max Stirner suggested in the nineteenth century. Stirner argued that the concept of self represents a link between culture and institutionalized power. If the self cannot validate its understanding through the belief in transcendent truth, and if social discourse consists of metaphors, traces of reified metaphysics, and power, then the self has only the self through which to validate being. As a result, Stirner embraced the concept of the ego.

There is a parallel between this idea of Stirner's and Foucault's idea of 'power/knowledge', but some distinction is also required. The post-structuralists would deny that any concept of self can be independent of language. The anarchistic conclusions for post-structuralism stem from a belief in the multiplicity of possible languages out of which the content for subjectivity can be formulated. The imposition of any of those languages as a metalanguage appears as a force alien and opposed to the multitextual nature of discourse.

Stirner claimed that the state imposes its will, its thoughts and its concepts on the individual body. In defending his 'skin' against the tyranny of the concept (1973: 148), Stirner is defending the sensing being against the process of objectification at the hands of the state. It is again Foucault who comes closest to the assertions of Stirner in his research on the control of 'bodies' in prisons and mental institutions. Foucault described his work as an inquiry into the 'technology of the self' (Foucault cited in Rabinow, 1984: 229). He was concerned with the various objectification strategies that have been used to control bodies. Because the technologies of the self imposed by institutions are both contingent and speculative, Foucault concludes that they should be resisted (1977: 211).

The post-structuralist critique of modernism undermines the project of constructing a universal human identity. In the absence of a metaconcept of human nature, the discourse on human subjectivity moves from a search for fact to a discussion of multiple interpretations. This shift constitutes a movement from science to aesthetics in the discourse about human beings.

Those who base their attacks on post-structuralism in the claim that the denial of a singular subjectivity makes the formulation of an ethics of resistance impossible misunderstand the focus of the post-structuralist argument. Resistance is formulated against a background of plurality. It is plurality that cultural and political institutions oppose as they promote one form of subjectivity over another. This is precisely why post-structuralism can support liberation movements even though a specific definition of power remains elusive. The struggle for liberation has the character of political resistance to a process of semantic and metaphorical reductionism that serves the interests of control and manipulation.

Ultimately, post-structuralism offers a new opportunity to reformulate the claims of anarchism. By demonstrating how political oppression is linked to the larger cultural processes of knowledge production and cultural representation, post-structuralism conveys a logic of opposition. By defending uniqueness and diversity, post-structuralism stands against any totalizing conception of being. Its liberating potential derives from the deconstruction of any concept that makes oppression appear rational.

NOTE

1. Andrew M. Koch. *Philosophy of the Social Sciences* 23(3): 327–51 (1993). Copyright © 1993 by SAGE Publications. Reprinted by permission of SAGE Publications.

REFERENCES

Arac, Jonathan (ed.) (1986). *Postmodernism and Politics*. Minneapolis: University of Minnesota Press.

Benhabib, Sela (1987). Epistemologies of Postmodernism: A Rejoinder to Jean-François Lyotard. *New German Critique* 33: 103–26.

Deleuze, Gilles (1983). *Nietzsche and Philosophy*. New York: Columbia University Press.

Derrida, Jacques (1982a). *Margins of Philosophy*. Chicago: University of Chicago Press.

—— (1982b) 'Sending: On Representation'. *Social Research* 49: 294–326.

Foster, Hal (ed.) (1983). *The Anti-Aesthetic: Essays on Postmodern Culture*. Port Townsend, WA: Bay Press.

Foucault, Michel (1981). 'Questions of Method: An Interview with Michel Foucault'. *Ideology and Consciousness* 8 (Spring): 4–13.

—— (1980). *Power/Knowledge* (C. Gordon, ed. and trans.). New York: Harvester/Pantheon.

—— (1977). *Language, Counter-Memory and Practice* (D.F. Bouchard, ed.; D.F. Bouchard and S. Simon, trans.). New York: Cornell University Press.

—— (1973). *The Order of Things: An Archaeology of the Human Sciences*. New York: Vintage Books/Random House.

Godwin, William (1971) [1798]. *Enquiry Concerning Political Justice* (reprint). Oxford: Oxford University Press.

Gould, James A., and Truitt, Willis H. (1973). *Political Ideologies*. New York: Macmillan.

Habermas, Jürgen (1990). *The Philosophical Discourse of Modernity* (F. Lawrence, trans.). Cambridge, MA: MIT Press.

Kaufmann, Walter (ed.) (1968). *The Portable Nietzsche*. New York: Viking.

Kropotkin, Peter (1987) [1903]. *Mutual Aid: A Factor of Evolution*. London: Freedom Press.

Lyotard, Jean-François (1984). *The Postmodern Condition: A Report on Knowledge*. Minneapolis: University of Minnesota Press.

Nietzsche, Friedrich (1967) [1901]. *The Will to Power* (W. Kaufman, ed. and trans.). New York: Random House.

—— (1957) [1874]. *The Use and Abuse of History*. New York: Macmillan.

—— (1956) [1872, 1887]. *The Birth of Tragedy and the Genealogy of Morals*. Garden City, NY: Doubleday/Anchor.

Proudhon, Pierre J. (1966) [1840]. *What Is Property? An Enquiry into the Principle of Right and of Government*. New York: Howard Fertig.

Rabinow, Paul (ed.) (1984). *The Foucault Reader*. New York: Pantheon.

Ross, Andrew (ed.) (1988). *Universal Abandon? The Politics of Postmodernism*. Minneapolis: University of Minnesota Press.

Stirner, Max (1973) [1845]. *The Ego and His Own* (J.J. Martin, ed.; S.T. Byington, trans.; reprint). New York: Dover.

Strong, Tracy B. (ed.) (1988). *Friedrich Nietzsche and the Politics of Transfiguration*. Berkeley: University of California Press.

White, Stephen K. (1988). 'Poststructuralism and Political Reflection'. *Political Theory* 16(2): 186–208.

2
Is Post-Structuralist Political Theory Anarchist?[1]

Todd May

The difficulty in evaluating the political philosophy of the French post-structuralists – Foucault, Deleuze and Lyotard in particular – is inseparable from the difficulty in understanding what their general political philosophy is. That they have rejected Marxism as an adequate account of our social and political situation is clear. But what they have substituted for it is still a subject of contention. This is because, rather than offering a general political theory, the post-structuralists have instead given us specific analyses of concrete situations of oppression. From Foucault's *Histoire de la folie* to Lyotard's *The Differend*, the focus has been upon madness, sexuality, psychoanalysis, language, the unconscious, art, etc., but not upon a unified account of what politics is or how it should be conducted in the contemporary world.

This absence or refusal of a general political theory has led some critics to accuse the post-structuralists of a self-defeating normative relativism or outright nihilism.[2] The question these critics raise is this: if the post-structuralists cannot offer a general political theory which includes both a principle for political evaluation and a set of values which provide the foundation for critique, don't their theories lapse into an arbitrary decision, or worse, mere chaos? The assumption behind this question is that in order to engage in political philosophy adequately, one must first possess a set of values which are either generally accepted or can be defended by recourse to generally accepted values. Then, one must construct one's political philosophy using those values as foundations. Last, one should compare the present political situation with the constructed one in order to help understand the deficiencies of the present and possible routes to remedy those deficiencies.[3]

The challenge to post-structuralism is to offer an account of itself as a theoretical political practice. It is a challenge that cannot be answered within the terms of the two traditions that have defined the space of political theory in the twentieth century: liberalism and Marxism. Both these traditions have been rejected by the post-structuralists. However, there is a tradition, though not cited by the post-structuralists, within which their thought can be situated and thus better understood and evaluated. That tradition is the neglected 'third way' of political theory: anarchism.

Anarchism is often dismissed in the same terms as post-structuralism for being an ethical relativism or a voluntarist chaos. However, the theoretical tradition of anarchism, though not as voluminous as Marxism or liberalism, provides a general framework within which post-structuralist thought can be situated, and thus more adequately evaluated.

[...]

The post-structuralist analyses of knowledge, of desire and of language, subvert the humanist discourse which is the foundation of traditional anarchism. Moreover, they consider humanism's emphasis on the autonomy and dignity of the subject to be dangerous (except for Lyotard, for whom it is mostly irrelevant), continuing in a subtler guise the very mechanisms of oppression it sought to resist. Humanism is the nineteenth-century motif, and individual autonomy and subjectivity its concepts, that must be rejected if a politics adequate to our age is to be articulated. This motif and its concepts are not peculiar to anarchism; they provide the foundation both for liberalism, with its emphasis on freedom and autonomy, and for traditional Marxism, with its focus on labour as a species-being, as well. (It is no accident that recent Marxists such as Althusser have tried to reformulate Marxism by divesting it of all humanist categories.) Humanism is the foundation of all political theory bequeathed to us by the nineteenth century. In rejecting it, post-structuralism has questioned not only the fundamental assumptions of such theory, but also the very idea that political theory actually requires foundations. That is why post-structuralism is so often misunderstood as an extreme relativism or nihilism.

However, it is not in favour of chaos that post-structuralism has abjured the notion of foundations, humanist or otherwise, for its political theorizing. What it has offered instead is precise analyses of oppression in its operation on a variety of registers. None of the post-structuralists' claims offer unsurpassable perspectives on oppression; indeed their analyses raise doubts about the coherence of the concept of an unsurpassable perspective in political theory. Instead, they engage in what has often been called 'micropolitics': political theorizing that is specific to regions, types or levels of political activity, but makes no pretensions of offering a general political theory. To offer a general political theory would in fact run counter to their common contention that oppression must be analysed and resisted on the many registers and in the many nexuses in which it is discovered. It would be to invite a return to the problem created by humanism, which became a tool of oppression to the very degree that it became a conceptual foundation for political or social thought. For the post-structuralists, there is a Stalin waiting behind every general political theory: either you conform to the concepts on which it relies, or else you must be changed or eliminated in favour of those concepts. Foundationalism in political theory is, in short, inseparable from representation.

This is the trap of an anarchist humanism. By relying on humanism as its conceptual basis, anarchists precluded the possibility of resistance by those who do not conform to its dictates of normal subjectivity. Thus it is no surprise when in Kropotkin's critique of the prisons he lauds Pinel as a liberator of the insane, failing to see the new psychological bonds Pinel introduced and which Foucault analyses in *Histoire de la folie* (Kropotkin, 1970: esp. 234; Foucault, 1972: 511–30). For traditional anarchism, abnormality is to be cured rather than expressed; and though far more tolerant of deviance from the norm in matters of sexuality and other behaviours, there remains in such an anarchism the concept of the norm as the prototype of the properly human. This prototype, the post-structuralists have argued, does not constitute the source of resistance against oppression in the contemporary age; rather, through its unity and its concrete operation it is one form of such oppression.

Traditional anarchism, in its foundational concepts – and moreover, in the fact of possessing foundational concepts – betrays the insights which constitute its core. Humanism is a form of representation; thus, anarchism, as a critique of representation, cannot be constructed on its basis. Post-structuralist theorizing has, in effect, offered a way out of the humanist trap by engaging in non-foundationalist political critique. Such a critique reveals how decentralized, non-representative radical theorizing can be articulated without relying upon a fundamental concept or motif in the name of which it offers its critique. However, one question remains which, unanswered, threatens the very notion of post-structuralism as a political critique. If it is not in the name of humanism or some other foundation that the critique occurs, in what or whose name is it a critique? How can the post-structuralists criticize existing social structures as oppressive without either a concept of what is being oppressed or at least a set of values that would be better realized in another social arrangement? In eliminating autonomy as inadequate to play the role of the oppressed in political critique, has post-structuralism eliminated the role itself, and with it the very possibility of critique? In short, can there be critique without representation?

To the last question, the answer must be: in some sense yes, and in some sense no. There can be no political critique without a value in the name of which one criticizes. One practice or institution must be said in some way to be wrong relative to another. Simply put, evaluation cannot occur without values; and where there are values, there is representation. For instance, in his history of the prisons, Foucault criticizes the practices of psychology and penology for normalizing individuals. His criticism rests on a value that goes something like this: one should not constrain others' action or thought unnecessarily. Lyotard can be read as promoting the value, among others, of allowing the fullest expression for different linguistic genres. Inasmuch as these values are held to be valid for all, there is representation underlying post-structuralist theorizing.

However, these values are not pernicious to the anarchist project of allowing oppressed populations to decide their goals and their means of resistance within the registers of their own oppression. They do not reduce struggles in one area to struggles in another. They are consonant with decentralized resistance and with local self-determination. The values that infuse the works of Foucault, Deleuze and Lyotard are directed not toward formulating the means and ends of the oppressed considered as a single class; they try to facilitate the struggles of different groups by offering analyses, conceptual strategies and political and theoretical critique. Foucault observes that '[t]he intellectual no longer has to play the role of an advisor. The project, tactics and goals to be adopted are a matter for those who do the fighting. What the intellectual can do is to provide the instruments of analysis' (1980: 62). Post-structuralism leaves the decision of how the oppressed are to determine themselves to the oppressed; it merely provides them with intellectual tools that they may find helpful along the way.

And to those who say that even the minimal values of the post-structuralists are too much, who refuse to be represented as people who think others should not be constrained unnecessarily, or would like to allow others their expression, the post-structuralists have nothing to offer in the way of refutation. To seek a general theory (outside any logical conflict or inconsistency between specific values) within which to place such values is to engage once again in the project of building foundations, and thus of representation. Beyond the point of local values that allow for resistance along a variety of registers, there is no longer theory – only combat.

Thus post-structuralist theory is indeed anarchist. It is in fact more consistently anarchist than traditional anarchist theory has proved to be. The theoretical wellspring of anarchism – the refusal of representation by political or conceptual means in order to achieve self-determination along a variety of registers and at different local levels – finds its underpinnings articulated most accurately by the post-structuralist political theorists. Conversely, post-structuralism, rather than comprising a jumble of unrelated analyses, can be seen within the broad movement of anarchism. Reiner Schürmann was correct to call the locus of resistance in Foucault an 'anarchist subject' who struggles against 'the law of social totalization' (Schürmann, 1986: 307). The same could be said for Deleuze and Lyotard. The type of intellectual activity promoted by the traditional anarchists and exemplified by the post-structuralists is one of specific analysis rather than of overarching critique. The traditional anarchists pointed to the dangers of the dominance of abstraction; the post-structuralists have taken account of those dangers in all of their works. They have produced a theoretical corpus that addresses itself to an age that has seen too much of political representation and too little of self-determination. What both traditional anarchism and contemporary post-structuralism seek is a society – or better, a set of intersecting societies – in which people are not told who they are, what they want, and how they shall live, but who will be able to determine these things for themselves. These societies constitute an ideal and, as the post-structuralists recognize, probably an impossible ideal. But in the kinds of analyses and struggles such an ideal promotes – analyses and struggles dedicated to opening up concrete spaces of freedom in the social field – lay the value of anarchist theory, both traditional and contemporary.

NOTES

1. Todd May. *Philosophy and Social Criticism* 15(2): 167–81 (1989). Copyright © 1989 SAGE Publications. Reprinted with permission from SAGE.
2. See for example Dews (1987), Habermas (1987) on normative relativism and Merquior (1985) on nihilism. For accounts of the Habermas–Lyotard debate for which this is a core issue, see Ingram (1987–88) and Watson (1984).
3. Of course, one need not proceed in this order. However, contemporary political philosophy – both Anglo-American and continental – has been guided by the predominance of these three intertwined elements, with Rawls and Habermas providing perhaps the most enlightened examples.

REFERENCES

Dews, Peter (1987). *Logics of Disintegration*. London: Verso.
Foucault, Michel (1980). *Power/Knowledge: Selected Interviews and Other Writings, 1972–88* (C. Gordon, L. Marshall, J. Mepham and K. Soper, trans.). New York Pantheon.
—— (1972). *Histoire de la folie à l'âge classique*. Paris: Gallimard.
Habermas, Jürgen (1987). *The Philosophical Discourse of Modernity* (Frederick Lawrence, trans.). Cambridge: MIT Press.
Ingram, David (1987–88). 'Legitimacy and the Post-Modern Condition: The Political Thought of Jean-François Lyotard'. *Praxis International* 7(3–4): 286–305.
Kropotkin, Peter (1970). *Kropotkin's Revolutionary Pamphlets* (R. Baldwin, ed.). New York: Dover.
Merquior, J.G. (1985). *Foucault*. Berkeley: University of California Press.
Schürmann, Reiner (1986). 'On Constituting Oneself an Anarchist Subject'. *Praxis International* 6(13).
Watson, Stephen (1985). 'Jürgen Habermas and Jean-François Lyotard: Postmodernism and the Crisis of Rationality'. *Philosophy and Social Criticism* 10(2): 1–24.

3
Post-Anarchism and Radical Politics Today

Saul Newman

In a recent series of exchanges between Slavoj Žižek and Simon Critchley, the spectre of anarchism has once again emerged. In querying Critchley's proposal in his recent book *Infinitely Demanding* (2007) for a radical politics that works outside the state – that take its distance from it – Žižek (2007a) says:

> The ambiguity of Critchley's position resides in a strange non sequitur: if the state is here to stay, if it is impossible to abolish it (or capitalism), why retreat from it? Why not act with(in) the state? [...] Why limit oneself to a politics which, as Critchley puts it, 'calls the state into question and calls the established order to account, not in order to do away with the state, desirable though that might be in some utopian sense, but in order to better it or to attenuate its malicious effects'? These words simply demonstrate that today's liberal–democratic state and the dream of an 'infinitely demanding' anarchic politics exist in a relationship of mutual parasitism: anarchic agents do the ethical thinking, and the state does the work of running and regulating society.

Instead of working outside the state, Žižek claims that a more effective strategy – such as that pursued by the likes of Hugo Chávez in Venezuela – is to grasp state power and use its machinery ruthlessly to achieve one's political objectives. In other words, if the state cannot be done away with, then why not use it for revolutionary ends? One hears echoes of the old Marx–Bakunin debate that split the First International in the 1870s: the controversy of what to do about the state – whether to resist and abolish it, as the anarchists believed, or to utilize it, as Marxists and, later, Marxist–Leninists believed – has returned to the forefront of radical political theory today. The question is why, at this political juncture, has this dilemma become important, indeed vital, again? And why, after so many historical defeats and reversals, has the figure of anarchism returned to haunt the radical political debates of the present?

This is not to suggest that Critchley is an anarchist (or even that Žižek is a Marxist, for that matter) in any simplistic sense, although both thinkers claim inspiration from, and a degree of affinity with, these respective traditions of revolutionary thought. It is to suggest, however, that the conflict between these thinkers seems to directly invoke the conflict between libertarian and more authoritarian (or rather statist) modes of revolutionary thought. Moreover, the re-emergence of this controversy signifies the profound ambivalence of radical politics today: after the decline of the Marxist–Leninist project (or at least of a certain form of it) and a recognition of the limits of identity politics, radical politics is uncertain about which way to turn. My contention is that anarchism can provide some answers here – and, moreover, that the present moment provides an opportunity for a certain revitalization of anarchist theory and politics.

There is an urgent need today for a new conceptualization of radical politics, for the invention of a new kind of radical political horizon – especially as the existing political terrain is rapidly becoming consumed with various reactionary forces such as religious fundamentalism, neoconservatism/neoliberalism and ethnic communitarianism. But what kind of politics can be imagined here in response to these challenges, defined by what goals and by what forms of subjectivity? The category of the 'worker', defined in the strict Marxian economic sense, and politically constituted through the revolutionary vanguard whose goal was the dictatorship of the proletariat, no longer seems viable. The collapse of the state socialist systems, the numerical decline of the industrial working class (in the West at least) and the emergence, over the past four or so decades, of social movements and struggles around demands that are no longer strictly economic (although they have often had economic implications), have all led to a crisis in the Marxist and Marxist–Leninist imaginary. This does not mean, of course, that economic issues are no longer central to radical politics, that the desire for economic and social equality no longer conditions radical political struggles and movements. On the contrary, as we have seen in recent years with the anti-globalization movement, capitalism is again on the radical political agenda. However, the relationship between the political and the economic is now conceived in a different way: 'global capitalism' now operates as the signifier through which diverse issues – autonomy, working conditions, indigenous identity, human rights, the environment, etc. – are given a certain meaning (cf. Newman, 2007a).

The point is, though, that the Marxist and Marxist–Leninist revolutionary model – in which economic determinism met with a highly elitist political voluntarism – has been largely historically discredited. This sort of authoritarian revolutionary vanguard politics has led not to the withering away of state power, but rather to its perpetuation. Žižek's attempt to resurrect this form of politics does not resolve this problem, and leads to a kind of fetishization of revolutionary violence and terror.[1] Indeed, one could say that there is a growing wariness about authoritarian and statist politics in all forms, particularly as state power today takes an increasingly and overtly repressive form. The expansion of the modern neoliberal state under its present guise of 'securitization' represents a crisis of legitimacy for liberal democracy:[2] even the formal ideological and institutional trappings of liberal checks and balances and democratic accountability have started to fall away to reveal a form of sovereignty which is articulated more and more through the state of exception. This is why radical political movements are increasingly suspicious of state power and often resistant to formal channels of political representation – the state appears to activists as a hostile and unassailable force through which there can be no serious hope of emancipation.

Indeed, radical political activism today seems to be working in the opposite direction. Instead of working through the state, it seeks to work outside it, to form movements and political relationships at the level of civil society rather than at the institutional level. This is not to deny, of course, that many more reformist-minded activists lobby and negotiate with the governments and state institutions on certain issues; but amongst the more radical anti-capitalist activists, the emphasis is on constructing autonomous political spaces which are outside the state, even while making demands upon it.[3] Moreover, social movements today eschew the model of the revolutionary vanguard party with its authoritarian, hierarchical and centralized command structures; rather, the emphasis is on horizontal and 'networked' modes of organization, in which alliances and affinities are formed between different groups and identities without any sort of formalized leadership. Decision making is usually decentralized and radically democratic.[4]

It is perhaps because contemporary modes of radical politics are often 'anarchist' in organizational form that there has been a renewed interest in anarchist theory. Anarchism has always been on the margins of political theory, even of radical political theory, often being historically overshadowed by Marxism and other forms of socialism.[5] This is perhaps because it is a kind of 'limit condition' for political theory, which, since Hobbes, has traditionally been founded on the problem of sovereignty and the fear of its absence. In Hobbes' state of nature, the conditions of perfect equality and perfect liberty – the defining principles of anarchism – led inevitably to the 'war of everyman against everyman', thus justifying the sovereign state (Hobbes, 1968: ch.13). For anarchists, however, the social contract upon which this sovereignty was supposedly based was an infamous sleight of hand in which man's natural freedom was sacrificed to political authority (see Bakunin, 1953: 165). Rather than suppressing or restricting perfect liberty and equality – which most forms of political theory do, including liberalism – anarchism seeks to combine them to the greatest possible extent. Indeed, one cannot do without the other. Étienne Balibar has formulated the notion of 'equal-liberty' (*egaliberté*) to express this idea of the inextricability and indeed, irreducibility, of equality and liberty – the idea that one cannot be realized without the other:

> It states the fact that it is *impossible* to maintain to a logical conclusion, without absurdity, the idea of perfect civil liberty based on discrimination, privilege and inequalities of condition (and, *a fortiori*, to institute such liberty), just as it is impossible to conceive and institute equality between human beings based on despotism (even 'enlightened' despotism) or on a monopoly of power. Equal liberty is, therefore, *unconditional*. (Italics in original; Balibar, 2002: 3)

However, it was the anarchists who took this formulation to its logical conclusion: if liberty and equality are to mean anything, then surely state power itself – whatever form it took – must be questioned; surely sovereignty was the ultimate blight upon equality and liberty. This is why, for Bakunin, equality of political rights instantiated through the 'democratic' state was a logical contradiction:

> [E]quality of *political rights*, or a *democratic State*, constitute in themselves the most glaring contradiction in terms. The State, or political right, denotes force, authority, predominance; it presupposes inequality in fact. Where all rule, there are no more ruled, and there is no State. Where all equally enjoy the same human rights, there all political right loses its reason for being. Political right connotes privilege, and where all are privileged, there privilege vanishes, and along with it goes political right. Therefore the terms '*democratic State*' and '*equality of political rights*' denote no less than the destruction of the State and the abolition of all political right. (Italics in original; Bakunin, 1953: 222–3)

In other words, there cannot be equality – not even basic political equality – while there is a sovereign state. The equality of political rights entailed by democracy is ultimately incompatible with *political right* – the principle of sovereignty which grants authority over these rights to the state. At its most basic level, political equality can only exist in tension with a right that stands above society and determines the conditions under which this political equality can be exercised. Political equality, if taken seriously and understood radically, can only mean the abolition of state sovereignty. The equality of wills and rights implied by democracy means that it is ultimately irreconcilable with any state, or with the structure and principle of state sovereignty itself. The demand for emancipation, central to radical politics, has always been based on the inseparability of liberty and equality. Anarchists were unique in their contention that this cannot be achieved – *indeed cannot even be conceptualized* – within the framework of the state.

CRITIQUE OF MARXISM

Anarchism's main contribution to a politics and theory of emancipation lies, as I see it, in its libertarian critique of Marxism. I have explored this elsewhere (see Newman, 2007b), and it has been extensively covered by other authors (see, for instance, Thomas, 1980); but, fundamentally, this critique centres around a number of problems and blind spots in Marxist theory. Firstly, there is the problem of the state and political power. Because, for Marxism – notwithstanding Marx's own ambivalence on this question[6] – political power is derived from and determined by economic classes and the prerogatives of the economy, the state is seen largely as a tool which can be used to revolutionize society if it is in the hands of the proletariat. This idea is expressed in Lenin's *State and Revolution* – a strange text which, in some places, seems to veer close to anarchism in its condemnation of the state and its celebration of the radical democracy of the Paris Commune; and at the same time reaffirms the idea of the seizure of state power and the socialist transformation of society under the dictatorship of the proletariat.[7] This ambiguity with regard to the state can be found in Marx's own thought, which shares with anarchism the goal of libertarian communism – an egalitarian society based on free association, without a state – and at the same time departs from anarchism in its belief that the state can and must be used in the 'transitional' period for revolutionary purposes. For anarchists, this position was fundamentally dangerous because it ignored the autonomy of state power – the way that the state was oppressive, not only in the form it takes, but in its very structures; and that it has its own prerogatives, its own logic of domination, which intersect with capitalism and bourgeois economic interests but are not reducible to them. For anarchists, then, the state would always be oppressive, no matter which class was in control of it – indeed, the workers' state was simply another form of state power. As Alan Carter says:

> Marxists, therefore, have failed to realise that the state *always* acts to protect its own interests. This is why they have failed to see that a vanguard which seized control of the state could not be trusted to ensure that the state would 'wither away.' What the state might do, instead, is back different relations of production to those which might serve the present dominant economic class if it believed that such new economic relations could be used to extract from the workers an even greater surplus – a surplus which would then be available to the state. (Carter, 1989: 176–97)

For anarchists, then, the state was not only the major source of oppression in society, but the major obstacle to human emancipation – which was why the state could not be used as a tool of revolution; rather, it had to be dismantled as the first revolutionary act. We might term this theoretical insight – in which the state is conceived as a largely autonomous dimension of power – the 'autonomy of the political'. However, here I understand this somewhat differently from someone like Carl Schmitt, for whom the term refers to a specifically political relation constituted through the friend/enemy antagonism (see Schmitt, 1996). For Schmitt, this entails an often violent struggle over power and identity, in which the sovereignty of the state is affirmed. For anarchists, it has precisely the opposite implication – a struggle of society *against* organized political, as well as economic, power; a general struggle of humanity against both capitalism and the state.

The second distinction between Marxism and anarchism follows from the first: while for Marxists, and particularly Marxist–Leninists, the revolutionary struggle is usually led by a vanguard party which, as Marx would say, has over the mass of the proletariat the advantage of correctly understanding the 'line of march' (Marx and Engels, 1978: 484), for anarchists, the vanguard party was an authoritarian and elitist model of political organization whose aim was the seizure and perpetuation of state power. In other words, according to anarchists, the revolutionary vanguard party – with its organized and hierarchical command structures and bureaucratic apparatuses – was already a microcosm of the state, a future state in waiting (see Bookchin, 1971). For anarchists, the revolution must be libertarian in form as well as ends – indeed, the former would be the condition for the latter; and so rather than a vanguard party seizing power, a revolution would involve the masses acting and organizing themselves spontaneously and without leadership. This does not mean that there would be no political organization or coordinated action; rather that this would involve decentralized and democratic decision-making structures.

The third major opposition between anarchism and Marxism concerns revolutionary subjectivity. For Marxists, the proletariat – often defined narrowly as the upper echelons of the industrial working class – is the only revolutionary subject because, in its specific relationship to capitalism, it is the class which embodies the universality and the emancipatory destiny of the whole of society. Anarchists had a broader conception of revolutionary subjectivity, in which could be included proletarians, peasants, lumpenproletariat, intellectuals déclassé – indeed, anyone who declared him- or herself a revolutionary. Bakunin spoke of a 'great rabble', a non-class which carried revolutionary and socialist aspirations in its heart (1950: 47). Indeed, Bakunin preferred the term 'mass' to class, class implying hierarchy and exclusiveness (ibid.: 48).

Of course, these disagreements do not cover all the points of difference between anarchism and Marxism – other questions, such as the role of factory discipline or Taylorism, as well as the value of industrial technology, were also important areas of dispute – and have indeed become even more prominent today with greater awareness about industrial society's impact on the natural environment.[8] However, the three major themes I have discussed – the autonomy, and therefore the dangers, of state power; the question of political organization and the revolutionary party; and the question of political subjectivity – constitute the main areas of difference between a Marxist and an anarchist approach to radical politics.

CONTEMPORARY DEBATES

The themes I have discussed are often reflected in debates in radical political theory today, particularly amongst key continental thinkers – such as Badiou, Rancière, Laclau, and Hardt and Negri. Amongst these contemporary theorists there is the recognition of the need to develop new approaches to radical politics in the face of the global hegemony of neoliberal capitalism and the increasing authoritarianism and militarism of 'democratic' states. Indeed, as I shall show, many of these thinkers seem to come quite close to anarchism in their approaches to radical politics, or draw upon anarchist themes – while at the same time remaining silent about the anarchist tradition. It is only Critchley who explicitly invokes anarchism in his notion of 'anarchic meta-politics' – although he has virtually nothing to say about the tradition of anarchist political thought itself, relying instead on a more philosophical and ethical reading of anarchy derived from Levinas.[9] There is a general and somewhat perplexing silence about anarchism – and yet, I would suggest that anarchism is the 'missing link' in a certain trajectory of radical political thought, one that is becoming increasingly relevant today. Here I will attempt to show the ways in which anarchism can inform some of these key debates in contemporary radical politics.

For instance, if we examine a thinker like Alain Badiou, we see a number of 'anarchist' themes emerging.[10] Despite his criticisms of anarchism, Badiou argues for a militant and emancipatory form of politics which does not rely on formal political parties and which works outside the state. For Badiou, the state has always been the rock upon which revolutionary movements in the past have foundered:

> More precisely, we must ask the question that, without a doubt, constitutes the great enigma of the century: why does the subsumption of politics, either through the form of the immediate bond (the masses), or the mediate bond (the party) ultimately give rise to bureaucratic submission and the cult of the State? (2005: 70)

This was precisely the same problem that was posed by the anarchists well over a century before – the tendency and danger of revolutionary movements (including Marxism) to reproduce, through the mechanism of the political party, the state power they claimed to be opposing. This is why Badiou proposes a post-party form of politics that, in his words, puts the state 'at a distance' (ibid.: 145). Here he points to historical events – such as the Paris Commune of 1871, May 1968 in Paris, the Chinese Cultural Revolution, and contemporary movements such as those which campaign for the rights of illegal immigrant workers[11] – in which egalitarian, autonomous and radically democratic forms of politics were achieved which avoided the party–state form. Here we see a critique of political representation and statism which has strong resonances with anarchism.

And yet there is a strange ambiguity here. While, for instance, Badiou celebrates some of the more libertarian aspects of the Cultural Revolution, such as the Shanghai Commune of 1966–67 which drew inspiration from the Paris Commune and which experimented with forms of radical democracy – at the same time he deliberately distances himself from anarchism:

> We know today that all emancipatory politics must put an end to the model of the party, or of multiple parties, in order to affirm a politics 'without party', and yet at the same time without lapsing into the figure of anarchism, which has never been anything else than the vain critique, or double, or the shadow, of communist parties, just as the black flag is only the double or the shadow of the red flag. (Badiou, 2006: 321)

One could certainly dispute Badiou's dismissal of anarchism that it is simply the 'double' of the communist parties. Anarchists departed from the Marxist and Marxist–Leninist movements in significant ways, developing their own analysis of social and political relations, and their own revolutionary strategies. Yet, what is more problematic – as well as paradoxical – about Badiou, is his highly idealized and abstract conception of politics, one that sees the political 'event' as such a rarefied experience that it almost never happens. The impression one gets from Badiou is that all genuine radical politics ended with the Cultural Revolution. Major political events, such as the 'Battle of Seattle' in 1999 and the emergence of the anti-globalization movement, are consigned to irrelevance in Badiou's eyes.[12] The problem with Badiou is his haughty disregard for concrete, everyday forms of emancipatory politics: genuine egalitarian experiments in resistance, autonomy and radical democracy are going on all the time, in indigenous rights movements, in food cooperatives, in squatters' collectives, in independent media centres and social centres, in innovative forms of direct action, in courageous acts of civil disobedience, in mass demonstrations and so on;[13] Badiou seems either oblivious to all of these or grandly contemptuous of them. As Critchley (2000) has observed, Badiou gestures towards a 'great politics' and an ethics of heroism, one that risks, as I would argue, a nostalgia for the struggles of the past. There is a kind of philosophical absolutism in Badiou's thinking, from which any form of politics is judged from the impossible standard of the 'event', akin to the Pauline miracle.[14] I agree that what we need today is a genuine politics defined by new practices of emancipation which break with existing forms, with the structures of the party and the state, and which invent new and innovative political relationships and ways of being. But the problem is that Badiou sets such an impossibly high and abstract standard for radical politics that almost nothing in his eyes lives up to the dignity of the event. For all his insistence that politics must be situated around the event, there is virtually no recognition of real, situated political struggles.

What is really behind this contempt for the politics of the everyday, I would argue, is a kind of elitism, which can be found in Badiou's fetishization of the militant. For Badiou (2001), the figure of emancipatory politics is not the people or the masses, but the isolated militant engaged in a heroic struggle against overwhelming odds, fighting his or her own impulse to give up, to capitulate. There is little emphasis here on building mass movements, on working to develop links between different groups, on the spontaneous self-organization of people, on grassroots direct action, on democratic decision making, on decentralized social organization, etc. There is an implicit vanguardism (not of the party, but of the militant) in Badiou's political thought. This is evident in his valorization of authoritarian revolutionary figures such as Lenin, Mao and Robespierre. In his critique of Rancière, whom we shall discuss later, Badiou says: 'He [Rancière] has the tendency to pit phantom masses against an unnamed State. But the real situation demands instead that we pit a few rare militants against the "democratic" hegemony of the parliamentary State' (2005: 122). There is no question that the 'democratic' hegemony of the parliamentary state must be challenged – but in the name of a more genuine democracy and through collective mass action.

For Ernesto Laclau (2005), on the other hand, the figure of 'the people' – rather than the militant – is central. His more recent work on populism shows the ways in which the notion of the people is discursively constructed in different situations through the development of hegemonic 'chains of equivalence' between different actors, groups and movements. Laclau's thought – along with Chantal Mouffe's – has developed out of a critique of Marxism, one that incorporates discourse analysis, deconstruction and new social-movement theory, and emphasizes the contingency of political identities and the importance of a radically democratic imaginary. Indeed, post-Marxism has a number of important parallels with anarchism – particularly in its rejection of economic determinism and class essentialism. Laclau and Mouffe, in *Hegemony and Socialist Strategy*, question the centrality of class to political subjectivity, and show that, even in Marx's time, the struggles and identities of workers and artisans did not always conform to his conception of the proletariat: many of these struggles were against relations of subordination generally, and against the destruction of their organic, communal way of life through the introduction of the factory system and new forms of industrial technology such as Taylorism. Even more so today, the category of 'class' has become less applicable to the multiplicity of struggles and identities:

> The unsatisfactory term 'new social movements' groups together a series of highly diverse struggles: urban, ecological, anti-authoritarian, anti-institutional, feminist, anti-racist, ethnic, regional or that of sexual minorities. The common denominator of all of them would be their differentiation from workers' struggles, considered as 'class' struggles. (Laclau and Mouffe, 2001: 159)

This is not to say, of course, that workers' struggles and economic issues are no longer important – indeed, Laclau has argued that economic globalization forms the new terrain around which political struggles are emerging. The point is that 'class', understood in the strict Marxist sense, is today no longer adequate to describe radical political subjectivity. As we have seen, precisely the same criticism of 'class' was made by anarchists like Bakunin well over a century before these post-Marxist interventions; as was the argument about the irreducibility (to the economic realm) of the political dimension of power, the notion that there were different sites of oppression – patriarchy, the family, industrial technology – as well as a number of other themes that later emerged as the central motifs of post-Marxism.

Yet, I also think it is important to draw certain distinctions between anarchism and post-Marxism. While post-Marxism makes an important contribution to the development of a new radical political terrain, it is also characterized by an underlying centralism which is inherent in the category of 'representation'. There are different ways of understanding the representative function in Laclau's argument, not all of which necessarily entail a notion of political representation or leadership. For instance, the notion that the empty universality of the political space can be filled temporarily with certain signifiers, like 'global democracy' or 'the environment' – or even the claims of a particular group – around which other struggles and identities are discursively constructed, is, in my view, a necessary and inevitable aspect of any kind of radical politics which hopes to transcend the position of pure particularism. In other words, when a particular signifier stands in for the empty universality of the political space, this is a representative function through which other identities, causes and struggles can achieve some form of coherent meaning and unite with one another. There is nothing necessarily authoritarian about this sort of symbolic representation. Indeed, without this function of the 'stand-in' there can be no real hope of radical politics. However, where this argument becomes problematic is when representation seems to translate into political leadership – into the idea that a radical political movement needs the figure of the leader to hold it together, and in whose person the disparate desires of the movement are temporarily united and imperfectly expressed. Indeed, the leadership function seems to be implicit in Laclau's model of populism, and the examples he gives of populist movements – particularly Peronism in Argentina, and, more recently, the popular movements which support Chavez in Venezuela, a figure whom Laclau admires – are all movements strongly identified with, and organized around, the figure of the leader. Of course, these are not *entirely* authoritarian political movements – indeed, even the Venezuelan experience, which certainly has authoritarian tendencies, has nevertheless been experimenting with forms of popular, grassroots democracy. But, from an anarchist perspective, the very notion of political leadership and sovereignty is inherently authoritarian – that is why anarchists rejected the idea of political representation. Representation always meant a leader, party or organization speaking for the masses, and thus a transfer of power from the latter to the former. Representation, for anarchists, always ended up with the state.[15] Perhaps this is also why for Laclau – as well as theorists of hegemony like Lenin and Gramsci – the state is always the stage for politics: hegemonic struggles always take place within the framework of the state, and are always fought with the aim of controlling state power.

Perhaps it is with a view of developing a new model of politics that is no longer reliant on notions of leadership, representation, sovereignty and the seizure of state power, that Michael Hardt and Antonio Negri have proposed the concept of the multitude. The multitude is a new revolutionary subject which is emerging out of the social relationships and knowledge and communication networks produced by biopolitical production and 'immaterial labour' – the increasingly dominant mode of production in our transnational world of global capitalism (whose political expression is Empire). These new post-Fordist modes of labour and production tend towards a 'being-in-common', which produces a new social and political commonality where singularities are able to spontaneously act in common. For Hardt and Negri, the multitude is a class concept, but one that is different from the Marxist notion of the proletariat: it refers to all those who work under Empire, not simply, or even primarily blue-collar workers. Its existence, moreover, is based on a becoming or immanent potential, rather than being defined by a strictly empirical existence; and it represents an irreducible multiplicity – a combination of collectivity and plurality – rather than a unified identity like 'the people'. This immanent multiplicity has a tendency to converge into a common organism which will one day turn against Empire and emancipate itself:

> When the flesh of the multitude is imprisoned and transformed into the body of global capital, it finds itself both within and against the processes of capitalist globalization. The biopolitical production of the multitude, however, tends to mobilise what it shares in common and what it produces in common against the imperial power of global capital. In time, developing its productive figure based on the common, the multitude can move through the Empire and come out the other side, to express itself autonomously and rule itself. (Hardt and Negri, 2004: 101)

There are a number of interesting themes here, themes which have a clear resonance with anarchism, as well as applying to the emerging reality of anti-globalization struggles. The notion of the multitude bears strong similarities to Bakunin's idea of the revolutionary mass, an entity defined by multiple identities and possibilities rather than by class unity and strict political organization. Furthermore, there is the idea of acting in common, spontaneously and without centralized leadership – an idea which derives from anarchism, and which, as many commentators have noted, is a characteristic of contemporary anti-capitalist movements, activist networks and affinity groups. The multitude, according to Hardt and Negri, rejects the very notion of sovereignty: indeed, in the paradoxical relationship that has existed between the multitude and the sovereign which supposedly represents and embodies it – as in the Hobbesian depiction of sovereignty – it is always the sovereign that depends on the multitude rather than the other way round. Here Hardt and Negri talk about the 'exodus' of the multitude, a simple turning away from, or refusal to recognize, sovereignty, upon which, as in Hegel's Master/Slave dialectic, the sovereign would simply no longer exist.

There are, at the same time, a number of problems with this notion of the multitude. For instance, there is some question over how coherent and inclusive the concept of the multitude actually is. Hardt and Negri argue that the conditions for this new subjectivity are being created by a 'becoming-common' of labour: in other words, people are increasingly working under the same conditions of production within Empire and are therefore melding into a commonality, defined by new affective relationships and networks of communication. However, surely this ignores the major divisions that continue to exist in the conditions of labour between a salaried white-collar worker in the West, and someone whose daily survival depends upon searching for scraps in garbage dumps in the slums of the global South. To what extent can we speak of any commonality between such radically different forms of 'work', such radically different experiences of oneself, one's body and one's existence? These two people live not within the same Empire but in *totally different worlds.* In the case of the white-collar worker, who perhaps works in the services sector, one can indeed speak of 'immaterial labour'; while the slum dweller in the Third World is completely removed from this experience. The two share no common language. While it is true that 'immaterial' biopolitical production is increasingly penetrating the global South, there are still major economic and social divisions in conditions of work and modes of production, and therefore in the social relationships and forms of communication that flow from this. Our world is not a 'smooth space' as Hardt and Negri maintain, but a dislocated, uneven space – a world beset by major divisions and inequalities, exclusions and violent antagonisms. Indeed, rather than creating a borderless world of smooth flows and transactions, economic globalization is producing new borders everywhere – symbolized by the Israeli 'security' wall, or the fence being constructed along the US–Mexico border. While capitalist globalization is a process that is affecting the entire world, it is at the same time creating savage divisions between people and continents, offering some an unprecedented degree of material comfort, while consigning others in the global South to a crushing poverty and a radical exclusion from the market and from global circuits of production. To what extent, then, is it possible to talk about a new commonality defined by one's incorporation into Empire and 'immaterial labour'? Given these disparities and socio-economic divisions, would the multitude not be a highly fractured, divided body – or perhaps even a body from which are excluded those subjectivities that cannot be defined by immaterial labour, or indeed by any form of labour at all?[16]

This highlights the problem of trying to construct a common politics across such radically different forms of life and experience. What is missing from Hardt and Negri's notion of the multitude is any account of how this can be constructed, how to build transnational alliances between people in the global North and South. Hardt and Negri simply assume that such a unity is already immanent within the productive dynamics of global capital, and therefore that the formation of the multitude is an inevitable and permanent potentiality. The problem, then, with Hardt and Negri's notion of the multitude is that it seems in some senses to be nothing more than a dressed up version of the Marxist theory of proletarian emancipation. The multitude is something that emerges organically through the dynamics of Empire and the hegemony of 'immaterial labour', just as, for Marx, the proletariat and proletarian class consciousness emerged according to the dynamics of industrial capitalism. In each scenario, moreover, this agency harnesses the economic forces of capitalism in order to transform them and create a new series of social relationships. In other words, there is an *immanentism* in Hardt and Negri's analysis which seems to parallel Marxian economism: both suggest a kind of automatic process in which a new revolutionary class develops through the capitalist dynamic, until it eventually transcends it through a general revolt. What is lacking in this understanding of the multitude is any notion of *political* articulation – in other words, any explanation of how this multitude comes together and why it revolts. Here I think Laclau is right when he says about Hardt and Negri's analysis, that 'we have the complete eclipse of politics' (2005: 242).

RANCIÈRE AND THE ANARCHISM OF EQUALITY

Jacques Rancière, on the other hand, proposes a very different notion of radical politics to that of the multitude – for him, politics emerges out of a fractured rather than smooth space, something that ruptures existing social relations from the outside rather than being immanent within them. Rancière's notion of politics also has strong, and at times explicit, parallels with anarchism, as well as having important implications for it, as I shall show. Indeed, Rancière at times describes his approach to politics as 'anarchic': for instance, he sees democracy – which for him has nothing to do with the aggregation of preferences or a particular set of institutions, but is rather an egalitarian form of politics in which all hierarchical social relationships are destabilized – as 'anarchic "government" [...] based on nothing other than the absence of every title to govern' (2006: 41). Moreover, his whole political project has been to disturb existing hierarchies and forms of authority, to unseat the position of mastery from which the masses are led, excluded, dominated, spoken for and despised. Any form of vanguard politics is, for Rancière, simply another expression of elitism and contempt for ordinary people. Indeed, these 'ordinary' people are actually extraordinary, being capable of emancipating themselves without the intervention of revolutionary parties.

We can see this idea particularly in Rancière's study of the French nineteenth-century schoolteacher Joseph Jacotot, who developed what was essentially an anarchist model of education where he was able to teach students in a language that he did not speak himself, and where students were able to use this method to teach themselves and others. The discovery that one did not need to be an expert in a subject – or even have any real knowledge of it – in order to teach it, undermined the posture of mastery and intellectual authority, a posture that all institutionalized forms of politics are based on (the authority of professional politicians, experts, technocrats, economists, those who claim to have a technical knowledge that the people do not). All forms of political and social domination rest upon a presupposed inequality of intelligence, through which hierarchy is naturalized and the position of subordination comes to be accepted. And so if, as Jacotot's experiment showed, there is actually an *equality of intelligence* – the idea that no one is naturally more or less intelligent than anyone else, that everyone is equally capable of learning and teaching themselves – this fundamentally jeopardizes the inegalitarian principle that the social order is founded upon. This form of intellectual emancipation suggests a profoundly egalitarian politics – a politics that not only seeks equality, but, more importantly, is founded on the absolute *fact* of equality. In other words, politics, for Rancière, *starts* with the fact of equality: 'Equality was not an end to attain, but a point of departure, a supposition to maintain in every circumstance' (1991: 138). Furthermore, emancipation was not something that could be achieved *for* the people – it had to be achieved *by* the people, as a part of a process of self-emancipation in which there was a recognition by the individual of the equality of others: '[T]here is only one way to emancipate. And no party or government, no army, school, or institution, will ever emancipate a single person' (ibid.: 102).

Clearly, these ideas of self-emancipation, autonomy and the destabilization of social and political hierarchies through the recognition and assertion of the fundamental equality of all speaking beings, have clear similarities with anarchism.[17] Rancière's thought *is* a kind of anarchism, in which the domination – and the 'passion for inequality' upon which it rests – is questioned at its most fundamental level. However, I would suggest that Rancière's conception of politics also allows us to rethink certain aspects of anarchism and to take it in new theoretical and political directions. Central here would be a certain realignment of anarchism, no longer around an opposition between society and the state, but between 'politics' and 'the police'. In other words, the central antagonism is not so much between two entities, but between two different modes of relating to the world. 'Police' refers to the rationality of 'counting' that founds the existing social order – a logic that partitions and regulates the social space, assigning different identities to their place within the social hierarchy. In this sense, police would include the usual coercive and repressive functions of the state, but it also refers to a much broader notion of the organization and regulation of society – the distribution of places and roles. In other words, domination and hierarchy cannot be confined to the state, but are in fact located in all sorts of social relationships – indeed, domination is a particular logic of social organization, in which people are consigned to certain roles such as 'worker', or 'delinquent', or 'illegal immigrant', or 'woman', to which are attributed particular identities.

Politics, on the other hand, is the process which disrupts this logic of social ordering – which ruptures the social space through the demand by the excluded for inclusion. For Rancière, politics emerges from a fundamental dispute or 'disagreement' (*mesentente*) between a particular group which is excluded and the existing social order: this excluded social group not only demands that its voice be heard, that it be included in the social order, but, more precisely, it claims in doing so to represent the whole of society. What is central to politics, then, according to Rancière, is that an excluded part not only demands to be *counted* as part of the social whole, but that it claims to actually embody this whole. Rancière shows the way that in ancient Greece the demos – or 'the people', the poor – which had no fixed place in the social order, demanded to be included, demanded that its voice be heard by the aristocratic order and, in doing so, claimed to represent the universal interests of the whole of society. In other words, there is a kind of metonymical substitution of the *part for the whole* – the part represents its struggle in terms of a universality: its particular interests are represented as being identical to those of the community as a whole. In this way, the 'simple' demand to be included causes a rupture or dislocation in the existing social order: this part could not be included without disturbing the very logic of a social order based on this exclusion. To give a contemporary example: the struggles of 'illegal' immigrants – perhaps the most excluded group today – to be given a place within society, to have their status legitimized, would create a kind of contradiction in the social order which refuses to include or even recognize them, which promises equal and democratic rights to everyone, and yet denies them to this particular group. In this way, the demand of the 'illegals' to be counted as 'citizens' highlights the inconsistency of the situation in which universal democratic rights are promised to all, but in practice are granted to only some; it shows that any fulfilment of the democratic promise of universal rights is at the very least conditional on their recognition also as citizens with equal rights. The discursive 'stage' upon which politics takes place is therefore an inconsistency within the structure of universality, between its promise and its actualization. To give a further example: the protests that took place in France in 2004 over the ban on Islamic headscarves in schools pointed to the inconsistency of a situation in which, on the one hand, everyone is formally recognized as having equal rights as citizens of the French Republic, while on the other hand, laws are introduced – *in the very name of this Republican ideal of equality* – which obviously discriminate against and target certain minorities. It was therefore a mistake to claim, as both conservative and socialist MPs did, that protests and acts of resistance against the headscarf law were anti-Republican: on the contrary, the Muslim women protesting against the headscarf ban waved the tricolor and held placards with the words *Liberté, Egalité, Fraternité*. By identifying with the ideals of the Republic, they highlighted, in a very effective way, the fact that they were excluded from these ideals. Their message was that they believe in the Republic *but the Republic does not believe in them*. Here we see the excluded part claiming to represent the universality of the egalitarian ideal through the simple demand to be counted. So, for Rancière, 'politics exists whenever the count of parts and parties of society is disturbed by the inscription of a part of those who have no part' (1999: 123).

While it might seem that the demand for inclusion into the existing social, legal and political order is not an anarchist strategy, the point is that this demand for inclusion, because it is framed in terms of a universality, of a part which, *in its very exclusion*, claims to be the whole, causes a dislocation of this order. In this sense, radical politics today might take the form of mass movements which construct themselves around particularly marginalized and excluded groups, such as the poor, or 'illegal' immigrants. This does not, of course, mean that mass movements should not be concerned with general global issues such as the environment; but mobilizing around particular structures of domination and exclusion, and around those who are most affected by them, can be an effective form of resistance. For instance, fighting for the rights of 'illegal' immigrants – as activist networks such as No Borders do – highlights broader contradictions and inconsistencies in global capitalism, a system which claims to promote the free movement of people (as well as capital and technology) across national borders, and yet which seems to be having precisely the opposite effect – the intensification of existing borders and the erection of new ones.[18] In other words, the situation of 'illegal' immigrants is a crucial point of antagonism and contradiction in the global capitalist system – and mobilizations around this can have potentially explosive and transformative effects.

However, the theoretical importance for anarchism of Rancière's understanding of politics lies in its account of political subjectification. For anarchists – particularly the classical anarchists – the subject revolts partly because, as Bakunin would say, there is a natural and spontaneous tendency to revolt, but, more precisely, because the subject is intrinsically and organically part of society, and society is conditioned by a certain essence – which is both rational and natural – which unfolds in the direction of revolution and emancipation. In other words, anarchism is based not only on a certain vision of human emancipation and social progress, but on the idea of a social rationality which is inexorably moving in that direction. This idea might be seen in Bakunin's materialist understanding of natural and historical laws – laws that are scientifically observable (see Bakunin, 1953: 69) – or Kropotkin's (1972) belief that there is an innate and evolutionary tendency towards mutualism within all living beings, or, in Murray Bookchin's (2005) conception, the potential for 'wholeness' that is central to his idea of 'social ecology'. What we find here is the idea of social progress, whether driven by the dialectic, or the laws of nature or history. Central here is the view of the human subject as not only essentially benign (for Kropotkin, humans had a natural tendency towards cooperation) but as inextricably part of the social fabric. Radical political subjectivity, for anarchists, is an expression of this inherent sociality.

Rancière's view of political subjectification would be somewhat different from this. There is no natural or social tendency towards revolution; instead, what is important is the unpredictability and contingency of politics. Furthermore, the political subject is not founded on essentialist conceptions of human nature; rather, the subject emerges in an unpredictable fashion through a rupturing of fixed social roles and identities. This last point is important. For Rancière, political subjectification is not the affirmation or expression of an innate sociality, but rather a break with the social. It is a kind of de-subjectification or 'dis-identification' – a 'removal from the naturalness of place' – in which one distances oneself from one's normal social role:

> [P]olitical subjectification forces them out of such obviousness by questioning the relationship between the *who* and the *what* in the apparent redundancy of the positing of an existence [...] 'Worker' or better still 'proletarian' is similarly the subject that measures the gap between the part of work as social function and the having no part of those who carry it out within the definition of the common of the community. (1999: 36)

Rather than political subjectivity emerging as immanent within society, it is something that, in a sense, comes from 'outside' it – not in terms of some metaphysical exteriority, but in terms of a process of disengagement from established subject positions and social identities.

POST-ANARCHISM

What I am pointing to here – via Rancière – is not some kind of radical or existential individualism, in which the subject is an isolated monad who acts in a political vacuum.[19] Obviously, radical politics involves developing links with others, and building new political relationships, new understandings of community. But the point is that these cannot be understood as being founded on a certain conception of human nature, or as emerging inevitably from social processes. Rather, they are always to be constructed, and they often have unpredictable and contingent effects. There is no inevitability in this process, as there was for classical anarchists.

It is this idea of unpredictability, invention and contingency that I see as central to a new way of thinking about anarchism – one that avoids the sort of humanist essentialism and positivism that characterized much of classical anarchism. My contention has been that anarchism, as a political philosophy, is in need of renewal, and that it can take advantage of theoretical moves such as deconstruction, post-structuralism and psychoanalysis in the same way that, for instance, certain post-Marxist perspectives have done[20] (notwithstanding the differences that I have already pointed to between anarchism and post-Marxism). This would mean a *partial* abandonment – or at least a revising – of the Enlightenment humanist discourse that anarchism has been indebted to: an abandonment of essentialist ideas about human nature, of social positivism, of ideas about an immanent social rationality that drives revolutionary change. Instead, anarchist theory would have to acknowledge that social reality is discursively constructed, and that the subject is situated, and even constituted, within external relations of language and power, as well as unconscious forces, desires and drives which often exceed his rational control.[21] However, this does not mean – as many have wrongly suggested in reference to thinkers like Foucault – that the subject is determined by social structures or caught in 'disciplinary cages'. On the contrary, post-structuralist approaches seek openings, interstices, indeterminacies, *aporias* and cracks within structures – points where they become displaced and unstable, and where new possibilities for political subjectification can emerge. Indeed, this view of the relationship between the subject and social structures, I would suggest, actually allows for a greater degree of autonomy and spontaneity than that posited by classical anarchists. That is to say, the 'post-structuralist' approach breaks the link between subjectivity and social essence, allowing a certain discursive space in which subjectivity can be reconfigured. The aim, from a post-structuralist point of view, would be for the subject to gain a certain distance from the discursive fields in which his/her identity is constituted – and it is precisely this distance, this gap, which is the space of politics because it allows the subject to develop new forms and practices of freedom and equality.

The term 'post-anarchism' therefore refers not so much to a distinct model of anarchist politics, but rather to a certain field of inquiry and ongoing problematization in which the conceptual categories of anarchism are rethought in light of such post-structuralist interventions. This does not, in any sense, refer to a superseding or moving beyond of anarchism – it does not mean that the anarchist theoretical and political project should be left behind. On the contrary, I have argued for the ongoing relevance of anarchism, particularly to understanding contemporary political struggles and movements. The prefix 'post-' does not mean 'after' or 'beyond', but rather a working at the conceptual limits of anarchism with the aim of revising, renewing and even radicalizing its implications. Post-anarchism, in this sense, is still faithful to the egalitarian and libertarian project of classical anarchism – yet it contends that this project is best formulated today through a different conceptualization of subjectivity and politics: one that is no longer founded on essentialist notions of human nature or the unfolding of an immanent social rationality.

There are a number of other thinkers who seek to reconstruct anarchism along these or similar lines, most notably Lewis Call[22] and Todd May. May, in particular, develops a post-structuralist approach to anarchist politics, highlighting the connections between classical anarchism's critique of representation and post-structuralist thinkers like Foucault, Deleuze and Lyotard, whose 'tactical' rather than 'strategic' approach to politics emphasizes particular and situated 'micropolitical' practices. There are clear parallels between May's approach to post-anarchism and mine. But there are also differences, most noticeably in the different thinkers and perspectives we draw upon. While I deploy the ideas of Foucault and Deleuze, I have also drawn upon thinkers like Derrida – whom May explicitly rules out on the grounds that he has no clearly articulated political position[23] – and Lacan. In May's work, there is a general avoidance of psychoanalysis. However, while many anarchists might be sceptical about psychoanalysis, pointing to what they perceive as its generally apolitical conservatism, its focus on the individual psyche, and, as some feminists, would claim, its 'phallogocentrism'[24], I would argue that psychoanalytic theory – particularly that of Freud and Lacan – can offer important resources for radical political theory. Indeed, rather than focusing on the isolated individual psyche, psychoanalysis stresses the social dimension, the individual's relations with those around him or her – not only with family members but with society more broadly. As Freud (1921: 69) demonstrates, psychoanalysis is concerned with 'social phenomena', including the formation of groups, and is thus eminently equipped for socio-political analysis. For Lacan, the individual (partially) constructs his or her subjectivity through a relationship with the external world of language, the symbolic order through which all meaning is derived – and, therefore, for Lacan, the unconscious was 'structured like a language' (1998: 20). The psychoanalytic unconscious is not individualizing and therefore reactionary, as Deleuze and Guattari alleged in Anti-Oedipus. On the contrary, it is intersubjective and can therefore be applied not only to an analysis and critique of existing socio-political relationships, but also to an understanding of radical political identities. Indeed, I do not think it is possible to get anywhere near a full conception of political agency and subjectivity without an understanding of the unconscious forces and desires which in large part drive political action, structure our political, ideological and symbolic identifications, or impel our psychic attachments – 'passionate attachments' as Judith Butler would put it (1997) – to authority and domination, as well as the ways that we at times break with and resist them. Psychoanalysis, in my view, is crucial to developing a fuller account of the potentialities of the subject – one that goes beyond the Foucauldian notion of 'subject positions'.

Moreover, the focus on the unconscious does not lead, as some would suggest, back to an essentialism of the subject. On the contrary, the Freudian and Lacanian understanding of the unconscious shows that the subject is always, as it were, 'at a distance' from him- or herself, and that one cannot achieve a full and completely unalienated and transparent identity. As Lacan showed, rather than there being an essence at the base of subjectivity, there was a lack, an absence, a void in signification (1998: 126).

If the only issue here was a different philosophical genealogy, then this question of the alternative approaches chosen by me and Todd May would hardly be worth mentioning. However, what is invoked by this difference is the broader debate that has been recently emerging in radical political philosophy over the question of ontology: to be more precise, the debate around *abundance* and *lack* – or, thought about slightly differently, *immanence* and *transcendence* – as the two rival conceptions of radical political ontology today. This question has, according to Lasse Thomassen and Lars Tønder, been at the base of different understandings of radical democratic politics:

> [E]xisting literature has failed to appreciate the way in which the conceptualization of radical difference has led to significantly different versions of radical democracy – what we refer to as the ontological imaginary of abundance and the ontological imaginary of lack respectively. These two imaginaries share the idea of a radical difference and the critique of conventional conceptualizations of universality and identity; yet they also differ in the manner in which they approach these questions. For instance, they disagree on whether political analysis should start from the level of signification or from networks of embodied matter. And they disagree on the kind of politics that follows from the idea of radical difference: whereas theorists of lack emphasise the need to build hegemonic constellations, theorists of abundance emphasise never-receding pluralisation. (2005: 1–2)

This debate has some relevance to post-anarchism today, as many post-structuralist-inspired theorists of contemporary activism – Hardt and Negri being among the most prominent, but also Richard J.F. Day (2005) – tend to see a Deleuzo-Spinozian motif of immanence, abundance, flux and becoming as the most appropriate way of thinking about the decentralized affinity groups and 'rhizomatic' networks that characterize anti-capitalist radical politics today.

Although I have always considered the anti-statist thought of Deleuze (and Guattari) to be invaluable for radical politics,[25] my own approach tends to place more emphasis on the idea of a 'constitutive outside': the idea – theorized in different ways by thinkers like Lacan and Derrida – of a kind of discursive limit or void which exceeds representation and symbolization. I do not agree with Andrew Robinson that it posits a myth-like abstraction which leads to an apolitical conservatism (2005). If one accepts the idea that social reality is constructed at some level discursively – that is through relations of language through which we form meaning and identities – then this idea is only consistent if one posits a logical limit or outside to discourse; and it is at this limit that new ways of understanding the world politically can emerge. This can produce conservative and pragmatist articulations of the political, certainly – or even conservative positions in the guise of ultra-radicalism, in the way we have seen with someone like Žižek. But there is nothing intrinsically conservative or apolitical about the idea of negativity and lack, as Robinson seems to suggest – and, indeed, a certain understanding of negativity, as Stirner and even Bakunin themselves showed, can have radical implications. Nor do I agree with May that this sort of ontology leads to a politics of indeterminacy that makes it unsuitable for collective action.[26] On the contrary, I would suggest that the idea of an 'outside' allows for a space or terrain in which new practices of emancipation can be developed.

CONCLUSION

What I see as particularly important is the need to develop a universal dimension for collective politics – one which is built upon localized practices of resistance, but which also goes beyond them and allows links to emerge between actors on a politico-ethical terrain defined by an unconditional liberty and equality. This is why the question of radical democracy is central: radical democracy – seen as a series of mobilizations and practices of emancipation, rather than as a specific set of institutional arrangements[27] – is the form of politics that allows liberty and equality to be combined and rearticulated in all sorts of unpredictable ways. However, I would also suggest that anarchism can be seen as providing the ultimate politico-ethical horizon for radical democracy. As anarchism shows, the central and fundamental principle of democracy – collective autonomy and egalitarian emancipation – is something that cannot be wholly contained within the limits of state sovereignty. At its very least, it is a principle which always challenges the idea of political authority.

NOTES

1. See Žižek (2000: 326) and his more recent writings on Lenin (Žižek, 2004) and Mao Tse-Tung (Žižek, 2007b).
2. See Wendy Brown's excellent essay on neoliberalism (2003).
3. See once again Simon Critchley's description of 'anarchic metapolitics' in *Infinitely Demanding*. This idea of developing alternative spaces outside the state has been developed by a number of thinkers, especially Hakim Bey with his notion of the 'temporary autonomous zone' (see Bey, 2003).

4. The 'anarchist' forms of organization and decision-making procedures which characterize many activist groups today are discussed in David Graeber's article, 'The New Anarchists' (2002).
5. This was not always the case, though: for instance, during the Spanish Civil war, anarchist groups were in many parts of the Spain the dominant political force (see Leval, 1975).
6. I am referring to Marx's theory of Bonapartism, in which the state achieves a degree of autonomy from bourgeois class interests. See 'The Eighteenth Brumaire of Louis Bonaparte', in Karl Marx and Friedrich Engels (1976). See also Saul Newman (2004).
7. This work (Lenin, 1932/1943) is really a kind of dialogue with anarchism – Lenin's attempt to distance himself from anarchism, to which he seems at times to be in close proximity.
8. More recently there have been important attempts to develop an anarchist approach to the environment, and to understand the relationship between social domination and environmental devastation. See Murray Bookchin's concept of 'social ecology' in *The Ecology of Freedom: The Emergence and Dissolution of Hierarchy* (2005); as well as John Zerzan's writings; for example, *Future Primitive* (1994).
9. Here Critchley cites Levinas's pre-political or a-political notion of anarchy as the absence of an *archè* or organizing principle. See *Infinitely Demanding* (2007: 122).
10. As Ben Noys (2008) argues, Badiou is a thinker who, despite being highly critical of anarchism, has much in common with it.
11. See, for example, L'Organisation Politique, an organization which Badiou is involved with, and which campaigns for the rights of undocumented immigrant workers – *sans papiers*.
12. Critchley makes a similar point about Badiou in *Infinitely Demanding* (2007: 131).
13. See Day (2005) for a survey of some of these groups and activities.
14. See Badiou's discussion of the 'event' in *Being and Event* (2003a). See also his discussion of Pauline universalism in *St Paul: The Foundation of Universalism* (2003b).
15. Todd May (1994) sees the critique of representation as being central to classical anarchism.
16. This query has also been raised by Jason Read (2005) in his review of Hardt and Negri's *Multitude*. See also Malcolm Bull (2005: 19–39).
17. Todd May (2007: 20–35) has also recognized the importance of Rancière's thought for anarchism.
18. See explorations of the politics of borders, migration and globalization in the work of Étienne Balibar (2004), as well as Sandro Mezzadra (2003).
19. Max Stirner's notion of egoism, for instance, while it offers an important philosophical intervention in anarchist theory – particularly in developing a critique of essentialism – does not necessarily offer a convincing or complete model of political action. See *The Ego and Its Own* (1995).
20. See, primarily, the work of Laclau and Mouffe.
21. Cornelius Castoriadis (1997), a psychoanalytic theorist whose political thought has close affinities with anarchism, talks about the role of imaginary significations in constructing social reality.
22. See Lewis Call (2003). One could also mention John Holloway (2005) here, although he comes more from the libertarian Marxist – rather than strictly anarchist – tradition.
23. See May (1994: 12). Here I would disagree with May – in recent years Derrida had been increasingly engaged with political questions regarding law, justice, democracy, Marxism, human rights and sovereignty.
24. However, a number of major feminist critiques of 'phallogocentrism' have at the same time been inspired by psychoanalysis. I have in mind here thinkers such as Luce Irigary and Julia Kristeva.
25. See, for instance, my article 'War on the State: Deleuze and Stirner's Anarchism' (2001).
26. See Todd May's review (2002) of my book *From Bakunin to Lacan*.
27. I have in mind here something like Derrida's notion of the 'democracy to come', which, so far from being a way of putting off or postponing political decision making (as May seems to be implying) actually invokes the immediacy of the present, and calls for a militant critique of all existing articulations of democracy in the name of an infinite perfectibility. See *Rogues: Two Essays on Reason* (Brault, 2005: 886–90).

REFERENCES

Badiou, Alain (2006). *Polemics* (S. Corcoran, trans.). London: Verso.
—— (2005). *Metapolitics* (J. Barker, trans.). London: Verso.
—— (2003a). *Being and Event* (O. Feltham, trans.). London: Continuum.
—— (2003b). *St Paul: The Foundation of Universalism* (R. Brassier, trans.). Stanford, CA: Stanford University Press.
—— (2001). *Ethics: An Essay on the Understanding of Evil* (P. Hallward, trans.). London: Verso.
Bakunin, Mikhail (1953). *Political Philosophy: Scientific Anarchism* (G.P. Maximoff, ed.). London: Free Press of Glencoe.
—— (1950). *Marxism, Freedom and the State* (K.J. Kenafick, trans.). London: Freedom Press.
Balibar, Étienne (2004). *We the People of Europe: Reflections on Transnational Citizenship* (J. Swenson, trans.). Princeton: Princeton University Press.
—— (2002). *Politics and the Other Scene*. London: Verso.
Bey, Hakim (2003). *T.A.Z.: The Temporary Autonomous Zone*. New York: Autonomedia.
Bookchin, Murray (2005). *The Ecology of Freedom: The Emergence and Dissolution of Hierarchy*. Oakland: AK Press.
—— (1971). 'Listen Marxist!'. In *Post-Scarcity Anarchism*. Berkeley: The Ramparts Press.
Brault, Pascale-Anne (2005). *Rogues: Two Essays on Reason* (M. Naas, trans.). Stanford, CA: Stanford University Press
Brown, Wendy (2003). 'Neoliberalism and the End of Liberal Democracy'. *Theory and Event* 7(1).
Butler, Judith (1997). *The Psychic Life of Power: Theories in Subjection*. Stanford, CA: Stanford University Press.
Bull, Malcolm (2005). 'The Limits of the Multitude'. *New Left Review* 35 (September–October): 19–39.
Call, Lewis (2003). *Postmodern Anarchism*. Manchester: Lexington Books.
Carter, Alan (1989). 'Outline of an Anarchist Theory of History'. In *For Anarchism: History, Theory and Practice* (D. Goodway, ed.). London: Routledge.
Castoriadis, Cornelius (1997). *The Imaginary Institution of Society* (K. Blamey, trans.). Cambridge: Polity Press.
Critchley, Simon (2007). *Infinitely Demanding: Ethics of Commitment, Politics of Resistance*. London: Verso.
—— (2000). 'On Alain Badiou', *Theory and Event* 3(4).
Day, Richard J.F. (2005). *Gramsci Is Dead: Anarchist Currents in the Newest Social Movements*. London: Pluto Press.
Freud, Sigmund (1921). 'Group Psychology and the Analysis of the Ego'. In *The Standard Edition of the Complete Psychological Works of Sigmund Freud* (J. Strachey, trans.). London: Hogarth Press.
Graeber, David (2002). 'The New Anarchists'. *New Left Review* 13 (January–February).
Hardt, Michael, and Negri, Antonio (2004). *Multitude: War and Democracy in the Age of Empire*. London: Penguin.
Hobbes, Thomas (1968) [1651]. *Leviathan* (C.B. Macpherson, ed.). London: Penguin.
Holloway, John (2005). *Change the World Without Taking Power: The Meaning of Revolution Today*. London: Pluto Press.
Kropotkin, Peter (1972). *Mutual Aid: A Factor in Evolution*. London: Allen Lane.
Lacan, Jacques (1998). *The Four Fundamental Concepts of Psychoanalysis: The Seminar of Jacques Lacan, Book XI* (J.A. Miller, ed.; A. Sheridan, trans.). London: W.W. Norton & Co.
Laclau, Ernesto (2005). *On Populist Reason*. London: Verso.
—— and Mouffe, Chantal (2001) [1985]. *Hegemony and Socialist Strategy: Towards a Radical Democratic Politics*. London: Verso.
Lenin, V.I. (1932/1943). *The State and Revolution*. New York: International Publishers.
Leval, Gaston (1975). *Collectives in the Spanish Revolution* (V. Richards, trans.). Freedom Press.
Marx, Karl, and Engels, Friedrich (1978). 'Manifesto of the Communist Party', *The Marx–Engels Reader* (R.C. Tucker, ed.). New York: W.W. Norton & Co.

—— (1976) [1848]. *Collected Works of Karl Marx and Friedrich Engels, vol.7: Demands of the Communist Party in Germany*. New York: International Publishers.

May, Todd (2007). 'Jacques Rancière and the Ethics of Equality'. *SubStance* (Issue 113) 36(2): 20–35.

—— (2002). 'Lacanian Anarchism and the Left'. *Theory and Event* 6(1).

—— (1994). *The Political Philosophy of Poststructuralist Anarchism*. Pennsylvania: Penn State University Press.

Mezzadra, Sandro (2003). 'Migration, Detention, Desertion: A Dialogue', with Brett Neilson. *Borderlands* 2(1). <http://www.borderlands.net.au/vol2no1_2003/mezzadra_neilson.html>

Newman, Saul (2007a). *Unstable Universalities: Poststructuralism and Radical Politics*. Manchester: Manchester University Press.

—— (2007b) [2001]. *From Bakunin to Lacan: Anti-Authoritarianism and the Dislocation of Power*. Lanham MD: Lexington Books.

—— (2004). 'Anarchism, Marxism and the Bonapartist State'. *Anarchist Studies* 12(1): 35–59.

—— (2001). 'War on the State: Deleuze and Stirner's Anarchism'. *Anarchist Studies* 9(2).

Noys, Ben (2008). 'Through a Glass Darkly: Alain Badiou's Critique of Anarchism'. *Anarchist Studies* (unpublished manuscript currently in draft form).

Rancière, Jacques (2006). *Hatred of Democracy* (S. Corcoran, trans.). London: Verso.

—— (1999). *Disagreement: Politics and Philosophy* (J. Rose, trans.). Minneapolis: University of Minnesota Press.

—— (1991). *The Ignorant Schoolmaster: Five Lessons in Intellectual Emancipation* (K. Ross, trans.). Stanford: Stanford University Press.

Read, Jason (2005). 'From the Proletariat to the Multitude: Multitude and Political Subjectivity'. *Postmodern Culture* 15(2). Retrieved from <http://muse.edu/journals/postmodern_culture/v015/15.2read.html>

Robinson, Andrew (2005). 'The Political Theory of Constitutive Lack: A Critique'. *Theory and Event* 8(1).

Schmitt, Carl (1996). *The Concept of the Political* (G. Schwab, trans.). Chicago: University of Chicago Press.

Stirner, Max (1995). *The Ego and Its Own* (D. Leopold, ed.). Cambridge: Cambridge University Press.

Thomas, Paul (1980). *Karl Marx and the Anarchists*. London: Routledge & Kegan Paul.

Tønder, Lars, and Lasse Thomassen (eds) (2005). *Radical Democracy: Politics Between Abundance and Lack*. Manchester: Manchester University Press.

Žižek, Slavoj (2007a). 'Resistance is Surrender'. *London Review of Books*. 15 November.

—— (2007b). *On Practice and Contradiction*. London: Verso.

—— (2004). *Revolution at the Gates*. London: Verso.

—— (2000). 'Holding the Place'. In Slavoj Žižek, Judith Butler and Enersto Laclau (eds) *Contingency, Hegemony, Universality: Contemporary Dialogues on the Left*. London: Verso.

Zerzan, John (1994). *Future Primitive*. New York: Autonomedia.

4
Post-Anarchism Anarchy

Hakim Bey

The Association for Ontological Anarchy gathers in conclave, black turbans & shimmering robes, sprawled on shirazi carpets sipping bitter coffee, smoking long chibouk & sibsi. QUESTION: What's our position on all these recent defections & desertions from anarchism (esp. in California-Land): condemn or condone? Purge them or hail them as advance-guard? Gnostic elite ... or traitors?

Actually, we have a lot of sympathy for the deserters & their various critiques of anarchISM. Like Sinbad & the Horrible Old Man, anarchism staggers around with the corpse of a Martyr magically stuck to its shoulders – haunted by the legacy of failure & revolutionary masochism – stagnant backwater of lost history.

Between tragic Past & impossible Future, anarchism seems to lack a Present – as if afraid to ask itself, here & now, WHAT ARE MY TRUE DESIRES? – & what can I DO before it's *too late?* ... Yes, imagine yourself confronted by a sorcerer who stares you down balefully & demands, 'What is your True Desire?' Do you hem & haw, stammer, take refuge in ideological platitudes? Do you possess both Imagination & Will, can you both dream & dare – or are you the dupe of an impotent fantasy?

Look in the mirror & try it ... (for one of your masks is the face of a sorcerer) ...

The anarchist 'movement' today contains virtually no Blacks, Hispanics, Native Americans or children ... even tho *in theory* such genuinely oppressed groups stand to gain the most from any anti-authoritarian revolt. Might it be that anarchISM offers no concrete program whereby the truly deprived might fulfil (or at least struggle realistically to fulfil) real needs & desires?

If so, then this failure would explain not only anarchism's lack of appeal to the poor & marginal, but also the disaffection & desertions from within its own ranks. Demos, picket-lines & reprints of 19th century classics don't add up to a vital, daring conspiracy of self-liberation. If the movement is to grow rather than shrink, a lot of deadwood will have to be jettisoned & some risky ideas embraced.

The potential exists. Any day now, vast numbers of americans are going to realize they're being force-fed a load of reactionary boring hysterical arti-ficially-flavored *crap*. Vast chorus of groans, puking & retching ... angry mobs roam the malls, smashing & looting ... etc., etc. The Black Banner could provide a focus for the outrage & channel it into an insurrection of the Imagination. We could pick up the struggle where it was dropped by Situationism in '68 & Autonomia in the seventies, & carry it to the next stage. We could have revolt in our times – & in the process, we could realize many of our True Desires, even if only for a season, a brief Pirate Utopia, a warped free-zone in the old Space/Time continuum.

If the A.O.A. retains its affiliation with the 'movement,' we do so not merely out of a romantic predilection for lost causes – or not entirely. Of all 'political systems,' anarchism (despite its flaws, & precisely because it is neither political nor a system) comes closest to our understanding of reality, ontology, the nature of being. As for the deserters … we agree with their critiques, but note that they seem to offer no new powerful alternatives. So for the time being we prefer to concentrate on changing anarchism from within. Here's our program, comrades:

1. Work on the realization that *psychic racism* has replaced overt discrimination as one of the most disgusting aspects of our society. Imaginative participation in other cultures, esp. those we live with.
2. Abandon all ideological purity. Embrace 'Type-3' anarchism (to use Bob Black's pro-tem slogan): neither collectivist nor individualist. Cleanse the temple of vain idols, get rid of the Horrible Old Men, the relics & martyrologies.
3. Anti-work or 'Zerowork' movement extremely important, including a radical & perhaps violent attack on Education & the serfdom of children.
4. Develop american samizdat network, replace outdated publishing/ propaganda tactics. Pornography & popular entertainment as vehicles for radical re-education.
5. In music the hegemony of the 2/4 & 4/4 beat must be overthrown. We need a new music, totally insane but life-affirming, rhythmically subtle yet powerful, & we need it NOW.
6. Anarchism must wean itself away from evangelical materialism & banal 2-dimensional 19th century scientism. 'Higher states of consciousness' are not mere SPOOKS invented by evil priests. The orient, the occult, the tribal cultures possess *techniques* which can be 'appropriated' in true anarchist fashion. Without 'higher states of consciousness,' anarchism ends & dries itself up into a form of misery, a whining complaint. We need a practical kind of 'mystical anarchism,' devoid of all New Age shit-&-shinola, & inexorably heretical & anti-clerical; avid for all new technologies of consciousness & metanoia – a democratization of shamanism, intoxicated & serene.
7. Sexuality is under assault, obviously from the Right, more subtly from the avant-pseudo 'post-sexuality' movement, & even more subtly by Spectacular Recuperation in media & advertizing. Time for a major step forward in SexPol awareness, an explosive reaffirmation of the polymorphic eros – (even & especially in the face of plague & gloom) – a literal glorification of the senses, a doctrine of delight. Abandon all world-hatred & shame.

8. Experiment with new tactics to replace the outdated baggage of Leftism. Emphasize practical, material & personal benefits of radical networking. The times do not appear propitious for violence or militancy, but surely a bit of sabotage & imaginative disruption is never out of place. Plot & conspire, don't bitch & moan. The Art World in particular deserves a dose of 'Poetic Terrorism.'

9. The despatialization of post-Industrial society provides some benefits (e.g. computer networking) but can also manifest as a form of oppression (homelessness, gentrification, architectural depersonalization, the erasure of Nature, etc.) The communes of the sixties tried to circumvent these forces but failed. The question of *land* refuses to go away. How can we separate the concept of *space* from the mechanisms of *control*? The territorial gangsters, the Nation/States, have hogged the entire map. Who can invent for us a cartography of autonomy, who can draw a map that includes our desires?

AnarchISM ultimately implies anarchy – & anarchy is chaos. Chaos is the principle of continual creation ... & *Chaos never died.*

(March '87, NYC: A.O.A. Plenary Session)

Part 2
Post-Anarchism Hits the Streets

5
Empowering Anarchy:
Power, Hegemony and Anarchist Strategy[1]

Tadzio Mueller

PROLOGUE: ANARCH-Y/-ISTS/-ISM

How does one define something that draws its lifeblood from defying convention, from a burning conviction that what is, is wrong, and from the active attempt to change what is into what could be? Definitions necessarily try to fix the 'meaning' of something at any given point, and they imply that I, who do the defining, have the power to identify the limits of 'anarchism', to say what is legitimately anarchist. It is probably better, then, to start with clarifying what anarchism is not: it is definitely not a question of ancient Greek etymology, as in: 'the prefix "an" linked to the word "archy" suggests that "anarchism" means ...'; neither is it a question of analysing the writings of one dead white male or another, a type of approach that would look at books written by anarchist luminaries like Kropotkin or Proudhon, and would then proclaim that the essence of anarchism can be found in either one, or a combination of the two;[2] nor is it, finally, a question of organizational continuity with the rebels who were killed in Kronstadt or the anarchists who fought in the Spanish civil war.

This is not to say that a historical approach to anarchism is not relevant – only that an attempt to seek a purely historical definition of anarchism would in some sense commit an act of intellectual violence against those people who today think of themselves as anarchist, anarchist-inspired, or as 'libertarian socialists': most of those have not read Kropotkin, Bakunin, or even more contemporary anarchists such as Murray Bookchin, or did not read any of their works prior to thinking of themselves as anarchists. Barbara Epstein has tried to come to terms with this relative lack of 'ideological purity' by arguing that today's anarchism is not really ideologically proper anarchism, but rather a collection of what she terms 'anarchist sensibilities' (Epstein, 2001: 4). However: in suggesting that today's anarchists are not really anarchists, even if they think of themselves as such, Epstein has made precisely the mistake that academics frequently make when talking about activists, that is, to define a 'proper' way of doing/being/thinking, and then identifying the ways in which activists diverge from the true path as identified by the intellectual elite.[3]

How can we then avoid this type of definitional 'violence', but still have something to talk about, that is, something that is identifiably 'anarchist'? First, I suggest, by letting those people who actually think of themselves as anarchists or acknowledge certain anarchist influences in their political work speak and act for themselves. Because if anarchism is anything today, then it is not a set of dogmas and principles, but a set of practices and actions within which certain principles manifest themselves.[4] Anarchism is not primarily about what is written, but about what is done: it is the simultaneous negation of things as they are, the anger that flows from viewing the world as riddled with oppression and injustice, and the belief that this anger is pointless if one does not seek to do something different in the here and now. What makes these practices specifically anarchist in the eyes of today's activists does of course vary from group to group, from person to person. For now, however, I will understand anarchist practices in the realm of political organization and expression as those practices that consciously seek to minimize hierarchies and oppose oppression in all walks of life, a desire which manifests itself in various organizational forms such as communes, federations, affinity groups and consensus-seeking structures.[5] In other words, anarchism is a scream, not one of negation,[6] but of affirmation: it is about going beyond rejecting, about starting to create an alternative in the present to that which triggered the scream in the first place ('prefigurative politics').[7] This is not to say that anarchist practices always achieve that – in fact, the main body of this chapter will deal with the question of which barriers there are in anarchism itself to reaching its own goal. Instead, this merely gives a broad frame of reference to a discussion of anarchism, a frame that will be refined as the chapter develops.

One disclaimer before the discussion starts: since I have suggested that it is only by letting today's anarchists talk and act that we can find out what anarchism 'really' is, I have been forced to rely on the anarchists that I have met, and those anarchist texts that I have been able to get and read, to gather my 'data'. These are, for a number of reasons, mostly from Europe and the United States. The questions faced by anarchists that I will discuss in this chapter come from this context, and the answers will be relevant, if at all, only in that context.

ANARCHISTS, HEGEMONY AND POWER

Having suggested what anarchism is about, the next question is: where is anarchism to be found? It is not, to begin with, the same as the globalization-critical movement (below: globalization movement), or even the latter's biggest part. However, because many anarchists have been very engaged with this movement, many of the examples used here will be drawn from its mobilizations. Anarchism is also not the same as the by now internationally (in)famous 'black bloc', although some of the voices on which I will draw here will emanate from under a balaclava. Anarchists, then, should be seen as a 'submerged network' of groups, people and identities (Melucci, 1989), as a counter-community (Gemie, 1994) that gets involved in mobilizations (e.g. against the International Monetary Fund) and tactics (e.g. the black bloc), but does not exhaust itself in these: the subcultures where people are attempting to construct different ways of life, that centre around cafes and squats, groups and individuals, that can be found in Berlin or London, Malaga or Stockholm – that is where anarchists and therefore anarchism can be found.

Anarchism might today be back on the agenda after some decades in the political wilderness, but its existence is far from trouble-free, with challenges coming from the 'outside', from the engagement with dominant structures of power, as well as from the inside, in terms of the ability to sustain itself as a subculture/movement. The first of these problems is that, from Seattle to Genoa, and now to the 'war on terror', anarchists have found themselves at the receiving end of rapidly escalating state repression without having any effective mechanisms to defend themselves against this onslaught. Linked to this policy of repression is the challenge of cooptation of more moderate groups within the globalization movement, leaving anarchists isolated on the radical fringes. Finally, the last problem is demonstrated by the fact that there is hardly anyone over 30 who is interested in anarchism. In other words: the anarchist subculture is plagued by its inability to sustain participation, by its limited size and mobilization capacities, its social isolation, and the vulnerability to repression that this produces.

These political challenges have been widely discussed within anarchist circles, and many proposed solutions have emerged, most of which can be summarized under two headings: they focus on the need firstly to overcome the isolation of the anarchist/left-libertarian subculture (extensive organizing), and secondly to deepen that subculture's political and social structures so as to strengthen its capacity of maintaining participation, or simply: to allow for people above, say, 29 to live an 'anarchist' life (intensive organizing).

Today's anarchists are obviously not the first radical force encountering the problem of how to maintain its strength over time and in the face of attacks, and how to grow beyond its current strength. About 80 years ago, the Italian Communist Party's strategist Antonio Gramsci asked himself the same question – and came up with an analysis of structures of power in advanced capitalism that I believe make him an important touchstone for any project of resistance operating under such conditions. His starting point was: why did the revolution succeed in Russia, and not in Italy or anywhere else in Western Europe, where classical Marxism had predicted it would be more likely to occur due to the more advanced development of capitalism? He argued that the reason for this failure was an incorrect understanding of the workings of power in modern capitalism: while Marxist revolutionary practice had assumed that political power was concentrated in the state apparatus, Gramsci suggested that power also rested in the institutions of 'civil society' (Gramsci, 1971: 210–76), or the structures and organization of everyday life. The revolution would therefore have to aim not only to conquer state power, but much more importantly, to create an alternative civil society, which would have to be able to attract the majority of people by convincing them of the validity of the project, which was in turn premised on its ability to perform 'all the activities and functions inherent in the organic development of a society' (ibid.: 16). This alternative society has come to be referred to as a 'counter-hegemony',[8] a term I would translate as 'sustainable communities of resistance'. The key to Gramsci's analysis therefore was the suggestion that the organization of resistance would somehow have to mirror the structures of power.

What is the relevance of this to anarchist practice? First of all, Gramsci's alternative society would involve both extensive and intensive political organizing, as suggested in the proposals cited above: to extend the appeal of anarchism/communism by opening up to other groups and individuals,[9] and to increase the sustainability of the anarchist/communist subculture by strengthening its social functions. There is, however, a major problem involved in transporting this concept into anarchist practice: Gramsci was a Leninist, and as such did not really have a problem with an anti-capitalist strategy that entailed hierarchies both internally and externally. It was in essence setting one power up against another. This clearly creates a problem for anarchists, if we understand anarchism as the struggle against all forms of hierarchies and power. If (1) a strategy of counter-hegemony, of building sustainable communities of resistance, is in essence a strategy of power, and if (2) anarchism is understood as rejecting all forms of power, and (3) the strategy outlined here in the crudest terms (internal and external expansion) is necessary to sustain the radical project of anarchism, have we then not reached the end of anarchism as a political project? Is anarchism as the rejection of hierarchies and power dead because it needs hierarchies and power in order to survive?

ANARCHISM, PARTS 1 AND 2

1. No Power for No-One!

The question therefore becomes, is anarchism really the rejection of all forms of power? The obvious difficulty with this question lies in the word 'really': for if it is true that anarchism is not a unified body of theory but a set of practices, it might be quite difficult to figure out anything that anarchism 'really' is. A look at any flyer written by an anarchist group will usually reveal the coexistence of a variety of conceptual positions, some of which may even be mutually contradictory. In order to pick apart the various 'strands' existing in anarchist discourse, then, it will be necessary to engage after all with anarchism as a historically created set of practices, that is: to critically analyse the various ideas and discourses that have shaped today's practices.

Anarchism developed to some extent both parallel to and in opposition to Marxism, and some of its guiding principles can best be illustrated as a critique of Marxist theory. The latter argued that all oppression fundamentally derived from one source, that is, control of the means of production. It was therefore able to suggest that, if the proletariat were first to seize the reins of the state (which was held to be a mere support structure for capitalist class power) and then to socialize the means of production in one fell swoop, it could offer a deliverance from all forms of oppression. For Marxism, there was only one enemy, one struggle, and one final and complete victory. In response, anarchists argued that oppression flowed not only from control of the means of production, but also from control of the means of physical coercion – in other words, the state was a centre of power whose interests were not fully reducible to those of 'capital' (Miller, 1984: 47–9). This created a problem for anarchism, as its identification of at least two enemies, capital and the state (and frequently the church as well (Marshall, 1992: 4–5)), splintered the political field, creating difficulties in terms of (1) who was the privileged agent of revolution, and (2) how this revolution could be made in one go if there were so many centres of power, so many enemies, so many struggles. The first question had been easy to answer for Marxism, or any analysis that operated with the notion that there is one main/central source of social conflict, because the oppressed part in that relationship (concretely: the proletariat in the labour–capital relation) becomes the necessary agent of revolution, but difficult for an analysis that identified a diffusion of power centres. Similarly, for such a position, the answer to the second question apparently had to be: 'not at all'.

One strand of anarchism, probably the one most identified with dead white males such as Bakunin, Kropotkin and Proudhon, responded to this shattering of the unity of power/oppression and the subsequent diffusion of struggles by simply reconstituting the unity of power on a higher level. Where previously the contradiction between capital and labour was paramount, the new key contradiction became one between a benign human nature/society and an unequivocally bad logic of oppression merely manifesting itself in different structures of power (capitalism, the state, religion) (Marshall, 1992: 4). This assumption at the core of what I will call the 'classical' strand of anarchism has important politico-theoretical implications: having posited a pure human essence in a constant struggle against forces that seek to oppress it, the possibility of anarchist practice leading to a total liberation from power after some sort of revolution is maintained. This conclusion is based on a conception of power as being external to human essence, as coming from institutions that impose themselves on an organically free humanity (Newman, 2001: 37).

And indeed, many of today's anarchists directly refer back to this dichotomous view of society when making political statements. In an essay written on the protests in Genoa, Moore asserts that for anarchists, 'power (be it economic or governmental) is the problem – not who holds it – and needs, therefore, to be overcome altogether' (Moore, 2001: 137). And to show that this question does not just manifest itself in the writings of anarchists, but also in practice: at a meeting at the largely anarchist-inspired 'No Border' camp in Strasbourg in July 2002, I witnessed a discussion about how to organize the set-up of toilets for the camp, where one speaker suggested that the question of who cleans the toilets was merely a 'technical' question. This may sound trivial, but if one considers that who cleans the toilets is very much a question of power, and therefore political rather than technical (whether it is the untouchables in India, or low-waged women both at their jobs and at home, it is almost always the oppressed who clean the toilets), then this argument must be seen as the articulation of a view that understands 'power' to reside only out there/up there, but not inside anarchism, with its privileged links to a naturally solidaristic human essence.

2. Multi-Sited Power, and Power among Anarchists

This 'classical' strand, however, is far from being the only or true anarchism. Above, I identified a crucial question for anarchists: how to respond to the diffusion of power centres that the critique of Marxism had led to? On the face of it, there is only one alternative to the answer given by the classical anarchists, namely to give up the ideas of a unity of struggles (against oppression) and of the revolution as one single, cataclysmic event. This, however, was a conclusion few – none to my knowledge – were willing to draw, and so an emerging second 'open' strand busied itself with introducing 'new' (or rather: newly recognized) centres of power/oppression. For example, Emma Goldman added the oppression of women by men/patriarchy (particularly within the institution of the (bourgeois) family) to the anarchist canon (Marshall, 1992: 5); later, Murray Bookchin brought an awareness of the environmental consequences of industrial capitalism to the anarchist worldview (Bookchin, 1989).

The upshot of all this activity was a challenge to the classical view of one top and one bottom in society, suggesting a more decentralized understanding of power, which resulted in a picture of 'a series of tops and bottoms' (May, 1994: 49). Whereas the classical view, even if it suggested a diversity of actual centres of power, usually resulted in the privileging of one social group as the authentic agent of revolutionary change – whether it was the working class, as Proudhon at some point held, or Bakunin's celebration of the 'great rabble' of urban centres (Gemie, 1994: 355; Newman, 2001: 30) – the image of a multitude of at least potentially equally important sites of struggle implies that no single group can claim that their fight is necessarily more important than others (Laclau and Mouffe, 2001).[10] This open strand of anarchism can therefore be summarized as opposing 'capitalism, inequality (including the oppression of women by men), sexual repression, militarism, war, authority, and the state' (Goodway, 1989: 2).[11] Note that this seemingly abstract debate has crucial political implications: the question of whether a left-libertarian counter-hegemony should ultimately focus on the working class – a view expressed for example in the influential pamphlet 'Give up activism' (Anonymous2, 2000a; 2000b) – is politically relevant, since it will determine which groups will become the focus of a political mobilization.

As with the classical strand, it is easy to point to examples of such an understanding of power as multi-sited in contemporary anarchists' statements: in a critique of the activities of 'authoritarian socialist' groups during and after the mobilizations in Seattle, an activist writes that anarchists 'want freedom from all forms of oppression and domination, including organizations that want to think and represent and act for us' (Anonymous6, 2000: 128). Similarly, the newly formed anarchist network Peoples' Global Action (PGA) – which emerged primarily as a coordinator of global mobilizations against elite summits but is now broadening its focus – states in its 'hallmarks' that seek to express its political philosophy that, in addition to being an anti-capitalist network, '[w]e reject all forms and systems of domination and discrimination including, but not limited to, patriarchy, racism and religious fundamentalism of all creeds' (PGA, n.d.). And finally, in keeping with a strong tradition of anarchism, the critique of power is here extended to encompass not only structures of power that are seemingly on the 'outside' of resistance, but also power that exists within anti-oppressive struggles. To highlight this, let me return to the discussion about who should clean the toilets at the activist camp in Strasbourg. The conception of power as multi-sited and also existing in the spaces of resistance is expressed by the response to the first speaker: 'No', the next discussant opined, 'it is a political question' – that is, it involves power.

WHITHER ANARCHISM?

Oppressive Anarchists

My contention is this: the view of power as external/opposed to some sort of 'human nature' has directly oppressive effects, as it serves to obscure the domination of one group of people/activists over another. In a comment about gender relations on so-called 'protest sites' (forest sites occupied by activists in order to prevent their clear-cutting for 'development' projects), a female activist begins by suggesting that the 'overall concept of a [protest] camp is one of a free society' – in keeping with the classical strand of anarchism. In reality, however, she points out that such camps become 'a patriarchy-dominated environment'. Specifically, this occurs in the field of sexual relations, where the discourse of free love (which is said to exist in a free society) ended up putting 'a certain amount of pressure [on women] to conform to the free love ideal, and not everyone wants such relations' (Anonymous7, 1998: 10, 12). What becomes clear here is that the idea of power as being external to human nature, expressing itself in the expectation that women could now, being liberated in the free space of the camp, finally conform to the ideal of free love, had become oppressive in itself: it put pressure on women to conform to the ideal of what the 'human essence' is, to live up to an ideal they never constructed.

Open Anarchism – Open, Yes, but Going Where?

So anarchist practice can in itself be oppressive, or at least entail relations of power, especially if that power is masked behind the idea of a possible power-free practice. But, one might wonder, what's the difference between the two 'strands' in this? After all, even if the open strand has a more subtle view of a multiplicity of centres of power, it still opposes these centres of power to some grouping of social forces, organized in what Gemie calls a 'counter-community', arrayed against the state (Gemie, 1994: 353) – and in this community, a power-free practice could, presumably, develop. It appears that there is no real difference then: both strands claim to be able to 'really' get rid of power.

There is, however, an important difference, a difference which will prove crucial in determining the further political development of each of these strands, and, I believe, of anarchism itself. As shown above, the view of anarchism as power-free practice, or at least as containing the possibility thereof, is an inherent and necessary component of the classical strand; the open strand, however, carried through to its logical conclusion, actually makes the belief in a power-free practice impossible. The argument starts again with and against Marxism: the latter posits the 'unity in the relations of power' as its defining criterion (Holloway, 2002: 40).

There might be two forces struggling, but there is only one real power centre that has to be conquered. As shown, anarchism originally opened up that monism to suggest the existence of two or three power centres. While the classical strand then proceeded to reduce these centres back into one (the 'logic' of power or oppression), the second strand maintained this openness, leading to the proliferation of centres of power described above: from two, to three, to five, to ... a multitude.

All's well thus far. But what happens now? Apparently, the diffusion of power centres that results from the original breaking of the monism has no logical endpoint, and does not even stop at the integrity of the individual that some anarchists value so highly: even a person who is oppressed on several counts (homosexuality, femininity) will be an oppressor on others (upper class, white). Therefore, flowing logically from the premises of the second strand, and from the political logic thus implied (no struggle is necessarily worth more than another), we get a picture of power relations criss-crossing all of society, penetrating even ourselves as subjects. Given this diffusion of power into our very own being, the conclusions must be that: (1) one cannot continue to think revolution as a one-off event, since that implies the existence of one or only a small number of centres of power. If power is also embedded in value structures as the example of patriarchy demonstrates, then 'revolution' must be seen as a process, since it is clearly impossible to 'revolutionize' values and attitudes from one day to the next;[12] and (2) we cannot escape power, because every human relation involves (but is not exclusively constituted by) power relations, and thus power 'over' someone. Therefore, power is everywhere.

From Open Anarchism to Post-Structuralist Anarchism

Having thus shown power as inescapable, we are faced with another point where anarchism could simply self-destruct, as its original project – the emancipation from all forms of hierarchies and power – seems to have become a theoretical and practical impossibility. However, this is where post-structuralist analysis can come in useful, in order, as it were, to think open anarchism to its logically and politically necessary conclusions. I do not so much seek to prove that anarchism and post-structuralism are compatible and even likely theoretical allies – that has been done[13] – but rather to understand how post-structuralism and anarchism can be practical allies, how post-structuralist analysis can be used to advance anarchist practice, and vice versa.

The point of departure for this discussion will be the end of the last: power is everywhere. But for anarchists, there is still that dualism of oppression vs. power-free practice that seems to contradict that conclusion. The work of Michel Foucault might offer us a way out of this dilemma.[14] But wait – isn't Foucault a 'postmodernist'? Doesn't that mean that he is essentially a petty-bourgeois nihilist, who, having deconstructed everything ends up with nothing to hold on to? As I will show below, this criticism, voiced frequently both by academics and activists,[15] is nothing but the theoretical equivalent of the familiar branding of anarchists as brainless 'rent-a-mob' types with no positive proposals. Believing this to be something of a slander, I would caution against such a wholesale rejection of post-structuralist analysis.

Post-structuralism developed at a historical juncture in some ways not unlike that where anarchism emerged as a distinct political movement. While the latter emerged in response to its critique of Marxism as a potentially oppressive practice (Miller, 1984: 79–93; Joll, 1969), which led to the split in the First International, the period during which post-structuralism developed also saw the emergence of the anarchist-inspired student movement of 1968 in France (Bookchin, 1989; Marshall, 1992: 539–57), and both the professors and the students struggled against an ossified, oppressive French Communist Party (PCF), in practice and in theory: one of Foucault's key concerns was to challenge the intellectual blockade on progressive thinking that the PCF had established on the basis of its claim that it alone held the key to a true understanding of the workings of capitalism, and therefore also to its ultimate overthrow. In particular, it was the question of internment in the Soviet Gulags that could not be discussed openly, suggesting that Marxism as a practice involved a number of unanalysed (and unanalysable) forms of oppression (Foucault, 1980: 109–10) – a critique that closely mirrors early anarchist critiques of Marxism, in particular Bakunin's scathing condemnation of Marxism's inherent scientistic elitism: 'As soon as an official truth is pronounced [...], a truth proclaimed and imposed on the whole world from the summit of the Marxist Sinai, why discuss anything?' (in Miller, 1984: 80).

Foucault's key critique of Marxism related to the way the knowledge claims inherent in Marxism are structured: that there is a reality out there, which is hidden under appearances (e.g. the oppression of the worker as reality is hidden under the appearance of alienation and commodity fetishism). Given that there is then one 'true' reality, it must be possible to gain knowledge of that reality, of course only after having absorbed the 'proper' doctrine of Marxism–Leninism. Foucault came to view the 'truth claims' made from this position, i.e.: the PCF knows the 'true' nature of the situation, while those who are not sufficiently steeped in theory cannot know the truth – all eternal truth claims, in fact – as fundamentally oppressive, because they immediately introduce hierarchies: I know, and you don't. Therefore, I am more powerful than you. 'Knowledge', that is the claim to know what 'really' is, is then a form of power (Foucault, 1980: 132–3). But, as suggested above, this is nothing particularly new, given that Bakunin had already made similar claims. Foucault's fundamental insight was that knowledge of the outside world (e.g. of the fact that there 'is' a political struggle out there, that patriarchy is a 'reality') is also what enables us to act politically, to act at all. Therefore, he came to see power not only as repressive, but also as productive, and began to look not only at the constraining effects of power, but also its 'productive effectiveness, its strategic usefulness, its positivity' (Foucault, 1990: 86). Foucault's focus of analysis was therefore not a set of power relations structured in the familiar top–bottom mode (whether there was one top or many, although he did not deny that power relations were always structured unevenly), but power as a web, a 'multiplicity of force relations' without tops or bottoms, and as 'the process, which, through ceaseless struggles and confrontations, transforms, strengthens, or reverses them' (Foucault, 1990: 92–4).

So, how does that link to anarchism? It allows us for example to understand the situation on the above-mentioned protest camp: Foucault suggests that the view of power as fundamentally repressive, and therefore opposed to something that can be called 'truth' (or 'anarchism', or a 'free society'), is actually one of the key methods of maintaining certain relations of power, for it allows them to be hidden behind the mask of their being the 'opposite' of power (Foucault, 1990: 86). In our example, anarchy as 'non-power' is merely a facade behind which certain groups of activists (the more experienced ones; the ones with more knowledge; men) hide their power. In turn, a Foucauldian analysis would understand the ability of the protest site's anonymous critic to deploy her argument as enabled by her having access to the knowledge necessary to write and disseminate her piece: if all truth claims are products of power, then the truth claims made by feminist analysis must be as well. 'Patriarchy' is then nothing that exists as a category before feminists constructed it, but was created in order to use it to alter the power relations between genders, by creating the 'absence of freedom for women' as a lack felt by women ('freedom' again being a category that does not pre-exist its social construction), which can then become the source of emancipatory activity.[16] The upshot: a post-structuralist analysis radicalizes anarchism as a critique of power relations by extending it into the very field of resistance. Whereas anarchism had previously viewed the existence of power relations within spaces of resistance as simply an aberration (e.g. Anonymous5, 2000; Levine, 1984), thus keeping open the possibility of a privileged place of freedom which anarchist practice could potentially reach, we have now arrived at a picture where a practice of resistance must itself be viewed as establishing a power relation (or altering an existing one) – from power being everywhere by default to power being everywhere by necessity.

Post-Structuralist Anarchism, Power and Identity

Having now understood any form of resistance as a form of power, where does this leave us? Do we have to give up resisting, simply because any statement to the effect that people are oppressed presupposes a power relation? This seems like a valid conclusion: even if we take power to be productive of our every action, and therefore unavoidable, we could still argue that it is necessary to minimize the power we exert over others. One way of doing this would be by avoiding the construction of common identities between people who would then engage in social struggle as a collective force.

But let me backtrack for a moment: from where did this 'identity' question suddenly appear? As I suggested above, the claims of feminists that all women in the world are oppressed by a power structure of patriarchy involved an attempt to restructure power relations between genders: the attempt to construct an identity common to all women by telling women that they ought to feel oppressed (because of course, in 'reality' they are), and that they therefore ought to struggle against this oppression, the attempt to create a political identity under the leadership of those who construct it. As Laclau and Mouffe put it: 'hegemonic articulations retroactively create the interests they claim to represent' (2001: xi). This is not to minimize or ridicule the oppression of women – only to suggest that political strategies that aim at mobilizing people for a struggle against this oppression involve attempts to construct collective identities, and therefore the establishment of power relations. And in turn, the strategies ask those who will have been successfully mobilized into this new collective identity, whether it is called 'a global sisterhood', 'the people', or 'the working class', to attempt to alter their power relations with those who are seen as oppressors. In short: politics is about the construction of collective identities as the basis for action, and therefore about power. The question now is quite simple: do we think that engaging in politics is still a good idea, or not?

Post-Structuralist Anarchism as Non-Political Non-Politics?

I will focus on the work of the German philosopher Peter Sloterdijk, whose work – influential and controversial in Germany, as exemplified by his public clashes with Jürgen Habermas – has been receiving increasing attention outside his home country as well.[17] Sloterdijk, in a typical post-structuralist move, first elaborates a very forceful critique of the power relations inherent in attempts to construct political identities, and then takes precisely the step that I hope to avoid: from a critique of politics to the abdication of politics. Starting with the assertion that knowledge has been revealed today as (a claim to) power, and 'truth' as merely strategy, he defines his project as carrying to a conclusion the task of the Enlightenment, that is, the exposure of power by dismantling the facades it hides behind (Sloterdijk, 1983: 12, 18). In terms of placing post-structuralism in general and Sloterdijk in particular in a relation to anarchism, this is quite significant: anarchism can similarly be said to be an attempt at a conclusion of the Enlightenment project (taking his definition), for it radicalized the critique of power put forth first by Enlightenment liberalism, and then Marxism, to extend to all realms of life.[18]

The final battle the Enlightenment has yet to win, Sloterdijk suggests, is to expose the power hiding behind the notion of identity, to expose the ego, or subject, as constructed (Sloterdijk, 1983: 131–2). Tracing the construction of a bourgeois class identity (and the somewhat less successful attempt to construct a positive working-class identity), Sloterdijk reveals these to have been political projects, altering and establishing relations of power by creating the very political force the leaders claimed to represent (ibid.: 133–54).

Politics, therefore, becomes a struggle between identities and power knowledges: any mobilization around any political topic, however anarchistic or progressive, necessarily involves not 'essences' (as in: we are all essentially oppressed workers), but the construction of 'a new knowledge-power and the creation of a new subject of power-knowledge'.[19] It is against this background that Sloterdijk's Enlightenment struggles to break open 'the frozen identities', celebrating against this necessary product of politics an 'existential anti-politics' that would seek to reject all attempts at identifying us, to break through the disciplinary mechanisms that make us conform to a particular view of what we should do, and how we should be. Because 'politics is, when people try to smash each others' heads in' (ibid.: 250; 315–19). Sloterdijk identifies his (non-)strategy to achieve this as 'kynicism': an attempt to break through social conditionings/disciplinary mechanisms by physically asserting our ability to enjoy life in spite of these conditionings – for example, he cites with great joy the example of Diogenes, who countered Plato's learned lectures on the 'Eros' by publicly masturbating on Athens's market square. Kynicism would never involve the construction of new identities, because all identities are disciplining, normalizing, shaming: it would rather be seeking an 'actual' (*eigentlich* – as opposed to constructed, *uneigentlich*) experience of life, which we can reach not through politics – Sloterdijk does quite clearly assert that his struggle is 'about life, not about changing history' (ibid.: 242) – but rather in 'love and sexual rapture, in irony and laughter, creativity and responsibility, meditation and ecstasy' (ibid.: 390).

So where does Sloterdijk's (non-)politics, which I will treat as representative for any tendency of anarchism and post-structuralism that moves from the critique of politics to abandoning politics, leave us? With, I would suggest, a number of glaring inconsistencies. The first and probably most damaging to Sloterdijk's position is the fact that even his non-politics are necessarily embedded in power relations, and are thus political. In order either to withdraw from 'established society' or to physically defy social disciplinary mechanisms, one has to have a good number of privileges: many anarcho-activists who are today on the dole tend to forget that this dole is the result of the state skimming off some of the surplus value produced by workers, either in their own countries, or in another; to establish a commune requires, at least, both intellectual and financial resources (skills and money), which are the products of power; and finally, while Sloterdijk's Diogenes may very well have masturbated and shit on the Athenian marketplace with a good deal of public success, we can assume that a person who has been defined by the authorities as 'mad', or 'homeless', would not have any effect with such an action, besides getting arrested, or worse, ignored. True, Prof. Sloterdijk's public masturbation would surely have an interesting 'kynic' effect, but that presupposes the very position he has achieved (chair of a department at a German university) as a result of power. Kynicism, or any apparently non-political 'non-practice' (ibid.: 939–53) that aims to avoid politics in order to avoid power, thus makes the old mistake of ignoring the power relations it is itself based on and that help produce it as a practice. In other words: to try to bypass power relations is to reaffirm them, and to deny yourself the ability to do anything about them.

The second criticism is linked to the first, but not identical: having affirmed that power is unavoidable, I will now argue that 'identity' – that is, a more or less conscious inside/outside distinction – is simply a general condition of communication and social existence, and it is not only unavoidable (by default), but enabling and necessary. Sloterdijk, however, has already anticipated this move: he asserts that the desire to dive back constantly into new identifications once an old one is shattered is itself part of a more fundamental 'programming' of ourselves, where we come to think of our subjectivity as necessarily linked to an identity. In addition, to state that such a tendency exists is identified by Sloterdijk as an exercise of 'master knowledge', which deviously suggests that most people would rather have more security than freedom, a position that in turn leads to claims to representing these 'poor people', to exercising power over them, to domination (ibid.: 155–6, 348). Again, in these seemingly esoteric questions we are not as far away from actual anarchist practice as it may seem: the pamphlet 'Give up Activism' recently demanded of left-libertarians that their politics should involve not the construction of new identities, but the breaking open of old ones (especially that of the 'activist') and the creation of a situation of fundamental openness for the expression of what might be called a 'non-identitarian identity' (Anonymous2, 2000a).

Three arguments can be deployed against this view. First, that in arguing that any claim to identity is oppressive and therefore concluding that it is the 'essence' of human freedom not to be tied to any identity, Sloterdijk has overshot his target. He has constructed a new 'identity' or human essence, that of the person who seeks constantly to escape his/her being forced into an identity. The necessary implication of this is that any search for 'sameness', community, for collective identity, is the expression of the 'deep programming' identified above, and therefore not 'essentially' free and human. From this follows directly that anyone who does not constantly seek to break through identities, to constantly redefine him-/herself ought to change his or her behaviour, and conform to the standards set down by Sloterdijk – or the author of 'Give up Activism'. Clearly, this claim to knowledge of a human 'essence' becomes yet another form of hierarchy building, with those who constantly escape identity at the top, and those who do not at the bottom. Having deconstructed all essences, we are back with a new essence, this time a hypermobile one. On the side, it appears that the practice of social 'hypermobility' is, somewhat like Sloterdijk's kynicism, premised on a whole lot of resources to maintain such a life: in other words, it is a strategy of the privileged.

The second argument against hypermobility is of course precisely the one Sloterdijk anticipated: that humans need identity. Let me start with the example of language. It seems clear that we understand ourselves to some extent in and through the use of language – Sloterdijk's arguments were, after all, expressed in German. Language being a powerful element in the construction of collective identities, Sloterdijk is evidently also caught in an identity: not that of 'a German', but of a German-language speaker. How is this an identity? Quite simply, insofar as it defines a group of 'ins' or a 'we' (those who speak a language) and of 'outs' or 'them/the others' (those who do not). In other words: writing is based on language, language on identity, identity on power, suggesting that if we at all try to communicate we are already involved in the construction of collective identities (Lyotard, 1984: 15), and therefore Sloterdijk cannot consistently claim to have escaped power and identity in his non-political non-practice.

But, one could claim here, maybe it is possible to construct identities that at least do not involve the disciplining/normalizing that (usually?) goes with identities. This leads to the third and final critique of non-political non-practice: not only is identity necessarily exclusive, as shown above, it is also undesirable not to have any form of disciplining mechanism in a society: from an anarchist point of view, for example, sexist behaviour is not a matter of legitimately asserting one's difference, but rather is simply unacceptable and oppressive. Therefore, one would have to create social structures, or disciplining mechanisms, that would prevent sexist behaviour from developing, and if it developed, there would have to be mechanisms to deal with that. In other words: even the most perfect anarchist community needs disciplining – anything else would imply everyone's freedom to do anything, no matter that such actions might be oppressive towards others. It is therefore one thing to make a theoretical claim to 'true' radicalism by proclaiming the desirability of non-identity based on the argument that identities are oppressive and disciplining (a point that is not even theoretically coherent, as shown above), and another to construct radical political spaces that seek to put into practice what anarchism and post-structuralism are all about: ongoing critiques of power and oppression.

BACK TO THE REAL WORLD: ANARCHIST PRACTICE, HETEROTOPIA AND COUNTER-HEGEMONY

It is now important to return to the discussion of concrete anarchist practices in order to demonstrate that the conclusions elaborated here have to some extent already been drawn by activists, both conceptually and in practice. That is to say that both an understanding of their own practices as power and the attendant modesty, as well as self-consciously 'powerful' attempts to establish counter-hegemonic structures, are currently visible in anarchist circles.

Let me begin with the 'conceptual' examples, that is, where ideas expressed in writing by anarchist activists resemble those developed here, and therefore imply similar strategies. First, in an essay discussing the use of direct action, an activist points out that direct action and the prefigurative community it is both based on and seeks to create are not necessarily good, because they could involve the exclusion of outsiders. For after all, 'how about a [community] that involves unacknowledged sexism, racism, being of the right class?' (Anonymous11, 2001: 137). The writer can never be totally sure that her action is 'good' (an acknowledgement of a loss of ultimate certainties) because it may involve an undue exercise of power over others. Nonetheless, she 'can't remain frozen; even in the midst of that uncertainty I have to act' and accept her fallibility in an exercise of power that is guided by the belief that something is important (Anonymous11, 2001: 138). Her right to act, in other words, derives from her ethics, and her activism therefore becomes a conscious relation of power guided by a modest ethics.

In the second example, the author defines the anarchist project as one that aims to construct 'non-hierarchical spaces and free and equal social relations', but goes on to criticise the exclusionary and homogenizing tendencies of the anarchist counterculture (Anonymous1, 2001: 551–2). It is argued that anarchists have to abandon the safety that comes with 'relatively closed and homogenous collective identities', which 'undermine the freedom and autonomy of the members of the collective, partially deny people's own particular identities, and introduce risky dynamics of power and leadership'. Rather, they should embrace 'diversity and respect for difference' as a necessary condition for autonomy (ibid.: 554–5). Having pursued this argument thus far, the author asks: what about 'behaviours, values and ideas that cannot be accepted', especially those whose acceptability is disputed? While some collective values are clearly necessary, the challenge is to give more space to disagreement, which is held to bring creativity and change. Finally, the author calls on anarchists to 'experiment, and improve ways to eliminate all forms and systems of oppression, domination and discrimination within our own circles (while keeping the right to difference and taking precautions against the formation of dominant collective identities)' (ibid.: 562). While this text mirrors many of the arguments developed above, it clearly does not ultimately reject the notion of a potentially power-free practice. However, since this potential is seen as one contained mostly in the striving, the author is able to criticise both external and internal power relations, and work towards a counter-hegemonic structure based on some collective values but aiming for the greatest possible difference, in other words, on modest values.

And finally, there are also practical examples of anarchists pursuing a strategy that can be called 'counter-hegemonic' in the sense discussed here. Three projects come to mind: the PGA; the so-called 'consulta process'; and the 'No Border' camps (the latter I mentioned already in the context of the toilets-and-power debate). The treatment of these examples will have to remain brief, even skeletal, as they are not intended to fully capture the meaning of these practices, but rather to understand their relation to the theoretical positions I established above.

The PGA, formed in 1998, is a global network of grassroots groups that act in ways consistent with the ground rules set down in the network's 'hallmarks': groups that build local alternatives to globalization; reject 'all forms and systems of domination and discrimination'; have a confrontational attitude towards dominant (governmental and economic) structures of power; organize based on principles of decentralization and autonomy; and employ methods of direct action and civil disobedience (PGA, n.d.). On the basis of these hallmarks, the network can clearly be said to be anarchist. Supporting this is its 'essentially' anarchist avoidance of claims to representation: it can neither be represented by someone, nor can it represent any persons or groups. As for the formal and informal structures of the PGA, they are limited to a rotating committee of convenors who organize the network's conferences, and an informal 'support group' of self-selected activists who support the convenors in their work. This network can be seen as a significant step in the possible construction of an anarchist counter-hegemony, as it tries to deepen the political linkages between various radical groups in order to strengthen both feelings of collective solidarity and anarchists' capacity to resist repression by acting as a tool of communication and coordination of radical activities and groups. It is then an example of 'intensive'/internal movement building, based on a set of defined principles that aim for the greatest possible diversity of practices and structures while also creating some limits in terms of what is acceptable.

Secondly, the 'social consulta' is, if anything, even more in flux, so that there is very little concretely to say about what is at best a 'process' and at worst so far only an idea, aiming at the spread of radical democratic practices from the anarchist subculture to other social groups.[20] Since local groups at this early stage of developing the idea have been almost totally 'free' in deciding what they want the consulta to be, disagreement is likely to continue. However, some principles may be distilled from one of the key documents in the debate about what shape the process could take, the 'Internal Consultation Guide' (ICG). This begins by pointing out that, in the face of increased repression, the libertarian left needs first to strengthen its networks, and secondly to 'connect to the rest of society'. The basic element of the consulta process should therefore be local 'popular' assemblies, based, like the PGA, on a set of 'hallmarks' in order to ensure that the consulta remain 'as open, democratic and horizontal as possible'. The consulta can then be said to be an example of extensive/external movement building, since it tries to widen the reach of the anarchists' message and mobilizing capacity, while at the same time increasing their public legitimacy. And as for the question of power, following the ICG, this aspect of the anarchist counter-hegemonic project even contains an acknowledgement of an act of power in laying down hallmarks in order to ensure difference and diversity.

The final project I will mention here is that of the No Border camps. These have been organized (mostly in Europe) by a loose network of groups campaigning around issues of freedom of movement and immigrant rights. For the purposes of my discussion, however, what is relevant about these camps is not so much the question of immigration but rather the attempt 'to implement a complete vision of the world(s) we're fighting for in the here and now, right down to the smallest details of daily life', as the 'handbook' to the camp in Strasbourg put it (No Border Camp, 2002: 2). Let me begin with this handbook then. Its telling subtitle designates it a 'manual of [intra-camp] geopolitics', a good sign if any of the recognition of the camp's organization as a matter of power struggles. Further on, the organizers ask that, while discussions about the organization of the camp should occur, 'the general functioning of the camp should not be called into question', even if the rules this entails 'will neither always convince everybody, nor avoid conflict'. Clearly, the organizers recognize the decisions they had taken as imperfect, but suggest that their acceptance is necessary to allow the camp (an embryonic form of an anarchist sustainable community of resistance) to perform its basic functions. Their call is for all 'to challenge racist, sexist, anti-Semitic and homophobic behaviour, and therefore [the organizers] expect everyone to make sure such attitudes find no room' in the camp (ibid.). The fact that it is so openly acknowledged that the rules laid down here are an ultimately arbitrary (but ethically motivated) exercise of power, taken together with the essay on direct action discussed above, suggests that it is the practical implementation of an anarchist project in community with others that is more likely to produce this 'post-structuralist' awareness, or simply 'modesty', than other forms of practice (writing, organization building, etc.). The reason for this appears to be that while it is possible to argue in theory for a power-free practice, any self-conscious anarchist practice will in reality turn out to be about power relations – a conclusion that is forced onto activists by anarchists' strong and salutary tendency to see oppression and domination everywhere, and to attack it vigorously. It takes only one hour-long meeting during which one's supposedly power-free proposal is ripped to shreds by people arguing that it oppresses women, newcomers, older people, physically challenged people, immigrants, or whomever, for the realization to hit home that nothing one could ever say would be devoid of power.

EPILOGUE: ANARCHISTS, MODEST AND UNCERTAIN – BUT STILL COUNTER-HEGEMONIC?

The Strasbourg camp accommodated between 2,000 and 3,000 activists over a period of over one week. In spite of massive disagreements, it represented a very successful example of anarchist living involving a large number of people, who developed bonds of solidarity based on common principles that allowed them to organize anarchistically the very details of everyday life – even who cleans the toilets: in the end, a functional group of volunteers was formed to do so. The camp operated under the constant threat (and fact) of police repression, and nonetheless managed to make some (albeit limited) contact with groups of illegal immigrants – although contact building with Strasbourg locals seemed, at least from my vantage point, woefully limited. The camp was certainly not perfect – but then, today's anarchism can no longer claim to be. All it can do is to try to create spaces and relations where domination and oppression are kept to a minimum.

As I have suggested above, this type of political modesty must ultimately flow from an acceptance of the unavoidability of power. The fundamental uncertainty this introduces into anarchists' political actions might be disconcerting at first, but can be used productively to recognize that all our politics are guided by our ethics, and that ethics, not historical truth or destiny, becomes the essence of political work. While there may be many who draw comfort from the belief that – as an anarchist graffiti put it – 'in the end, we will win', and the sense of historical mission, truth and inevitability this implies, surely we all realize in our daily political work that there is no historical inevitability in anything political: mobilizing means appealing to, and changing, people's perceptions of what is good and bad. Their ethics, in short.

From there, I have argued, it is only a short step towards accepting the necessity and ethical acceptability of a strategy of an anarchist counter-hegemony, or the creation of sustainable communities of resistance. Projects such as the PGA, the consulta, or the No Border camps suggest that there are people actively trying to construct such communities. In doing so, they will always have to return to the fundamental uncertainty of political organizing today, to find a route that negotiates between two types of oppression: that of too few rules/identities, and that of too many. This does not sound much like a political project; such projects seem somehow always to need certainty. But at a time when the project of neoliberalism is having obviously disastrous consequences; when social democracy is in a coma, if it hasn't quite kicked the bucket yet; when fascists and proto-fascists are on the rise; and when the authoritarian left cannot mobilize sufficient resistance; this uncertain and modest post-structuralist anarchism seems to be our best shot at a new emancipatory project.[21] In it, a movement (anarchism) found an analysis (post-structuralism) found a strategy (counter-hegemony) found a movement, etc. An uncertain synthesis, I admit. But uncertainty, perhaps even more than variety, is the real spice of life.

NOTES

1. This chapter originally appeared in *Anarchist Studies* 11(2) (2003). The author would like to thank three anonymous reviewers for *Anarchist Studies*, as well as Ben Day and Jamie Cross, for their insightful critiques and comments – some of which I ignored at my own peril.
2. Compare Gemie's condemnation of the 'now standard Godwin–Stirner–Proudhon–Bakunin–Kropotkin approach' (Gemie 1994: 350).
3. See also Cross 2002.
4. I am here employing a distinction between 'scriptural' and 'embodied' (i.e. practised) knowledge, suggested by Jon Mitchell in a presentation on the anthropology of religion during a seminar at the University of Sussex, Brighton, 24 May 2002.
5. For what can be called a 'scriptural' reading of anarchism, see e.g. Miller (1984) and Joll (1969).
6. Compare Holloway (2002: 1–10).
7. Graeber relates this notion of prefiguration directly to the anarchist wing of the globalization movement (Graeber, 2002: 62). It refers to a politics which in its current practice seeks to 'prefigure' the future society it struggles for – a notion of politics juxtaposed to a more 'systemic' approach, which would deny the possibility or efficacy of such 'utopian' communities.
8. See for example Gill (2000).
9. Gramsci held alliances of different social groups (classes/class fractions) under the leadership of one to be a key condition of hegemony (Gramsci, 1971: 53).
10. Whether any struggle is *concretely* more important than others is a question that has to be answered after a concrete analysis, as opposed to posited in advance.

11. Related analyses of anarchism as consisting fundamentally of two strands, one more monistic and one more pluralistic, can be found in Gemie (1994) and May (1994).
12. And there is indeed some disagreement as to whether the term 'revolution' should still be used by anarchists: compare Anonymous1 (2001: 546).
13. See Newman (2001), May (1994), Koch (1993), Schürmann (1986), Easterbrook (1997) and Mümken (1998). Habermas, too, recognized the anarchist potential of post-structuralist analysis (Habermas 1987: 4–5).
14. Many other post-structuralist thinkers could be, and have been, cited to make similar points, for example Lyotard, Deleuze and Guattari, or Derrida (see especially May, 1994 and Newman, 2001).
15. Beyond my personal experience, such examples can be found especially in Habermas (1987); for an overview of Habermas' and his associates' criticisms of post-structuralist thought, see Best and Kellner (1991: 240–55) and, from an anarchist point of view, Zerzan (n.d).
16. Foucault argues that the existence of a desire, in this case for the liberation of women, already presupposes a power relation, since the latter produces 'both the desire and the lack on which it is predicated' (Foucault, 1990: 81).
17. For a critique, see e.g. Bewes (1997), and for a positive appropriation, the work of Slavoj Žižek (1989).
18. Compare Joll (1969: 17–39).
19. All translations from non-English sources by TM.
20. General information about the consulta process can be found on the website (European Social Consulta, n.d.).
21. There are of course other projects on the left, which I have not discussed here – the 'list' suggested is therefore not conclusive, and not everyone who is a leftist is therefore an authoritarian or a social democrat (I thank Julian Mueller for pointing this out to me).

REFERENCES

Anonymous1 (2001). 'Replacing Capitalism with Networks of Free, Autonomous Spaces: A Western European Perspective'. In K. Abramsky (ed.). *Restructuring and Resistance: Diverse Voices of Struggle in Western Europe*. Self-published: 546–64.
Anonymous2 (2000a). 'Give up Activism'. *Do or Die 9*: 160–6.
—— (2000b). 'Postscript'. *Do or Die 9*: 166–70.
Anonymous5 (2000). 'Time to Take the Gloves off: Fuck the Civil, Let's Get Disobedient'. *Do or Die 9*: 15–19.
Anonymous6 (2000). 'This Is What Anarchy Looks Like'. *Do or Die 9*: 126–8.
Anonymous7 (1998). 'No Escape from Patriarchy: Male Dominance on Site'. *Do or Die 7*: 10–13.
Anonymous11 (2001). 'If Not You, Who? If Not Now, When?' In K. Abramsky (ed.). *Restructuring and Resistance: Diverse Voices of Struggle in Western Europe*. Self-published: 134–8.
Best, S. and Kellner, D. (1991). *Postmodern Theory: Critical Interrogations*. Houndmills and London: Macmillan.
Bewes, T. (1997). *Cynicism and Postmodernity*. London and New York: Verso.
Bookchin, M. (1989). 'New Social Movements: The Anarchic Dimension'. In D. Goodway (ed.). *For Anarchism: History, Theory and Practice*. London: Routledge: 259–74.
Cross, J. (2002). 'Anthropology and the Anarchists: Culture, Power, and Practice in Militant Anti-Capitalist Protests'. Unpublished manuscript.
Easterbrook, N. (1997). 'Anarchy, State, Heterotopia: The Political Imagination in Henlein, LeGuin and Delany'. In C. Wilcox and D. Hassler (eds). *Political Science Fiction*. Columbia: University of South Carolina Press.
Epstein, B. (2001). 'Anarchism and the Anti-Globalization Movement', *Monthly Review 53(4)*: 1–14.
European Social Consulta (n.d.). Retrieved 15 October 2002 from <http://www.europeansocialconsulta.org>.

Foucault, M. (1990) [1978]. *The History of Sexuality: An Introduction*. New York: Vintage Books.

—— (1980). *Power/Knowledge: Selected Interviews and Other Writings 1972–1977*. New York: Harvester Wheatsheaf.

Gemie, S. (1994). 'Counter-Community: An Aspect of Anarchist Political Culture'. *Journal of Contemporary History* 29: 349–67.

Gill, S. (2000). 'Toward a Postmodern Prince? The Battle in Seattle as a Moment in the New Politics of Globalization'. *Millennium* 29 (1): 131–40.

Goodway, D. (1989). 'Introduction'. In D. Goodway (ed.). *For Anarchism: History, Theory and Practice*. London: Routledge.

Graeber, D. (2002). 'The New Anarchists'. *New Left Review* 13: 61–73.

Gramsci, A. (1971). *Selections from the Prison Notebooks of Antonio Gramsci*. London: Lawrence & Wishart.

Habermas, J. (1987). *Lectures on the Philosophical Discourse of Modernity*. Cambridge, MA: MIT Press.

Holloway, J. (2002). *Change the World Without Taking Power: The Meaning of Revolution Today*. London and Sterling, VA: Pluto Press.

Joll, J. (1969). *The Anarchists*. London: Methuen.

Koch, A. (1993). 'Post-Structuralism and the Epistemological Basis of Anarchism'. *Philosophy of the Social Sciences* 23(2): 327–51.

Laclau, E. and Mouffe, C. (2001) [1985]. *Hegemony and Socialist Strategy: Towards a Radical Democratic Politics*. London and New York: Verso.

Levine, C. (1984). 'The Tyranny of Tyranny'. In Anonymous10 (ed.). *Untying the Knot: Feminism, Anarchism and Organization*. London: Dark Star & Rebel Press.

Lyotard, J.-F. (1984). *The Postmodern Condition: A Report on Knowledge*. Minneapolis: University of Minnesota Press.

Marshall, P. (1992). *Demanding the Impossible: A History of Anarchism*. London: HarperCollins.

May, T. (1994). *The Political Philosophy of Post-Structuralist Anarchism*. University Park, PA: Pennsylvania State University Press.

Miller, D. (1984). *Anarchism*. London: Dent.

Moore, R. (2001). 'Beyond Genoa: Where to Now?' In Anonymous3 (ed.). *On Fire: The Battle of Genoa and the Anti-Capitalist Movement*. One Off Press.

Mümken, J. (1998). 'Keine macht fuer niemand'. *Schwarzer faden* 19(1): 34–46.

Melucci, A. (1989). *Nomads of the Present: Social Movements and Individual Needs in Contemporary Society*. London: Hutchinson Radius.

Newman, S. (2001). *From Bakunin to Lacan: Anti-Authoritarianism and the Dislocation of Power*. Lanham, Boulder, New York and Oxford: Lexington Books.

No Border Camp (2002). *The Handbook: Manual of Inter-Barrio Geopolitics*. Strasbourg.

PGA (n.d.). Retrieved 19 July 2002 from <http://www.nadir.org/nadir/initiativ/agp/en/>.

Schürmann, R. (1986). 'On Constituting Oneself an Anarchistic Subject'. *Praxis International* 6(3): 294–310.

Sloterdijk, P. (1983). *Kritik der zynischen vernunft*. Frankfurt: Suhrkamp.

Zerzan, J. (n.d.). *The Catastrophe of Postmodernism*. Retrieved 18 July 2002 from <http://www.primitivism.com/postmodernism.htm>.

Žižek, S. (1989). *The Sublime Object of Ideology*. London and New York: Verso.

6
Hegemony, Affinity and the Newest Social Movements: At the End of the 00s

Richard J.F. Day

PREFACE

In writing this chapter, I've taken the opportunity to consolidate and update what I've had to say, over the past ten years or so, about two trends relevant to post-anarchism: the (re-)emergence of what I have called the 'newest' social movements, and the political logic that operates within and between them. In this time, the values and practices that guide the movements in which I've participated, and which I have written about, have not changed all that much. But I have. Probably the biggest change in me has been a slow but inexorable movement away from 'high' or 'meta' theory, that is, theory about theory, theory as abstraction from, well, more theory. Thus, some of what appears below now seems, to me, to go over the line between meta- and movement-theory; but given that I have accepted the task set before me, I feel compelled to reproduce the argument more or less as it was originally set out. At the same time, I will try to highlight the ways in which these abstractions not only can matter, but also do matter, to those of us working to create new worlds in the shells of the old.

INTRODUCTION

The energy behind the so-called 'anti-globalization' movements is mostly going into other things these days, but it had a pretty good run throughout the 00s, and led to a prodigious outpouring of academic texts. These range from writers continuing primarily in the tradition of functionalist analysis (Smith and Johnston, 2002; Cohen and Rai, 2000) to those attempting to discern a revitalization of Marxist struggles (Holloway, 2002; McNally, 2002; Panitch, 2001). In the middle, so to speak, we find commentators who have argued that these same forces are helping to create a universal 'cosmopolitan social democracy' (Held and McGrew, 2002), and there are of course important analyses emerging from the post-colonial/feminist and queer traditions (Hawley, 2001; Mohanty, 2003; Sassen, 1998). In this chapter, though, I want to focus on interpretations emerging from traditions that are less well-established, though definitely gaining more and more attention these days. Of particular interest for this article are works that deploy concepts from Italian autonomist Marxism (Dyer-Witheford, 1999; Hardt and Negri,

2000), and those that have begun to recognize the centrality of anarchist theory and practice to the social movements of the 90s and 00s (Antliff, 2003; Graeber, 2002; Jordan, 2002). My primary goal is to argue that the field in which these interventions are occurring is ordered by the relation of the various authors to what I will call the *hegemony of hegemony*. By this I mean the commonsensical assumption that meaningful social change – and social order itself – can only be achieved through the deployment of universalizing hierarchical forms, epitomized by the nation state, but including conceptions of the world state and other globalized institutions as well. As I will try to show, this assumption is challenged not only by some important and highly visible forms of contemporary activism, but also by a long-standing tradition of affinity-based direct action that has been submerged under (neo)liberal and (post-)Marxist theory and practice. Hence my secondary purpose: to contribute to the ongoing effort to destabilize the hegemony of hegemony, by exploring the possibilities of non-hegemonic forms of radical social change.

Of course, theorists and practitioners committed to the concept of the new social movements (NSMs) have been wary of the idea that something even newer is afoot. This is a position with which I share a certain amount of sympathy, since what is at issue here is a matter of genealogies of logics of struggle, not definitions and chronological novelty. Modes of social organization and social change have long existed that cannot be adequately understood by either (post-)Marxism or (neo)liberalism. What is different now, if anything is different at all, is that the hegemony of hegemony is being brought into question openly, massively, at the heart of precisely those struggles which currently seem to have more momentum than most others. When I refer to the political logic of the newest social movements, then, I am using the term 'newest social movements' guardedly and more than a little ironically. Indeed, my argument would suggest that the struggles in which I am most interested would not appear within some paradigms of analysis as 'social movements' at all.

Yet the question remains: if contemporary non-hegemonic struggles cannot be adequately characterized by the categories of the 'old' or 'new' left, then how are they to be understood? Is there anything they share, other than their difference from established practices? In this chapter I will argue that their commonalities can be best understood by tracing a genealogy of the logic of hegemony which shows how its own trajectory has cleared a space in which an ever-present, but relatively subterranean, logic of affinity has re-emerged. The discussion will begin with an analysis of the logic of hegemony as it has developed in Western Marxism, starting with Lenin and Gramsci and proceeding through the work of Laclau and Mouffe. I will then present several examples of constructive direct action tactics that are being used in contemporary radical social movements, and link these to a shift from a counter-hegemonic politics of demand to a non-hegemonic politics of the act. To focus attention on one site at which these two political logics productively collide, I will discuss the notion of constituent power of the multitude as it appears in Michael Hardt and Toni Negri's *Empire* (2000). The analysis will focus on their ambivalent position with regard to the logic of hegemony, as expressed in the acceptance of a Leninist dichotomy between revolution and reform. A genealogy of the logic of affinity will then be presented, to support the claim that in order to understand the newest social movements, it is necessary to move away from theories that emphasize the achievement of totalizing effects within the system of states and corporations and to focus instead on the possibilities offered by the *displacement* and *replacement* of this system. Only then are we able to recognize the particularity of a non-statist politics being practised by what Giorgio Agamben has called the 'coming communities' (1993). To begin, then, let us briefly recall some of the key developments that contributed to the shift from the theory and practice of the 'old' social movements that emerged in the mid-1800s, to the 'new' social movements of the 1960s–80s.

As previously mentioned, this discussion will be genealogical is in its intent. That is, while reference will be made to periods of time, the analysis is not based upon mere novelty or simple succession, but upon the observation of shifting 'regularities in dispersion' (Foucault, 1972: 38). Further, any shift in relations or regularities that might be noted should not be read as implying that previously dominant forms have been thrust into insignificance or even eradicated from the field. Proceeding in this way would be at odds with what I am trying to do, that is, to challenge the deference that is given to practices guided by a hegemonic logic. Underneath this mainstream flow, the careful observer can discern a logic that self-consciously seeks to remain emergent and unincorporated (Williams, 1973), that sets out to challenge not only the hegemony of the values and forms of the currently dominant order, as in counter-hegemonic struggles, but seeks to avoid the generalization of its own values and forms as well. Because they set out to challenge hegemonic forms as such, I prefer to use the term 'non-hegemonic' to describe these activities. Finally, it should be noted that in proceeding genealogically I make no claim to be producing an objectively correct or universally valuable narrative. Rather, I want to track an emergence that I find interesting and compelling due to my own ethico-political commitments and theoretical interests. Other genealogies are not only possible, they are necessary, and I welcome them.

HEGEMONY AND THE NEW SOCIAL MOVEMENTS

Gramscian Marxism, of course, never really caught on in Western Europe, as various forms of social democracy based on the so-called 'welfare state' captured the imagination and loyalty of the working classes. The Keynesian accommodation, along with a series of large-scale international wars, helped to maintain relative peace for a while. But this period ended, in Europe, North America, and the rest of the Euro-colonial world, with the emergence of the 'new social movements' of the 1960s and 70s. In order better to understand what is 'newest' about the social movements of the late 90s and early 00s, it is necessary to spend some time discussing what was 'new' about those of the 60s. This is far from a simple question, since various analysts have produced different and mutually contradictory lists of characteristics of NSMs, and disagreements on their applicability are rampant. There are observable regularities in the field however, some of which I will now try to tease out.

First of all, most commentators agree that NSMs differ from OSMs (old social movements) in addressing a wide range of antagonisms that cannot be reduced to class struggle, such as those generated by racism, patriarchy, the domination of nature, heterosexism, colonialism, and so on. The displacement of class as 'the fundamental antagonism' has led many commentators to see NSM politics as 'merely symbolic' (Melucci, 1989: 5; Touraine, 1992: 373; Pulido, 1998: 7–8). Paul Bagguley uses the term 'expressive politics' to describe the activities of those he sees as 'bearers of a new hedonistic culture' of 'personal freedom' (1992: 34). While there are certainly some individuals in some movements who relate to their activism on a purely personal level, it is not entirely clear to me how striving to improve the situations of women, people of colour, and non-heterosexual orientations, or working against military and ecological destruction, can be seen as individualistic pursuits. The burnout rate of activists in these movements would also seem to suggest that their struggles are not somehow less intense or difficult than those associated with class warfare. Hence, I would suggest that the most accurate description of NSMs is not that they have *no* analysis of or concern for socially structured antagonisms, but that they do not focus solely on class as *the fundamental* axis of oppression.

It has also been noted that NSMs are unlike their precursors in that they lack a totalizing conception of social change. They are single-issue movements 'not perceived to be struggling for a grand or universal transformation' (Pulido, 1998: 8). Once again, while there is certainly some value in this description, it is somewhat reductive and ignores long-standing analyses of relations between various struggles. As early as the 1970s socialist feminists were discussing links between patriarchy and capitalism (Firestone, 1970; Eisenstein, 1979), environmentalists were linking capitalism to the domination of nature (Bahro, 1986; Leiss, 1972), and so on. For these reasons, I do not accept without qualification the characterization of NSMs as single-issue struggles. However, I would agree that agitating for reforms across two or three axes of oppression is a very different thing from seeking the wholesale reconstruction of an existing order through revolutionary means.

This difference is manifested in various shifts in the orientation of NSMs to state power. One of these involves the opening up of new fronts outside of mainstream political institutions. With the acknowledgement of the micropolitical, capillary nature of macro-structures and processes of power, attention shifted to a 'politics of everyday life and individual transformation' (Melucci, 1989: 5). Also, and very importantly for the genealogy of the logic of affinity, the social movements emerging in the 1960s reflected a commitment to the long-standing anarchist idea that the means of radical social change must be consistent with its ends (Melucci, 1989: 5; Bagguley, 1992: 31; Offe, 1985: 829–31).

However, the absence of a totalizing conception of change and the recognition of the deep entwining of the personal and the political do not necessarily, or even usually, lead to a rejection of state power as such. As many commentators have pointed out, 1960s–1980s NSMs are characterized primarily by a politics of protest and reform (Bagguley, 1992: 32; Touraine, 1992: 392–3). Those new social movements that are most commonly cited as exemplars of their type are like the old social movements in that they tend to desire irradiation effects across an entire social space, usually defined as a nation-state container – the changes most often cited as their successes have involved modifications to laws, bureaucratic structures, and shifts in hegemonic commonsense assumptions and practices. This is to say that in protest politics there is still a strong orientation to the state, and this is a crucial moment of commonality between the OSMs and NSMs. The difference between them is that the latter hope to achieve effects on a limited number of axes, rather than on all axes at once. Thus I would argue that the dominant stream of the new social movements remains within a hegemonic conception of the political, and is only marginally and nascently aware of the possibilities inherent in actions oriented neither towards achieving state power nor towards ameliorating its effects.

HEGEMONY DECONSTRUCTED: LACLAU AND MOUFFE

In order to aid the reader in placing my argument, I have provided a quick enumeration of some of the characteristics of the movements usually studied by NSM theory. For the purpose of the genealogy I am trying to construct, though, the most important theoretical development at this time was the reworking of Gramsci's concept of hegemony by a new generation of social and political theorists who were steeped in Lacanian psychoanalysis and Derridean deconstruction. One product of this effort was Laclau and Mouffe's *Hegemony and Socialist Strategy* (1985), which pushed Gramsci's theory to its limits in an attempt to understand and provide guidance to the new social movements. Their work has been widely read and cited, and has been a major influence on how the concept of hegemony has been deployed in critical social, political and cultural theory.

While celebrating the fact that 'in Gramsci, politics is finally conceived as articulation' (1985: 85), Laclau and Mouffe objected to Gramsci's assumption that 'there must always be a *single* unifying principle in every hegemonic formation, and this can only be a fundamental class' (69, emphasis in original). In their anti-essentialist reworking of the theory of hegemony, the socialist revolution and its privileged agent – the working class – are displaced from the centre of the political, to be considered instead as one of many struggles that form a broad and indeterminate 'project for radical democracy'. This project is explicitly linked to the new social movements, which are taken to include the peace movement, as well as 'older struggles such as those of women or ethnic minorities' (165). But this list is not complete, and is indeed impossible to complete, since new struggles are constantly emerging, 'questioning the different relations of subordination ... and demanding ... new rights' (165). Laclau and Mouffe see the new social movements as working towards a 'democracy to come' (Derrida, 1994: 59), via a progressive expansion of the realm of application of the values of the French revolution – liberty, equality, community.

Many Marxist critics have questioned whether this project is indeed radical, given its abandonment of the centrality of class struggle and its adherence to what appear to be explicitly bourgeois values (Bertram, 1995; Geras, 1987). I want to raise a similar question, but on a different basis. I want to ask whether Laclau and Mouffe's theory takes us *far enough away* from classical Marxism and the old social movements, far enough from irradiation effects and the orientation to state power, to remain applicable in the context of the emerging struggles of the 1990s and 00s. To this end I will discuss the exposition of the theory of hegemony found in Ernesto Laclau's contributions to *Contingency, Hegemony, Universality* (Butler, Laclau and Žižek, 2000).

In these essays, Laclau argues that there are four interlocking 'dimensions' of hegemony. First, he states that 'unevenness of power is constitutive of the hegemonic relation' (Butler, Laclau and Žižek, 2000: 54). This is to say that hegemony occupies a middle ground between the war of each against each, where power is widely and evenly distributed, and the totalitarian regime, where individuals and groups are entirely subordinated to an overarching apparatus. The logic of hegemony, therefore, operates only in societies where there is a 'plurality of particularistic groups and demands' (55), i.e. in *liberal* societies. In one sense, the first dimension of hegemony can be seen as a mere acknowledgment that something like a (post?)modern condition exists within the liberal–capitalist world.[1] That is, it simply points out that the political today is a complex terrain of overdetermined relations within and between particular identities, states, and groups of states. But, as I shall argue later, there is also a normative component to the first dimension of hegemony, in the assumption that today's liberal societies represent the best, or perhaps the *only possible* mode of social organization that acknowledges and thrives upon this condition of unevenness of power.

The second dimension of hegemony holds that 'there is hegemony only if the dichotomy universality/particularity is superseded' (56). For Laclau, no political struggle can be truly universal, since it is impossible for those who advance a cause to fully transcend their particular interests. Similarly, there is no such thing as a pure particularity, since no identity can exist without establishing relationships with what it is *not* (the 'constitutive outside').[2] In a hegemonic articulation, particular interests 'assume a function of universal representation', leading to a mutual 'contamination' of the universal and the particular (56). This process operates via the establishment of 'chains of equivalence', extended systems of relationships through which identities compete and cooperate, each seeking to enlarge itself to the point of being able to represent all of the others. It is crucial to note that while the universalizing element is itself part of the chain, it simultaneously sets itself above it, via the metaphorical elevation of its particular concerns (302). In practical terms, we can think of this as an extension of Gramsci's notion of hegemony to cover situations in which the 'fundamental social group' is not a class, but any kind of identity at all. To the extent that the Green movement has been successful in its programme, for example, a diverse array of social groups have lined up under the banner of 'ecological sustainability', each expressing its own particular concerns about environmental destruction: parents as guardians of the well-being of vulnerable young children; people of colour as those affected by environmental racism; and so on.

As a corollary of the contamination of the universal and the particular, hegemony 'requires the production of tendentially empty signifiers' which articulate chains of equivalence (207). The empty signifier – not to be confused with Lacan's floating signifier[3] – has a dual aspect. Empty signifiers are signifiers to the extent that they resonate within existing discourses; they do participate in the production of meaning. But they *tend* towards emptiness, or lack of meaning, due to the stresses placed upon them by the exigencies of hegemonic articulation. That is, in order to be seen as a general equivalent for an increasing number of struggles, they must be ever further removed from their point of origin in a particular discourse. As an excellent example of an empty signifier, the term 'Green' will again suffice. It manages, with apparent ease, to refer to mainstream political groupings oriented to parliamentary reform (Green Party), underground movements that carry out direct action against the destruction of the environment and in defence of non-human beings (Green Warriors), and niche-marketed products in the capitalist marketplace (Green Detergent). The result of all of this overtime is that most of us are not at all sure what it means to 'be Green'.

Finally, Laclau argues that '[t]he terrain in which hegemony expands is that of a generalization of the relations of representation as condition of the constitution of the social order' (207). With this thesis, we appear to have returned to the empirical realm of the first dimension; under conditions of (post)modernity, representation – or the delegation of power in the economy, cultural production and political will formation – becomes 'the only way in which universality is achievable' (212). However, once again, we must be aware that this is no mere description. The claim being made is not only that representation is necessary, but that it is *desirable*, because it is through processes of representation that equivalential chains are expanded, hegemonic blocs are formed and social transformations are achieved.

This theoretical argument has been taken up in interventions related to many counter-hegemonic struggles, such as those against Thatcherism in the United Kingdom (Hall, 1983b), Reagan–Bush conservatism in the United States (Grossberg, 1992: 377–84) and studies of the role of television in maintaining consent to the established order of racist, sexist capitalism (Kellner, 1990; Press, 1991). The strength of these interventions is that they move beyond the Frankfurt School's postulation of a one-dimensional apparatus of ideological domination, in which possibilities for resistance are negligible or non-existent. Their weakness is that, in valorizing contestation as such, they do not always pay enough attention to the logic of various forms of contestation, or acknowledge that a diversity of logics of struggle exists. More precisely, they tend to advocate only for *counter*-hegemonic struggles against various modes of subordination. Grossberg's 'affective politics', for example, sees the struggle for hegemony as a 'struggle for authority' (Grossberg, 1992: 380–1). And Kellner echoes Laclau's thesis on representation quite closely in claiming that '[b]ecause of the power of the media in the established society, any counter-hegemonic project whatsoever – be it that of socialism, radical democracy, or feminism – must establish a media politics' (Kellner, 1990: 18).

These deployments of Laclau and Mouffe's theory of hegemony show explicitly how the theory/practice of NSMs moved away from the coercion/consent politics of Lenin and Gramsci, into a territory of hegemony by what appears as pure consent, i.e. into the territory of liberal reform. Rather than seeking state power, subordinated groups began to focus more on persuading an existing hegemonic formation to alter the operation of certain institutions, or on infiltrating those institutions with a different set of values and thereby constructing a counter-hegemony. This practice achieved some important reforms in the countries of the global North, which undoubtedly helped to motivate the post-Marxist rereading of the theory of hegemony. Over the past 20 years, however, the situation has changed drastically. Struggles against racism, sexism and homophobia, as well as attempts to ameliorate some of the worst effects of capitalist exploitation, have been successfully resisted by a reaction against state intervention and so-called political correctness. All the signs point not only to continuing success on the part of social conservatism and political–economic neoliberalism, but to a resurging and deepening of their hold on what used to be called the masses of the First World. Therefore, just as it was necessary in 1985 to rethink radical politics in the light of the successes of the new social movements, it is necessary to do so again, in the light of their failure to effectively limit the continued rise of neoliberal ideology and the societies of control.

THE POLITICAL LOGIC OF THE NEWEST SOCIAL MOVEMENTS

'The term new social movements is rapidly approaching its sell-by date' (Crossley, 2003: 149).

Just as some 'new' social movements perpetuate certain characteristics of the 'old', it can also be argued that some of them anticipate the 'newest'. I am particularly interested in two aspects of NSMs that have already been mentioned, i.e. the tendency to work outside of state forms, and the desire to express chosen ends in the means used to achieve them. In this section I want to expand the discussion of these shifts to include their contextualization within a more global conception of the arena of social struggle. On this latter point, many critics have noted that NSM theory has tended to focus on 'one particular, albeit interesting, subset of social movements that happen to be predominantly white, middle class, and located in Western Europe and North America' (Gamson, 1992: 58; c.f. Pulido, 1998: 12). However, some of the most high-profile and intense struggles in the 90s and 00s are characterized by currents that transcend the boundaries of the nation state, and thus, some analysts argue, should be considered as 'transnational social movements' (Smith and Johnston, 2002; Keck and Sicknick, 1998; Tarrow, 2001). This brings us to an important cusp or discontinuity, an axis of differentiation between the two discursive fields I am trying to discuss using the signifiers 'new' and 'newest' – that is, the transcendence of the orientation to what I have called the nation-state container.

This tendency has been prominently noted in analyses of 'the anti-globalization movement', a disparate and ever-changing network of activist groups and communities which, like the 'new' social movements, have resisted easy identification (Holloway, 2002; McNally, 2002; Starr, 2000). Indeed, it is often suggested that the term 'anti-globalization movement' is a crippling misnomer (Buchanan, 2002; Klein, 2001; Milstein, 2002).[4] While I certainly share these concerns, I also believe that we need some way to talk about the resurgence of struggle which has coincided with the intensification of the global reach of capitalism and its electronic systems of exchange and surveillance. This resurgence has been made visible in the mass media by way of certain punctuating events, including: the emergence onto the world stage of the Zapatista Army of National Liberation in Chiapas, Mexico in 1994; massive strikes in response to neoliberal reforms in France in 1995; similar mass actions in Korea in 1996–97, this time on the heels of what many saw as the orchestrated collapse of the East Asian economies; and, in North America, the surprisingly powerful direct action struggle against the WTO meetings in Seattle in 1999 (McNally, 2002: 13–23). What all of these events have in common is their opposition to the agenda of globalizing capital and the neoliberal ideology associated with it, which brings privatization, deregulation, and unemployment to the global North, and structural adjustment programmes and increased impoverishment to the global South. This opposition has come from all classes, identity groups and causes, from every part of the world, and it has reinvigorated both activists and academics, who see in it a return of the countercultural spirit of the 1960s.

Already, though, the energy built up over the 1990s and released so formidably at the end of the millennium has been dissipated by clampdowns on dissent, or redirected against the adventures of the US/UK global police force in Afghanistan and Iraq, the Russians in the Caucasus, the Chinese in Tibet and Mongolia, Israel in Palestine, to name only a few of the more prominent. Yet, despite the fact that the regularity and intensity of street protests have diminished, the same forces of change still exist, as do the antagonisms that drive them. Thus, I would suggest that the reactionary consolidation of the status quo and the clampdown on dissent mean that it is more important than ever to take stock of what has been achieved and what remains to be achieved in the struggles against globalizing capital and the societies of control.

As previously noted, the NSMs were seen by many commentators as adopting a mode of social change that did not focus only on achieving irradiation effects via the state form. While accepting that this is an important observation, I have argued that: (i) NSM-style politics still involves expending a significant amount of energy in trying to ameliorate state power; (ii) the way in which the personal is made political within the rubric of NSMs tends to *bracket* the state form, rather than presenting a challenge to it. That is, the fact that the state itself is a system of interpersonal relationships is overlooked. I would also argue that the commitment to means/ends identification has tended to dissipate with time and 'success' – the devolution of Greenpeace from a consensus-based direct action group to a multinational pseudo-capitalist NGO provides just one example among many. Perhaps this is a result of what Pareto called the iron law of oligarchy or what Weber referred to as the routinization of charisma. But I would like to offer up a different interpretation, which would hold that it is the result of an insufficient awareness of the dangers of the logic of hegemony. What I'm calling the newest social movements are very aware of these dangers, and take active steps to respond to them at the deepest levels of their structure and process of organization. In order to understand precisely how the logic of hegemony is being superseded by certain elements of the anti-globalization movement, I want to return to the discussion of Laclau's dimensions of hegemony.

As mentioned previously, I have no quarrel with the thesis that unevenness in relations of power is characteristic of the liberal–capitalist system of states. However, in its normative component, the first dimension of hegemony implies much more than this mere description, as is evident in the claim that since 'power is the condition of emancipation', there is 'no way of emancipating a constellation of social forces except by creating a new power around a hegemonic centre' (Butler, Laclau and Žižek, 2000: 208). Following Foucault, it is easy to accept the first part of this proposition ('power is the condition of emancipation'). Sufficient work has been done within post-structuralist and psychoanalytic theory to convince most of us that the desire to achieve a transparent society is based on a phantasmatic relation to the social and the political. However, I do have a problem with the second part of the proposition ('no way of emancipating ... except by creating a new power around a hegemonic centre'), because it assumes that all political struggles must be hegemonic in their intent and realization.

This assumption is what makes it difficult to apply Laclau and Mouffe's theory of hegemony to the analysis of many contemporary forms of activism. In the case of many anarchist and indigenist movements, for example, the goal is not to create a new power around a hegemonic centre, but to challenge, disrupt and disorient the processes of global hegemony, to *refuse, rather than rearticulate* those forces that are tending towards the universalization of the liberal–capitalist *ecumene*. As David Graeber has pointed out in a recent article in *New Left Review*, many of today's activists have rejected 'a politics which appeals to governments to modify their behaviour, in favour of physical intervention against state power in a form that itself prefigures an alternative' (2002: 62). There are many examples of this kind of affinity-based, direct-action politics, which take us beyond both reform *and* revolution, i.e.

which take us beyond the logic of hegemony. John Jordan of Reclaim the Streets (RTS) notes that

> RTS does not see Direct Action as a last resort, but a preferred way of doing things ... a way for individuals to take control of their own lives and environments ... If global capitalism does not manage to destroy the ecosphere and human civilization ... and a new culture of social and ecological justice is developed, RTS would hope that direct action would not stop but continue to be a central part of a direct democratic system. (Jordan, 1997)

At this point it may be helpful to clarify a few points of interpretation. Graeber's article appeared under the title 'The New Anarchists', which could be taken to imply that every individual or every group that participates in contemporary radical activism or anti-globalization struggles should be seen as 'anarchists'. I would not want to give this impression, since not all of these activists or the groupings in which they participate self-identify in this way, and since 'anarchism', like any tradition of theory and practice, is multiple and internally contested. Thus I will refer to these practices as 'anarchistic', meaning that they partake of a logic that can be found within certain self-identified strains of anarchist theory and practice, which will be identified and discussed later on in this chapter. It should also be noted that I am not claiming that RTS is a 'social movement' in the sense that this term is given within the relevant literature on either side of the Atlantic. Rather, I see RTS as a *non-branded tactic* that is being used by various groups and communities to achieve various ends.[5] The relation of 'tactics' to 'social movements' is of course another question that requires further analysis, which I can delve into only briefly here. Analysed in certain combinations, some might see some of the groups and communities that make use of non-branded tactics as constituting one or more social movements. Certainly, in the quote from John Jordan above, we can see that there is a hope, on the part of some activists, that what currently registers as an activist tactic could one day become an accepted part of daily life.

This is precisely what is being done through the use of tactics which not only prefigure non-hegemonic alternatives to state and corporate forms, but create them here and now. The burgeoning network of Independent Media Centres (IMCs) is an excellent example of this kind of 'productive' direct action. IMC aims to combat corporate concentration in media ownership through the creation of alternative sources of information, and in so doing to participate directly in the negation and reconstruction of mass-mediated realities. Not only is each centre independent from the corporate world, it is also independent from the other centres – there is no hub which disseminates a particular editorial line, and on some parts of some sites, there is no editorial line at all. Each centre tends to be driven by the interests and resources of the local communities it serves, thus building a high degree of differentiation into the system at its most basic level. Again, what makes this tactic important in the context of social movements is its political logic, as the following account from a participant–researcher involved in the Vancouver, Canada IMC makes clear:

> Independent Media Centre is, I think, one of the most important recent examples where grassroots movements, particularly those in the North, work to create spaces that are autonomous from capital and the state, where processes unfold according to logics dramatically opposed to the instrumentalist logics of accumulation and centralized decision making, even while these movements use technologies created for these purposes. It is also an instance of a subtle shift in political activism and struggle, a move from strategies of demand and representation to strategies of direct action and participation. (Uzelman, 2002: 80)

Like RTS, the IMCs show the possibilities of reconstructive community in action, and orient to a model which can be, and has been, adapted to other institutions where corporate and state control are endemic.[6] Other examples of non-branded tactics that prefigure and/or create autonomous alternatives include the dissemination and development of the Italian 'social centre' model throughout the world, Food Not Bombs, and countless long-standing and newly emerging cooperative social and economic experiments. What is important about all of these ventures is that they consciously defy the logic of hegemony by warding off the appearance of overarching centres of power/ signification that would place themselves above the constituent groups. That is, to use Laclau's terminology, *there is no general equivalent standing within but above* these networks, and their members are committed to maintaining this situation as a key value of their communities.

It is important to note that the use of productive direct action to prefigure and create autonomous alternatives is not limited to privileged subjects of the global North. The Zapatistas have been particularly adept in this regard, most famously by making use of (relatively) autonomous means of mass communication such as the internet to advance awareness of their cause both within mainstream Mexican society and around the world (Cleaver, 1998; Ronfeldt et al., 1998). But at the same time they have been wary of the politics of recognition, and have proceeded apace with many local, sustainable projects for autonomous control of their affairs (Lorenzano, 1998; Rochlin, 2003). Indigenous decolonization movements in Australia and New Zealand are also interesting on this point. To supplement mainstream strategies, some groups are pursuing forms of self-determination that run counter to the dominant paradigm of integration within the system of states. These groups often shun both capitalism and socialism, and their goals are not necessarily liberal, or even democratic, in the European sense of these terms. Their difference poses difficult problems for Western theory, problems that have so far not been adequately addressed (Day, 2001a).

Autonomy-oriented indigenous theorists have also advanced a radical critique of the integration of their nations within the liberal–capitalist system of states. As in Western political theory, these critiques focus on issues of race, class, gender and rational–bureaucratic domination of human beings and the land (Alfred, 1999; Monture-Angus, 1999; Kickingbird, 1984; Maracle, 1996; Marule, 1984). Unlike many of their Western counterparts, however, indigenist theorists also link these relations of subordination to the concept of sovereignty that serves as the horizon of the system of states itself. This approach is guided by the reflection that while redistribution of sovereignty may indeed challenge a particular colonial oppressor, it will not necessarily challenge the tools of his oppression. According to Taiaiake Alfred, sovereignty, as an 'exclusionary concept rooted in an adversarial and coercive Western notion of power', is itself deeply problematic (Alfred, 1999: 59). Taken to its limit, this critique approaches that of the activist communities described above, in positing – and positively valuing – modes of social organization in which there is 'no absolute authority, no coercive enforcement of decisions, no hierarchy, and no separate ruling entity' (Alfred, 1999: 56).[7]

POLITICS OF DEMAND VS. POLITICS OF THE ACT

Having discussed both the role of hegemonic thought in the history of radical politics and the recent challenges to this paradigm, it is now possible to specify precisely what I mean by the term 'newest social movements'. I am talking about direct-action-oriented formations that are neither revolutionary nor reformist, but seek to block, resist and render redundant both corporate *and* state power in local, national and transnational contexts. These formations do not seek irradiation effects on any spectrum at all, except perhaps in the sense of a postmodernist performative contradiction – they might be seen as motivated by a desire to universalize an absence of universalizing moments, that is, to undo the hegemony of hegemony as it is dispersed within (neo) liberal and (post-)Marxist theory and practice.

As a shorthand description of this complex and nascent set of transformations in the logic of radical struggle, I would like to introduce a distinction between what I will call a *politics of the act* and a *politics of demand*. By the latter I mean to refer to actions oriented to ameliorating the practices of states, corporations and everyday life, through either influencing or using state power to achieve irradiation effects. 'Pragmatic' as it may be, and despite its successes during the heyday of the welfare state in a few countries, the politics of demand is by necessity limited in scope: it can change the content of structures of domination and exploitation, but it cannot change their form. As Laclau points out, without a hegemonic centre articulated with apparatuses of discipline and control, there is no force to which demands might be addressed. But the converse is also true – every demand, in anticipating a response, *perpetuates* these structures, which exist precisely in anticipation of demands. This leads to a positive feedback loop, in which the ever increasing depth and breadth of apparatuses of discipline and control create ever new sites of antagonism, which produce new demands, thereby increasing the quantity and intensity of discipline and control.

It is at this point that a politics of the act is required to break out of the loop. This politics can be productively understood in terms of what Lacan has called the *ethics of the real* (Lacan, 1992). According to Slavoj Žižek, the force of this ethic derives from 'going through the fantasy', from 'the distance we are obliged to assume towards our most "authentic" dreams, towards the myths that guarantee the very consistency of our symbolic universe' (Žižek, 1994: 82). Clearly, the fundamental fantasy of the politics of demand is that the currently hegemonic formation will recognize the validity of the claim presented to it and respond in a way that produces an event of emancipation. Most of the time, however, it does not; instead it defers, dissuades or provides a partial solution to one problem that exacerbates several others. Thus the politics of demand can be seen as driven by an ethics of desire, in that it seeks primarily to reproduce the conditions of its own emergence. Crossing the fantasy in this case means giving up on the expectation of a non-dominating response from structures of domination; it means surprising both oneself – and the structure – by inventing a response which precludes the necessity of the demand and thereby breaks out of the loop of the endless perpetuation of desire for emancipation. This, I would argue, is precisely what is being done by those who are participating in the forms of direct action I have mentioned above.

HARDT AND NEGRI: THE MULTITUDE WITHIN EMPIRE

The central argument being developed in this chapter is that groups and movements that are oriented to a politics of the act cannot be adequately understood by existing paradigms of social-movements analysis and therefore require the development of new modes of theorization. In this section I will address the strengths and deficiencies of one of the most influential recent attempts to carry out this task, Michael Hardt and Toni Negri's *Empire*. *Empire* is a huge text, in more ways than one. I cannot hope to engage with all, or even most, of the issues it raises or to provide an overview of its argument.[8] Rather, I will focus my attention on the ways in which Hardt and Negri's book, and the debates it has spawned, help and hinder our understanding of the political logic of the newest social movements.

One important contribution Hardt and Negri have made is to introduce into the English-speaking world some key concepts associated with Italian autonomist Marxism. Autonomist theory argues that workers have created and sustained capitalism, not only through allowing their productivity to be captured, but also by their struggles to overthrow and reform the system that captures it. Each time it is presented with a new challenge, capital responds by adjusting its structures and processes, deepening its sophistication and its hold on our lives (Hardt and Negri, 2000: 51). Although this may sound like a recipe for despair, it is not necessarily so. Rather, the goal of autonomist struggles is, as Nick Dyer-Witheford so elegantly puts it, to 'rupture this recuperative movement, unspring the dialectical spiral, and speed the circulation of struggles until they attain an escape velocity in which labour tears itself away from incorporation within capital' (Dyer-Witheford, 1999: 68). This action of tearing away is referred to within autonomist theory as auto- or self-valorization, and it appears in Hardt and Negri's work as the 'constituent power of the multitude' (2000: 410).

Constituent power, I would suggest, is something very similar to what I have called direct action; it involves communities of various sorts working together in a circulation of struggles which are simultaneously *against* capitalism and *for* the construction of alternatives to it. In their response to the authors who participated in a special issue of *Rethinking Marxism* devoted to critiques of *Empire*, Hardt and Negri further clarify what they mean to encompass by the term constituent power. For them, the project of the multitude involves action on three levels: 'resistance, insurrection, and constituent power'. They go on to identify each of these elements, respectively, with 'micropolitical practices of insubordination and sabotage, collective instances of revolt, and finally utopian and alternative projects' (Hardt and Negri, 2001: 242). Constituent power thus appears to be strongly identified with constructing concrete alternatives to globalizing capital here and now, rather than appealing to state power or waiting for/bringing on the Revolution.

While it does seem that Hardt and Negri are aware of and positively value what I have called a politics of the act, it is not at all clear how they perceive the practical political logic of the project of counter-Empire. On the one hand, the multitude is theorized as a multiplicity in the Deleuzean sense, that is, as a formation of subjects in 'perpetual motion', sailing the 'enormous sea' of capitalist globalization in a 'perpetual nomadism' (2000: 60–1). The multitude is supposed to exist as 'creative constellations of powerful singularities' (61), that is, as something unknowable, untotalizable, ungraspable. Thus '[o]nly the multitude through its practical experimentation will offer the models and determine when and how the possible becomes real' (411). At the same time, however, Hardt and Negri's language often shifts into a totalizing mode in which the multitude appears as an entity that needs 'a centre', 'a common sense and direction', a 'prince' in the Machiavellian sense (65). The philosophical answer to this conundrum of course lies in the Spinozian notion of immanence, through which the dichotomy between singularity and totality is supposed to be transcended. But the practical answer seems to lie in a rather orthodox conception of the logic of hegemony.

This observation is based on a few scattered passages in *Empire*, but is reflective, I would claim, of a general impasse in Hardt and Negri's work together. They are highly critical, for example, of Laclau and Mouffe's 'revisionist' reading of Gramsci: 'Poor Gramsci, communist and militant before all else, tortured and killed by fascism ... was given the gift of being considered the founder of a strange notion of hegemony that leaves no place for a Marxian politics' (235 n.26). What would a properly Marxian reading of hegemony look like? Hardt and Negri approvingly cite Lenin's analysis of imperialism, and give him credit for recognizing, at least implicitly, the existence of a fundamental dichotomy in modes of radical struggle: '*either world communist revolution or Empire*' (2000: 234, italics in original). It is somewhat jarring to see two autonomists reaching back behind Western Marxist readings of Gramsci to recover a properly Leninist conception of hegemony. Yet it seems clear that the project of counter-Empire is to be guided by this Leninist conception. That is, although it may be internally differentiated and fluid, the goal of the multitude is to counter one totalizing force with another totalizing force. This reading is adequately supported, I think, both in *Empire* and in subsequent interviews and responses by the authors. Near the end of *Empire*, Hardt and Negri suggest that 'the actions of the multitude against Empire' already 'affirm [the] hegemony' of an 'earthly city' that is replacing the modern republic (2000: 411). This eschatological tone is maintained in a later interview, where the authors argue that 'a catholic (that is, global) project is the only alternative' (2002: 184). This is not to say that they fall into the trap of advocating a Leninist vanguard *party* – they explicitly state that they 'have no desire ... to reconstruct the Party' (2001: 237). And it is certainly the case that the strain of Italian autonomist Marxism with which Negri is strongly associated rejects centralized forms of organization, striving instead towards a 'lateral polycentric concept of anticapitalist alliances-in-diversity, connecting a plurality of agencies in a circulation of struggles' (Dyer-Witheford, 1999: 68).

And yet ... what are we to make of the many ways in which the multiplicity of the multitude seems to be overwritten by a desire to create a 'coherent project' (Hardt and Negri, 2001: 242), to '*give* to these movements of the multitude of bodies, which we recognize are real, a power of expression that can be shared' (243, italics added)? Perhaps the answer lies not in the autonomist elements of Hardt and Negri's brand of autonomist Marxism, but in their Marxism. Perhaps to descend out of the realm of metatheory and engage with actually existing struggles in their specificity, it is necessary to indulge in even more historical revisionism, to reach back behind not only Laclau and Mouffe, Gramsci and Lenin, but also behind Marx, to the decisive moment when 'socialism' came to mean 'Marxism', and all other logics of struggle were relegated to a subsidiary position.

'UTOPIAN' SOCIALISM AND THE LOGIC OF AFFINITY

In liberal and post-Marxist theories of democracy, it is only when a civil society is externally 'mediated' by a state form that the defining – and highly desirable – situation of liberal pluralism arises (Shalem and Bensusan, 1994). Polities in which this distinction has been eliminated must become either 'totalitarian' (excessively ordered) or 'anarchic' (excessively disordered), depending upon whether it is the state or civil society that usurps its proper boundaries. A similar perception exists in classical Marxism, where state coercion is seen as an unfortunate, but necessary, evil on the way to a transparent society. Within these paradigms, then, it is impossible to imagine that sufficient order can be achieved in (post)modern societies without recourse to the state form.

But this kind of stateless order is precisely what Hardt and Negri propose via their notion of constituent power. While, as I have noted, this concept emerges out of the tradition of autonomist Marxism, it bears a striking resemblance to certain branches of anarchist theory. As early as 1949, Martin Buber argued that the crucial feature of the rise of the state was not that it displaced existing forms of association, but that 'the political principle with all its centralistic features percolated into the associations themselves, modifying their structure and their whole inner life' (Buber, 1958: 131). Buber had thus identified, in its nascent form, the situation which Habermas would later describe as the colonization of the lifeworld (1987: 301–73), and which Hardt and Negri have characterized as the 'real subsumption' of society in the state (1994). Buber's use of the term 'political principle' marks a crucial point of differentiation between anarchist theory and its (neo)liberal and (post-)Marxist counterparts: for anarchists, it is both possible *and* desirable for human beings to live without state intervention, if sufficiently strong non-state (and of course non-corporate!) modes of organization exist to take on the tasks assigned to state coercion in the other paradigms.[9] On the further assumption that the character of a transformation will have a strong effect on its outcome, anarchist thought has tended to privilege 'social' revolutions based on the construction of affinities (constituent power) over 'political' revolutions based on achieving hegemony (constituted power).[10]

In *Paths in Utopia* (1958) Buber presents a genealogy of the anarchist concept of social revolution, under the rubric of what he calls *structural renewal*. This line of theory and practice springs from the so-called Utopian socialism of Saint Simon and Fourier, and runs through Proudhon and Kropotkin to Gustav Landauer. While the details of this development are important to recent trends in social theory and activism, limitations of space restrict me to the task of considering how Landauer's theory links up with a politics of the act and constituent power, that is, to showing how this expression of the 'classical' anarchist logic of structural renewal resonates with those elements of contemporary radical social movements that are guided by a logic of affinity.[11]

Not well known outside of anarchist circles, Landauer lived and wrote in Germany in the late nineteenth and early twentieth centuries.[12] Against the grain of both Marxist orthodoxy and social-democratic revisionism, and against the more voluntarist anarchists of his time, he argued in *For Socialism* (1978) that a radical transformation of capitalist society could not be achieved by either instantaneous revolution or slow reform. Anticipating Gramsci, Landauer insisted that the appropriate social institutions and relations had to be in place *before* any change in the political order could occur. Contrary to Gramsci, however, Landauer did not rely upon the existing institutions of civil society as a source of raw material, nor did he rely upon state coercion to achieve hegemony. For him, new institutions had to be created 'almost out of nothing, amid chaos' (1978: 20); that is *alongside*, rather than *inside*, the system of states and corporations.

For this strategy the appropriate tactics involved a complementary pairing of disengagement and reconstruction. 'Let us destroy', Landauer suggested, 'mainly by means of the gentle, permanent, and binding reality that we build'

(93). To the extent that it does not seek an abrupt and total transition away from capitalist modes of social organization, the strategy of structural renewal shares with reformism a willingness to coexist with its 'enemies'. However, structural renewal is more akin to constituent power, in that it does not provide positive energy to existing structures and processes in the hope of their amelioration. Rather, it aims to reduce their efficacy and reach by rendering them redundant. Structural renewal therefore appears simultaneously as a negative force working against the colonization of everyday life by the state and corporations (what Hardt and Negri call insurrection and resistance) and a positive force acting to reverse this process (constituent power). Just as what Habermas calls 'system' advances by percolating into everyday relations, structural renewal proceeds as we (re-)make our own connections to each other and the land.

If existing social relations are to be rendered redundant, then what will take their place? Like Hardt and Negri, Landauer does not offer a vision of a New Harmony. Rather, he always refused to say how a new socialist reality 'should be constituted as a whole' (29). 'We need attempts', he argues. 'We need the expedition of a thousand men to Sicily. We need these precious Garabaldi-natures and we need failures upon failures and the tough nature that is frightened by nothing' (62). Again, the resonances with the subject of constitutive power – a 'labouring subject, a creative, productive affirmative subject' – are strong (Hardt and Negri, 1994: 309). But where Hardt and Negri seem to maintain a faith in what used to be called the masses, Landauer did not accept the revolutionary qualifications of the proletariat as an abstract entity.[13] Rather, he believed that the revolutionary subject could only be created via a process that must begin *and continue* as a proliferation of a large number of small and relatively disparate struggles. These struggles could be linked by a commitment to the construction of non-statist socialist alternatives, but never totalized – or even pluralized or quasi-universalized – through the mediation of an overarching identity.

The final point I would I like to make deals with Landauer's insight into the nature of the links between everyday life and social and political structures and processes. In a formulation of which post-structuralist theorists would have to approve, Landauer asserts that capitalism 'is not really a thing, but a nothing that is mistaken for a thing' (1978: 132). That is, he understands capitalism as a set of relations between human individuals and groups, a reality or way of being in common. Landauer analyses the state, law and administration in the same way: not as institutions in the sociological sense, but as 'names for force between men [and women]' (132). For Landauer, then, because capitalism and the state – and of course socialism as well – are all modes of human coexistence, changing these macro-structures very much involves changing micro-relations: new forms 'become reality only in the act of being realized' (138). As a practice of changing reality, of giving oneself and one's communities new realities in the context of other selves and communities, I hope to have made it clear that structural renewal is intersubjective and deeply ethical in the Lacanian sense I have outlined above.

To summarize and clarify the main argument of this chapter, I am suggesting that the logic of affinity should be seen as emerging out of an anarchist tradition of theory and practice which rejects the struggle for hegemony, both as domination over others via the state form and as 'consensual' direction of others via ideological sway or 'consciousness raising'. Such a logic, I have argued, is discernible in tactics such as IMC, RTS, FNB (Food not Bombs), Zapatismo and indigenism, which are widely influential in contemporary radical activist circles. The key elements of this (post-)anarchistic logic of affinity are: a desire to create alternatives to state and corporate forms of social organization, working 'alongside' the existing institutions; proceeding in this via disengagement and reconstruction rather than by reform or revolution; with the end of creating not a new knowable totality (counter-hegemony), but of enabling experiments and the emergence of new forms of subjectivity; and finally, focusing on relations between these subjects, in the name of inventing new forms of community (Day, 2001b).

CONCLUSION

In closing, and in response to many people who have commented upon my work, I would like to reiterate that I am not claiming that the social movements of the 1960s–1980s have been entirely superseded by a political logic that has no precursors. As is always the case with a genealogical analysis, it is not a matter of a clean break, but of a precarious coexistence, a series of subtle shifts in the alignment of forces, which show the limits of a hegemonic logic for certain kinds of social transformation. This is to say that I am fully aware (a) that a relatively hegemonic order exists and (b) that counter-hegemonic struggles are necessary in order to achieve totalizing changes within that order. I part ways, however, with (neo)liberalism and (post-)Marxism when I suggest that non-hegemonic struggles also have their place, inasmuch as they are most effective in creating new worlds in the shells of, on the margins of, in the cracks of, the currently dominant order. For me, it is not a matter of discovering the 'best' mode of social change that will be superior anytime, anywhere. Rather, I advocate for, and practice in my own life, what Arundhati Roy has called a 'biodiversity of resistance'. The purpose of this chapter, then, is not to establish a hegemony of non-hegemonic practices, for that would clearly be ridiculous. It is, rather, to displace the hegemony of hegemony, in order to make more room for the creation of alternatives. In my experience, this is the most difficult and least rewarding of all modes of social change. It is, however, also one of the most important, and this is why it is emerging, once again, out of the shadows.

NOTES

1. In *Hegemony and Socialist Strategy*, Laclau and Mouffe suggest that the

> new struggles ... should be understood from the double perspective of the transforma-
> tion of social relations characteristic of the new hegemonic formation of the post-war

period, and of the effects of the displacement into new areas of social life of the egalitarian imaginary constituted around liberal–democratic discourse. (1985: 165)

My reading is that they believe that hegemony began to become possible with Western modernity, and becomes in some sense mandatory with the advent of postmodernity.

2. One might say that modern nation states have long 'known' this to be the case; but the logic of hegemony moves beyond this unconscious, fearful awareness by *acknowledging and celebrating*, rather than dissimulating, the impossibility of achieving a pure identity.

3. That is, the unfixity of the floating signifier arises from the contestation over meaning that occurs *between* competing discourses; that of the empty signifier is a result of its function as a general equivalent *within* a particular chain. (See Laclau in Butler, Laclau and Žižek 2000: 305.)

4. If 'the anti-globalization movement' is not a movement itself in the accepted meaning of this term, then the question of whether it is composed of one or more 'movements' becomes moot. My own interest, as I have tried to make clear, is in logics of struggle and tactics, and their relations with established traditions of theory and practice.

5. The term 'non-branded tactic' was evolved in conversations with Ryan Mitchell, a graduate student in the Department of Sociology at Queen's University at Kingston.

6. See <www.indymedia.org> for a list of affiliated sites and for accounts of the genesis of some of the more well-known IMCs.

7. This is to say that both classical anarchism and Native American political theory could benefit from further engagement with post-structuralist theory in general and the Foucauldian analytics of power in particular.

8. For an excellent and wide-ranging collection of commentary and criticism, see 'Dossier on Empire', a special issue of *Rethinking Marxism* (13(3/4), 2001).

9. The anarchist literature on this question is far more rich and complex than is generally recognized and goes far beyond simply 'wishing away' the state. Rather, it is focused on how actually existing human societies, from the 'premodern' to the 'postmodern', can and do function without state (or corporate) intervention.

10. Unfortunately this terminology could lead to the assumption that social revolutionaries are, or believe themselves to be, 'apolitical'. This, however, would be impossible, since all modes of social transformation must both challenge existing relations of power and instantiate new ones. Thus the term 'social revolution' should be read in the restricted sense of describing social change achieved through methods of affinity rather than hegemony.

11. For an extended discussion, see my *Gramsci Is Dead* (London: Pluto Press, 2005).

12. Much more of Landauer's work is now available in English, in the excellent collection edited by Gabriel Kuhn, *Revolution and Other Writings: A Political Reader* (PM Press, 2010).

13. In fact, in his moments of high anti-Marxist polemicism, Landauer sounds rather classist. Since socialism aims at the abolition of the proletariat, he argued, 'we need not find [the proletariat] to be an institution especially beneficial to the mind' (1978: 49). For him, the proletariat was not a class of 'natural revolutionaries', but of 'born uncultured plodders' (69).

REFERENCES

Alfred, Taiaiake (1999). *Peace, Power, Righteousness: An Indigenous Manifesto*. Don Mills, Ontario: Oxford University Press.

Agamben, Giorgio (1993). *The Coming Community* (M. Hardt, trans.). Minneapolis and London: University of Minnesota Press.

Antliff, Allan (2003). 'Anarchy in Art: Strategies of Dissidence'. *Anarchist Studies* 11(1):66–83.

Bagguley, Paul (1992). 'Social Change, the Middle Class and the Emergence of "New Social Movements": a Critical Analysis'. *Sociological Review* 40(1): 26–48.

Bahro, Rudolf (1986). *Building the Green Movement*. Philadelphia: New Society Publishers.

Bertram, Benjamin (1995). 'New Revolutions on the "Revolutionary" Politics of Ernesto Laclau and Chantal Mouffe'. *Boundary* 2 22(3): 81–110.

Buber, Martin (1958) [1949]. *Paths in Utopia*. Boston: Beacon Press.
Buchanan, Ian (2002). 'What is "Anti-Globalization?" I Prefer Not to Say'. *Review of Education, Pedagogy and Cultural Studies* 24: 153–5.
Butler, J., Laclau, E. and Žižek, S. (2000). *Contingency, Hegemony, Universality: Contemporary Dialogues on the Left*. London and New York: Verso.
Cleaver, Harry (1998). 'The Zapatistas and the Electronic Fabric of Struggle'. In J. Holloway and E. Peláez (eds). *Zapatista: Reinventing Revolution in Mexico*. London: Pluto Press.
Cohen, Robin and Rai, Shirin (2000). *Global Social Movements*. London: Athlone.
Crossley, Nick (2003). *Making Sense of Social Movements*. Buckingham: Open University Press.
Day, Richard J.F. (2001a). 'Who Is This We that Gives the Gift? Native American Political Theory and the Western Tradition'. *Critical Horizons* 2(2): 173–201.
—— (2001b). 'Ethics, Affinity and the Coming Communities'. *Philosophy and Social Criticism* 27(1): 21–38.
Derrida, Jacques (1999). *Cyber-Marx: Cycles and Circuits of Struggle in High-Technology Capitalism*. Urbana and Chicago: University of Illinois Press.
—— (1994). *Specters of Marx*. London and New York: Routledge.
Eisenstein, Z. (1979). 'Developing a Theory of Capitalist Patriarchy and Socialist Feminism'. In *Capitalist Patriarchy and the Case for Socialist Feminism*. New York and London: Monthly Review Press.
Firestone, S. (1970). *The Dialectic of Sex: The Case for Feminist Revolution*. New York: William Morrow.
Foucault, Michel (1972). *The Archaeology of Knowledge*. London: Routledge.
Gamson, William A. (1992). 'The Social Psychology of Collective Action'. In A. Morris and C. Mueller (eds). *Frontiers in Social Movement Theory*. New Haven, CT: Yale University Press.
Geras, Norman (1987). 'Post-Marxism?' *New Left Review* 163: 40–83.
Graeber, David (2002). 'The New Anarchists'. *New Left Review* 13: 61–73.
Grossberg, Lawrence (1992). *We Gotta Get out of This Place*. New York and London: Routledge.
Habermas, Jürgen (1987). *The Theory of Communicative Action*, vol.2. Boston: Beacon Press.
Hall, Stuart (1983b). 'The Great Moving Right Show'. In S. Hall and M. Jacques (eds). *The Politics of Thatcherism*. London: Lawrence & Wishart.
Hardt, Michael and Negri, Antonio (2001). 'Response'. *Rethinking Marxism* 13(3/4): 236–43.
—— —— (2000). *Empire*. Cambridge, MA: Harvard University Press.
—— —— (1994). *Labour of Dionysus: Critique of the State Form*. Minneapolis: University of Minnesota Press.
Hawley, J (ed.) (2001). *Postcolonial, Queer: Theoretical Intersections*. Albany: SUNY Press.
Held, David, and McGrew, Anthony (2002). *Globalization and Anti-Globalization*. Oxford: Polity Press.
Holloway, J. (2002). *Change the World Without Taking Power: The Meaning of Revolution Today*. London and Sterling, VA: Pluto Press.
Jordan, John (1997). 'Interview with Naomi Klein'. *The Anarchives* 4(9). <www.ainfos.ca/A-Infos97/4/0552.html>.
Jordan, Tim (2002). *Activism! Direct Action, Hacktivism and the Future of Society*. London: Reaktion Books.
Keck, Margaret and Sikknik, Kathryn (1998). *Activists Beyond Borders*. Ithaca, NY: Cornell University Press.
Kellner, Douglas (1990). *Television and the Crisis of Democracy*. Boulder and San Francisco: Westview Press.
Kickingbird, K. (1984). 'Indian Sovereignty: The American Experience'. In Leroy Little Bear, Menno Boldt and J. Anthony Long (eds). *Pathways to Self-Determination*. Toronto: University of Toronto Press.
Klein, Naomi (2001). 'Reclaiming the Commons'. *New Left Review* 9: 81–9.
Lacan, Jacques (1992). *The Ethics of Psychoanalysis*. London: Routledge.
Laclau, Ernesto and Mouffe, Chantal (1985). *Hegemony and Socialist Strategy*. London: Verso.
Landauer, Gustav (1978) [1911]. *For Socialism*. St. Louis: Telos Press.
Leiss, William (1972). *The Domination of Nature*. Boston: Beacon Press.

Lorenzano, Luis (1998). 'Zapatismo: Recomposition of Labour, Radical Democracy and Revolutionary Project'. In J. Holloway and E. Peláez (eds). *Zapatista: Reinventing Revolution in Mexico*. London: Pluto Press.

Maracle, Lee (1996). *I Am Woman: A Native Perspective on Sociology and Feminism*. Vancouver: Press Gang Publishers.

Marule, Marie Smallface (1984). 'Traditional Indian Government: Of the People, by the People, for the People'. In Leroy Little Bear, Menno Boldt and J. Anthony Long (eds). *Pathways to Self-Determination*. Toronto: University of Toronto Press.

McNally, David (2002). *Another World Is Possible: Globalization and Anti-Capitalism*. Winnipeg: Arbeiter Ring.

Melucci, Alberto (1989). *Nomads of the Present*. London: Hutchinson Radius.

Milstein, Cindy (2002). 'What's in a Name?' *Harbinger* 2(1). <http://www.social-ecology.org/harbinger/vol2no1/name.html>.

Mohanty, Chandra T. (2003). *Feminism Without Borders: Decolonizing Theory, Practicing Solidarity*. Durham, NC and London: Duke University Press.

Monture-Angus, Patricia (1999). *Journeying Forward: Dreaming First Nations' Independence*. Halifax: Fernwood.

Offe, C. (1985). 'New Social Movements: Challenging the Boundaries of Institutional Politics'. *Social Research* 52(4): 817–68.

Panitch, Leo (2001). *Renewing Socialism: Democracy, Strategy and Imagination*. Boulder: Westview Press.

Press, Andrea Lee (1991). *Women Watching Television: Gender, Class and Generation in the American Television Experience*. Philadelphia: University of Pennsylvania Press.

Pulido, Laura (1998). *Environmentalism and Economic Justice: Two Chicano Struggles in the Southwest*. Tucson: University of Arizona Press.

Rochlin, James F. (2003). *Vanguard Revolutionaries in Latin America: Peru, Colombia, Mexico*. Boulder and London: Lynne Rienner.

Ronfeldt, David, Arquilla, John, Fuller, Graham and Fuller, Melissa (1998). *The Zapatista 'Social Netwar' in Mexico*. Santa Monica, CA: Rand Corporation.

Sassen, Saskia (1998). *Globalization and Its Discontents*. New York: The New Press.

Shalem, Yael, and Bensusan, David (1994). 'Civil Society: The Traumatic Patient'. *Angelaki* 1(3): 73–92.

Smith, Jackie and Johnston, Hank (eds) (2002). *Globalization and Resistance: Transnational Dimensions of Social Movements*. New York and Oxford: Rowan & Littlefield.

Starr, Amory (2000). *Naming the Enemy: Anti-Corporate Movements Confront Globalization*. London and New York: Zed Books.

Tarrow, Sidney (2001). 'Transnational Politics: Contention and Institutions in International Politics'. *Annual Review of Political Science* 4: 1–20.

Touraine, Alain (1992). 'Beyond Social Movements?' *Theory, Culture and Society* 9:125–45.

Uzelman, Scott (2002). *Catalyzing Participatory Communication: Independent Media Centre and the Politics of Direct Action* (MA thesis). Burnaby, BC: Simon Fraser University.

Williams, Raymond (1973). 'Base and Superstructure in Marxist Cultural Theory'. *New Left Review I* 82: 3–16.

Žižek, Slavoj (1994). *The Metastases of Enjoyment*. London: Verso.

7
The Constellation of Opposition

Jason Adams

INTRODUCTION: THE CONSTELLATION OF N30

The protests that occurred around the world on 30 November 1999 (N30) were truly without precedent. They marked an important turning point in what had become increasingly fragmented struggles of new social movements constructed around various forms of anti-authoritarian politics, identity politics and ecological politics as well as traditional class-struggle politics. In the cultural rebound against universalism after the 1960s, new social movements continuously sought to create autonomous space for the particularity of youth, queers, women and people of colour, as well as for the general ecology of the planet. While there have been enormous strides made since that time, the downside has been that in general, they have not successfully articulated the intersectionalities of these various oppressions and resistances. This failure has resulted in fragmented, single-issue politics with no visible option other than reformist – rather than transformational – political activity. At the same time, traditional class-oriented movements have been in continual decline due to the rise of a global neoliberal economy since the 1980s. Faced with such circumstances, labour unions have often opted merely to 'protect their own', leaving most low-income women, people of colour, immigrants and students to fend for themselves. Throughout the three decades following the 1960s and lasting well into the final years of the twentieth century, it seemed that reformism was destined to become the new reality of social movements.

N30 was a turning point because it articulated for the first time the irreducible interconnectedness experienced but not recognized within the praxis of contemporary social movements. Never before had so *many* divergent groups and perspectives converged, successfully swarming and disrupting a 'common enemy', as did the tens of thousands who filled the streets of Seattle and dozens of other cities around the world (de Armond, 2001: 201).

[...]

THE DISINTEGRATION OF HEGEMONY

Several years after the events of May 1968, Michel Foucault argued that they had fundamentally transformed the grounds on which the game of war would be played (Foucault, 1980: 116). Rather than conflict emerging primarily on the macropolitical level of the workplace or the nation state, there was a downward shift into the micropolitical realm of everyday life embodied in the intermeshed and conflictual capillary practices of individual subjects. This empirical realization was interwoven with Foucault's theoretical analysis that since the eighteenth century, the shape of power begins to transform from one of repression of individual subjects to one of both repression *and* creation of individual subjects. Consequentially, a movement to liberate the working class as a subjectivity might not really be liberating at all; without an analysis of the web of power, the 'emancipated' workers might still impose authoritarian, racist, sexist, heteronormative policies in the new society that they create.[1] The reason is that 'workers' as a subjectivity have been created by power. While he argued that power had been operating in this fashion for over two centuries by the time he was writing, he also argued that this understanding of power as a web did not become thinkable until the events of May 1968. Strangely, for some this perspective is fundamentally bleak in that with the death of the subject there is said to also be a concomitant death of resistance as well; yet Foucault argued that far from limiting resistance, this transformation multiplied its possibilities into literally thousands of new arenas of conflict (Foucault, 1980: 111). These arenas are the political spaces in which the new social movements emerged as fragments in the 1970s and 1980s, each reductively defining its unique particularity in the shape of a new form of universality.

Like Foucault, André Gorz argued that fundamental changes in society were leading towards the displacement of the industrial proletariat as *the* agent of social change and towards a fragmented 'non-class of non-workers' instead. Yet for Gorz, the shift was primarily an economic one; that of the global shift to a neoliberal service economy under the global tutelage of Ronald Reagan and Margaret Thatcher. Of course this was to have great implications, since the left had argued since its inception that the industrial proletariat was the central pillar of social change due to its strategic position in the economy. In the post-Fordist world of temporary labour, just-in-time production and ever increasing automation this hope was clearly becoming less and less of a possibility. Yet, like Foucault, Gorz argued that rather than spelling the end of the logistical possibility of transformational social conflict, this change would allow a broad array of new social movements outside the normalizing bounds of 'class struggle' to emerge freely. These movements were largely constituted by those who had already been marginalized out of the system for some time; such positionalities could thus lead to a common movement for 'autonomous production' (i.e. local production for local use) outside the bounds of the wage-labour system. Gorz hoped that this economic change would paradoxically serve as the midwife of a future 'post-capitalist, post-industrial, post-socialist' society centred on the common theme of 'the liberation of time and the abolition of work' (Gorz, 1982: 2).[2]

Between the two of them, Gorz and Foucault helped to lay some of the theoretical groundwork for the new social-movement theories that emerged in subsequent years. The primary theorists in this vein, such as Alain Touraine and

Alberto Melucci, largely came out in agreement with these basic observations regarding the shift to a post-hegemonic, post-industrial society. Touraine, for instance, argued that the dissolution of a primarily economic foundation for power meant that the identity of the former industrial worker would become transformed into that of the 'individual, a member of primary communities' (Touraine, 1988: 5).[3] These fragmented individuals would subsequently become the new centres of social upheaval; in other words, what had been a more or less cohesive society 'turns completely into a field of conflicts' in the post-industrial era. As a result of this change in the centre of conflict, he became convinced that 'the era of Revolutions [...] is coming to an end', while a new era of permanent conflict and participatory democracy would emerge to replace it (ibid.: 148). Yet Touraine did not see these emergent conflicts as entirely decentralized; in fact he felt that in each historical period, a competition amongst movements for the position of the hegemony would emerge. Perhaps illuminating some residual authoritarian Marxian aspects within his thought, he extrapolated further from this that the role of the researcher was to determine before the fact which movement it was likely to be in order to help bring it into its own. Yet the one movement that could never become central for Touraine was anarchism, which he blindly associated with terrorism, in order to justify his rejection of any anarchist sensibility as a major aspect of the new social movements (ibid.: 129). This rather problematic point is precisely where Melucci's more unorthodox, anti-authoritarian, egalitarian perspective becomes particularly useful as a means of correcting the limitations in Touraine.

Melucci had been a student of Touraine and thus held a number of concurrent perspectives with him; yet, as might be expected, there were also major aspects of Touraine's thought that he rejected. He agreed, for instance, that new social movements dwelt in the space of everyday life and that they reject the aspiration to 'seize power' that had so captivated the movements that came before them. Yet he rejected Touraine's idea that the rise and fall of the hegemonic movement necessarily results in the periodization of history, since this would imply that there was some sort of natural hierarchy of oppression underlying social life. Against this essentially Marxian analysis, he argues that 'Touraine's idea of the central movement still clings to the assumption that movements are a *personnage*, unified actors playing out a role on the stage of history' (Melucci, 1989: 202). He also rejected his teacher's belief that the role of the researcher was to pedagogically 'convert' actors to a higher level of understanding somehow unavailable to them; like Foucault, he argued that the role of the researcher was instead one of mutuality and equal exchange. And in line with Gorz, Melucci argued that contra classical Marxism, the 'class struggle' of the early 19th century was not so much one between the newly proletarianized and the bourgeoisie as it was one between the elites and the non-proletarianized traditional subsistence communities (ibid.: 189). In arguing this, he amply demonstrated his belief that 'new' social movements in fact had roots reaching back centuries to the struggles of those whose means of existence had always proved superfluous and extraneous (rather than fundamental) to the official structures of capitalism. In doing so, Melucci went beyond Foucault by showing that micropolitics ultimately had an effect not only on the practices of everyday life but on the functioning of institutions as well (ibid.: 208).

In recent years, the works of Gorz, Touraine, Melucci and other new-social-movement theorists of the 1980s have come under somewhat of an attack for their exclusive focus on fragmentation of social movements and their avoidance of how this has led to new forms of reductionism and therefore cooptation as well. Peyman Vehabzadeh's phenomenological analysis of contemporary social movements is perhaps one of the most unique and challenging to have emerged amongst these, employing the insights of Martin Heidegger and Reiner Schürmann for the first time in this field. His argument is basically that the positivist sociological theories that emerged before him tended to take individual identity, 'ultimate referentiality' and liberal democracy for granted: this lack of critical spirit is seen as contradicting the 'new' in their theory and ultimately reinforcing the continuity of what currently is. This is because they 'cannot see the great implications of their claim that society as a totality has come to an end', which is that sociology – in its historical role as the legitimation of existing society – has come to an end as well. Vahabzadeh's contribution goes beyond these 'sociologies of action' to what he calls a 'sociology of possibilities' that 'prepares itself for the turning' by studying 'the present entities and phenomenal arrangements' (Vehabzadeh, 2000: 343–5). In this project of redefining new-social-movement theory within a more critical, post-foundationalist framework, Vehabazadeh questions most of the underlying assumptions of those that preceded him; rather than accepting the subjectivity of identity as 'natural' he points out that in fact it is constructed, since, as Schürmann argues, 'identity does not precede conflict, but is born out of conflict' (ibid.: 71).

This birth of identity is what he refers to as the 'articulation of experience' that makes the collective action of contemporary social movements possible. It is important to remember however that the articulation of experience in this sense is not merely an act of the will, but is primarily a reflection of the epoch in which subjects are situated. In order to illustrate this more clearly, Vehabzadeh uses the Zapatistas; in order to construct the possibility of a relevant social movement, a Zapatista identity was constructed by 'articulating the experience of injustice and oppression' suffered by Mayan Chiapanecos. This was made possible by the 1992 land reform, which 'collapsed the hegemonic social imaginary' of the *Mexico de las tres culturas* that had been won by Emiliano Zapata and his comrades in the Mexican Revolution. As the Zapatistas advanced towards the new counter-hegemonic social imaginary, their articulated experience as Mayan Chiapanecos 'receded' into the general population, thus widening and diversifying the struggle. In short, the Zapatistas were able to break out of the boundaries of the hegemony of the Mexican neoliberal regime by building a counter-hegemonic parallel power autonomous from the officiality of liberal democracy (Vahabzadeh, 2000: 259); therefore they can be seen to 'offer the world the first non-teleocratic revolutionary praxis' of 'utopia unnamed' (ibid.: 315). This sort of transgressive praxis is precisely what Vehabzadeh sees as the most promising aspect of social movements more recently. By rejecting the discourse of rights under liberalism, contemporary social movements also reject their transformation into subjects of the existing order, which is a major step beyond the new social movements that Gorz, Touraine and Melucci were focusing on.

We now have a brief schematic of how various theorists have conceptualized this shift on a theoretical level; yet we would not really understand the full complexity of this without examining at least a couple of examples in greater detail. Therefore, we will look first at deep ecology and then at third-wave feminism through Vehabzadeh's 'sociology of possibilities' in order to begin to bring this emerging map into greater relief. Radical deep-ecology movements have in the past decade articulated a common experience into a movement through the 'primitivist' critique of industrial civilization laid out by John Zerzan and others sympathetic to his vision (Zerzan, 1994: 145).[4] Primitivists argue that the totality of industrial civilization should be abolished in order to recreate the space in which humanity and the rest of earth could potentially regain the 'free nature' that it had so thoroughly domesticated (ibid.: 146). According to Zerzan, this domestication emerged as a direct result of the specialization and division of labour, beginning with the advent of agriculture and then increasing with each technological development. Specialization thus 'works to dissolve moral accountability as it contributes to technical achievement', which, as Zygmunt Baumann has argued, ultimately allows events such as the Holocaust or the mass clear-cutting of forests to occur without opposition (Zerzan, 1999: 2). A provocative argument to say the least, yet what is not understood by many of his supporters is that Zerzan bases much of his critique of civilization on the work of deep ecologists such as Arne Naess, who in turn rely on a Heideggerian understanding of being. In addition, Zerzan leans heavily on early Frankfurt School theorists such as Max Horkheimer and Theodor Adorno, in their book *Dialectic of Enlightenment*.[5] It is to this book, followed by a consideration of Arne Naess, that we now turn in order to understand some of the fundamental theoretical bases of the primitivist movement.

In this book, Horkheimer and Adorno examine the nature of a society based on 'rationality' in a deeply critical way that challenges many of Western civilization's basic beliefs and exposes their hidden uses. They point out for instance, that Enlightenment philosophers such as Francis Bacon hoped to 'disenchant' the world through a notion of universal rationality which ultimately rationalized the domination of all of nature and reality through the pursuit of knowledge. The result, they say, is that all attempts at Enlightenment have finally become bound up in relations of domination and unfreedom; 'the power of the system over human beings increases with every step they take away from the power of nature', since nature, like man, is reduced to that which is useful to the economic apparatus (Adorno and Horkheimer, 2002: 31). After the Enlightenment, all pre-agricultural societies are defined as 'barbaric', since rather than 'mastering nature' in the Baconian sense, they let nature self-organize its own abundance and consciously live within the patterns of its natural cycles. Against what Zerzan calls the domesticating precepts of civilization, they point out that 'abundance needs no law, and civilization's accusation of anarchy sounds almost like a denunciation of abundance' (ibid.: 51). The new domination that emerges with Enlightenment is reinforced tautologically so that the defencelessness of women, Jews and nature at various points in history merely naturalizes their continued exploitation and oppression. Meanwhile, the concomitant rise of the culture industry ensures that any divergence outside the realm of the civilization it enforces is totally and immediately stamped out; 'existence in late capitalism is a permanent rite of initiation. Everyone must show they identify wholeheartedly with the power which beats them' (ibid.: 124). This 'stamping out' occurs through their redeployment as exemplars 'condemned to an economic impotence [...] of the eccentric loner' (ibid.: 106), though it is also true that even those who do not resist become increasingly isolated as well. An important point, which Zerzan builds on, is that this occurs through the advance of technology and communications; radio, television and cars ironically create subjects that 'become more and more alike. Communication makes people conform by isolating them' (ibid.: 184).

Though the critique is profound and important in its analysis of civilization, Horkheimer and Adorno still cling to Vehabzadeh's ultimate referentiality – in this case it is a 'dialectical' critique in which civilization replaces capital as the base, in order to reduce all other 'superstructural' oppressions down to a single location. This comes out in those sectors of the deep ecology movement today which fail to see how flora and fauna forms of being could be of equal importance to human forms of being and who shrug off instances of mass human carnage as a 'natural' corrective of some form or another. One attempt to remedy this situation, if their rhetoric is taken at face value, is found in Murray Bookchin's life-long project, the Institute for Social Ecology; in theory, it was supposed to be a sort of synthesis of human and ecological social movements. Yet, as with Horkheimer and Adorno, Bookchin's perspective is actually yet another form of ultimate referentiality; rather than a biocentric framework it is based on an anthropocentric one which states that man exploits nature because man exploits man as a central feature of capitalism (Bookchin, 1990: 24). Today, however there are signs that this polarization is beginning to dissolve; Arne Naess, who coined the term deep ecology in 1973, has in recent years disavowed the more polarized threads of the movement. He has argued instead for a more pragmatic approach in the hopes that social movements would not be forced to come out in direct opposition to one another. In a 1997 interview he stated that 'there is no contradiction between humans and wilderness' (Naess, 1997: 20), citing the thousands of years of pre-industrial human presence in Alaska as evidence. He goes further in arguing that due to the fundamental interconnectedness of contemporary social movements, people in the South should not be expected by Northern ecologists to engage policies that would threaten their very survival. Rather, he argues for a pragmatic cooperation between different types of activists in various parts of the world in order to maximize the potential transformation embodied within (ibid.: 21). This statement undoubtedly would come as a surprise to some, since Naess's definition of deep ecology is essentially that all forms of being have an intrinsic right to exist regardless of the Baconian clarion call to level flora and fauna merely to satisfy human desire. Yet it is precisely this type of pragmatic willingness to revise in order to develop a more thoroughly anti-foundationalist perspective that will allow for the interconnections between different movements to be rendered visible and practicable.

[...]

Like Horkheimer and Adorno, (many) feminists persistently cling to an ultimate referentiality, in this case one where patriarchy substitutes for civilization, or capital, or something else that is seen as the fundamental oppression in order to introduce the reduction of all other oppressions down to a single location. The consequences of this can be seen in the way in which Riot Grrrl was eventually recuperated back into the American cultural spectacle; by the late 1990s domesticated, corporate-concocted 'Riot Grrrls' such as Courtney Love dominated the media environment constructed around the subject. The increasingly tame magazines *Bitch* and *Bust* also bear testimony to the legacy the reductionist aspects of the movement have left behind. The flipside of this is that many of those who resisted this incorporation did so only to then embrace what became for them a new universalism, leading to the valorization of a rather shallow, subjectivist militancy over the deeper, more intersubjectivist radicalism that had been its early potential. However, just as with the deep ecology movement, recent years have brought signs that this corrosive, deradicalized polarity had begun to unravel as newer, more pragmatic forms began to emerge. One obvious example would be contemporary Riot Grrrl Nomy Lamm who was featured in Naomi Klein's first book for her fanzine *I'm so fucking beautiful* (Klein, 1999: 289).[6] Lamm has become increasingly involved in the anti-globalization and anti-war movements even as she continues her activism in the continuing Riot Grrrl community. And, as is well known, the Lesbian Avengers have become one of the most visible nodes of the anti-globalization movement throughout the continent as well.[7]

The deep-ecology and Riot Grrrl movements examined here demonstrate quite well the way in which the fragmentation of universality – characterized by the replacement of economism with new forms of ultimate referentiality – eventually polarized the new social movements into a dichotomous prison of ideology. The choice became one of either cooptation through increasing willingness to compromise in 'superstructural' issue areas on the one hand, or immobilization through non-strategic, separatist militancy on the other. Richard Day has produced a challenging genealogy of the emergence of Canada's official multiculturalism that illuminates some of the weaknesses of the former tendency. His argument is that multiculturalism as a project traces back to Herodotus, Plato, St. Augustine and their successors' classifications of various human types in order to render them as subjects of domination and control (Day, 1998: 61). In the Canadian context, the multiculturalist agenda engaged in this project to construct a 'problem of diversity' that could only be solved within the normalized discourse of Canadian unity and liberal democracy through a definition of the English–Canadian Self in terms of its Others. Day argues that the only real way to create 'multicultural' political space would be outside of such normalized discourse, leaving open a multiplicity of possibilities – including the breakup of the Canadian nation state (ibid.: 23). Rather than taking the commonly accepted linear 'history' of multiculturalism for granted, Day uses Foucault's genealogical method, which 'fragments what was thought unified' in the evolution of a particular discourse as a tool. In the process, he draws a parallel between the Roman Empire and its Others and the Greek method of 'war to the end' practised in the extermination of indigenous peoples in what eventually became Canada. Of course, it was precisely acts such as these and later events such as the October Crisis of 1970 that finally solidified the English as the cultural backbone of what was later constructed as an 'already achieved' Canadian diversity, what Day calls a 'design theory of identity'. In the years after this event a new Canadian identity arose, centred on the metaphor of the mosaic as a 'free emergence' theory of identity, in which Canada finally began to 'grant recognition' to its non-canonical Others, a move applauded by liberal philosophers such as Taylor and Kymlicka. This rise of the mosaic occurred through the separation of language from culture, in Trudeau's announcement that 'although there are two official languages there is no official culture'. Yet as Day points out, when Canada requires the learning of one of two official languages, it cannot also say that language and culture have been separated without the implication that the victorious colonial cultures are somehow more 'worthy' of recognition than immigrants or First Nations (ibid.: 251). Therefore, he argues, like Vehabzadeh, that multicultural movements must ultimately go beyond the various liberal democratic recuperations to a post-hegemonic conception of a 'designerless mosaic' consisting of 'decentralized, non-hierarchical, participatory [...] settlements that would be capable of defending themselves [...] against the operation of state forms' (ibid.: 295). Rather than by 'citizens', the designerless mosaic would be inhabited by 'smiths', characterized neither by a nomadic nor a sedentary nature but rather one that is hybrid and interacts with both. The smith is not the subject of particularistic identity politics but is that hybrid form which goes beyond both the universal and the particular, taking a *line of flight* with which to escape the empire (ibid.: 293).

Throughout this section I have demonstrated that the fragmentation of universality was a transformative development with implications reaching deep into the dimensions in which new social movements came to operate. While on the one hand the period introduced an increasing immiseration as a result of the dismantling of Keynesianism, on the other it opened up new spaces in which more transgressive movements could emerge. These new spaces allowed for the articulation of a more radical critique of centralized power, industrial civilization, white supremacy, patriarchy, heteronormativity and multiple other oppressions. It is in this sense that one could say that with the worldwide fall of communism and Keynesianism, the hegemonic pillar of economism fell as well. Yet, as Day has amply explained, this period was also characterized by a new polarity within the ultimately universalist frameworks that each social movement had articulated separately. On the one hand this meant that these movements became increasingly militant, positing their various single issues as primary, which led in turn to more militant forms of resistance in the process. But on the other hand, it also meant that they became increasingly vulnerable to cooptation, since other forms of domination necessarily held comparatively less importance, thus allowing compromise in these 'external' dimensions to become more widely accepted as a norm. In short, what this polarity meant was that new social movements in this period became either more militant or more reformist, but very rarely did they become more radical. In saying this, I use the term 'radical' in a very specific sense; here I do not simply mean getting to the immediately apparent 'root' cause of a particular issue. Rather, I mean taking as a starting point the Foucauldian realization that power is always both repressive and creative and that it is not necessarily concentrated in any one dimension, but is always multidimensional; and that therefore resistance is always interconnected and irreducible as well. If Foucault argued that the web of power had existed since the eighteenth century yet did not become visible until May 1968, I would argue that the web of resistance had existed since that time yet did not become visible until November 1999.

THE EMERGENCE OF OPPOSITION

[...] As Day demonstrated and Agamben confirmed, the recuperation of new social movements is made possible by the fact that rather than reducing their particular oppressions down to the classic site of 'class-struggle', these movements merely reduced them down to a more particular category, such as race, sex or civilization. In the process they did exactly what the working-class movements of the past had done; they fundamentally negated the real multi-dimensionality of singularity and in the process severely curtailed important potentialities. One of the earliest attempts to challenge both the particular and universal tendencies through a conceptualization of the interconnected-ness of social movements was the 1986 book *Liberating Theory*, compiled by Michael Albert, Noam Chomsky, and several others connected with South End Press. The book proposes a theory of social change that would move beyond both particular and universal forms of foundationalism in order to be more in line with recent explanations of reality such as chaos theory, while still retaining the humanist spirit of the Enlightenment (Albert, 1986: 116). Specifically, the authors argue that the 'separate' parts of reality always act together, as an interconnected, unbroken whole, whether one is referring to an ecosystem or a social movement. Throughout history, they say, movements for social change have been primarily either of a 'monist' (universal) nature or of a 'pluralist' (particular) nature, which, they say, is a reflection of the fundamentally reductionist conceptual tools that were available at the time. They go on to explain that these monistic and pluralistic concepts emerged primarily within four general theories, each focusing on four general social spheres: Marxism (class and the economy), Anarchism (the state and authority), Feminism (gender and the family), and Nationalism (race and the world-system) (ibid.: 12).

When used completely separately as reductionist theories they all become problematic quite quickly; this is the perspective that is dismissed as monist. But a similar problem occurs in the understanding of the pluralist; the pluralist uses all of these theories but only as they are 'appropriate' to the primary dynamics of a particular situation. Against both of these, the authors propose a 'Complementary Holism' in order to explain why it is that one cannot even understand, for instance, the economy, without using an interwoven combination of the multiple critiques employed by feminists, anarchists, Marxists and nationalists. Despite the tendencies of many activists towards economism, they argue, the fact is that Marxism alone will not lead to very deep insights since all 'spheres' are combined into one unbroken whole (Albert, 1986: 52). In *Liberating Theory*, the authors illustrate the importance of the intersectionalities between spheres as a precarious balance of 'auton-omy-within-solidarity', where social movements understand themselves as autonomous movements for self-determination on the one hand, *as well as* the different facets of a still larger 'movement of movements' on the other (ibid.: 144). In this sense, 'Complementary Holism' offers social movements a powerful conceptual tool in that it engages with all four spheres simultane-ously, in a complex, interconnected fashion, recognizing that movements from within each sphere continually reinforce one another in ways that are not always readily apparent and which must be articulated. This concept becomes especially important in the anti-globalization movement, where just such an interconnected movement of movements has begun to emerge for the first time.

Though credit is given where it is due in the realm of physics, there are good reasons to suspect that this book may also be an attempt to claim the insights of post-structuralist theories of social movements for those radical intellectuals who see some value in them, but who refuse to move beyond the security offered by Enlightenment precepts. Because while the book emphatically claimed to be 'the first to put forward a coherent, radical politics that gives activists and theorists a framework for understanding the complex, integrated character of modern oppressions' (Albert, 1986: back cover), just one year earlier, Ernesto Laclau and Chantal Mouffe had released a suspiciously similar set of conceptualizations about social movements in their classic book *Hegemony and Socialist Strategy*. In fact, the single biggest difference between the two books is that Laclau and Mouffe make no effort to try to preserve the sanctity of Enlightenment precepts, since, like other post-structuralists, they see these as being one of the primary sources of universalism in the first place. Other differences include that they make no effort to positivistically justify their theories through a purportedly 'scientific' foundation, nor do they argue that these movements can be simply reduced down to four all-encompassing spheres. Yet, like the authors of *Liberating Theory*, Laclau and Mouffe were on the whole responding to the 'crisis in Marxism' that was largely a result of the new social movements after May 1968. Not wanting to reject Marxism entirely in this process, they worked through the finer points of Gramsci's theory of hegemony in order to articulate what they hoped could become a common struggle between both the working-class movements and the new social movements, a project which they described as 'counter-hegemony' (Laclau and Mouffe, 2002).

The impetus for this theorization was the growing sense that there was a 'need to understand that there are different sides to antagonism; that one cannot just think that class antagonism is the only one'. Against the classical Marxist conception of 'equality' based on the obliteration of all difference, counter-hegemony takes conflict and plurality as a necessary given, 'a logic of what we call equivalence'. This is an important concept, because it creates space in which social movements can finally transcend the twin traps of extreme particularism marked by the complete obliteration of commensurability on the one hand, and extreme homogeneity marked by the complete obliteration of difference on the other. The logic of equivalence is articulated further in the central concept of 'agonistic pluralism', which is defined as 'a real struggle against different positions [...] in order to have a vibrant democracy' based on the centrality of conflict and diversity. Agonism differs from antagonism in that the latter is 'the limit of social objectivity [...] between two social forces', where relations of equivalence have not yet been articulated in the shape of a counter-hegemony. Since class antagonism thus becomes only one form among many, the resolution of class struggle ceases to take the form of the 'final conflict' and is thus spread into all social spaces. All of this focus on conflict should not be misinterpreted as a negative, however; as Mouffe has argued elsewhere, if there were no social divisions, there would be no freedom because everyone would think alike. The result instead is that there is no teleological 'goal' and social movements become focused on means rather than ends, a point which Melucci, Vehabzadeh and Agamben have all recognized as well. The project of counter-hegemony is thus a process of turning antagonisms into agonisms or enemies into adversaries; it is constructed through 'complex strategic movements requiring negotiation among mutually contradictory discursive surfaces' (Laclau and Mouffe, 2001: 93).

In order to articulate such a counter-hegemony, the common belief that there is some objective society 'out there' that has not been constructed by power would be one of the first things to be challenged. The articulation of equivalence is based on this understanding since the articulation of a counter-hegemony establishes a relationship among elements that thus modifies their identity, resulting in a shared discourse and a common project. But rather than occurring through the simplistic notion of four primary spheres 'the practice of articulation [...] consists in the construction of nodal points which partially fix meaning [...] every social practice is therefore [...] articulatory' (Laclau and Mouffe, 2001: 113). Relations of equivalence are thus necessary to bridge the multiplicity of differences that will emerge between virtually infinite social practices, since social movements that have arisen out of these practices have embraced a particularist epistemology. The building of a counter-hegemony, therefore, 'should take place through a confrontation with antagonistic articulatory practices' based on relations of equivalence in which antagonisms can be transformed into agonisms through a recognition that each practice is necessarily partially outside of the greater counter-hegemonic whole that is under construction (ibid.: 135). This conception demonstrates how new social movements make a new use of the concept of autonomy, that of an autonomy linked to radical democratic pluralism, or as Albert et al., refer to it, 'autonomy-within-solidarity'. Because 'if these identities depend on certain precise social and political conditions of existence, autonomy itself can only be defended and expanded in terms of a wider hegemonic struggle' (ibid.: 141). Clearly the ideas utilized in *Liberating Theory* were not without precedent; this fact leads one to wonder what other relevant insights into the counter-hegemonic project might be found in the works of other theorists who move beyond the Enlightenment precepts of 'humanism' and positivism.

Ian Angus agrees with much of Laclau and Mouffe; he argues that although the dissolution of universalism has been of fundamental importance in the creation of new possibilities, the rise of social movements organized around particularity is ultimately a 'rebound from universality', and without a concept of totality, critique inevitably falls into reformism (Angus, 2000: 29). Instead he argues for a sort of pragmatic balance between the two, since 'one cannot simply discard universality for particularity [...] but must radically deconstruct and reformulate the particularity–universality nexus itself' (ibid.: 48). The difference with Angus is that what he endorses is not strictly counter-hegemony per se, but a new contingent totality conceived as a Husserlian 'horizon' made up of the multiple subject-positions of new social movements and the intersectionalities that they articulate. It is yet another way of conceptualizing autonomy-within-solidarity due to the increasing sense that so-called 'organic unity is [...] a "tyranny of the part" elevated to an organization of the whole' (ibid.: 72). In the current media environment, this tyranny of the part is reproduced in yet another way even with the dissolution of that unity since 'it is much easier for the new pluralist apologists to celebrate the ingenuity of "people" to use the products of mass culture in diverse ways despite their control by increasingly fewer hands, than for critical theorists to define precisely the constraints that foreclose political alternatives' (ibid.: 133). One key problem then is the continuing configuration of the media environment as a centralized, one-way system; against this, Angus calls for a transformative media ethic that would recognize not only the right to speak but also the right to be heard. This demand for the right to be heard does not imply that the teleological goal of such a project would necessarily be the emergence of an 'organic unity' however. In fact, a key aspect of Angus's project is the construction of a paradoxical 'border [...] which lets one's own territory appear [...] animated by an active love of diversity' (ibid.: 180).

Connecting with the notion of relations of equivalence, this is the point at which he rejoins Laclau and Mouffe in the project of radical democracy; unlike them, however, Angus has taken it a step further in this direction by considering the question in the context of the anti-globalization movement. He argues that in this context, 'the politics of alliance' requires a neo-Proudhonian framework of federalism in order to construct a counter-hegemony capable of recognizing a Levinasian principle of equality outside the dichotomy of particularity/ universality, in which groups come together for the purpose of solidarity without giving up their autonomy (Angus, 2002). Such a politics, he argues, is invested in the formation of alternative identities outside the normalized world of self-referentiality and conformity, which therefore decentres the importance of the continual maintenance and expansion of that world. Because that world is always adapting to new shapes that emerge on the social field, these new identities have a tendency towards recuperation and therefore must be continually reinvented and restated so that they do not become hardened and frozen into a recuperable shape. The new identity that Angus argues is being produced in this movement is that of the 'anti-globalization activist' who, like Day's 'smith', also becomes a 'post-national person'. The anti-globalization activist thus maintains membership in a plurality of movements and communities and therefore in his/her singularity forms the real intersectionalities between them as the ontological appearance of Proudhonian alliance. Yet the notion of alliance used here may be insufficient for the type of radical democracy being proposed; though it is constituted for a specific purpose, is avowedly temporary and is open to change, for Proudhon this federalist alliance is also a formal one; his definition of federalism clearly describes 'contracting' groups that 'bind' themselves together into 'agreements'. As outlined by Angus, an alliance of this sort would involve questions of when a group would be allowed to join, as well as questions of when a group would be expelled. While the call for an alliance that does not subsume singularity is imperative, the Proudhonian formulation is only one possibility amongst several others, some of which involve lesser degrees of officiality and organization and therefore subsume singularity to an even lesser degree.[8]

One counter-hegemonic 'alliance' of this sort that has the potentiality to fulfil Angus's requirements without the messy business of expulsions, memberships and contracts, is that theorized by Jacques Derrida. Within the volatile political context of the worldwide collapse of state communism, he first began to articulate the concept of a 'New International' in the 1994 book *Specters of Marx*. Against the triumphalist demands for a universal 'exorcism' of Karl Marx, Max Stirner, and other critics of capitalism and liberal democracy, Derrida argued that the collapse of dogmatic formulations of radical critique in fact presented an unprecedented opportunity to reclaim their best elements from the rubble of their disassembled pieces. As he describes it, the New International would reflect such an eclectic spirit, as it would no longer bear the dogmatic marks of purges, denunciations and cults of personality that plagued the First International of the classical Marxists and anarchists, but would instead move beyond this to an order-out-of-chaos that would not require 'administration' at all. This New International would be an 'alliance of a rejoining without conjoined mate, without organization, without party, without nation, without state, without property' (Derrida, 1994: 29). In a further elaboration, he described it as

> a link of affinity, suffering, and hope, a still discreet, almost secret link, as it was around 1848, but more and more visible, we have more than one sign of it. It is an untimely link, without status, without title, and without name, barely public even if it is not clandestine, without contract, 'out of joint,' without coordination, without party, without country, without national community (International before, across, and beyond any national determination), without co-citizenship, without common belonging to a class. The name of the new International is given here to what calls to the friendship of an alliance without institution. (ibid.: 85)

The key difference with Derrida then, is that his conceptualization of an alliance is one that is 'without institution' and 'without organization'. In this case, the question of official expulsions of groups would not arise since it would not be technically possible in an International that is both 'without coordination' and 'without co-citizenship'. For Derrida, nearly everything becomes opened up to both deconstruction and reconstruction with the collapse of dogmatism; yet there *is* one thing that cannot be deconstructed, that being the 'emancipatory promise', which not only must not be rejected, but 'is necessary to insist on [...] now more than ever' (ibid.: 75). The primary change then, seems to be the emergence of a new attitude of mutual acceptance of pluralism and conflict between social movements, a concept endorsed by Angus, Laclau and Mouffe, but extended beyond the assumptions of the positivity of organization.

In recent years, it has been argued further that this decentring of the party, the union, the alliance and other officialistic forms of organization has been brought about by the fact that they are 'radically unadapted to the new – tele-techno-media – conditions of public space' (Derrida, 1994: 102). This line of thought is a reflection of Angus's central theory of communication; that the dominant medium of communication that defines a given epoch ultimately determines the materiality of discourse as well (Angus, 2000: 12). In the current epoch then, the primary medium of the internet results in ever multiplying, increasingly interlinked yet, paradoxically, also increasingly decentralized social movements. This describes the core issues in the quickly expanding subject of 'netwar', which argues further that contemporary actors become increasingly interlinked through 'network forms of organization, doctrine, strategy and technology', thus allowing for multiple possibilities that would not have been thinkable previously (Ronfeldt and Arquilla, 1998: xi).[9] Despite being a relatively new subject, netwar has become the central focus of a growing number of books, articles and discussions across a field ranging from elites fearful of the potentialities involved to the social movements that seem to be excited by these same potentialities. Theorists from the former camp who have published studies include John Arquilla, David Ronfeldt, Kevin Kelly and Steven Johnson; those writing from the perspective of the latter include Gilles Deleuze, Félix Guattari, James Der Derian, Paul Virilio and Harry Cleaver.

Of these, the rather unique perspective offered by the last of them is directly related to the theory of the constellation of opposition that I propose as a means of understanding why a notion of counter-hegemony is inappropriate to the contemporary context. Cleaver argues that the leading metaphors of the rhizome and the network used by his colleagues are ultimately inappropriate, since, like Angus, Laclau and Mouffe's conceptualizations, they rely on a prioritization of formal, organizational forms which then either form the 'sprouts' of the rhizome on the one hand or the 'nodes' of the network on the other. As has been argued by Derrida, in contemporary interlinked social movements, formal organization, to the extent that it is a factor, is usually only a momentary, incidental aspect and is not a solidified central feature. Today, informal affinity groups, multiply-linked individuals and spontaneous street formations form the primary basis of resistance, while increasingly anachronistic formal organizations act as a mere shell structure, sometimes enabling and sometimes hindering such activity.

It's for this reason that Cleaver invokes the far more dynamic metaphor of water. Like civil society (understood in the broadest sense) water is an 'all-channel network' – it is constantly moving and constantly changing form. The tidal waves, the currents, the whirlpools, the freezing, the thawing, the ebbing and the flowing; all of these features allow theorists and activists to move beyond the organizationalist notions of counter-hegemony and formality into a form of thought far more reflective of post-hegemonic, post-organizationalist social movements of today. In such movements, Cleaver says, 'resistance flows not from the unified class seeking to form a new unified hegemony, but rather from myriad currents seeking the freedom of the open seas' (Cleaver, 2002).[10] While Ernesto Laclau, Chantal Mouffe, Ian Angus and Jacques Derrida argue in favour of different formations of counter-hegemony, it is clear from these statements that for Cleaver the current 'movement of movements' is increasingly post-hegemonic rather than counter-hegemonic. So what we have mapped out here, then, is a spectrum of organizationalism as a way of understanding the nature of the anti-globalization movement; in this sense, Angus's perspective is closer to post-organizationalism than Laclau and Mouffe's perspective, while Derrida's perspective is closer to it than Angus's. It is important to point out however that post-organizationalism as a means of understanding the constellation of opposition is both *post*-organizationalist and post-*organizationalist*; this means that it does not reject organization completely, but only the currently dominant forms in which decision making and execution are separated through various means of representation (Landstreicher, 2002)[11]. Though this argument has been actualized recently in the new forms social movements have begun to take, one can trace an anti-organizationalist argument going back several decades at least.

Less than a year after the Paris uprisings of May 1968, Jacques Camatte argued that 'the mystique of organization' led to a sort of *groupthink* in which the state form is redeployed in miniature in the form of the political gang.

This political gang, he argued, puts forward the appearance of a democratic, level-headed, open entity that is 'in touch' with the trials and tribulations of 'average people'. Yet behind this façade, the recruitee soon discovers the cult of the clique, the cult of personality, a pervasive low-opinion of the average person, and a mutual distrust between other recruitees and the ruling cliques or personality. As in the culture industry, these features manifest practically in banal propaganda formulated with the patronizing goal of reaching 'the masses' at the level of the lowest common denominator, with the sole intention of the limitless expansion of the organization, while actual *social change* takes the back seat. Ultimately though, Camatte argued, the political gang becomes recuperated, since it 'seduces itself by its own bullshit and it is thereby absorbed by the surrounding milieu' (Camatte, 1995: 27).

Camatte's critiques centred primarily on orthodox Marxist organizations; yet recently, Bob Black has made a strong case that traditional anarchist organizations have been subject to these gang-like tendencies of the traditional left as well, located primarily in calls for internal homogeneity. In practice, he argued, direct democracy tended to function as a mere tyranny of the majority (as Socrates learned) perhaps at least partially because it is based originally on a society in which being a slave meant that one could not vote (as the vast majority of Greeks learned). This tendency can be seen clearly in the Spanish CNT–FAI, for instance – though it is considered by many anarchists to be the high point of their history – in that it actually had eight separate levels of redundant, hierarchical bureaucracy organized around multiple aspects of geography and economy; when push came to shove, the movement's leaders took positions in the government (Black, 1997: 63). The history of the CNT–FAI is sadly typical; during the first half of the twentieth century, organizationalist anarchists regularly converted to fascism, as happened in Italy; Maoism, as happened in China; Bolshevism, as happened in Russia; or liberalism, as happened in Spain and Mexico. Given the reluctance of most people today to engage in formal organization-building activity or official parliamentary politics (perhaps for good reasons) it is clear why anti-organizationalist ideas are beginning to take hold in the social movements emerging in the post-organizationalist wake of N30.

Yet, contrary to the majority of the anti-organizationalists, I would argue that one would be foolish to rush headlong into such an explicitly declared project; although the coming community is as likely to be one beyond categorization as it is beyond organization, it is also true that the present moment is one of *transition* marked by a continually uneven, unpredictable hybrid tension between the old and the new. In fact, some theorists have argued that this is always the case; that the moment of the present is perpetually shaped as much by the 'dead hand' of the past as it is by the 'open sky' of the future. This is why even Bob Black, who claimed to support a cleansing within anarchism of its 'Marxist residues', ironically cites dozens of unorthodox Marxists such as Jacques Camatte, Herbert Marcuse, Theodor Adorno, Guy Debord and Anton Pannekoek in order to do so. As Derrida taught us in *Specters of Marx*:

If he loves justice at least, the 'scholar' of the future, the 'intellectual' of tomorrow should learn it and learn it from the ghost. He should learn to live by learning not how to make conversation with the ghost but how to talk with him, with her, how to let them speak or how to give them back speech, even if it is in oneself, in the other, in the other in oneself; they are always there, spectres, even if they do not exist, even if they are no longer, even if they are not there yet. (Derrida, 1994: 176)

The spectres of which Derrida speaks are thus not merely the ghosts of the past but also the ghosts of the future, both of which inform and shape the living moment of the present. Therefore, within the context of the subject at hand, we glean that it is in the uneasy relationship *between* the organizationalist/ counter-hegemonic and the anti-organizationalist/anti-hegemonic elements of contemporary movements that we can begin to speak of a 'constellation of opposition' as it actually appears in the present moment as post-organizationalist/post-hegemonic.

This constellation is not constituted exclusively by normalizing formal organizations nor uncoded, spontaneous whatever-beings alone, but only that which its diverse, constituent elements articulate at a given moment, in a given situation. This articulation, of course, is how the constellations of stars we are familiar with today first came to be accepted as givens; while there have always been 'clusters or groups of stars' in the night sky, they need not have been articulated as official entities. These canonical constellations might just as easily *not* have been articulated as such; in that case the world would know a completely different set of constellations. So at any given moment a constellation of opposition might consist primarily of the various officialistic organizations brought about by the working class and new social movements (like the canonical twelve constellations of the Zodiac paired with the 88 semi-canonical constellations). In another moment a constellation might consist primarily of informal and unofficial spontaneous assemblies, street riots or other unpredictable manifestations (the non-canonical 'unofficial' constellations invented and promptly forgotten by imaginative laymen since the emergence of humanity). Most often today, however, a constellation of opposition is that which one finds in the uneven, unmapped space between and outside; in this case, it may be an unspoken reality that is embraced by some and regretted by many or it may be a clearly articulated reality that is regretted by some and embraced by many.[12] Depending on the circumstances, at a given moment a constellation of this sort may fill up an entire night sky – on another night it may fill just a small section; it may include large stars, distant planets, a passing satellite. This is a useful way of conceptualizing the 'anti-globalization movement' in its local, regional and global dimensions; because while a constellation might be mappable globally, in fact it is primarily a simultaneous emergence of thousands of local movements, which therefore may not be, or may not care to be, on the same map. During daylight or cloudy weather the constellation may be temporarily invisible, yet it may or may not still be there, behind the silence and the invisibility of circumstances that are never permanent and always temporary.[13]

More clearly, we might consider the second definition of the term as 'a configuration, of related items, properties, ideas, groups or individuals' characterized not by the internal orthodoxy demanded by Proudhon's federalist alliance, but precisely the opposite: an authentic manifestation of 'autonomy-within-solidarity', as in Derrida's or Camatte's post-organizationalist alliance. Unlike in the metaphors of the rhizome or the network, relationships between elements need not occur through 'organizations' per se, but might just as easily occur through individuals, ideas or properties as suggested in Angus. Unlike in the metaphor of water, there is no need to assume that the transition to a politics beyond hegemony and organization is somehow already fully complete. The powerful, undecidable tension that defines this concept of constellation has emerged repeatedly in the past several years in major protests, uprisings and conferences such as those in Seattle, Quebec City, Genoa, Buenos Aires and Porto Alegre. In Seattle the constellation was defined by the primary tension between the semi-official Direct Action Network and the unofficial black bloc; the secondary tension being that between the highly officialistic AFL–CIO and its unofficial rank-and-file formations. As confirmed by the security apparatus in charge of N30, it was *precisely* this tension between the official, the semi-official and the unofficial that allowed the protests ultimately to succeed in shutting down the city.[14] In Quebec City, the constellation was similarly constituted by a semi-official 'anti-capitalist' network, an unofficial black bloc, a highly officialistic labour federation and unofficial rank-and-file elements. It is here that the logic of the constellation of opposition reached its highest level of expression yet in the North; a general agreement emerged between all participating elements to respect a 'diversity of tactics' through colour-coded zones of conflict intensity. In Genoa, the constellation was composed of the same elements, yet this time the police did everything possible to disrupt and neutralize this powerful tension, including the liberal use of murder, infiltration, provocation and violent repression.

Perhaps even more inspiring are the constellations that have emerged in South America as of late; there, they have moved beyond street demonstrations to toppling entire governments, while building grassroots alternatives in the process. In the streets of Buenos Aires, the slogan *'que se vayan todos'* (they all must go) quickly became the rallying cry of a constellation so large and diverse that it brought together marginalized squatters, angry students and a mass of distraught yuppies, playfully dubbed the 'bourgeois bloc'.[15] With such a massive base, the country has since seen the emergence of a sprawling network of hundreds of autonomous neighbourhood assemblies, over 450,000 community gardens, over 100 collectivized factories, and hundreds of bartering circles. In Porto Alegre, Noam Chomsky described the 2002 World Social Forum as 'the most exciting and promising realization of the hopes of the left [...] for a true international [...] unprecedented in scale, in range of constituency, and in international solidarity' (Chomsky, 2002).[16] While this description reflects quite well what is meant by a constellation of opposition, I would argue that this was probably the most reserved form that it has taken has thus far, with local anarchists and other undesirables being deliberately excluded from the planning committees. However, I would agree with Chomsky that it had great potential, due to the fact that it accomplished the unprecedented feat of bringing together over 50,000 grassroots activists from every corner of the globe in order to develop viable alternatives to the current order. None of these events would have emerged in the unique way that they have in the past several years had the processes outlined in this chapter not taken place in the way that they have – from the deconstruction of the working-class movements to the reconstruction of the new social movements, and from the deconstruction of the new social movements to the reconstruction of a constellation of opposition. Several new landscapes of conflict have emerged over the past three decades; what action social movements might take in this new landscape will form the subject of the conclusion.

CONCLUSION: THE CONSTELLATION OF OPPOSITION AND THE TWENTY-FIRST CENTURY

The project of counter-hegemony envisioned by Laclau and Mouffe thus serves as a bridge between divergent epistemologies and social movements based on universality, particularity and singularity; yet while it is useful in its explanation of the current transitional moment, the constellation of opposition emerging today indicates a larger move toward post-hegemony. The balance of the official, semi-official and unofficial formations in the contemporary constellation of opposition is thus the actualization of the balance of universality, particularity and singularity in contemporary counter-hegemonic theory. While we began with the key insight from Foucault that power is both dispersed and interconnected, it is my hope that in the course of this chapter it has been demonstrated that today resistance is also dispersed and interconnected. Overall, there are five key points that can be gleaned from this study that I feel will be particularly important for the continuing anti-globalization movement:

1. Older social movements organized around the industrial working class should drop their universalistic pretensions, and recognize that they represent a constituency that is just as particularistic as are the movements organized around so-called identity politics. They should further recognize that today they are no more 'strategically located' in the economy than are the constituencies of the new social movements, which is also to say that the post-Fordist economy has been developed in part to preclude that very possibility.

2. New social movements organized around gender, race, immigration, sexuality, education and the ecology should similarly drop their universalistic pretensions and recognize that, like the working-class movements, they too represent particularistic identities that have been constructed

by power, and thus universal aspirations of 'liberation' from their new foundations are equally invalid.

3. All social movements should re-examine how and why the subjects around which they organize have been historically constructed by power in the first place, in order to actively seek out the interconnections that may become possible once particularities have been deconstructed into singularities and the multidimensionality of each constituent element has been released.

4. In this process of singularization and the release of multidimensionality, divergent social movements should begin to spontaneously reconstruct relations of equivalence between themselves, thus forming a self-organizing constellation of opposition based on the general principle of autonomy-within-solidarity.

5. The constellations which emerge based on these ideas ought not be automatically accepted as constituted only by officialistic organizations of particularities or post-organizational manifestations of singularities alone, but should recognize that in the transition to the coming community there will necessarily exist an uneasy tension between the two, which, far from being catastrophic, can become (and has been) a source of immense power and possibility.

NOTES

1. The empirical record of class-reductionist 'emancipation' in Russia, China, Cuba and the rest of the Soviet Empire speaks for itself in this regard. See Marcuse (1985).

2. The subsistence economy as an alternative to global neoliberalism has been defended more recently – and in much more detail – by eco-feminists such as Maria Mies and Veronka Bennholdt-Thomsenn.

3. Barbara Epstein and many other commentators have confirmed the anti-authoritarian nature of the anti-globalization movement.

4. Primitivism and its related ideologies have since developed into an important philosophical basis for movements such as Earth First and the Earth Liberation Front.

5. The irony here is that while he argues emphatically against 'postmodernism' and Marxism in favour of a more 'anarchistic' anarchism, he rarely quotes anarchist thinkers and often quotes post-structuralists and unorthodox Marxists in order to back up his theories.

6. This, of course, was one of the first books to outline the possible shape of what at that time was an emerging anti-globalization movement.

7. The Lesbian Avengers were founded in 1992 in New York City, around the same time as the Riot Grrrl movement, with whom they share numerous members and philosophical bases.

8. Though the attempt to bring in an anarchist framework for understanding some of the new forms of solidarity emerging in the anti-globalization movement certainly makes sense, both the 'movement of movements' and its more specifically anarchist threads are presently caught up in an intense debate over the question of 'organizationalism', which means that the ideas of a more recent theorist such as Jacques Camatte might be more appropriate than a classical anarchist like Pierre-Joseph Proudhon.

9. Netwar is increasingly understood as the emerging twenty-first century *modus operandi* of social movements, terrorist organizations, international mafias, intelligence services, police departments and militaries.

10. Hakim Bey makes a similar argument regarding 'counter-hegemony', while Michael Hardt and Antonio Negri use the metaphor of the virus as an alternative to the clunkiness of the network metaphor.

11. Landstreicher's essay is one of the key texts that has helped to define the emerging post-organizationalist current in radical North American social movements; while this essay is clearly anti-organizationalist, social movements tend in practice to be more pragmatically post-organizationalist.
12. The former refers to the positionality of the black bloc in Seattle, while the latter refers to its positionality in Quebec City.
13. After 11 September 2001, it seems clear that this is what has happened to large sections of the movement, especially in the North; this is what Melucci would refer to as a 'submerged network'.
14. The final decision was to allow the AFL-CIO parade to proceed from the Seattle Center to downtown. This sealed the fate of the street actions as a victory for the Direct Action Network [...] several thousand people broke away from the march, just in time to run into the renewed police push to move people away from the Convention Center. (De Armond, 2001: 218)

The rank-and-file union members, Wobblies and anarchists that led this breakaway march had planned ahead of time to subvert the official plans, which confirms the importance of the tension between the official, the semi-official and the unofficial which is also the tension between universality, particularity and singularity.
15. It was impossible to tell the demonstrators from the passersby. Men in suits and ties with briefcases in one hand and hammers in the other, women with gold bracelets, handbags, and high heels sharing cans of spray paint, anonymous suits on their lunch break joining the fracas and then melting back into the crowd. (Jordan and Witney, 2002)
16. Clearly Chomsky had not examined Derrida's description of the New International – or maybe he *had* and this was something of a reply in favour of greater officiality.

REFERENCES

Adorno, Theodor, and Horkheimer, Max (2002). *Dialectic of Enlightenment*. New York: Continuum.
Albert, Michael (1986). *Liberating Theory*. Boston: South End Press.
Angus, Ian (2002). 'Globalization Versus Social Movements: Towards a New Alliance?' Retrieved 28 November 2002 from <http://poeticguerrillas.com/articles/arcade.html>.
—— (2000). *(Dis)figurations: Discourse/Critique/Ethics*. London: Verso.
Armond, Paul de (2001). *Networks and Netwars: The Future of Terror, Crime and Militancy* (J. Arquilla and D. Ronfeldt, eds). Santa Monica: RAND.
Black, Bob (1997). *Anarchy after Leftism*. Columbia: CAL Press.
Bookchin, Murray (1990). *Remaking Society: Pathways to a Green Future*. Boston: South End Press.
Chomsky, Noam (2002). 'A World Without War'. Retrieved 20 November 2002 from <http://www.zmag.org/content/ForeignPolicy/chomwsf2t.cfm>.
Day, Richard (1998). 'Multiculturalism and the History of Canadian Diversity' (dissertation). Simon Fraser University.
Derrida, Jacques (1994). *Spectres of Marx: The State of the Debt, the Work of Mourning in the New International*. New York: Routledge.
Camatte, Jacques (1995). *This World We Must Leave*. Brooklyn: Autonomedia.
Cleaver, Harry (2002). 'Computer-Linked Social Movements and the Global Threat to Capitalism'. Retrieved 26 November 2002 from <http://www.antenna.nl/~waterman/cleaver2.html>.
Foucault, Michel (1980). *Power/Knowledge: Selected Interviews and Other Writings 1972–1977* (Colin Gordon, ed.). New York: Random House.
Gorz, André (1982). *Farewell to the Working Class: An Essay on Post-Industrial Socialism*. London: Pluto Press.
Jordan, John, and Whitney, Jennifer (2002). 'Que se vayan todos: Argentina's popular uprising'. Self-published.

Klein, Naomi (1999). *No Logo: Taking Aim at the Brand Bullies.* New York: Picador.

Laclau, Ernesto, and Mouffe, Chantal (2002). Interview by Ian Angus. Conflicting Publics. Retrieved 29 November 2002 from <http://www.english.ilstu.edu/strickland/495/laclau2.html>.

—— (2001). *Hegemony and Socialist Strategy: Towards a Radical Democratic Politics.* London: Verso.

Landstreicher, Wolfi (2002). 'From Politics to Life'. Retrieved 2 December 2002 from <http://www.infoshop.org/inews/stories.php?story=02/12/03/6279028>.

Marcuse, Herbert (1985). *Soviet Marxism: A Critical Analysis.* Columbia University Press.

Melucci, Alberto (1989). *Nomads of the Present: Social Movements and Individual Needs in Contemporary Society.* Philadelphia: Temple University Press.

Naess, Arne (1997). Interview by Ian Angus. *Alternatives Journal* 23(3).

Ronfeldt, David, and Arquilla, John (1998). *The Zapatista Social Netwar in Mexico.* Santa Monica: RAND.

Touraine, Alain (1988). *Return of the Actor: Social Theory in Post-Industrial Society.* Minneapolis: University of Minnesota Press.

Vehabzadeh, Peyman (2000). 'Articulated Experiences: Toward a Radical Phenomenology of Contemporary Social Movements' (dissertation). Simon Fraser University.

Zerzan, John (1999). *Against Civilization: Readings and Reflections.* Eugene: Uncivilized Books.

—— (1994). *Future Primitive.* Brooklyn: Autonomedia.

8

Acracy_Reloaded@post1968/1989: Reflections on Postmodern Revolutions[1]

Antón Fernández de Rota

POST '68–'89 WORLDS AND GALAXIES

I write without being able to pinpoint my *cultural localization* (Bhabha, 2002). Male, young, white, university graduate, precarious worker, activist. Catholic upbringing. Atheist. I am localized. Sitting before a computer in Galicia, Spanish state, connected to the Net. *Cyborg. Galicia@Cyberspace.* Localization: Iberian Peninsula, but with constant reminders of my life on the other side of the Pond. I suffered racist attacks in Chicago: once for being a white middle-class *teenager*; another time for being a *Hispanic* migrant. *Windy City.* Back to Europe, and, later, a journey into Hell. A *redneck* town in South Illinois: four months. Drugs and unemployment everywhere. Deep America. Back in Europe I became a punk rocker. Metropolitan Mohawk. *East Cost:* A brief, wintry stay in icy New Hampshire. Family visit. Idyllic stay in Gainesville, a university city: vegetarian hamburgers and alligators. Dawning of the new millennium. A couple of months in the Sunny State surrounded by stars and stripes on flags, shortly after that terrible attack: 9/11. I wouldn't know how to decide if I enjoyed the new world or the old world more, Heaven or Hell, the Windy City or the City of Ice. I think that with every step I took, the Mohawk sunk further within me. (Cyber)punk, and later *post-*. University scholar, part-time undeclared waiter, at first lucky in love then unlucky. *Recycling.* Post-lover. Post(cyber)punk. Pirate. *Reloading* … Current localization: *Acracy 2.0@post68/89.*

From my perspective, I look to the past that I did not live, but that strangely makes up my cultural and desiring body. I understand that the decade of the 60s was not so much the 'birth of a counterculture' (Roszak, 1973) but the generalization and the creative refounding of another culture which pulsed beneath it. That substratum had been forged with the heat of the artistic innovations of the first third of the twentieth century (from dada/surrealism to black *jazz* and cross-bred *bebop*) and the evolution of a chain of social struggles. Whether they wanted to or not, these struggles culminated in the emergence of the *welfare state*: almost full employment, certain social benefits and rights, etc. These struggles had transformed the technical and technological composition of work, and, moreover, the cultural form and content of social creativity itself. 1968 symbolized a pause between the modern and the postmodern periods, both of which had certainly been prepared a little while before. 1968 obliges us to think of the left and the revolution in a different way. The bohemian *underground*, and later the *hipsters*, *beatniks* and *hippies* of the Forties, Fifties and Sixties; the young workers who throughout the Sixties and Seventies rejected political and economic Fordism *en masse*; the students and the intellectuals, the Frankfurtian and post-structural critics, all of them emerged from the new sediments prepared by these styles of creativity and antagonistic struggles which finally brought about the passage to postmodernity. 1968 symbolically marked the mass dawning of a contra-cultural trend. Approximations bordering the limits of everything modern. Singular fluxes in each territory: mass and cultural unrest in the USA, with successive explosive uprisings in the spring of 1964 in the black *ghettos*; uprisings in Italy until – and especially in its prolongation until – 1977; radically imaginative in the Holland of the *Provos*, intense in the Germany of the Sixties, and especially *mythopoietic* in 1968, French. Common to all of the global uprisings (from Brazil to Japan) was the widely extended rejection of authoritarianism, of all bureaucracies, of Marxist modernism and its proletarian dictatorship. The rebels, in general, bet on ideas and practices which took them much closer to those put forward by the socialist utopianists and anarchists: self-managed movements, prefigurative and assembly-based politics instead of the politics of representation; direct and participative democracy, extra-parliamentary struggle, etc.

The classical organizations of the working class, the mass unions and the workers' parties, entered a deep crisis with the proliferation of the new flows of subjectivities, desires and values. They would never recover. Before the start of the Sixties, this crisis could be seen coming. The horror of Stalinist crimes was made public with the arrival of Khrushchev to power in 1953. The Bolshevik aura was fading. And for many of the militants from the older generations, Stalinism was not a motive sufficient for further disillusion-ment; from the start of the Sixties, the tedium caused by political–unionist bureaucracies and different types of liberal authoritarianism (the school, factory, etc.) ended up making the counter-cultural politics and the old left-wing politics irreconcilable. *Post*-1989 marked the end of Real Socialism, but the beginning of the end should be looked for in the passage to political postmodernity from the Sixties.

The counter-cultural revolts of 1967/68/69 or 1977 were rebellions against 'disciplinarian society', against *panopticism*, its exclusions and its normali-zations: against marriage, psychiatrists, school and university, factories, jail, family, etc. (Foucault, 1984). These historical fissures meant the end of the (industrial) proletariat in as much as the privileged 'revolutionary subject' was concerned. The Sixties and the Seventies also meant the arrival of new battle fronts, and although its first expressions have been nationalized and disarmed, its final declinations (its *post*) remain alive and kicking today: feminism, anti-racism, pacifism, ecologism, *gay* movement turned to *queer*, etc. The anti-militarist and neo-utopian (in urban or rural squats) movements are also heirs of this period of struggle. All of these movements unify into a collage with – not excluding – the traditional working-class subjectivity:

working-class subjectivity is now nothing more than one component among various others; however, this subjectivity has done away with the old economic centrality which placed the rest of the causes under its monopoly. All these singularities now aspire to become a transversal federation; their articulations emanate from different antagonistic singularities without the predominance of any one of them or the subordination of any of the others.

In a certain way, this configuration mirrors what some have called the 'multitude' (Virno, 2003; Negri and Hardt, 2006). That is to say, the multitude is not just a social class but *a class and something more*, a composition of multiple incompatible singularities that, in order to persevere their singularity, must fuse horizontally and dynamically. Like a net. The rising of the *multitude* means that it won't be possible to construct a 'political subject' in the terms of the old identity, which imposed a central symbol (class, proletariat) and a practice of power which was in a position to explain the rest. Hereafter, the Movement will have to deal with a variety of powers which are combated by a multitude of desires and identities incompatible with the overarching unit. The multitude is always diverse and plural. A multiplicity of subjective leaks and counter-powers which embrace the feminist slogan 'the personal is political' to such an extent that it becomes impossible to locate political rivals *only* in the big institutions (state, school, etc.); power does not descend from these central institutions but rather emanates from a variety of directions. In the societies of accelerated media (Virilio, 1996), ploughed by endless migrant dispersion and *transcultural routes* (Clifford, 1999), a long and proliferating series of subjectivities and identities emerges. Intensely hybrid and heterogeneous societies and social movements. Multitude versus Mass. This heterogeneous multitude, in the same way that it is unable to permit a reduction in its singularities for the overarching unit, will not permit a reduction in its differences with the old unitary forms of the masses: the party, the union, and in the last instance, the state. The crisis of the *politics of representation*. The end of the masses, the birth of the multitude. The ambiguous flesh of the *multitude*: the anti-globalization movement, Reclaim the streets and the Critical Mass, the EZLN in Chiapas, the Parisian *banlieusards*, the Argentinian insurrection of 2001, the movement for free culture and free software, the *hackers*, the global protests against war, the assembly of migrants, the fight of the French against the First Job Contract in 2006, the Aymara movement before Evo Morales, the squatters, networks against frontiers and the 'climate action camps', etc. The step from mass politics to the politics of the multitude: the essence of the masses is indifference, their acting together under one representative bureaucracy (the political party or the one-big-union), their walking in unison, their vertical integration, even if only under the heading of direct democracy. The essence of the multitude is its form of network, their unyielding singularities under one sole flag and their disregard of representative politics. Crisis of representation. 'Qué se vayan todos!' – they shouted in Argentina. 'Not in our name' – shouted those opposed to the war in Iraq.

LINES OF FLIGHT AND EXCESSES

With the revolutions and transformations symbolized by the years '56–'68–'77–'89, and finally in 1999 one belonging to Seattle, the previous workerist period finalized. In the cycle of the workerist fights the political space was triangulated by three groups with monopolistic pretences: parties/state, corporations and mass labour unions. We said that in the workerist mode, the discourse forged itself through economic categories and that worker subjectivity subsumed the rest of subjectivities beneath the hegemonic relationship. Post-'68 changes it all. Subjectivities which had before been a minority become now the main characters in the antagonistic drama (feminist, ecologist, anti-racist, pacifist, indigenous subjectivities) and other emerging ones (*queer*, post-feminists, *hackers*). They all transformed the class composition with the emergence of a new set of multiple hegemonic figures: precarious and cognitarian workers, sex-related and 'feminized' labour, post-colonial positions and migrants status. The triangulation of the political space breaks with new invasion of new collective actors. A new way of doing politics appears, the *politics of the multitude*, daughter of the forms that emerged during the beginning of the postmodern caesura, that is, those extra-parliamentary and anti-imperialist fights of the Sixties and the fights of the Autonomy of the Seventies. In Seattle, a movement of the heterogeneous, decentralized, organized into a network form, comes onto the scene definitively.

At this new scene, the old hope of forming a massive labour union that would head a revolution no longer seems to make sense. The route of the revolution via the political party makes even less sense. The very idea of a revolution associated with parties had long before become obsolete. The virtual and present-day possibilities of the revolutionary syndicalism have got smaller and smaller and nothing can make us imagine that in the future its expectations will get better. With each great conflict that breaks out, labour unions (who are about as much revolutionaries as those integrated in the logics of control and command of capital!) are, time after time, surpassed. In these fights the workforce looks for and sometimes finds other forms of association, more in agreement with the times. The Argentina 'piquetes' and neighbourhood assemblies in 2001, the Brazilian Sem Terra movement or the Uruguayan housing cooperatives, the networks for Social Rights, such as the 'V de Vivienda' movement or the rise of Offices of Social Rights in Spain, the proliferation of squatters and rebel social centres, the Nomadic Universities and groups of self-management of knowledge are all examples of a new type of emergent *bio-syndicalism*. Syndicalism as such, that is, the bureaucratic syndicalism centred around the working-class subjectivity, will never be able to aspire to anything more than being just one more element, another small collective, of the revolutionary *collage*. (Let me make things clear. Although my political localization is closer to the bio-syndicalist forms, I do not believe that the period for antagonistic traditional labour unions has passed. I do not want to disqualify syndicalism or base syndicalism. My historic story limits itself to specify their present-day possibilities, which have been reduced to being one more element in the collage. And, in the same way, my story aims towards the need to update its old syndical structures, its forms of behaviour and its political theories. This *per se* could be said for the rest of the modern anarchist segments or anarchism in aggregate. *Anarchism reloaded.*)

As we have already said, it was the excesses and flights of antagonistic desire which caused the crisis of the classical leftist forms (anarchist or communist). Towards the end of the Seventies and the beginning of the Eighties, Félix Guattari and Michel Foucault tried to consider this caesura. Guattari defined a series of features of the new post-socialist struggles: (1) they will focus not only on quantitative features, rather they will call into question the purposes of work, leisure and culture, and they will politicize the everyday and domestic life; (2) they will no longer be focused around the industrial-qualified-white-masculine-adult-classes; (3) they will not focus on a political party, a labour union or a vanguard; (4) they will not become centred inside the national scene, rather they will happen globally; (5) they will not focus on only one theoretical corpus; (6) they will refuse the departmentation between exchange values, use values and desiring values (Guattari, 2004: 56–7). Foucault emphasised another series of features. Among others, for example, the importance of fighting against the forms of power/knowledge (the fight of the patients against medical or pharmaceutical-industry authority). I believe that all these features remain valid.

We are surrounded by a multitude of excesses. Global migration, as a consequence of the repression of desire on the part of worldwide geopolitics, is creating excesses which flow against the restrictions of state-owned space, of the national citizenship and governamentality, while at the same time it weaves and spreads trans-cultural routes that surpass nationalistic desires of purity everywhere. Excesses always imply the creation of a crisis in the capturing dispositives of subjectivities, of the institution that they exceed, of the concept or the desire that they exceed. The crisis is an ambiguous moment that is debated between two poles. A *carcinogenic pole* in which the excess of the body is turned against itself, that turns it into a black hole (the *sadness* in Spinoza's philosophy), and a *delirious pole* that reinvents the body (Spinozian *joy*). The migrant excess is debated between a point of fascist reaction and another one characterized by the smooth space of the global citizenship, the suppression of the frontiers and the joyful affirmation of crossbreeding. The same thing happens with the excess in sexes and sexualities. Transsexuals create alternative sexes, but their real importance goes further: they create the possibility of considering that which is sexual in several terms of biological moralism (nature/anti-natural). A transsexual is always a techno-nature-culture, that is, *a cyborg.* The transsexual is the new figure and symbol of the embodiment in the era of cyberspace, the biotechnology, the techno-political production of bodies, sexes and genres (implants, operations, hormones and synthetic oestrogens, etc.). We are all *cyborg. Cyberpunk* capitalism. The *trans* and *cyborg-becomings*, in their excess of dichotomies such as human/machine, human/animal, man/woman, homo/hetero, demand us to redefine our sexual, scientific, ecological and gender politics.

In this day and age in which the old left wing sees nothing more than the 'ruins and defeats' of that which was once revolutionary possibilities, their eyes still brimming with tears for the end of the working-class period, they are not able to understand the possibilities of the excesses that surround us, those that were produced in the antagonistic flights and fights. We commented on the lines of flight related to sex and sexuality and we mentioned the excesses relative to the molarity of gender. Hand in hand with that which is *queer*, the (post-)feminist theories, instead of defending a natural sex beneath the culturally constructed gender, radically deconstruct the sex/gender relation. They understand that by nature there is neither masculinity nor femininity, neither man nor human, but rather that these categories are politically, culturally and technologically elaborated, and that in the same way that they were produced, can be reconstructed and converted into something different. A good example of this would be the queer and post-feminist Judith Butler's position (2006) and Donna Haraway's work (1995), with her allegations in favour of a *cyborg* feminism, with which the barriers between science and politics, or that which is human and that which is non-human, implode and articulate themselves and politicize themselves in innovative ways.

The Great Refusal in the Sixties (Marcuse, 1984), which put in check the institutions of the disciplinary and puritan society, still today has consequences that are shown in 'the crisis of authority at school', in the 'crisis of the family', in the 'crisis of the paternal figure', etc. – also in the democracy crisis, given that the new social movements have moved away from representative politics and no longer accept unitary representatives who act as spokespeople on behalf of the 'masses'. The movements have forged their own space where they can exercise and reinvent their own politics; a space that expresses a true political excess.

The lines of flight projected by the molecular, social and cultural revolutions have bequeathed a whole galaxy of possible worlds to us. In recent years we have seen other excesses emerging. The productivity of the multitude also exceeds the dispositives of contemporary capitalism. A valid example of that cybernetic excess is 'piracy', the free software movement, free cooperation of brains and the free culture to share: excess and exodus from the economical mechanisms of capture. All of this is, without any doubt, made good use of by certain cyber-companies to gain ample profits. That's the case with YouTube, or that whole host of companies that profited greatly thanks to Linux (magazines, technical services, etc.). However, piracy and free software also suppose a big movement of exodus from the capitalistic control dispositives. Such excess once again challenges that which classical socialism began to make problematic: private property. The *copyleft* movement (Creative Commons, etc.) supposes an interesting attempt to constitute, with the general flight of piracy, a political vector.

To enumerate all the present-day flights and exoduses would be a task of encyclopaedic volume, a vast work above and beyond the possibilities of a chapter like this and also, of course, above and beyond my capacities. I am aware of some of the errors that I am committing. One of them is to part from and scarcely try to leave behind my own localization. This account is also 'Western', to give it a name of sorts. However, it is important to take into account that lines of flight happen everywhere, throughout the world, each with its own singularity according to its geopolitical and subjective *localization*. In fact, many of the most powerful expressions can be found outside of what might be labelled 'Western'. The indigenous movements, for example, are innovating (post)modern alternatives everywhere. The European localization in which this article is more or less located has left to one side the experiences on a global level that are most interesting, such as the experiences which take place, for example, in all those 'down-and-to-the-left' antagonistic South American subjectivities, 'anonymous' behind the balaclavas in the jungles and the neighbourhoods. But also on other continents. From the Marxist tradition they have studied these movements profusely through subaltern studies and post-colonial studies. Over the past years, a series of contributions has been put forward which tries to consider anarchist politics from an angle that is not centred on European knowledge and situations (see for example, Adams, 2009; Evren, 2008; Mbah and Igariwey, 2000; Alston, 2003).

In the world today, there is *much more than ruins*. The issue, now, as Hakim Bey has said, is picking up from where the anti-colonial movements, the counter-cultural movements of the Sixties and the Autonomous movements of the Seventies and Eighties left off. This is to achieve accomplishments that are *post*-1968, *post*-1977, and, above all, *post*-1989. The first promising sparks express themselves in (1) the proliferation of a political autonomous space, independent of state politics and para-state institutions (that is to say, independent of NGOs and labour unions integrated into governmentality); (2) the explosion of the first cycle of the global *becoming* of fights that took place during last decade; (3) the whole set of new theoretic enunciations thus far commented on, although they cannot be named by themselves (post-structuralism, post-feminism, post-Marxism, post-anarchism, etc.). The three elements point at several passages towards postmodernity: space postmoderni-zation, political passage to postmodernity, postmodernization of the discourse of the desiring and antagonistic politics.

Finally in our enumeration of the lines of flight and the excesses that we encounter like political first-rate challenges we should recognize that the *agencement* of the fights for a proper autonomous/global space requires today more than ever an articulation with ecological problems. A new transversal and non-natural ecologism (beyond nature/culture dichotomy and essentialism) is needed to articulate the environmental, psychological and social ecologies and to do so in terms of constituent power and the molecular revolutions of desire (Guattari, 1990). Such a proposal, intimately enchanted by creativity, will have to interchange the madness of the industrial productionism for a new *poietical* ethic (*desirepolitik*) and an ecological material *poiesis* (innovating convivial relations with the rest of the biospheric bodies).

ANARCHY *RELOADED*

We have rejected the utopian projection of anarchism, and also its concept of revolution. We have rejected the logic of the possibility/realization pair, and the idea of 'human nature' on which it was founded. We could legitimately ask what is left of anarchism after the criticism and the reinvention that is offered in this article. In a recent book, Benedict Anderson wrote:

> Following the collapse of the First International, and Marx's death in 1883, anarchism, in its characteristically variegated forms, was the dominant element in the self-consciously internationalist radical Left. It was not merely that in Kropotkin [...] and Malatesta [...] anarchism produced a persuasive philosopher and colorful, charismatic activist-leader from younger generation, not matched by mainstream Marxism. Notwithstanding the towering edifice of Marx's thought, from which anarchism often borrowed, the movement did not disdain peasants and agricultural laborers in an age when serious industrial proletariats were mainly confined to Northern Europe. It was open to 'bourgeois' writers and artists – in the name of individual freedom – [which,] in those days, institutional Marxism was not. Just as hostile to imperialism, it had no theoretical prejudices against 'small' and 'ahistorical' nationalism, including those in the colonial world. Anarchists were also quicker to capitalize on the vast transoceanic migrations of the era. Malatesta spent four years in Buenos Aires – something inconceivable for Marx or Engels, who never left Western Europe. May Day celebrates the memory of immigrant anarchists – not Marxists – executed in the United States in 1887. (Anderson, 2007: 2)

The anarchism of the end of the nineteenth century has often been depicted under the image of the *propaganda par le fait* ('propaganda of the deed').[2] It goes without saying that I refuse this political practice. What I vindicate is this youth, this opening, and this will to articulate with the different subjectivities and cultural global expressions that Anderson indicates, and that now more than ever, in postmodernity, are necessary for a revolutionary *desirepolitik*. Without this articulation nothing is possible. In like manner, its anti-authoritative spirit of anarchism remains present throughout this narrative. The criticism of capitalism too. However, it would also be correct to suggest than *post*-anarchism is no longer *stricto senso* anarchism. The same is true of post-Marxism. Curiously, *post*-Marxism sometimes re-vindicates the kind of anarchism Anderson was talking about. In short, Negri and Hardt vindicate the legacy of the Wobblies (the IWW) of the early twentieth century. Negri and Hardt vindicate its opening toward migrants, its organizational dynamism and its first experiments with a kind of networking organization. Nowadays, *post*-anarchism and *post*-Marxism tend to converge. In my opinion, both the post-anarchists (May, 1994; Call, 2002; Newman, 2001, etc., etc.) and the post-Marxists alike, at least those that I have cited up to this point (Negri, Haraway, Lazzarato, Guattari), coincide on two issues: the redefinition of revolution in terms of the event, a revolution without utopia, and the defence of practices and political forms that can be summarized under the term *multitude*.

Post-anarchism (or Acracia 2.0) is, and at the same time is not, anarchist. It is no longer what it used to be, although it owes a lot to that past. Just as the post-socialist revolution has to redefine itself in terms of the event and the constituent power, now anarchy has to redefine itself also in terms of *multitude*. Starting from the dispute between Hobbes and Spinoza, authors such as Antonio Negri and Paolo Virno have defined the *multitude* as a form opposed to the people. The multitude is a set of singularities that persevere as singularities during their political and productive exercise. The multitude is a *garden of peculiarities* (Sepúlveda, 2002). The Hobbesian 'people' deals with the reduction of this multiplicity down to One. The One: The monarch, Sovereignty, the General Will, etc. If democracy implies the reduction of this multiplicity under the representation of the One, 'only acracy is constituted in the social body like the procedure which guarantees the material conditions of deliberation, participation and decision that the politics of the movement needs' (Viejo, 2005: 114). In this sense, and only in this sense, that is, in terms of the constituent power of the multitude, 'acracy was, is and will continue to be the political regime of communism' (ibid.). Both, post-anarchism and post-communism, now go hand in hand under their respective postmodern forms. To tell them apart is almost impossible, because as many differences exist *within* the two categories as between them.

We live in a moment of transition. Rather than the end of metanarratives, it can be confirmed that postmodernity is the frenetic place of post-socialist mitopoietic simmering. Still, we cannot give ourselves new names. We are *post* and we are *anti*. But this nihilism is active, although not as much as is wanted. It affirms its new values again and again, at the time that the walls of Rome are falling apart. If we are no longer what we were, why do we defend something like post-anarchism? For strategic purposes. I prefer the label 'post-anarchism' to a simple anarchist label (without adjectives, and a prefix) because it localizes us during a period of transition. Post-anarchism is an excess of anarchism. Anarchy 2.0. *Intermezzo* politics. Post-anarchism flights and deterritorializes its forefathers, but without stopping to recognize its kinship.

Rather than a fixed status, with this expression we refer to a flow of intensities. A never-ending route. Also, a de/re/construction that, at the same time, preserves what the old meaning still has of its symbolic force, and reformulates it to take it to the other side. *Postmodernity* is an *intermezzo*. Post-anarchism is being *in-between*, with one foot in the dying world and the other in the world that is coming. It should not be understood as a mere conjunction of anarchism plus post-structuralism alone, no matter how much it drinks from both fountains. Rather, it is a flag around which to express the desire to transcend the old casts, of *becoming-other* and of procuring our bodies in the virtual and actual flow of the eternal antagonistic differentiation. Leaving behind the world that abandons us, with all our hagiographies and relics, in order to create new worlds through the actual unfolding of virtual possibilities. To follow lines of flight and to recombine them with friendly *others* to innovate excesses to come. *Reloading movement*. Galloping on smooth plateaus and between sharp wire fences of that which is common to everyday routines. That is what it means today: the *joy* of being an 'anarchist'.

NOTES

1. Translated from Spanish by Salome Rebunal and Duane Rousselle.
2. 'Propaganda of the deed' entailed physical violence against the state and/or bourgeoisies as a way to inspire revolt amongst the working class.

REFERENCES

Adams, Jason (2009). 'Non-Western Anarchism: Rethinking the Global Context'. Retrieved 22 December 2009 from <http://raforum.info/article.php3?id_article=3229>.
Alston, Ashanti (2003). 'Towards a Vibrant and Broad African-Based Anarchism'. *New Formulation* 2(1). Retrieved 22 December 2009 from <http://www.newformulation. org/3alston.htm>.
Anderson, Benedict (2007). *Under Three Flags: Anarchism and the Anti-Colonial Imagination*. New York: Verso.
Bhabha, Homi (2002). *El lugar de la cultura*. Buenos Aires: Manantial.
Butler, Judith (2006). *Deshacer el género*. Barcelona: Paidós.
Call, Lewis (2002). *Post-Modern Anarchism*. Lanham, MD: Lexington Books.
Clifford, James (1999). *Itinerarios transculturales*. Barcelona: Gedisa.
Evren, Süreyyya (2008) 'Postanarchism and the Third World'. In Antón F. de Rota (ed.). *Antologia de Postanarquismo*. Barcelona: Wordpress (in press).
Foucault, Michel (1984). *Vigilar y castigar*. Madrid: Siglo XXI.
Guattari, Félix (2004). *Plan sobre el planeta*. Madrid: Traficantes de Sueños.
—— (1990). *Las tres ecologías*. Valencia: Pre-Textos.
Haraway, Donna (1995). *Ciencia, cyborgs y mujeres*. Madrid: Cátedra.
Marcuse, Herbert (1984) [1955]. *Eros y civilización*. Barcelona: Ariel.
May, Todd (1994). *The Political Philosophy of Poststructuralist Anarchism*. University Park, PA: The Pennsylvania State University.
Mbah, Sam, and Igariwey, I.E. (2000). *África rebelde: Comunalismo y anarquismo en Nigeria*. Barcelona: Alikornio.
Negri, Antonio, and Hardt, Michael (2006). *Multitud*. Barcelona: Debolsillo.
Newman, Saul (2001). *From Bakunin to Lacan*. Lanham, MD: Lexington Books.
Roszak, Theodore (1973). *El nacimiento de una contracultura*. Barcelona: Kairós.
Sepúlveda, Jesús (2002). *El jardín de las peculiaridades*. Buenos Aires: Ediciones del Leopardo.
Viejo Viñas, Raimundo (2005). 'Del 11-S al 15-F y después: Por una gramática del movimiento ante la guerra global permanente'. In José Angel Brandariz and Jaime Pastor (eds). *Guerra global permanente*. Madrid: Catarata.
Virilio, Paul (1996). *El arte del motor*. Buenos Aires: Manantial.
Virno, Paolo (2003). *Gramática de la multitud*. Madrid: Traficantes de sueños.

Part 3
Classical Anarchism Reloaded

9
Things to Do with Post-Structuralism in a Life of Anarchy: Relocating the Outpost of Post-Anarchism

Sandra Jeppesen

In the cultural production of anarchism, a variety of interrelated anti-authoritarian practices are important. These practices are informed, directly or indirectly, by post-structuralism, and post-structuralism has also been and continues to be influenced by contemporary anarchism. The two are coextensive in a variety of heterogeneous ways. Post-structuralist anarchist writers such as Todd May, Saul Newman and others bring them together, but their work has been limited to the Eurocentric masculine sphere – writers that include Deleuze and Guattari, Lacan, Derrida, Foucault and the like, as well as the 'classical anarchists', including Proudhon, Bakunin and Kropotkin. Nonetheless post-structuralism also includes theorists of gender, sexuality, race and nation. Judith Butler, for example, deconstructs the gender/sex binary extensively in *Gender Trouble*; Eve Sedgwick introduced Queer Theory into post-structuralist thought in *Epistemology of the Closet*; Gloria Anzaldua deconstructs borders of identity, nation state and language as extensions of post-structuralism in *Borderlands/La frontera*; Gayatri Spivak deconstructs the colonial aspects of silence and voice in 'Can the Subaltern Speak?'; and bell hooks deconstructs the category of woman with respect to racialized groups, particularly black people in the United States, in *Ain't I a Woman*. These are all important post-structuralist thinkers who may be read by anarchists.

Furthermore, contemporary anarchist theory has moved beyond nineteenth-century anarchism. Theorists in this category comprise a wide range of global thinkers and activists who again are not just straight/white/middle-class/male, including Cindy Milstein, Jamie Heckert, Ashanti Alston, Lorenzo Erven, and many more, to be discussed below.

The omission of issues such as anarcha-feminism, black anarchism, queer anarchism, disability anarchism, etc. from post-anarchist theorizing, as well as the omission of such a multiplicitous range of theorists (contemporary post-structuralist white and non-white women writers, and both historical and contemporary anarcha-feminists and/or anti-racists, etc.) results in a serious misrepresentation of both post-structuralist and anarchist philosophy theory and practice in contemporary times.

Furthermore, among anarchists there are many 'organic intellectuals' who produce theory and action in written and dialogical texts that are not primarily academic, including zines, blogs, workshops, teach-ins, counter-summits, indymedia web sites, and other anarchist spaces. I would argue that this work is also informed by and important to the formation of post-structuralism. Thus, in considering post-anarchist theory, we need to extend the spaces that we investigate as post-anarchist or we risk seeing only a partial picture that looks neither beyond the male European classical anarchists to contemporary anarchist thinkers, including anarcha-feminists and/or queer anarchists and/ or anarchists of colour, nor beyond the male European post-structuralists to a wide range of feminist, queer, post-colonial and/or anti-racist post-structuralist thinkers, nor at current social movements in which anarchists are playing agenda-setting roles.

All of that being said, in this short chapter I can only present a preliminary broad survey of what might be included in an in-depth consideration of anarchist culture and its admixture with post-structuralism. What I will do here is to suggest some starting points for investigation, including texts, events and theorists, if post-anarchist theory is to be relevant to post-structuralism taken more broadly and to anarchy as it is theorized and practised in the streets today.

Axiom X. Anarchism Is Not a White Movement

To ask better questions about anarchist organizing in relation to racialized groups, we might turn to an article by Elizabeth Martinez called 'Where was the color in Seattle?', first printed in *ColorLines* and reprinted in *Colours of Resistance* zine. Martinez suggests that white people need to unlearn the condescending ways in which they have typically attempted to organize people of colour, and move toward an understanding of the notion of organizing 'with'. Making anarchist groups relevant to people of colour by taking on anti-racist organizing projects, and taking leadership from people of colour in their own struggles are two concrete suggestions.

As anti-racists we need to take a global perspective. There are broad networks of anarchist movements all over the world which have not followed Euro-American anarchism, but have developed their own struggles, theorists and actions. Jason Adams' zine *Non-Western Anarchisms* presents a historical analysis of the development of anarchism in many disparate countries. The assumption among (white) anarchists that anarchism is a white-dominated movement tends to be a racist assumption at worst, or at best a kind of self-absorbed inability to see beyond whiteness into the broader global anarchist movement. That said, some Western anarchist groups are white-dominated, and certainly this is an issue that needs to be addressed.

Axiom 6. Anarchism Is Not a Movement of Two-Gendered Heterosexual Monogamy

Historical anarcha-feminists such as Emma Goldman and Voltairine de Cleyre put gender roles, sex, free love, non-monogamy, birth control, sex work, relationships and bodies on the anarchist political agenda a century ago. Anarcha-feminism has grown since then to include queer anarchy, and radical gender queer anarchists play key roles in anarchist organizing. Beyond the regular set of socially constructed binaries that post-structuralist feminists deconstruct, including sex (male/female), gender (masculine/feminine), and sexuality (heterosexual/homosexual), anarchist sexuality includes non-monogamy, polyamory and radical monogamy. Bodies themselves can be pangender, transgender, intersex, trans-sexual and other forms beyond cis-gendered or cis-sexed. In anarchism there is a whole range of new sex/gender/sexuality categories of resistance, and/or resistances to categorization, two different ways of approaching intersectionality. Much sex/gender/sexuality/queer theory derives from post-structuralism.

Axiom de. Anarchism Is a Movement toward Decolonization

If post-colonialism is a theoretical terrain that, in at least some of its forms, theorizes contemporary struggles for decolonization, then the indigenous sovereignty struggles of Turtle Island (aka North America) may be seen as one aspect of its practice. Anarchists have formed alliances with indigenous struggles for self-determination in places such as Grassy Narrows, Cold Lake, Six Nations, Kanehsatake, Akwesasne and Tyendinega. To take one example, in Akwesasne, a territory that spans the US/Canada border, indigenous people have been fighting against the arming of Canada Border Services Agency guards because they do not believe in the existence of a border between two other nations superimposed on indigenous land. Anarchists, as part of the Indigenous Solidarity Group within PGA-bloc (People's Global Action) in Montreal are working with indigenous people in this struggle, by participating in protests, organizing public forums, and other solidarity actions. The indigenous self-determination movement is consistent with anarchist anti-state politics and the commitment to self-determination and collective autonomy for all.

Globally, there are other movements for decolonization and to end occupations, such as the Free Palestine movement in Palestine–Israel, where a group called Anarchists Against the Wall is organizing against the apartheid walls that are being built explicitly to prevent, disrupt and control the movement of Palestinians. Anarchists are actively involved in Boycott, Divestment and Sanctions (BDS) organizing against Israeli apartheid, putting on events such as Israeli Apartheid Week in cities across Canada.

Colonization and occupation takes place in the context of gender. Gayatri Spivak is a feminist post-structuralist post-colonial writer who is widely read by anarchists, particularly anarcha-feminists, as she links post-colonialism with women's struggles, asking the question (in the context of India): 'Can the subaltern speak?' The linking of voice to power comes from Foucault's analysis of discourse and power, Derrida's analysis of writing and speaking as absence and presence, and many feminist analyses of the importance of self-representation to self-empowerment and ultimately self-determination. Edward Said, in *Orientalism*, also poses questions around Western constructions of the East, or what Spivak calls the subaltern, through cultural colonization and a lack of self-representation in scholarship and research. Post-structuralist anarchism needs to engage this kind of intersectional analysis of decolonization as it is taken up in contemporary social movements involving indigenous and other non-white anarchists.

Axiom a. Anarchy Is Not a Movement of Able-Bodied, Healthy-Minded Folks

Disabled and differently-abled folks, both in body and in mind, play an important role in anarchist organizing. Health and wellness, including mental health, need to be redefined to eliminate disempowering assumptions of normativity. Health and wellness need to be things we are all working toward, and that we mutually support each other in achieving, regardless of our ability levels, mental health issues, allergies, etc.

Disability anarchist activists draw attention to the fact that we all have disabilities. None of us is perfectly physically or mentally healthy every day of our lives. Many of us hide our disabilities because the world does not accept them and will make our lives more difficult for us than the disability itself. In other words, the barriers to full participation caused by disabilities are the fault of infrastructure and other people's attitudes more often than they are the result of a physical or mental disability. For example, people who use wheelchairs could easily get to a job if the transit, buildings, walkways, taxis, public washrooms, and other public spaces were fully accommodated to wheelchairs. Furthermore, people with anxiety attacks, panic disorders and other post-traumatic behaviours would not be so freaked out if the people around them had an understanding of what this means and could help them through it, rather than tasering them, as the police do regularly, or making the assumption that the person is therefore incapacitated, dysfunctional, not intelligent, unable to work, etc.

Axiom ⅃. Anarchism Is Not a New Type of Marxism

Anarchists made a break from Marxism when Bakunin was ejected from the First International. Bakunin's controversial proposition was that not just capitalism but also the state should be a site of political critique and action. Seizing state power would simply replicate relations of domination, whereas organizations and institutions, for Bakunin, needed to be shifted, decentralized, and regrouped into federations. This was looked upon poorly by the Communists, who executed many anarchists after the Russian revolution, including Nestor Makhno, who was organizing workers' collectives in the Ukraine. Anarchism, however, is not the poor underachieving little sister of Marxism.

Axiom ⅃+. Anarchy Is Not about the Worker

Anarchist class politics tend to focus on anti-poverty issues rather than labour or the working class. Many anarchists live by squatting, shoplifting, table-diving, dumpstering, in precarious work and/or housing situations. This is what anarchists have started to theorize and practice as precarity activism, activism against the precarity of housing work, legality, sexuality, ecology, bodies, social relationships, financial stability, geographical mobility, forced migration, criminalization and the like, while also claiming social space in the public sphere for precarious subjectivities in self-determination. While these spaces are sometimes concerned with the precarity of work, they are not wrapped up in the identity of being a worker *per se*, as so many other aspects of the lives of precarious subjectivities are at stake, and these aspects are intertwined and mutually defining, not dependent on the overarching aspect of work.

Axiom *11*. Anarchism Is Not a Men's Movement (That's Capitalism)

Anarchism is a movement full of women. Strong women, feisty women, women committed to struggle. Women who might go to the fence and withstand tear gas, police brutality, rubber bullets, pepper spray and keep on fighting. Women who might freight hop, build houses, hitchhike, have multiple partners, and sometimes also keep the home fires burning or take care of children, each other and each other's children. In meetings women listen carefully as people speak, build consensus, share resources, speak their minds. Sometimes anarchist women are wymyn or womyn or wimmin, taking a cue from radical feminism, removing 'men' from the word itself so that it is not a diminutive.

Anarchist theory will have to include intersectional anarcha-feminism, and not as an afterthought or an additional chapter (like, Oops! Almost forgot the women/queers/people of colour/indigenous peoples/people with disabilities) but in understanding the crucial role women (queers/people of colour/indigenous peoples/people with disabilities) play in anarchist organizing structures, theoretical development, direct action tactics, anti-oppression commitments, cultural production, etc.

Axiom *&*. Anarchists Use Language Differently

The awareness of language and how language constructs the possible, determines norms and constrains our lives in so many ways, which Guattari identifies as 'semiotic subjugation', is strong in anarchist circles. In our day-to-day lives, anarchists use language differently. Examples abound. We use the term 'regular' when we mean that the way a person is being is okay, instead of the term 'normal' with the oppressive psychoanalytical discourse of normativity it implies. As we have seen above, we use the term 'queer' as a positive term to imply gender revolutionaries, turning it from its original usage to mean weird or eccentric, although that might also be included and reclaimed in the term. Indeed, anarchists reject norms, as we have seen, and this applies to body norms as well, in terms of body configurations, shapes and sizes. There are also words that apply to things that we do and who we are in relation to others, both of which are radically transformed practices by anarchists. We use the word 'spectacular' not to mean that something was really great, but exactly the opposite, drawing the meaning from the Situationists (more French theorists who were also political activists) – we often suggest that it was all just a big recuperated spectacle with no possibility of participation by regular folks.

Axiom ~. Anarchy Is about Cultural Production

Anarchists make things, things that are not theory and not practice. Anarchists make art, and might even send it off travelling around the country, like the Drawing Resistance art show that travelled like a punk band around the United States in a tour bus. Anarchists make zines and comix and trade them with other anarchists, or sell them at book fairs for a nominal fee. Anarchists anthologize, so that the privilege of publication is de-hierarchicalized, in books like *Drunken Boat, Resist!, Quiet Rumors, Our Culture Our Resistance* or *Only a Beginning.* Anarchists write poetry and read it out loud to their friends as bedtime stories or around the campfire, or in public black cat cafes, punk shows, Reclaim the Streets, community festivals or radical readings. Anarchists write stories about struggles for political and personal freedom. Bourdieu's notion of consecration by the avant-garde is of interest here in that anarchists are often engaged in avant-garde experimental art production.

Axiom ^. Anarchy Is Not a Protest Movement

The anarchist movement today is in no way reducible to the so-called anti-globalization movement, nor is that the space from which it has emerged, nor does it seek to be a central player in it. Anarchy is not about confronting the centralized leadership of the World Bank or the American government or the European Union, although anarchists might choose to participate in protests against these forms of oppression and domination. But anarchist movements are not about protest: anarchists do not concede power to anyone and are not concerned with becoming involved in negotiating the terms of our own oppression by being incorporated into the decision-making processes of the International Monetary Fund or the Free Trade Area of the Americas.

When anarchists do protest, we do not accept the state directives on how to protest ('How to be a Good Protester', by Bill Clinton), rather we protest on our own terms. This is called direct action. It is not a form of protest, it is a way of life.

Axiom >2. Anarchism Is Not Violent/Non-Violent, Nor Is It Legal/Illegal

Post-structuralism can be helpful here in deconstructing the legal/illegal and violent/non-violent binaries. Peter Gelderloos, in his book *How Non-violence Protests the State*, argues that it is not easy to define what is violent and what is non-violent, but that nonetheless this discourse has been mobilized by some activists or protesters in favour of 'non-violent direct action' to in effect demobilize activists and limit their tactics. In the organizing that led up to the Quebec City anti-FTAA protests, instead of violence versus non-violence, this debate was framed as a 'diversity of tactics'. People who wanted to engage in festival-like modes of protest including theatre and puppets were accommodated in the 'green' zone, non-violent direct action such as sitting street blockades took place in the 'yellow' zone, and unconstrained direct action took place in the highly mobile 'red' zone. The division of these diverse tactics into three zones shows already that the violent/non-violent debate is a false binary. This issue has also been written about in other contexts by academics such as Ward Churchill, for example, in *Pacifism as Pathology*, where he argues in favour of armed struggle as a possible tactic of decolonization, or Frantz Fanon, who similarly argued for 'violent' tactics as an appropriate response to the systemic physical, emotional and mental violence of poverty and colonization as experienced in countries such as Algeria. Theories (from post-structuralism) that challenge binaries sit comfortably side by side with activism and activist thinkers.

Axiom E. Anarchy Is about Events

Anarchists organize events, in fact we organize literally thousands of events every year, from street parties to theatre productions, from book fairs to jail and court solidarity, from film screenings to book launches to urban direct-action protests to rural-logging road blockades. Anarchists make things happen. They burn things down, they blow things up, they shut things down, they build things, they interact and participate. Temporary autonomous zones, radical gatherings, anarchist book and freedom fairs, anarchist soccer games, anarchist street parties – these events are our lives, and they change our lives. We become participants rather than consumers. We meet fellow life participants with whom to share in these events, with whom to share our lives. Anarchist theory must consider the importance of these kinds of events and texts in shaping anarchist culture, theory and practice.

Axiom undo. Anarchism Is about Unlearning

Anarchist organizing, like all radical organizing, and indeed all of society, is rife with internal oppressions. We have all internalized modes of domination, which we unwittingly use in our daily interactions with each other, from being raised in a racist, capitalist, sexist, heterosexist, ableist society that teaches us how to exercise power over each other in order to get what we want. We need to unlearn all of this. Unlearning is a lifelong process. Many of the things we need to unlearn come to us in binaries such as those that have been deconstructed above. But post-structuralist thinkers also take on issues critical to unlearning and rebuilding, crucial to what I call social sustainability, such as friendship, revolutionizing poetic language, unlearning racism, sexism, heteronormativity and ableism, and living in loving respectful relationships.

These axioms are not comprehensive, nor are they any kind of directive. Rather they are just a few observations about the multiplicities of anarchy in practice and their relationship with post-structuralism. They are also a call to all anarchists and post-structuralists to keep thinking/feeling about these things, to write your thoughts/feelings down and make this wealth of material that we live available to each other in cultural forms.

Each anarchist text, event and debate challenges hegemonic cultural production through a reorganization of practices. Several characteristics of anti-authoritarian cultural practice emerge, including: social relationships that are anti-hierarchical and transformative; mutual accountability among texts and actions and community; the destabilization of binaries (producer/consumer, writer/reader, legal/illegal, violent/non-violent, personal/political) into heterogeneous connected multiplicities; anti-authoritarian non-professional authorship; collective production and distribution; distancing from capitalism; and the elimination of mediation.

None of the struggles or ideas I have outlined occurs independently of the others; rather they are all interrelated nodes in a rhizomatic network. Furthermore, there should be as many theorists as possible, working together or separately; indeed every person is a theorist of anarchy, which they express as they put their ideas and beliefs into transformative social, political and cultural action. These debates must also continue in oral form, at teach-ins, reading groups, radical gatherings, anarchist conferences, kitchen tables, pot-luck dinners, book fairs, workshops, bike-repair spaces and anarchist free schools.

With so many potential theorists, there should also be as many anarchist theories as possible. We might say that there is a lot of work to be done, but, following Barthes and Heckert, let's say instead that there is a lot of play to be done. Anarchist theory, like anarchist practice, at its rhizomatic roots, is about play. From playing anarchist soccer to sex and gender play and playing with words to playing with a diversity of tactics, playing with the legalities of border-crossings, or playing with fire – play has always been an anti-authoritarian practice.

FURTHER READING

Adams, Jason. *Non-Western Anarchisms: Rethinking the Global Context*. Johannesburg: Zabalaza, 2001
Alston, Ashanti. *Anarchist Panther*. Self-published, n.d.
Anzaldua, Gloria. *Borderlands/La frontera*. San Francisco: Aunt Lute Books, 1999.
bell hooks. *All about Love: New Visions*. New York: William Morrow, 2000.
Blechman, Max (ed.). *Drunken Boat: Art Rebellion Anarchy*. New York: Autonomedia, 1994.
Block, Diana. *Arm the Spirit: A Woman's Journey Underground and Back*. San Francisco: AK Press, 2009.
Brown, L. Susan. 'Beyond Feminism: Anarchism and Human Freedom'. In Howard J. Ehrlich (ed.). *Reinventing Anarchy, Again*. San Francisco: AK Press, 1996.
Butler, Judith. *Gender Trouble*. New York: Routledge, 1990.
—— *Bodies that Matter*. New York: Routledge, 1993.
Churchill, Ward. *A Little Matter of Genocide: Holocaust and Denial in the Americas, 1492 to the Present*. City Lights, 1998.
—— *Pacifism as Pathology: Reflections on the Role of Armed Struggle in North America*. Winnipeg: Arbeiter Ring, 1998.
Cohn, Jesse, and Shawn P. Wilbur. 'What's Wrong with Postanarchism?' <http://www.anarchist-studies.org/publications/theory_politics>.
Colors of Resistance Collective. *Colors of Resistance* (zine). Self-published, 2000. <http://zinelibrary.info/colours-resistance>.
CrimethInc. *Days of War, Nights of Love: Crimethink for Beginners*. Olympia: CrimethInc, 2000. Workers' collective.
Dark Star Collective (ed.). *Quiet Rumours: An Anarcha-Feminist Reader*. San Francisco: AK Press, 2002.

Deleuze, Gilles, and Félix Guattari. *A Thousand Plateaus: Capitalism and Schizophrenia, vol. 2.* Minneapolis: University of Minnesota Press, 1987.

Dunbar-Ortiz, Roxanne. *Outlaw Woman: A Memoir of the War Years 1960–1975.* San Francisco: City Lights, 2002.

Ehrlich, Howard J. (ed.). *Reinventing Anarchy, Again.* San Francisco: AK Press, 1996.

Ervin, Lorenzo Komboa. *Anarchism and the Black Revolution.* Toronto: Third Force Pirate Editions, 2005.

Fanon, Frantz. *The Wretched of the Earth.* New York: Grove, 1968.

Gelderloos, Peter. *How Nonviolence Protects the State.* Boston: South End Press, 2007.

Goldman, Emma. *Living My Life, vols 1 and 2.* New York: Dover, 1970 [1931].

—— *Anarchism and Other Essays.* New York: Dover, 1969 [1917].

Guattari, Félix. *Soft Subversions.* New York: Semiotext(e), 1996.

—— *Chaosophy.* New York: Semiotext(e), 1995.

Hansen, Ann. *Direct Action: Memoirs of an Urban Guerrilla.* Toronto: Between the Lines, 2001.

Heckert, Jamie. 'Sexuality/Identity/Politics'. In Jonathan Purkis and James Bowen (eds). *Changing Anarchism: Anarchist Theory and Practice in a Global Age.* Manchester: Manchester University Press, 2004.

—— *Ain't I a Woman: Black Women and Feminism.* Boston: South End Press, 1981.

Leeder, Elaine. 'Let Our Mothers Show the Way'. In Howard J. Ehrlich (ed.). *Reinventing Anarchy, Again.* San Francisco: AK Press, 1996.

Martinez, Elizabeth (Betita). 'Where Was the Color in Seattle?' *Color Lines* 3(1). Spring 2000.

May, Todd. *The Political Philosophy of Poststructuralist Anarchism.* Pittsburgh: Pennsylvania State University Press, 1994.

McCann, Anthony. 'I Always-Already Make a Difference'. <http://www.anthonymccann.com/craftinggentleness.html>.

McQuinn, Jason. 'Post-Left Anarchy: Leaving the Left Behind'. <http://theanarchistlibrary.org/HTML/Jason_McQuinn__Post-Left_Anarchy__Leaving_the_Left_Behind.html>.

Newman, Saul. 'The Politics of Postanarchism'. <http://theanarchistlibrary.org/HTML/Saul_Newman__The_Politics_of_Postanarchism.html>.

—— *From Bakunin to Lacan: Anti-Authoritarianism and the Dislocation of Power.* Oxford: Lexington, 2001.

Nguyen, Mimi (ed.). *Evolution of a Race Riot, vol.1.* Berkeley: self-published, 2000.

—— *Race Riot 2.* Berkeley: self-published, 2003.

—— *Race Riot Project Directory.* Berkeley: self-published, 2003.

Said, Edward. *Orientalism.* Toronto: Random House, 1978.

Sedgwick, Eve Kosofsky. *Epistemology of the Closet.* Berkeley: University of California Press, 1990.

Shakur, Assata. *Assata: An Autobiography.* Westport, CT: L. Hill Books, 1987.

Smith, Linda Tuhiwai. *Decolonizing Methodologies: Research and Indigenous Peoples.* London: Zed Books, 1999.

Spivak, Gayatri. 'Can the Subaltern Speak?'. In Cary Nelson and Lawrence Grossberg (eds.) *Marxism and the Interpretation of Culture.* Champaign, IL: University of Illinois Press, 1988.

Staudenmaier, Peter. 'Anarchists in Wonderland: The Topsy-Turvy World of Post-Left Anarchy'. <http://www.anarchist-studies.org/publications/theory_politics>.

Sycamore, Matt Berstein (ed.). *That's Revolting! Queer strategies for Resisting Assimilation.* Brooklyn: Soft Skull, 2004.

10
Anarchy, Power and Post-Structuralism

Allan Antliff

As a corollary to Todd May's praise for anarchism's thoroughgoing attack on domination in all its forms, May argued that anarchism (theoretically) was not up to the task of realizing its political potential. Referencing 'classical' figures from the nineteenth-century European wing of the movement, May suggested that anarchists had yet to come to terms with power as a positive ground for action. The anarchist project, he argued, is based on a fallacious 'humanist' notion that 'the human essence is a good essence, which relations of power suppress and deny'. This impoverished notion of power as ever oppressive, never productive, was the Achilles heel of anarchist political philosophy (May, 1964: 62). Hence May's call for a new and improved 'post-structuralist anarchism'. The post-structuralist anarchist would not shy away from power: she would shed the husk of humanism the better to exercise power 'tactically' within an ethical practice guided by Habermas's universalist theory of communicative action (ibid.: 146).

My purpose is not to further May's positioning of anarchism as post-structuralist. Rather, I am interested in the claim that 'classical' anarchism – and by extension, contemporary anarchism – founds its politics on a flawed conception of power and its relationship to society. Based on this premise, May has urged anarchist-oriented theorists to press on without looking back – and some, notably Lewis Call and Saul Newman, have done just that.[1] But surely, if one claims to be fundamentally revising a political tradition, then one has an obligation to familiarize oneself with that tradition's theoretical foundations. This is my modest aim: to provide a brief corrective meditation on 'classical' anarchism and power.

Let us begin with Emma Goldman's (1869–1940) closing summary of anarchist principles, circa 1900, from her essay, 'Anarchism: What it Really Stands for':

Anarchism, then, really stands for the liberation of the human mind from the domination of religion; the liberation of the human body from the domination of property; liberation from the shackles and restraint of government. Anarchism stands for a social order based on the free grouping of individuals for the purpose of producing real social wealth, an order that will guarantee to every human being free access to the earth and full enjoyment of the necessities of life, according to individual desires, tastes, and inclinations. (Goldman, 1969: 62)

Goldman's statement certainly confirms May's point concerning how anarchism widens the political field (May, 1994: 50). Goldman critiques religion for oppressing us psychologically, capitalist economics for endangering our corporal well-being, and government for shutting down our freedoms. She also asserts that the purpose of anarchism is to liberate humanity from these tyrannies. That said, one searches in vain for any suggestion that Goldman's liberated individuals are, as May would have it, *a priori* good. Rather, she posits a situated politics in which individuality differentiates endlessly, according to each subject's 'desires, tastes and inclinations'.

Goldman counted anarchist–communist Peter Kropotkin (1842–1921) among her most important influences, so it is appropriate we turn to him for further insight regarding the anarchist subject. In his 1896 essay, 'Anarchism: Its Philosophy and Ideal' (Kropotkin, 1970: 143), Kropotkin wrote that anarchism was synonymous with '*variety, conflict*'. In an anarchist society 'antisocial' behaviour would inevitably arise, as it does at present; the difference being that this behaviour, if judged reprehensible, would be dealt with according to anarchist principles, as he argued in his 1891 'Anarchist Morality' (ibid.: 106). More positively, the libertarian refusal to 'model individuals according to an abstract idea' or 'mutilate them by religion, law or government' allowed for a specifically anarchist type of morality to flourish (ibid.: 113). This morality entailed the unceasing interrogation of existing social norms, in recognition that morals are social constructs, and that there are no absolutes guiding ethical behaviour. Quoting 'the unconsciously anarchist' Jean-Marie Guyau (1824–1882), Kropotkin characterized anarchist morality as 'a superabundance of life, which demands to be exercised, to give itself . . . the consciousness of power' (ibid.: 108). He continued: 'Be strong. Overflow with emotional and intellectual energy, and you will spread your intelligence, your love, your energy of action broadcast among others! This is what all moral teaching comes to' (ibid.: 109). Shades of Friedrich Nietzsche? Kropotkin is citing a passage from Guyau's *Esquisse d'une morale sans obligation, ni sanction* (1884), a book that also influenced Nietzsche's 'overman' concept and the related idea of going 'beyond good and evil' – an interesting confluence, to say the least, given post-structuralism's indebtedness to the German philosopher.[2] More to the point, Kropotkin's subject, who exercises power by shaping her own values to accord with a 'superabundance' of life, is antithetical to May's claim regarding 'classic' anarchism: 'human essence is a good essence, which relations of power suppress and deny'. Kropotkin, *contra* May, embeds power in the subject and configures the unleashing of that power on morality as the marker of social liberation, predicting that it will generate both 'antisocial' (to be debated and resolved) and 'social' (socially accepted) behaviour in the process.

Indeed, it is worth underlining that the anarchist subject's power, situated socially, is not reactive; it is *generative*. Kropotkin wants power to 'overflow'; it has to if a free social order is to be realized. Anarchist social theory develops out of this perspective.

Again, a reading of anarchist theory exposes the mischaracterizations put forth by the post-structuralist anarchists. In 'Anarchism and the Politics of Resentment', Saul Newman asserts that 'classical' anarchism assumes 'society and our everyday actions, although oppressed by power, are ontologically separate from it' (Newman 2004: 120). But if power is separate from society, why has so much theorizing been devoted to the social conditions through which libertarian power can be realized? The post-structuralist anarchists have yet to acknowledge, let alone address, this issue.

How do we account for the 'classical' blind spot in their field of vision? I would conjecture that it arises from a particular genealogy. As Jonathan Purkis relates, in the 1960s the key theorists of post-structuralism emerged from and were reacting to the radical wing of a structuralist movement dominated by Marxism. Having adopted the structuralist critique of the Enlightenment subject as unitary and absolute, they then rejected the Marxist hierarchy of social forces that determined, in the last instance, the subject's formation (Purkis, 2004: 50).[3] Seeking to develop a more dynamic notion of the decentred subject while deepening their critique of authoritarianism in all its guises, post-structuralists drew, in the first instance, on Nietzsche as the understudied alternative to Marx (see Purkis, 2004: 51–2). Anarchism, it appears, never showed itself on the political horizon. Perhaps this can be attributed to a lingering misreading of the anarchist subject as just another variation of the humanist individual, autonomous from the social forces, which structuralism attacked.[4] This, after all, was the accusation levelled by Marx and Engels in their polemics against the anarchists of their day – notably Bakunin and Max Stirner (1806–1856).[5] It is ironic indeed, then, to encounter the same claim being levelled over 150 years after the fact by post-structuralist anarchists.

Be that as it may, 'classical' anarchism offers some promising avenues for exploration, as a brief examination of anarchist theory and practice in Moscow during the Russian Revolution (1917–1921) reveals. From its founding in 1917 until its untimely demise, the locus of anarchist activity in Russia's capital was the Moscow Federation of Anarchist Groups. The Federation was founded in March 1917 after the Russian Tsar's abdication and eventually dissolved around 1919 due to repeated attacks (raids, arrests, etc.) by the Communist government under Lenin's leadership.[6] During its short existence, the Federation's secretary, Lev Chernyi, was the organization's leading theorist. Chernyi expounded an 'associational' anarchism based on Max Stirner's anti-statist manifesto, *The Ego and Its Own* (1915), and this brand of anarchism was also discussed in the Federation's newspaper, *Anarkhiia*.[7]

Stirner posited that an anarchist social order would be based on voluntary associations ('unions') of 'egoists' acting co-operatively (Stirner, 1915: 414–15). Regarding the Federation from this perspective, we can begin by noting that it grew by bringing disparate groups together to 'unionize' on a foundation of shared criminality. Its headquarters, 'The House of Anarchy', was the old civic Merchants' Club, 'confiscated' and communalized in March 1917. From there it expanded spontaneously as anarchists organized themselves into clubs, joined the Federation, and began contributing to the collective welfare. By way of furthering mutual aid within the Federation, detachments of 'Black Guards' continued to carry out expropriations – building occupations in the main – into the spring of 1918 (Avrich, 1967: 179–80; 184–5). In April 1918 these activities would serve as the excuse for Lenin's Communist government to conduct a series of police raids against the Federation. The official goal was to arrest and charge 'robber bands' in the anarchist ranks – an assertion of the power of the Communist state over anarchist direct action – but the authorities quickly expanded the scope of illegality, announcing that 'entire counter-revolutionary groups' had joined the Federation with the aim of 'some covert action against Soviet [government] power' (Antliff, 2001: 200). Following this logic, smashing the organizational structure of the state's most determined opponents 'just happened' to go hand in hand with law enforcement. From an anarchist perspective, of course, the raids were tantamount to 'executing' freedom, to paraphrase the editors of the anarchist *Burevestnik* (*The Petrel*) (ibid.) Certainly they underlined the stark contrast between the anarchist exercise of social power and state power in its Marxist guise. After the attack in Moscow and similar raids in St Petersburg, the legality of anarchist activity was subject to the whims of the state police and the Cheka. Criminalization effectively brought an end to anarchism as an above-ground movement within territories controlled by the Communist Party, and the last instance of libertarian-inspired resistance in March 1921 – an uprising of workers, soldiers and sailors at the Island Fortress of Kronstadt – was destined to be put down in 'an orgy of blood-letting'.[8]

The Ego and Its Own singled out the proletariat – the 'unstable, restless, changeable' individuals who owe nothing to the state or capitalism – as the one segment of society capable of solidarity with those 'intellectual vagabonds' who approached the condition of anarchistic egoism (Stirner, 1915: 148–9). Liberation for the proletariat did not lie in their consciousness of themselves as a class, as Marx claimed. It would only come if the workers embraced the egotistic attitude of the 'vagabond' and shook off the social and moral conventions that yoked them to an exploitive order. Once the struggle for a new, stateless order was under way, the vastness of the working class ensured the bourgeoisie's defeat. 'If *labor* becomes *free*', Stirner concluded, 'the state is lost' (ibid.: 152).

This class orientation was reflected in the make-up of the Federation's clubs and communes, most of which were located in Moscow's working-class districts (Avrich, 1967: 180). Indeed, the Federation's conceptualization of free individuality was indebted to Stirner's theory of class (an issue that falls by the wayside in much post-structuralist thinking) (Callinicos, 1990: 121–62). Among Moscow's anarchists, A.L. and V.L. Gordin distinguished themselves in this regard. The Gordins were arch-materialists who argued that religion and science were social creations, not eternal truths. *Manifest Pananarkhistov* (Pan-anarchist Manifesto), a collection published in 1918, opened with the following declaration:

The rule of heaven and the rule of nature – angels, spirits, devils, molecules, atoms, ether, the laws of God-heaven and the laws of Nature, forces, the influence of one body on another – all this is invented, formed, created by society. (Gordinii, 1918: 5–7)

Here the Gordins took a page from Stirner, who condemned metaphysics and dismissed the idea of absolute truth as a chimera. Stirner argued that the metaphysical thinking underpinning religion and the notions of absolute truth that structured a wide range of theories laid the foundation for the hierarchical division of society into those with knowledge and those without. From here a whole train of economic, social and political inequalities ensued, all of which were antithetical to anarchist egoism. The egoist, he countered, recognized no metaphysical realms or absolute truths separate from experience; 'knowledge', therefore, was ever-changing and varied from individual to individual (Stirner, 1915: 421). The Gordins agreed, arguing that the individualistic 'inventiveness' of the working class made for a sharp contrast with the 'abstract reasoning' of the bourgeoisie and its 'criminal dehumanization' of the individual (Gordinii, 1918: 28).[9]

Stirner also drew distinctions between insurrection and revolution, reasoning that whereas revolutions simply changed who was in power, insurrection signalled a refusal to be subjugated and a determination to assert egoism over abstract power repeatedly, as an anarchic state of being. 'The insurgent', wrote Stirner, 'strives to become constitutionless', a formulation that the programme of the Moscow Federation put into practice (1915: 287). Autonomous self-governance, voluntary federation, the spread of power horizontally – these were the features of its insurgency. As a result, wherever the Federation held sway, power remained fluid, unbounded by central authority, and ever creative in its manifestations.

No wonder the state-enamoured Communists felt compelled to stamp it out. They saw themselves as the vanguard disciplinarians of the proletariat, building socialism by moulding the masses under the aegis of state dictatorship. As Lenin put it during the assault on Kronstadt:

Marxism teaches . . . that only the political party of the working class, i.e., the Communist Party, is capable of uniting, training, and organizing a vanguard of the proletariat and of the whole mass of the working people . . . and of guiding all the united activities of the whole of the proletariat, i.e., of leading it politically, and through it, the whole mass of the working people. (Lenin, 1921: 327)

'The dictatorship of the proletariat' was established to combat the 'inevitable petty-bourgeois vacillations of this mass' towards anarchism during the initial revolutionary upheaval and to create a socialist society in its aftermath (ibid.: 326–7). The 'practical work of building new forms of economy' required a state, Lenin reasoned (328), because whenever and wherever 'petty-bourgeois anarchy' reared its head, 'iron rule government that is revolutionarily bold, swift, and ruthless' had to repress it (Lenin, 1972: 291). And repress it, it did.

Complementing the power of social insurrectionism, Stirnerist egoism also called for our psychological empowerment through the cultivation of a critical consciousness that would, metaphorically, devour oppression. In *The Ego and Its Own*, Stirner deemed belief in a transcendent unchanging ego to be an alienating form of self-oppression. Libertarian 'egoism', Stirner wrote, 'is not that the ego is all, but the ego *destroys* all. Only the self-dissolving ego . . . the *finite* ego, is really I. [The philosopher] Fichte speaks of the "absolute" ego, but I speak of me, the transitory ego' (Stirner, 1915: 237). Much like Kropotkin's moralizing anarchist, the liberated egoist's 'free, unruly sensuality' overflowed with ideas – 'I am not a mere thought, but at the same time I am full of thoughts' – a fecund multiplicity that defied absolutes (453). Stirner characterized the internalization of authoritarian psychology as a mode of self-forgetting, a desire to escape the corporeal that found ultimate expression in the other-worldly delusions of immortality prescribed by Christianity (451–3). The liberated ego, on the other hand, would never subordinate itself to an abstract truth, because it was conscious of its finitude and gained power from this knowledge.

Russian anarchism's engagement with the psychological dimensions of Stirner's theory has barely been documented, and the historical and theoretical threads are too complex to recapitulate here.[10] For now it will suffice to note that during the movement's last bid for power in March 1921, the rebels at Kronstadt issued two statements, 'What We Fight For' and 'Socialism in Quotation Marks', protesting not only against political and economic oppression, but also against 'the moral servitude which the Communists have inaugurated' as they 'laid their hands also on the inner world of the toilers, forcing them to think in the Communist way'.[11] While state power grew,

[t]he life of the citizen became hopelessly monotonous and routine. One lived according to timetables established by the powers that be. Instead of the free development of the individual personality and a free labouring life, there emerged an extraordinary and unprecedented slavery. [...] Such is the shining kingdom of socialism to which the dictatorship of the Communist Party has brought us.[12]

Anarchist subjectivity was a threat to the regime because freedom was, and is, its essence.

To conclude, the history of the Russian Revolution makes abundantly clear that 'classical' anarchism does have a positive theory of power. Not only that, it offers an alternative ground for theorizing the social conditions of freedom and a critical understanding of power and liberation as perpetually co-mingling with and inscribed by a process of self-interrogation and self-overcoming that is pluralistic, individualist, materialist and social. Finally, it has the advantage of a historical record: this theory has been put into practice, sometimes on a mass scale.

Arguably, then, contemporary radicals would do better marshalling anarchism to critique post-structuralism, rather than the other way around. As it stands, the continual rehashing of May's spurious characterizations in a bid to theorize 'beyond' anarchism has merely set up a false-God adjective, 'post-structural', at the price of silencing the ostensive subject.

CODA

Since this essay first appeared (2007), a subtle shift has taken place in the post-anarchist discourse. May's claim that 'classical' anarchism lacks a theory of power has been quietly dropped. Now we are told 'post-' merely signals the intent to infuse anarchism with contemporary post-structuralist currents (Newman, 2008: 101). Of course this sort of theorizing has many precedents (Nietzsche's historical influence being a case in point). Whether it leads to a critical reworking of post-structuralism remains to be seen.

NOTES

1. See, for example, Lewis Call, *Postmodern Anarchism* (Lanham, MD: Lexington Books, 2002), 15–24 and Saul Newman (2005: 107–26). For a more extended variation of the same argument, see Newman, *From Bakunin to Lacan: Anti-Authoritarianism and the Dislocation of Power* (Lanham, MD: Lexington Books, 2001).
2. Hans Erich Lampl, *Zweistimmigkeit-Einstimmigkeit? Friedrich Nietzsche und Jean-Marie Guyau (Esquisse d'une morale sans obligation, ni sanction)* (Cuxhaven: Junghans-Verlag, 1990), passim. For further documentation of Nietzsche's ownership and interest in this book, see <http://muse.jhu.edu.ezproxy.library.uvic.ca/journal_of_the_history_of_ideas/v058/58.4brobjer_append01.html>, accessed 10 January 2006. On Nietzsche and post-structuralism see Alan D. Schrift, *Nietzsche's French Legacy: A Genealogy of Poststructuralism* (London: Routledge, 1995), passim.
3. Purkis is referring to Jean-François Lyotard, Jean Baudrillard, Jacques Derrida, Michel Foucault, Gilles Deleuze, Félix Guattari, Julia Kristeva and the later work of Roland Barthes.
4. On the anti-humanist subject and post-structuralism see Callinicos (1990: 62–91).
5. Anarchist theories of subjectivity and individualism are critiqued at length in ch.3 of Karl Marx and Frederick Engels's polemic, *The German Ideology*, written between 1845 and 1846 and published posthumously. See Karl Marx and Frederick Engels, 'Saint Max', *Collected Works, vol.5* (New York: International Publishers, 1976).
6. On the founding of the Federation, see Avrich (1967: 179). The Communists were relentless. Avrich writes that the cycle of arrests, executions, and imprisonments of anarchists intensified in 1919, and that by 1920 the 'dragnet had swept the entire country', effectively crushing the anarchist movement in Russia (in the Ukraine, Nestor Makhno's anarchist insurgent army continued to contest Communist hegemony until the summer of 1921). Avrich (1973: 138; 1967: 177).
7. Chernyi's book on 'Associational Anarchism' includes two chapters dealing with anarchist egoism and collectivism; Lev Chernyi, *Novoe Napravlenie v Anarkhizme: Asosiatsionnii Anarkhism* (Moscow, 1907; 2nd edn, New York, 1923).
8. The uprising lasted 18 days and was put down at a cost of approximately 10,000 dead, wounded or missing on the Soviet side. No reliable estimate exists of the number of Kronstadt deaths, but it was substantial. See Paul Avrich (1974: 211).
9. Stirner argued that the privileged 'cultured' segments of society distinguished themselves from the downtrodden 'uncultured' on the basis of supposed superior knowledge (1915: 94–5).

10. I discuss the artistic dimensions of this issue in *Art and Anarchy: From the Paris Commune to the Fall of the Berlin Wall* (Vancouver: Arsenal Pulp Press, 2007), 71–96.
11. 'What We Fight For' (March 8, 1921) in Avrich (1974: 241).
12. 'Socialism in Quotation Marks' (March 16, 1921) in Avrich (1974: 245).

REFERENCES

Antliff, Allan (2001). *Anarchist Modernism: Art, Politics and the First American Avant-Garde.* Chicago: University of Chicago Press.

Avrich, Paul (1974). *Kronstadt 1921.* New York: Norton.

—— (ed.) (1973). *The Anarchists in the Russian Revolution.* Ithaca: Cornell University Paperbacks.

—— (1967). *The Russian Anarchists.* Princeton, NJ: Princeton University Press.

Callinicos, Alex (1990). *Against Postmodernism: A Marxist Critique.* London: St. Martin's Press.

Engels, Frederick, Marx, Karl and Lenin, Vladimir Illich (1972). *Anarchism and Anarcho-Syndicalism.* Moscow: Progress Publishers.

Goldman, Emma (1969). 'Anarchism: What It Really Stands for'. In *Anarchism and Other Essays* (Richard Drinnon, intro.). New York: Dover Press.

Gordinii, Brat'ia (1918). *Manifest Pananarckhistov.* Moscow. Cited in Avrich (1967: 177–8).

Kropotkin, Peter (1970). *Kropotkin's Revolutionary Pamphlets: A Collection of Writings* (Roger N. Baldwin, ed.). New York: Dover.

Lenin, Vladimir Illich (1972) [1918]. 'The Immediate Tasks of the Soviet Government' (*Pravda*, 28 April 1918). In Engels, Marx and Lenin (1972).

—— (1921). 'Preliminary Draft Resolution of the Tenth Congress of the R.C.P. on the Syndicalist and Anarchist Deviation in Our Party'. In Engels, Marx and Lenin (1972).

May, Todd (1994). *The Political Philosophy of Poststructuralist Anarchism.* University Park, PA: Pennsylvania State University Press.

Newman, Saul (2008). 'Editorial: Postanarchism'. *Anarchist Studies* 16(2): 101–5.

—— (2004). 'Anarchism and the Politics of Resentment'. In *I Am Not a Man, I Am Dynamite! Nietzsche and the Anarchist Tradition* (John Moore and Spencer Sunshine, eds). New York: Autonomedia.

Purkis, Jonathan (2004). 'Towards an Anarchist Sociology'. In Jonathan Purkis and James Bowen (eds). *Changing Anarchism: Anarchist Theory and Practice in a Global Age.* Manchester: Manchester University Press.

Stirner, Max (1915) [1848]. *The Ego and Its Own* (S.T. Byington, trans.; J.L. Walker, intro.). London: A.C. Fifield. Text available online at <www.lsr-projekt.de/poly/enee.html#secondii2>.

11
Post-Anarchism: A Partial Account[1]

Benjamin Franks

Anarchism was not a major concern for political theory/philosophy from the 1930s to the fall of the Berlin Wall. It was only with the disintegration of the Soviet Union, and the corresponding decline in the hegemonic primacy of orthodox Marxism, that other radical socialist movements, including anarchism, were (re)discovered by academia. Alongside this renewed interest in anarchism, there has also been a small but significant departure with the development of an identifiable 'post-anarchist' movement, which includes most prominently Lewis Call, Todd May and Saul Newman, polemicists such as Bob Black and Hakim Bey, and many of the post-millennial contributors to the Institute for Anarchist Studies' *Perspectives on Anarchist Theory* and journals such as *Anarchist Studies*. Articles informed by post-anarchism can be found in Jonathan Purkis and James Bowen's collection *Changing Anarchism*, and defenders of post-anarchism appear on bulletin boards and discussion groups.[2] This 'cottage industry in "post-anarchism"' (Creagh, 2006) is the product of artisans working individually and collectively, through associations like the Anarchist Academic Network and the Anarchist Studies Network (2008), a specialist group of the Political Studies Association. There is also a useful collation of key authors on the 'What Is Post-Anarchism?' website (Anonymous, 2006).

The emphasis in post-anarchism has been on a rejection of essentialism, a preference for randomness, fluidity, hybridity and a repudiation of vanguard tactics, which includes a critique of occidental assumptions in the framing of anarchism (Adams, 2004; Anderson, 2005). Despite many excellent features of post-anarchist writings, not least their verve, sophistication and their opening up of new terrains for critical investigation and participant research, there are, nonetheless, a number of concerns, which this paper is designed to articulate and help to resolve. The first is to determine where post-anarchism is positioned in relation to the other 'orthodox' or 'classical' versions of anarchism. The second concern of this analysis of post-anarchism is to illustrate that, despite the post-anarchists' commitments to non-vanguard and anti-hierarchical practices, many reconstruct a strategic supremacy to particular types of action and overlook or underemphasize certain forms of oppression and resistance. These lacunae are especially relevant in light of the current policies of dominating powers. The argument presented is that although post-anarchism does accurately identify certain deficiencies in particular types of classical anarchism, post-anarchism is not a transcendence of traditional anarchism by a variant of classical anarchism. Post-anarchism represents the particular responses of particular subjected groups in a limited historical context. The clusters of concepts (and their structures) that characterize the main strands of post-anarchism are indicative of it being part of the wider ideological family of anarchism, rather than representing a substantive break,[3] in the same way that environmental anarchism (also known as 'green anarchism') is not a surpassing of anarchism, but a re-ordering and re-emphasizing of certain principles (and de-emphasizing of others) as a result of wider cultural changes.[4]

Given the bewildering range of interpretations of 'anarchism' it is hardly surprising that 'post-anarchism' is also a hotly disputed term. The prefix, 'post-', of 'post-anarchism' has referred to either, or both, 'post-structuralism' and 'postmodernism'. Both 'postmodernism' and 'post-anarchism' are also problematic headings: as the critical theorist Jon Simons notes, it is not easy to divide thinkers into these neatly separated categories (Simons, 2002: 16). However, Terry Eagleton's definition of 'postmodernism' from *After Theory* acts as a good starting point for unravelling the multiple meanings of 'post-anarchism'. Eagleton interprets the postmodern as

> the contemporary movement of thought which rejects totalities, universal values, grand historical narratives, solid foundations to human existence and the possibility of objective knowledge. Postmodernism is skeptical of truth, unity and progress, opposes what it sees as elitism in culture, tends towards cultural relativism, and celebrates pluralism, discontinuity and heterogeneity. (Eagleton, 2004: 13)

Eagleton's definition is useful in its scope as well as its brevity, historically contextualizing postmodernism within the wider economic and political framework of the rise of neo-liberalism without the constraints of a competing set of collectivist values. However, Eagleton's brief description collapses together the realm of (primarily) academic theory with wider social movements and phenomena.

For heuristic purposes, therefore, it might be better to disentangle 'post-structuralism' from 'postmodernism'. The first, the preferred term for the most prominent post-anarchist theorists, such as Adams, May and Newman,[5] is one closely associated with the writings of Jean Baudrillard, Gilles Deleuze, Jacques Derrida, Michel Foucault, Félix Guattari, Jacques Lacan and Jean Lyotard.[6] The latter term, 'postmodernism', can refer to the range of movements that adopt the tropes identified by Eagleton in the quotation earlier (and elsewhere in his book) – namely a commitment to contingency, discontinuity, fluidity, hybridity and pluralism (Eagleton, 2004: 13, 16, 117–19). As such, postmodernism can be regarded as referring to wider cultural phenomena rather than just academic theory. In addition, postmodernism's championing of polymorphous sexual identities and cultural diversity was frequently viewed as a less radical alternative to resisting hegemonic power relations and challenging material inequalities; thus, postmodernism can be considered more conservative than the critical theory that preceded it (Simons, 2002: 10).

Those participating in and constructing practices consistent with postmodernism need not be informed by post-structural theory. However, those identifying, explicating and (on rare occasions) evaluating these postmodern phenomena, particularly for a largely academic audience, often apply methods, concepts and philosophical insights derived from post-structuralism. Just as the developments of the wider postmodern culture were not necessarily directly informed by post-structural theory, although such theory has latterly helped to clarify and evaluate such recent developments, so too the wider post-anarchist canon often concentrates on applying anarchist principles to the contemporary cultural context. Post-anarchism, thus, considers issues and forms of action that are thought to lie outside of traditional anarchism, such as environmentalism, lesbian and gay rights and anti-nuclear campaigns (Bowen and Purkis, 2004: 5). This therefore gives rise to some distinctions within post-anarchism, which are redolent of the differences within post-Marxism.

Post-anarchism's relationship to anarchism shares key characteristics with post-Marxism's relations to Marxism, as Newman (2003) suggests, not least a potentially bewildering mixture of dispositions, outlooks and methodologies that are present in this particular combination of prefix to the stem. The combination of anarchism and post-structuralism is potentially less problematic than that attempted in post-Marxism. Anarchism, for the most part, has not been reduced to a single identifiable dogma with a singular strategy, in the way that orthodox Marxism has been wrongly, but popularly, condensed into a vulgar economic determinism, with the singular party-based stratagem.

We can identify three types of post-anarchism. First, a strident, Lyotardian *Post*-anarchism, that rejects traditional anarchist concerns, and instead proposes the adoption of new critical approaches and tactics that lie beyond the remit of anarchist orthodoxy, using as their basis those post-structural theorists who are antipathetic to traditional anarchism. Second, a redemptive post-*anarchism* that seeks the adoption into anarchism of post-structural theory to enrich and enliven existing practices, one which sees 'anarchism' as it currently stands as lacking, but amenable to change. Third, and finally, a postmodern anarchism (which corresponds to the last version of post-*Marxism*), that reapplies anarchist analyses and methods to the new globalized political economy, and concentrates on the actions of oppressed subjects.

It is primarily within the first two interpretations that Call, Newman and May lie. They prioritize the theoretical developments of post-structuralism over the mere reapplication of anarchist principles to postmodern cultural phenomena. Newman, for instance, refers to post-anarchism as constructing an intersection between anarchist and post-structuralist discourses (Newman, 2004). Dewitt, in conversation with May, regards post-anarchism as a 'grafting [of] French poststructuralist thought onto anarchism' (Dewitt, 2000). By contrast, sociological papers, from Karen Goaman, for instance, tend towards the third, 'postmodern' account of post-anarchism, by concentrating on the anarchist features of relatively recent phenomena, such as the alternative globalization movements which coalesced to form anti-capitalist carnivals. Others, such as Graeme Chesters, Ian Welsh and Purkis, combine the different versions. They present a theoretical reappraisal of anarchism through an analysis of contemporary cultural movements (Welsh and Purkis, 2003; Chesters, 2003, 2005). In addition, some commentators slip from one presentation of post-anarchism to another – presenting it at one point as a reapplication and clarification of longstanding anarchist principles, whilst at others as a development of anarchism and at others as a transformation and negation – within a single paper.[7]

However, another prominent post-anarchist, Jason Adams, offers an alternative perspective. He sees post-structuralism as having 'emerged out of a much larger anti-authoritarian milieu', one which was actively involved in applying anti-authoritarian theory to the political movements of the 1970s and 1980s. Thus, post-structuralism did not require 'grafting onto' radical social theories or reapplication to radical movements; it was always part of post-structuralism's orientation. For Adams, however, this transformed radical theory is still a surpassing over the 'more closed and ideological anarchisms' of the past, which Adams identifies as anarcho-syndicalism and anarchist communism (2006). But, one can still accept Adams's initial premise that post-structuralism and, consequently, post-anarchism are part of a progression from earlier anti-authoritarian theories and practices without accepting his conclusion regarding its ultimate superiority to all previous anarchisms.

An alternative position to that of Adams and Lyotardian post-anarchists is feasible and consistent. This approach to post-anarchism is much more modest and contextual. It regards certain forms of post-anarchism as being consistent with the most coherent forms of practical 'classical' anarchism. Whilst post-anarchism has highlighted some weaknesses in certain forms and traditions within anarchism, and reapplied anarchism to new social forms, it is often less adequate at developing a cogent account of oppression, prioritizing its own post-Pruitt–Igoe institutional outlook and discourse over that of other, equally contemporary, subject identities. In different environments alternative forms of anarchism might be more appropriate in providing a discourse and repertoire of identities than post-anarchism. Thus, the transcendent versions of post-anarchism are guilty of universalizing a particular set of radical identities and discursive tactics. It is better, therefore, to regard post-anarchism as another modification of anarchist principles and discourses as part of a wider anarchist 'family', not a superior new form which replaces all before it.

Those who adopt the more strident transcendent post-anarchist position have been subject to numerous critiques. These criticisms of post-anarchism fall into two main groups. The first type of critical assessment of post-anarchism, from Sasha K. Villon (2003), and Jesse Cohn and Shawn P. Wilbur (2003), is that, in adopting a separate demarcation, it is merely claiming for itself a distinction without a difference: that anarchism and post-anarchism are identical in all major respects, and in order to maintain a differentiation, post-anarchists misrepresent classical anarchism, either as an essentialist philosophy or one corresponding to Leninist economic reductivism. The second, from South Africa's Zabalaza Anarchist Communist Federation (ZACF, 2003), takes a different approach. It maintains that there are substantial differences between anarchism and post-anarchism, in which the latter is inferior, as it either recreates liberalism, or, by being so wedded to postmodern cultural assumptions, is incapable of responding to changes in the current political climate.

One set of replies to the post-anarchists is that they misrepresent both the epistemological and programmatic features of classical anarchism. Critics such as Villon and Cohn highlight how some post-anarchists reduce classical anarchism, regarding it as promoting an essentialist view of the individual (as fundamentally good), and thus advancing a simplistic and highly regressive political strategy. These critics, consequently, argue that there is a rejection of essentialism present in 'classical' anarchism, and that the diversity of tactics, characteristic of post-anarchism, was already an existing feature of anarchism.

In a review of Newman's influential post-anarchist book *From Bakunin to Lacan*, Villon identifies Newman's text with the type of post-anarchism that corresponds to the *post*-Marxism described by Sim (n.d.), with a surpassing of anarchism (a transcendence), rather than its mere reapplication or updating. Newman's account of his own position is more complex and potentially more perplexing; he claims that anarchism would 'greatly benefit' from the adoption of post-structuralism and argues that post-anarchism also actually represents a 'new paradigm', one that is no longer wedded to a 'limited [...] Enlightenment humanism' (Newman, 2003). This is resolved by claiming that post-anarchism is an attempt to salvage the 'central insight' of classical anarchism, expressed as 'the autonomy of the political', that is to say a continuous resistance to hierarchical control in its irreducible, myriad forms (ibid.). These forms of opposition are nevertheless distinguished from classical anarchism, because, according to Newman, this earlier form of libertarian struggle is wedded to a limited epistemology that concentrates on only limited domains of power. In other words, Newman posits that classical anarchism has a core, absolute commitment to a humanist essentialism, and that post-anarchism, which rejects this principle, represents a wholly different morphology of concepts and practices.

Classical anarchism is, then, for Newman an inherently authoritarian movement, because of its epistemological weakness. This deficiency – namely that there is an ideal form of the individual, which grounds the classical anarchist project – is, he argues, one common to other Enlightenment political theories (Newman, 2003; 2001: 38–49). This is a view also shared by May (1994: 63–5). By viewing the individual as *naturally* rebellious (Bakunin) or *essentially* co-operative (Kropotkin), this predetermined trait limits freedom, fixing the ideal for all humanity, and restricts legitimate political action to opposing power in order to allow the expression of 'natural goodness'. It recreates, as Villon notes, a strategic 'Manichean' battle between the forces of good (nature) and those unnatural powers (state or capitalism) seeking to subvert it (Newman, 2001: 47–8; Villon, 2003). Thus, the old conflicts, as identified by Newman, of state versus individual (Bakunin) or proletariat against capitalism (Marx), are not only outmoded but also recreate hierarchies, in which only certain, specific subject identities take priority in the battle for liberation (Newman, 2001: 23–9).

Villon's contention is that Newman, and by implication Call and May, has misrepresented classical anarchism as wedded to a primitive essentialism. Villon argues that such a position is not common, nor critical to all classical anarchisms, and as a result post-anarchism is not distinct from them. Villon's contention is that Newman's choice of the quotations from Kropotkin, Bakunin and Godwin is too selective and de-historicized and that there are interpretations of Kropotkin that view him as 'break[ing] human nature open with his critique' (Villon, 2003).[8] William Godwin too is quoted by Cohn and Wilbur as explicitly rejecting an essentialist account of agency and that 'ontologically [...] all that Proudhon, Bakunin and Kropotkin really require [is]: the *possibility* of free co-operation' (emphasis added; Cohn and Wilbur, 2003). Anarchism does not require a metaphysical fixed certainty, which post-anarchism assigns it – and therefore post-anarchism's anti-essentialist critique of anarchism is redundant.

Whilst there are examples of essentialism in anarchism, which are worthy of criticism, these do not represent the whole of the non-post-anarchist libertarian canon. Concentrating on just these aspects risks overlooking the varied politics of 'classical' anarchism. Indeed, one can equally find essentialisms reappearing in certain post-anarchist texts. For instance, in Purkis and Bowen's collection there are references to both 'inherent creative' and 'critical' defining human traits (Gore, 2004: 145–61, esp. 156, 146),[9] or appeals to a shared 'humanity' that inspires anti-capitalist resistance (Q. Graeber in Goaman, 2004: 165).

Deleuze and Guattari's rhizome metaphor from *A Thousand Plateaus* is particularly popular among post-anarchists (Adams, 2006; Bowen and Purkis, 2004: 14; Call, 2002: 1, 123–4; Chesters, 2003: 192–3; Gordon, 2005; May, 1994: 96–7; Newman, 2001: 105–7; Purkis, 2004: 50). Like a rhizome, power works through 'connection and heterogeneity' (difference). Its roots intersect and sometimes merge (Deleuze and Guattari, 1998). Consequently, as multiple forms of power do not operate uniformly, or to the same degree at different points, different political identities develop. Thus, post-anarchists argue that social terrain is constructed out of a multitude of intersecting hierarchical practices rather than a single root of oppressive power. In addition, the rhizomic analysis proposes that there is no central political struggle, nor a universal group that represents all struggles. Thus, strategies based on a group with a singular identity contesting a single source of heteronomous power, such as Leninist accounts of the proletariat challenging bourgeois rule, are bound to be incomplete, as they ignore other oppressions, or recreate forms of domination (May, 1994: 20–3).

This rejection of a single sphere of conflict and consequent denial of a single universal vanguard identity of resistance, post-anarchists claim, distinguishes their transcendent theory from classical anarchism. Classical anarchism, they argue, regards one set of oppression as the major origin of all types of domination and thus prioritizes one type of oppressed agent's struggle over other forms of oppression. In the eyes of post-anarchists, classical anarchism privileges singular oppositions, either the fight against the state or workers' opposition to capitalism (May, 1994: 43; Morland, 2004: 37; Newman, 2001: 106–9; Purkis, 2004: 50).[10]

Again, following the critical route of Villon and Cohn and Wilbur, one could point to those aspects of classical anarchism which do not identify a singular source to all oppressions, nor place strategic centrality on a sole agent of change. Emma Goldman, for instance, on some occasions prioritized sexual dynamics and at others the class struggle (Goldman, 1969: 177–94). Other examples of a multiplicity of vectors and domains of struggle include the early Jewish immigrant anarchists, *Der Arbeiter Fraint* (The Workers' Friend), who set up cultural and self-educational groups and confronted religious hierarchies as well as creating radical trade unions to contest economic hierarchies (Fishman, 1975). In addition, there is a significant environmental disposition, which characterizes works of advocates of syndicalism, such as Kropotkin, an outlook that remained central to the 'workerist' Murray Bookchin (Kropotkin, n.d.: 24–7; see for example Bookchin, 1997: 31–6).

The earlier 'class struggle' classical anarchists tended not to be the economic determinists portrayed by many of the post-anarchists, nor indeed are their contemporaries, but instead they see a multitude of interacting, irreducible oppressions.[11] As such, Newman's 'salvaging' of anarchism is not only unnecessary, but also potentially misleading. However, anarchists, both classical and contemporary, were (and are) often centrally concerned with economic conflict, for good reason: class domination, in the domains they operated within, was (and is) one of the major forms of control. This awareness of the importance of the economic struggle leads to the second category of criticism of post-anarchism, that rather than representing a transcendence, it is an inappropriate reformulation of anarchism. Transcendent *post*-anarchism is consequently condemned for re-establishing the hierarchies of liberalism.

In rightly rejecting Leninist economic reductivism, however, some post-anarchists mistakenly reject class analysis wholesale. In other words, by rejecting class as the sole determinant, they erroneously ignore its influence altogether. This carries the risk either, as ZACF accuse them, of collapsing into naive liberalism, or of asserting an inappropriate, and often elitist, alternative agency for making social change. The shortcomings of post-anarchist alternative accounts of agency are highlighted by recent changes in the political landscape. In part, the altered political terrain is the result of dominant state agencies responding oppressively to the movements endorsed by post-anarchists (ZACF, 2003).

Following Bey and Black and their denunciation of 'leftism' within anarchism (Bey, 2003: 62–3; Black, 1997), many post-anarchists highlight their rejection of class analysis as constituting their difference from classical anarchism. For instance, Bowen claims that his anarchism is not a 'class movement' (Bowen, 2004: 118) and Gordon demarcates his contemporary anarchism, marked by the influence of Foucault, from 'old-school' working-class anarchism (Gordon,

2005: 76). These are indicative of a trajectory in significant sections of post-anarchism. So whilst oppressions of race, gender, sexuality, species or (dis-) ability are rightly highlighted in post-anarchism, class is largely absent. As Call proclaims: 'Postmodern anarchism begins with a premise: a Marxist or classical-anarchist 'radical' position which insists upon the primacy of economics and class analysis lacks meaningful revolutionary potential' (Call, 2002: 21). Or as Sandra Jeppesen more prosaically expresses it: 'Anarchy is not about the worker' (Jeppesen, 2006; see too Black, 1988).

Part of the reason for this denial of class as a major vector[12] lies in the history of Leninist, and later Stalinist hegemony, in which the discourse of 'class oppression' was monopolized and came to symbolize state communism's official discourse, one that played an ideological function of attempting to legitimize systematic structural oppression. As Glen Rhys, writing in the late 1980s class-conscious anarchist magazine *The Heavy Stuff*, explained: 'The more talk of class struggle the more Stalinist' (Rhys, 1988: 26).[13] Goaman similarly associates class discourse and imagery with a macho patriarchal attitude to (anti-)political struggle (Goaman, 1995: 165–8). As a result of this patriarchal, reductivist hegemony, many anarchists felt that even entering into a class-based discourse was to identify with state oppression or sexism. Another facet of the rejection of class as an explanatory category is that post-anarchists are in agreement with their Leninist opponents in their inter-pretation of Marx, viewing him as a historicist and economic reductivist.

The post-anarchist rejection of 'class', with its Leninist overtones, is under-standable in creating an important distance from the Leninist legacy, and those sections of anarchism which followed such a totalistic discourse. However, in doing so it risks ignoring not only the extremes of economic oppression that continue in both the occidental and oriental domains, but also the more sophisticated and wide-ranging forms of economic oppressions and class dynamics which take place beyond the realm of immediate production. Deleuze and Guattari in their powerful rhizome metaphor acknowledge that in some contexts there are more powerful encoding structures. Flows are not equal in force, as their other metaphor of the Amsterdam canal system indicates: at some points certain stem-canals are more significant than others (Deleuze and Guattari, 1998: 15).

A more significant potential weakness is that, inadvertently, post-anarchists start to prioritize certain elitist forms of resistance and agents of change. Having overlooked workers as potential revolutionary subjects, Bey, Call and Jeppesen, in keeping with the Deleuze and Guattari influence, promote a nomadic agent of change: one who can disappear, who is not bound by place, or past experiences (Bey, 2003: 128; Call, 2002: 128; Jeppesen, 2006). Such fleeting, drifting individuals represent, for these three theorists in particular, the post-anarchist ideal (Bey, 2003: 126; Call, 2002: 24; Jeppesen, 2006). Yet nomadic identities prioritize specific practices, namely those methods more suited to economically independent individuals. Not everyone is capable of drifting; there are those who are physically, socially or economically restrained or have responsibilities to particular locales or to more vulnerable others.[14]

The call to nomadic models overlooks the different socio-historical constructs that create individuals, differences in power relations, and the social nexuses of responsibility and dependence. Rosi Braidotti, in her criticism of the Deleuzean nomad, points out that this fleeting, fleeing 'radical identity' assumes an equivalence between classes, genders and (dis)abilities that is little different to the gender-, race-, class- and (dis)ability-blind abstract agent of liberalism (Braidotti, 1993: 49). Nomadism, rather than providing an anti-hierarchical strategy, can instead, through its over-emphasis by post-anarchists, recreate a vanguard elite.

We have witnessed a dramatic change in the operations of power, quite to the contrary of Bey's assumption that the state 'must [...] continue to deliquesce' (Bey, 2003: 132). Under the pretext of fighting 'terrorism', anti-capitalists and radical environmentalists have been subjected to greater state and private-sector surveillance, and stronger legislative control. Thus, many of the cultural assumptions that underlie many post-anarchist theories have been undermined. As Newman acknowledges, rather than dissolving, the state has, instead, switched to a more oppressive paradigm, with greater centralized control, executive power and concentrated authority in the hands of military and police (Newman, 2003; 2004). The heroic nomenclature of postmodernism, of flexibility, openness, pluralism and risk-taking, has moved towards a more politically and philosophically conservative disposition, in which the dominant political terminology stresses safety, security and fixed identity and shared 'universal' values. In the face of this authoritarian turn, the favoured tactic of post-anarchists, seeking flight rather than contestation (see Bey, 2003: 130–2; Newman, 2001: 99–100), seems inadequate, as exodus is not always possible or desirable.

The desire to escape the state also influences the reluctance, in some quarters, to engage in critical scrutiny of state practices, engagements and consequences.[15] In the more relativistic forms of post-anarchism, which Gavin Grindon identifies in Bey's works, the evasion takes the form of viewing the state as a mere simulation (a mythic model with no connection to real powers) (Grindon, 2004: 158–9). The consequence of Bey's Baudrillardian analysis is that it ignores the personal and social consequences of state power, whether they be the torture of Abu Ghraib, Guantanamo Bay, rendition flights or daisy-cutter ordinance. Thus, it becomes an analysis that is indicative of a particular (rather comfortable) elite position, rather than one which seeks out alliances of the oppressed to create new, anti-hierarchical social relations.

Post-anarchism's great strengths have been in identifying the essentialisms and dogmatisms in classical anarchisms, opening up original areas for critical scrutiny, employing new amalgams of analysis and also reflecting on institutional research practices. Today, a more modest version of post-anarchism is required: one that views itself as (another) modification of anarchism, more pertinent for particular social and cultural contexts, but less so in others, rather than a categorical supersession. Post-anarchisms embody the interests of particular radical subjects, in a particular era, in resisting (and transforming) heteronomous power relations; but the discourses, modes of organization and types of identity that characterize post-anarchisms can be less relevant, and damaging to the creation of non-hierarchical social relationships, in other contexts. To universally prioritize the practices of post-anarchism would be to recreate vanguards and hierarchies, structures that both post-anarchism and more traditional anarchism reject.

NOTES

1. This is a revised version of the article 'Postanarchism: A Critical Assessment' that appeared in the *Journal of Political Ideologies* 12(2), June 2007. It has been reprinted by permission of the publisher (Taylor & Francis Group, http://www.informaworld.com). My thanks to Lesley Stevenson, Stuart Hanscomb, David Graeber and the anonymous reviewer for their careful reading and pertinent suggestions for the original article, to Duane Rousselle for his assistance on this version, and to the participants at the PSA Conference (2006) for their supportive advice.
2. See for instance Urban 75s *Is Postanarchism a Good Idea?* (2006) and the debates on postmodernism and anarchism found on the Post-anarchism Listserv (2006).
3. An account of 'ideology' based on Freeden (1996: 53–4).
4. The question could arise as to whether Green anarchism is a hybrid of environmentalism and anarchism. Freeden's account of hybridity and the absence of absolute boundaries is useful here; anarchism, like other ideologies, is fluid and green anarchism shares many of the histories as well as core concepts of non-prefaced anarchism (1996: 87–8).
5. See the title of May's book *The Political Philosophy of Poststructuralist Anarchism* (1994) and Newman's comments in his book (2001: 14–15). Call's preference for the term 'postmodernism', which he uses to stand for 'the philosophical or critical movement' as against the wider cultural 'postmodern condition' (2002: 13). See too J. Purkis (2004: 39–54, esp. 50–1).
6. Adams cites Foucault, Deleuze and Guattari and Paul Virilio; May prioritizes Deleuze, Foucault and Lyotard; Newman stresses Derrida, Deleuze and Guattari, Foucault and Lacan; Call focuses primarily on Foucault and Baudrillard (Adams, 2006).
7. See for instance Morland, who, like Newman (2004), views 'post-anarchism' as both a reapplication of key anarchist themes to the contemporary setting, but also as an 'evolution'; that is to say post-anarchisms are more highly developed variants, which junk an inappropriate Marxism (Morland, in Purkis and Bowen, 2004: 23–38, esp. 24–5). Such confusion may be because the main intent of the text is not to theoretically locate post-anarchism, but to concentrate on describing the main features or applications of post-anarchisms to assist practical struggles.
8. Cohn and Wilbur contribute to this critique of Newman (but also extend it to May and Call) by arguing that the selection of theorists is too narrow, omitting those authors such as Gustav Landauer and Emma Goldman who do not fit neatly into the post-anarchist framework for earlier 'anarchism' (Cohn and Wilbur, 2003).
9. Such as 'natural curiosity' and 'natural concern', which underpin children's behaviour (Gribble, 2004: 183).
10. For an example of the state-centred approach, look at Alan Carter (2000); for an example of an anarchist class-centred analysis, see Yaroslavsky (2006).
11. See for instance the Anarchist Federation of Great Britain and Ireland's self-description:

> Another important principle of the AF is that it is not just class exploitation and oppression that needs to be abolished. Though we do not necessarily use the concept of patriarchy, we believe that the oppression of women predates capitalism and will not automatically disappear with its end. (2006: 16)

12. A term used by Alan Carter in his account of 'analytical anarchism' to describe the influence and direction of particular forms of state interest; these vectors intersect to create 'a parallelogram of forces' (2000: 244).

13. See too Call's comments about the symbolic importance for postmodern anarchism to avoid the language of 'bourgeois political economy', in contrast to Marxism and classical anarchism (2002: 23).

14. Robert Young (2003: 53) criticizes Deleuze and Guattari's idea of nomadism, because such landless existences, rather than being an indication of liberation and transgression, are often an identity forced upon people by oppression and dispossession.

15. Although it should be noted that there are some examples of highly perceptive post-anarchist analyses of state techniques and strategies; see for instance Antliff and Milwright (2005), Evren (2005) and Gemie (2005).

REFERENCES

Adams, J. (2006). 'Postanarchism in a Nutshell'. Interactivist Infoexchange. Retrieved 30 May 2006 from <http://info.interactivist.net/article.pl?sid=03/11/11/1642242>.

—— (2004). Non-Western Anarchisms: Rethinking the Global Context. Johannesburg: Zabalaza Books.

Anarchist Federation of Great Britain and Ireland (2006). 'Thought and Struggle'. Anarkiisto Debato 0 (magazine of International of Anarchist Federations).

Anarchist Studies Network (2008). A PSA specialist group for the study of anarchism. Untitled. Retrieved 26 March 2008 from <http://www.anarchist-studies-network.org.uk/>.

Anderson, B. (2005). Under Three Flags: Anarchism and the Anti-Colonial Imagination. London: Verso.

Anonymous (2006). 'What is Post-Anarchism?' Retrieved 20 March 2006 from <http://www.geocities.com/ringfingers/postanarchism2.html>.

Antliff, A., and Milwright, W. (2005). 'The Public Humiliation of Saddam Hussein'. Anarchist Studies 13(1): 78–82.

Bey, H. (2003) [1990]. T.A.Z.: The Temporary Autonomous Zone, Ontological Anarchy, Poetic Terrorism (2nd edn). Brooklyn, NY: Autonomedia.

Black, B. (1997). Anarchy after Leftism. Columbia, MO: Columbia Alternative Library Press.

—— (1988). 'The Abolition of Work', Vague 20.

Bookchin, M. (1997). Social Ecology. The Murray Bookchin Reader. London: Cassell.

Bowen, J. (2004). 'Moving Targets: Rethinking Anarchist Strategies'. In Purkis and Bowen (2004).

—— and Purkis, J. (2004). 'Introduction: Why Anarchists Still Matter'. In Purkis and Bowen (2004).

Braidotti, R. (1993). 'Discontinuous Becomings: Deleuze on the Becoming-Woman of Philosophy'. Journal of the British Society of Phenomenology 24(1).

Call, L. (2002). Postmodernism Anarchism. Oxford: Lexington Books.

Carter, A. (2000). 'Analytical Anarchism: Some Conceptual Foundations'. Political Theory 28(2): 230–53.

Chesters, G. (2005). 'Complexity and Social Movement(s): Process and Emergence in Planetary Action'. Theory, Culture and Society 22(5): 187–211.

—— (2003). 'Shape Shifting: Civil Society, Complexity and Social Movements'. Anarchist Studies 11(1): 42–65.

Cohn, J., and Wilbur, S. (2003). 'What's Wrong with Postanarchism?' Institute for Anarchist Studies. Retrieved 20 March 2006 from <http://www.anarchist-studies.org/article/articleview/26/2/1/>.

Creagh, R. (2006). Research on Anarchism Forum. Specialist group for the study of anarchism. Retrieved 20 March 2006 from <http://raforum.apinc.org/article.php3?id_article=3482&lang=en>.

Deleuze, G., and Guattari, F. (1998). *A Thousand Plateaus: Capitalism and Schizophrenia*. London: Continuum.

Dewitt, R. (2000). 'Poststructuralist Anarchism: An Interview with Todd May'. Institute for Anarchist Studies. Retrieved 31 March 2006 from <http://perspectives.anarchist-studies.org/8may.htm>.

Eagleton, T. (2004). *After Theory*. Harmondsworth: Penguin.

Evren, S. (2005). 'The Spectacle of Torture'. *Anarchist Studies* 13(1): 70–8.

Fishman, W. (1975). *East End Jewish Radicals 1874–1914*. London: Duckworth.

Freeden, Michael (1996). *Ideologies and Political Theory: A Conceptual Approach*. Oxford: Oxford University Press.

Gemie, S. (2005). 'Occupation and Insurrection in Iraq'. *Anarchist Studies* 13(1): 61–70.

Goaman, K. (2004). 'The Anarchist Travelling Circus: Reflections on Contemporary Anarchism, Anti-Capitalism and the International Scene'. In Purkis and Bowen (2004).

—— (1995). 'Active Currents'. *Anarchist Studies* 3(2).

Goldman, E. (1969) [1911]. 'The Traffic in Women'. *Anarchism and Other Essays*. New York: Dover.

Gordon, U. (2005). *Anarchism and Political Theory: Contemporary Problems* (D. Phil. thesis). Mansfield College, Oxford.

Gore, J. (2004). 'In the Eye of the Beholder: Child, Mad or Artist?' In Purkis and Bowen (2004).

Gribble, D. (2004). 'Good News for Francesco Ferrer: How Anarchist Ideals in Education Have Survived Around the World'. In Purkis and Bowen (2004).

Grindon, G. (2004). 'Carnival Against Capital: A Comparison of Bakhtin, Vaneigem and Bey'. *Anarchist Studies* 12(2).

Jeppesen, S. (2006). 'Seeing Past the Outpost of Post-Anarchism: Anarchy Axiomatic'. Institute for Anarchist Studies. Retrieved 20 March 2006 from <http://www.anarchist-studies.org/article/articleview/55/1/1>.

Kropotkin, P. (n.d.). 'Syndicalism and Anarchism'. *Black Flag* 210: 24–7.

May, T. (1994). *The Political Philosophy of Poststructuralist Anarchism*. Pennsylvania, PA: Pennsylvania State University Press.

Morland, D. (2004). 'Anti-Capitalism and Postanarchism'. In Purkis and Bowen (2004).

Newman, S. (2004). 'Is There a Postanarchist Universality? A Reply to Michael Glavin'. Institute for Anarchist Studies. Retrieved 31 March 2006 from <http://www.anarchist-studies.org/article/articleprint/87/-1/9>.

—— (2003). 'The Politics of Postanarchism'. Institute for Anarchist Studies. Retrieved 21 March 2006 from <http://www.anarchist-studies.org/article/articleprint/1/-1/1/>.

—— (2001). *From Bakunin to Lacan: Anti-Authoritarianism and the Dislocation of Power*. Oxford: Lexington Books.

Postanarchism Listserv (n.d.). Retrieved 26 March 2006 from <http://groups.yahoo.com/group/postanarchism>.

Purkis, J. (2004). 'Towards an Anarchist Sociology'. In Purkis and Bowen (2004).

—— and J. Bowen (2004). *Changing Anarchism: Anarchist Theory and Practice in a Global Age*. Manchester: Manchester University Press.

Rhys, G. (1988). 'Class War's Rough Guide to the Left'. *Class War: The Heavy Stuff* 2.

Sim, S. (ed.) (n.d.). 'Introduction: Spectres and Nostalgia – Post-Marxism/Post-*Marxism*'. In *Post-Marxism: A Reader*. Edinburgh: Edinburgh University Press.

Simons, J. (ed.) (2002). 'Introduction'. In *Contemporary Critical Theorists: From Lacan to Said*. Edinburgh: Edinburgh University Press.

Urban 75 (2006). *Is Post-Anarchism a Good Idea?* Retrieved 26 March 2006 from <http://www.urban75.net/vbulletin/showthread.phpt=141865&highlight=postanarchism>.

Villon, S. (2003). 'Post-Anarchism or Simply Post-Revolution?' <http://theanarchistlibrary.org/HTML/sasha_k__Post-Anarchism_or_Simply_Post-Revolution_.html>.

Welsh, J., and Purkis, J. (2003). 'Redefining Anarchism for the Twenty-First Century: Some Modest Beginnings'. *Anarchist Studies* 11(1): 5–12.

Yaroslavsky, E. (2006) [1937]. 'History of Anarchism in Russia'. Retrieved 28 March 2006 from <http://dwardmac.pitzer.edu/anarchist_archives/worldwidemovements/anarchisminrussia6.html>.
Young, Robert (2003). *Postcolonialism: A Very Short Introduction*. Oxford: Oxford University Press.
ZACF (2003). Zabalaza Anarchist Communist Federation of Southern Africa. 'Sucking the Golden Egg: A Reply to Newman'. Interactivist Information Exchange. Retrieved 20 March 2006 from <http://slash.autonomedia.org/article.pl?sid=03/10/10/1220218>.

Part 4
Lines of Flight

12
Buffy the Post-Anarchist Vampire Slayer

Lewis Call

The publication of *Post-Anarchism: A Reader* confirms what many of us have suspected (and cautiously hoped for) these past few years: a kind of post-anarchist moment has arrived. Benjamin Franks has argued that this moment has already enabled a small but identifiable post-anarchist *movement* to emerge; he quite sensibly names Todd May, Saul Newman, Bob Black, Hakim Bey and me as members of this movement (2007: 127). Legend has it that Bey got the whole thing started back in the 1980s, when he called for a 'post-anarchism anarchy' which would build on the legacy of Situationism in order to reinvigorate anarchism from within (1985: 62). Interestingly, Bey identified popular entertainment as a vehicle for 'radical re-education' (ibid.). It is in this spirit that I offer my post-anarchist reading of Joss Whedon's popular fantasy programme *Buffy the Vampire Slayer*. My text will be *Buffy's* fourth season. This season undeniably represents Buffy's anarchist moment; I will argue that season four also offers its audience an accessible yet sophisticated post-anarchist politics.

But what does a post-anarchist politics look like? Newman has pointed out that post-anarchism is not 'after' anarchism and does not seek to dismiss the classical anarchist tradition; rather, post-anarchism attempts to radicalize the possibilities of that tradition (2008: 101). Broadly speaking, post-anarchists believe that an effective anarchist politics must address not only the modern forms of economic and state power, but also the more pervasive and insidious forms of power which haunt our postmodern world. These include what Foucault called bio-power (1978: 140ff.), and what Deleuze and Guattari called overcoding or the imperialism of the sign (1983: 199ff.). The kinds of power which structuralists and post-structuralists have located in the realm of language are of particular importance to post-anarchism. For example, Newman (2001) has shown that Lacan's concept of the Symbolic order is crucial to the post-anarchist project. For Lacan, the Symbolic is the place of language and thus of Law; the Symbolic order creates us as individuals, structures our desires and determines the limits within which resistance can happen. This has serious implications for radical thought: if Lacan's model is correct, then anarchist theory must offer an account of the Symbolic. Furthermore, if the Symbolic is the place where Law happens, and if Law is the speech of the state, then anarchists should seek to subvert the Symbolic order. In other words, if we really want to do something about *the Law*, we must find a way out of the Symbolic. Otherwise, we're just fighting *laws*, a losing proposition.

What I'm really saying is that we just want to let anarchism take its structuralist turn, because we think that will lead us to a place that's fascinating and possibly liberatory. This desire is motivated by what Franks has called one of the 'great strengths' of post-anarchism: its ability to spot the 'essentialisms and dogmatisms' of classical anarchisms, and its capacity to open up original areas for critical scrutiny (2007: 140). Yet Franks and others have also noted a serious potential problem with post-anarchism: it often rejects or ignores the concept of class, and thus disregards important forms of oppression (ibid.: 137). It seems that a dangerous elitism lurks within post-anarchism. My turn to popular culture was motivated, in part, by my desire to purge the project of this elitism. After all, it's true that the workers don't read much Lacan. They have better things to do. But in our postmodern world, everybody watches television. As post-anarchist ideas are represented on TV, they become accessible to a broad audience, which includes many working-class viewers. Pop culture in general, and television in particular, can take post-anarchism out of its bourgeois ivory tower and broadcast it into living rooms around the world.

This is where *Buffy the Vampire Slayer* comes in. *Buffy* is a pop-culture phenomenon. The show ran for seven seasons. Its spinoff, *Angel*, ran for five. Both narratives have continued in comic book form. *Buffy* has a large, loyal, dedicated audience. That audience does include many bourgeois academics: David Lavery (2004) has described Buffy Studies as an academic cult, and I am a card-carrying member of that cult. But Buffy is not just for scholar-fans; it is for everybody. *Buffy*'s most working-class character, Xander Harris, starts season four by stating his ethical imperative. He solves his moral dilemmas by asking himself, 'What would Buffy do?' (4.1).[1] The answer, I will argue, is that *Buffy* would launch a classical anarchist assault on the military–scientific complex, followed by an all-out post-anarchist attack on the Symbolic. And then have hot chocolate.

Not everyone agrees; *Buffy* criticism, especially in its early years, has often denied the show's revolutionary potential. Jeffrey Pasley equated Buffy and her demon-hunting friends with the 'primitive rebels' and 'social bandits' of leftist lore, but concluded that they ended up offering only 'piecemeal' resistance, not revolution (2003: 262–3). Reading the programme through the lens of Marxist historiography, Pasley failed to see the more radical elements of anarchist resistance in *Buffy*. Even less plausibly, Neal King (2003) denied that there was anything anti-authoritarian about Buffy's 'Scooby gang'; for him, Buffy and her (mainly female) friends were nothing more than fascist 'brownskirts'. This position was based largely on a tortured interpretation of *Buffy*'s first three seasons; by the fourth season, it had become quite impossible to identify Buffy with any kind of fascist politics.

Season four shows us Buffy's freshman year at the University of California, Sunnydale. As Bussolini has pointed out, this is the same U.C. that brought us the American nuclear arsenal (2005; paragraph 16). Buffy begins dating

Riley Finn, her handsome young teaching assistant. (Whoops!) Buffy soon discovers that Riley is actually a special forces soldier working for the U.S. government's secret demon-hunting project, the Initiative. Buffy tries to work with the Initiative, but soon finds that she can't handle its military hierarchies and authoritarian power structures. So season four actually establishes Buffy's politics as *anti*-fascist. Wall and Zryd have argued compellingly that Buffy's 'critical way of thinking about the fascistic and military-structured Initiative' facilitate Riley's transformation from loyal soldier to self-proclaimed anarchist by the end of the season (2001: 61). Riley's 'anarchism', they claim, is not rigorous, but rather represents a 'shorthand alternative to institutional logic' similar to that used by opponents of globalization (ibid.). The fact that it is non-rigorous or post-rational may be to its advantage, however. Bussolini makes the important point that the famous mass protests against the World Trade Organization, later known as the 'Battle of Seattle', took place while season four was originally being broadcast in November 1999 (2005; paragraph 29). Bussolini emphasizes, correctly, that the anti-globalization politics which were contemporary with season four criticize the kind of state-based, hierarchical politics which motivate the Initiative (ibid.). The show presents Seattle-style anarchism as a real and legitimate option for an Iowa farm boy like Riley Finn, or for a working-class carpenter like Xander Harris. The show thus makes anarchism an option for various non-bourgeois audiences. As the streets of Seattle filled with those who believed another world was possible, *Buffy* was broadcasting a radical endorsement of this belief – on network television!

If *Buffy*'s fourth season had 'only' portrayed a relevant form of contemporary anarchist politics in a highly positive light, that alone would secure the show a place in the history of popular culture. But this season did much more than that. In addition to its compelling narrative about the emergence of a classical anarchist consciousness, season four offered a bold post-anarchist vision. Kenneth Hicks has recently accused season four of assuming that 'government is incompetent because it's incompetent'; Hicks finds this assumption 'inconclusive and unsatisfying' (2008: 69). But there is, in fact, a perfectly convincing reason for the Initiative's failures. Richardson and Rabb have quite rightly interpreted Riley's rejection of the Initiative as a rejection of 'humanity's militarization of reason and scientific knowledge' (2007: 70). Riley's 'anarchism', then, is in part an anarchist critique of what Habermas and others have called instrumental rationality.

This is *Buffy*'s entry point into post-anarchism. A Habermasian critique of instrumental rationality, while certainly radical by the standards of network television, would nonetheless have remained wedded to the modernist position of the Frankfurt School. To avoid this, the show must take a post-structuralist turn. Amazingly, this is precisely what it does. The second half of season four takes as its central concern the operations of power within the realm of language and Law. *Buffy* has always shown a strong fascination with language (see M. Adams, 2003), but here that fascination takes on a specifically political form. The show enacts an escape from what Fredric

Jameson called the 'prison-house of language' (1972). This escape begins with the silent episode, 'Hush' (4.10), which performs the elimination of the Symbolic in order to stage a very post-anarchist return to the Lacanian Real. The alternate reality episode 'Superstar' (4.17) rewrites the Symbolic order, to make a minor character into the star of the show. *Buffy*'s post-anarchist project culminates in the season four finale, 'Restless' (4.22). This episode is a tour of the dreamworld, the world beneath the rational. As much as any symbolic artefact could, 'Restless' approaches the unrepresentable world Lacan called the Real.

So *Buffy*'s fourth season does not only provide a savvy, vibrant representation of an anarchist praxis which was real and relevant when the programme aired in 1999. The show also models a very viable post-anarchist politics, one which is based on a radical subversion of the dominant Symbolic regime. This politics is the heir of 60s Situationism and the 'ontological anarchy' of the 80s. It builds on radical street theatre and the symbolic interventions associated with Carnival against Capitalism and other contemporary anarchist movements. Most crucially, this post-anarchism challenges the hegemony of language. It locates the places where effective revolutionary action is still possible: in the space where there is no speech, and in the mystical space of the unconscious. Lacan named this last space the Real. We can never represent it, but if we approach it even obliquely, we contribute to our liberation from the tyranny of language. *This* is what Buffy would do. She would be an anarchist, certainly: after all, Riley and all the other kids are doing it. But being an anarchist means something specific in *Buffy*'s millennial moment. It means that she will be Buffy, the post-anarchist vampire slayer.

'WE'VE GOT IMPORTANT WORK HERE. A LOT OF FILING, GIVING THINGS NAMES.'

Post-Anarchist Themes in Late Season Four of *Buffy*

Jacques Lacan is justly infamous for his incomprehensible prose, but his structuralist version of psychoanalysis is nonetheless crucial to many contemporary intellectual projects, including post-anarchism. Thankfully, there is a rich secondary literature on Lacan. Marini (1992) provides a useful summary of Lacan's conceptual revolution. In 1953, Lacan replaced the traditional Freudian system with a structural system which divided human reality into a Symbolic realm of language and culture, an unrepresentable and unknowable Real, and an Imaginary composed of our fantasies of reality (ibid.: 43). Lacan reformulated the Oedipus complex; he made it our entrance into the Symbolic, which was the 'universe of the law' (ibid.). The Lacanian model should be of tremendous interest to contemporary anarchists, for it's just possible that Lacan located the place where Law happens. That place is the Symbolic, which we first enter via the name of the Father. As Elizabeth Grosz has pointed out, the Lacanian model implies that 'language alone is capable of positioning the subject as a social being' (1990: 99). Language does this by deploying the rules, structures and hierarchies of the social. Since these are also the conduits through which political power flows, language advances the statist agenda. That makes the Symbolic a legitimate target for post-anarchism.

If the Symbolic is post-anarchism's natural enemy, the Real is its natural ally. It was Saul Newman who first recognized this important point: 'this gap, this surplus of meaning that cannot be signified, is a void in the symbolic structure – the "Real"' (2001: 139). The Real ensures that the hegemony of the Symbolic is never complete. Thinking about the Real helps us to find fissure points in the structures of postmodern power. The Real is a jackpot for post-anarchists, suggesting as it does that 'there is always something missing from the social totality, something that escapes social signification – a gap upon which society is radically founded' (ibid.: 147). It's certainly a relief to realize that society and its myriad power structures must always remain incomplete. Society might appear to be monolithic and omnipotent, as might the state which claims to represent society. But both were built upon this gap in the system of signification: their foundations are hollow.

Newman uses this Lacanian notion of the gap 'to theorize a non-essentialist outside to power' (2001: 160). This is post-anarchism in a nutshell – or in a bombshell, as Jason Adams (2003) would have it. Post-anarchism seeks a space outside power, and endeavours to use that space as the staging area for a project of radical liberation. Like Newman, I believe that this space is to be found in the Lacanian Real. Of course, the Real is not a destination we can reach; it will always elude us. But we can think about the Real. We can develop an awareness of its effects. We can feel its presence in our lives. When we do these things, we challenge the authority of the Symbolic. We question its *jurisdiction*, in the most literal sense: we dispute its right and its ability to *speak the Law*. What could be more anarchist than that?

Buffy makes its post-anarchist move about halfway through season four, in Joss Whedon's celebrated silent episode 'Hush' (4.10). In this Emmy-nominated episode, an especially terrifying band of monsters descends on Sunnydale. The Gentlemen are neat, tidy and Victorian in their appearance. They are also completely silent. And the moment they arrive in Sunnydale, they steal everyone's voices. In Lacanian terms, the Gentlemen rip the Symbolic order away and lock it in a box. In an excellent Lacanian reading of 'Hush', Kelly Kromer notes that Buffy normally acts as the Law in Sunnydale: she creates the world by classifying creatures as wicked or good (2006: 1). Buffy wields the power of the Name, a weapon just as potent as her trusty stake, Mr. Pointy. From a post-anarchist perspective, of course, this power is problematic, since it is precisely the kind of power that underwrites the postmodern state. But Buffy, like all slayers, is a woman. And as Luce Irigaray (1985) has pointed out, women are connected to the Symbolic in a way which is tenuous at best. As Irigaray argues, women assure the possibility of the Symbolic without being recipients of it: 'their nonaccess to the symbolic is what has established the social order' (ibid.: 189). Buffy's gender is important here. As a woman, she's used to being denied access to the Symbolic. This denial of access is literalized in 'Beer Bad', (4.5) when magic beer causes Buffy to devolve into a cavewoman.[2] By the end of the episode, she is incapable of forming multi-word sentences. Xander asks her what lesson she has learned about beer; she replies, 'foamy'. When the womanizing Parker asks forgiveness for his use and abuse of Buffy, she is beyond language, and can only bonk him on the head with a club. At this point we realize that actually, Buffy is often outside the Symbolic. So when the Symbolic suddenly vanishes from Sunnydale in 'Hush', she can cope better than an old patriarch like Giles or a young one like Riley. In silent Sunnydale, the Real reigns supreme, and consequently social Law begins to disintegrate (Kromer, paragraph 8). This is bad news for Buffy, but good news for post-anarchists. Life would indeed be really good, if only the Real could be domesticated (Marini,1992: page 43). At least, that's how the state sees things. But 'Hush' argues powerfully that this domestication can never be achieved. Indeed, 'Hush' performs the polar opposite of this domestication: a radical release of the Real.

In 'Hush', the Real is dramatically erotic. That's understandable, since Eros always contains the excess of meaning which characterizes the Real. Erotic gestures thus approach the Real in a way that language never can. 'Hush' begins with a daydream. Buffy is in her psych class. Professor Walsh (the mad scientist who runs the Initiative) is lecturing about communication, language and the difference between the two. As part of a demonstration, Walsh asks Riley to kiss Buffy. 'If I kiss you, it'll make the sun go down', warns Riley. He does, and it does. Clearly this kiss has performative powers which language can't match. Of course, the Symbolic immediately tries to reassert itself. 'Fortune favours the brave', observes Buffy. She doesn't usually quote Virgil, so this looks like the voice of the Empire speaking through Buffy – in this case an Empire of Signs, as Barthes might say. 'Hush' is all about the kiss. Riley complains to Forrest that he has trouble talking to Buffy. 'Then get with the kissing', Forrest quite sensibly replies. But the really interesting thing about Buffy and Riley is that they actually *can't* kiss anywhere near the Symbolic. Their first kiss happened in the Imaginary, in Buffy's daydream. Their second kiss happens in the Real. Stripped of speech, the two mute heroes meet in downtown Sunnydale, which has become a chaotic no-man's-land. They hug. Each checks, silently, to see that the other is OK. They hear the sounds of nearby violence. Preparing to do their duty, they start to turn away from one another. They think better of this, turn back, and kiss. The entire kiss is negotiated and consummated without speech, which gives it a great deal of power. This kiss becomes the foundation of their relationship. Buffy and Riley never do get the hang of the talking. But when they are fighting demons together – and afterwards, when they are making love – they move with effortless grace. Buffy and Riley don't need speech; indeed, they are visibly better off without it. They show us that we can actually operate much closer to the Real than we typically believe.

The other major erotic event in 'Hush' is an incident of same-sex hand-holding, which represents the beginning of Willow's first lesbian relationship. In 'Hush' we meet a young witch named Tara. When Sunnydale goes silent, Tara seeks out Willow, the one person who might understand what's happening. Tara and Willow are attacked by the Gentlemen. They're forced to barricade themselves in the dorm laundry room. With the Gentlemen banging on the door, Willow tries to use her magic to move a soda machine up against the door. It's too heavy, and she fails. Then Tara takes Willow's hand. Their fingers intertwine. They look at each other. In a very well choreographed move, they turn simultaneously towards the soda machine, which flies across the room and blocks the door. (This shot would later reappear in the show's opening credits.) Willow and Tara don't stop holding hands after their spell is done, and they are basically inseparable from this moment. Their shared magical power illustrates the nature of their relationship: vital, energetic, and very much greater than the sum of its parts. All of this is accomplished without language. Indeed, 'Hush' makes us realize that if the Gentlemen hadn't come to Sunnydale, Willow and Tara might never have got together. Willow is a hyper-articulate nerdy type, and Tara has a stutter which gets worse when she's nervous. In normal times, the two of them live on two very different margins of the Symbolic. None of that matters in the laundry room. Here there is no language, only a Real composed of power and love.

'Hush' argues consistently that love happens where there is no language. Naturally, Buffy finds her voice at last, and her scream destroys the Gentlemen. The Law returns to Sunnydale. But no one is actually happy about that. 'Hush' concludes with a brilliant meditation on the misery of the Symbolic. During the reign of silence, Buffy and Riley have discovered each other's secret identities. At the end of the episode, Riley visits Buffy in her dorm room. He sits down awkwardly on Willow's bed. 'I guess we have to talk', he begins. 'I guess we do', Buffy agrees. The two of them then sit in complete silence, staring at one another across the gulf between the two beds. Their longing is palpable, and it is a longing for the Real. Their plight suggests that we should resist the Symbolic not only because it's the right thing to do, but also because it might be the only way that we can find happiness.

Jane Espenson's 'Superstar' (4.17) explores the fascist tendencies of the Symbolic. The teaser shows us a typical monster hunt, with one bizarre twist: Buffy can't handle things, so she has to get help from ... Jonathan Levinson? This geeky, alienated graduate of Sunnydale High has somehow been transformed into a super-suave James Bond type. Things get worse fast: Jonathan has even colonized the *opening credit sequence*, in which he gets as much screen time as any Scooby. This is big trouble, because it means that Jonathan has broken out of the Buffyverse's narrative space. The credits are the part of the programme which knows itself to be a television show. In the credits, Jonathan is not just part of the story; he is part of the real-world cultural artefact we call *Buffy the Vampire Slayer*. Ten minutes into this astonishing 'Espensode', Jonathan has taken control of the Symbolic in the Buffyverse and in our world, too.

Throughout 'Superstar', the image of Jonathan continues to proliferate across every available surface. We see rows and rows of identical Jonathan posters lining the walls of Sunnydale. The aesthetic is unmistakably fascist: infinite copies of Jonathan's sad, shy face gaze down on the population.

Jonathan has become all things to all people: brilliant musician, vampire slayer, author, basketball player. He is the subject of comic books and trading cards. Jonathan advertises sporting goods on billboards. A poster on the back of Riley's dorm room door shows Jonathan as a basketball superstar – like Michael Jordan, only short and Jewish. This infinite propagation of Jonathans slides smoothly into a very smart critique of consumer culture. Here is a radical assault on the corporate logo, for those who may never get around to reading Naomi Klein. In this strange and disturbing world, there is only one logo, and it is Jonathan. His image has monopolized the Symbolic system more effectively than Nike's swoosh ever did. And now we see where consumer capitalism is headed: towards a barren, totalitarian Symbolic, a world with only one sign. Here the Name has been distilled down to its most basic, oppressive essence. That essence is Jonathan.

Naturally, the magic which Jonathan used to rewrite the Symbolic order proves to be 'unstable'. It's one thing to disrupt the narrative of the show, but Jonathan's magic is threatening to spill over into *our* Symbolic, and that won't do. This is television, after all, and the name of the show must be identical with the name of its protagonist. So the spell is broken. Jonathan goes back to being a nobody, and Buffy's on top of the world once again. But the damage has been done. Buffy's viewers can no longer take the Symbolic for granted. 'Hush' has already taught us that the Symbolic comes and goes in the Buffyverse. Now we know that our own Symbolic is no safer than Buffy's.

The stage is set for season four's climactic post-anarchist battle. To defeat Adam, the Scoobies must use a spell which combines the strengths of Buffy, Willow, Xander and Giles. It's a moment of radical mysticism. 'We are forever', declares Combo Buffy. Here we see a powerful expression of *Buffy*'s typical argument: Buffy needs her friends, and is always better off when she has their help. She may be a kick-ass Stirnerean superhero, but she can't do it alone. A strong collectivist spirit lies deep at the heart of *Buffy*. Maybe this is what Fredric Jameson was talking about when he described the attempt to dissolve the subject into the Symbolic as an awareness of the 'dawning collective character of life' (1972: 196). By the end of season four, *Buffy* was post-Seattle and post-structuralist. The show increasingly pointed towards a radically collectivist politics, and it increasingly found space for such a politics in the place beyond the Symbolic.

This trend culminates in Joss Whedon's 'Restless' (4.22), the denouement of season four.[3] It turns out that the joining spell which created Combo Buffy has a price, as such spells often do. The Scoobies try to sleep off the spell's after-effects, but they are plagued by troubling dreams. These dreams reveal a persistent need to overcome language and embrace the Real. Willow dreams of 'homework' which requires her to cover every inch of Tara's skin with mysterious calligraphy. In this dream, Tara is over-inscribed. She is completely contained and constrained within the Symbolic. This reiterates the argument of 'Hush': Tara is always better off without language. Indeed, all the Scoobies are. Dream-Giles directs a play. He gives an inspirational speech just before the curtain goes up, and cheerfully instructs his troupe to 'lie like dogs'. Public speech is ridiculed here, dismissed as a pack of lies. Gradually the Scoobies start to realize the nature of their dilemma. 'There's a great deal going on, and all at once!' observes Giles. He's right: as the Symbolic erodes, everything becomes simultaneous. The Scoobies are entering the eternal Now of the Real. This world is seductive; it's hard to leave. Willow and Giles start to work out the fact that they are being pursued by some kind of primal force. Xander resists: 'Don't get linear on me now, man!' He doesn't want to re-enter the Symbolic – who would? That would mean going through the whole Oedipal thing again. 'Restless' literalizes Oedipal fear through Xander's pseudo-incestuous desire for Buffy's mom, and through his aggression towards his drunken father, who makes a rare and violent appearance in Xander's dream.

Buffy's dream provides the strongest challenge to the Symbolic. Buffy meets Riley in an Initiative conference room. He's dressed in coat and tie, as befits his new rank: 'They made me Surgeon General.' In the dreamworld, Buffy's critique of instrumental rationality can reach new heights of beautiful absurdity. It transpires that Riley is drawing up a plan for world domination with Adam (the season four 'Big Bad', now in human form). 'The key element?' Riley reveals: 'Coffee-makers that think'. It's a wonderful absurdist send-up, in the tradition of Situationism, Dadaism or Surrealism. When Buffy questions this plan to achieve the apotheosis of state power, Riley replies, 'Baby, we're the government. It's what we do.' It's important to note that Riley did not participate in the joining spell, and is not part of this dream voyage. What we are seeing here is Buffy's unconscious *perception* of Riley. This is the show's way of explaining how Riley could call himself an anarchist without actually understanding what that meant. Although Riley has rejected the external power structures which once ruled him, he has not yet killed his inner fascist. Riley remains a statist, and an especially nasty sort of statist at that. He dismisses his girlfriend: 'Buffy, we've got important work here. A lot of filing, giving things names.' The work he mentions, the filing and naming, are the distilled essence of bureaucracy. Buffy's dream becomes a nightmare as Riley embraces Symbolic power. The dream reveals to us that Riley's political education is not over. He may call himself an anarchist, but now he needs to learn how to be a post-anarchist.

Finally, Buffy meets the mysterious primal force which has been pursuing her and her friends through the dreamworld. This force turns out to be the spirit of the original Slayer, the woman who first took on the burden of slayerhood in the ancient world. Tara shows up to mediate between Buffy and the speechless Primal Slayer. As Tara says, 'Someone has to speak for her.' This ancient tribal woman confirms Irigaray's interpretation, for she is definitely outside the Symbolic. 'Let her speak for herself', Buffy demands. Buffy is still the voice of the Law here, constantly trying to reassert the Symbolic order. '*Make her speak*', Buffy insists. Speech is an imperative here, for the Symbolic order is in a state of crisis. The Primal Slayer is a creature of the radical Real. If she cannot be made to speak, she threatens to undermine the entire Symbolic regime. Speaking through Tara, the first Slayer insists upon her position outside language: 'I have no speech. No name. I live in the action of death, the blood cry, the penetrating wound. I am destruction. Absolute … alone.' She is pure action, and she has nothing to do with language. Buffy reasserts the Symbolic one more time, with a twinkling speech that rolls off Sarah Michelle Gellar's tongue like a waterfall in springtime: 'I walk. I talk. I shop. I sneeze. I'm gonna be a fireman when the floods roll back. There's trees in the desert since you moved out. And I don't sleep on a bed of bones. Now give me back my friends.' This is finally enough to force the first Slayer to speak. 'No … friends! Just the kill. We … are … alone!' But it's Buffy's position that prevails. She defeats her ancient ancestor, everybody wakes up, and things get back to normal.

Wait a minute. Doesn't that just mean that the Symbolic always wins in the end? What's revolutionary about that? Buffy's still the voice of the Law, and the space outside language has vanished once again. But here we have to look at the big picture. Baudrillard once observed that the events of May 1968 created a rift in the Symbolic order which remained open for years (1976: 34). The events of 'Restless' have a similar effect on the Buffyverse. 'Restless' appeared almost exactly halfway through Buffy's seven-season narrative. Seasons five, six and seven are largely concerned with Buffy's quest to understand the primal nature of her power. In a way, Buffy never wakes up from her dream. She now knows that the Real is out there. She continues to live in the Symbolic as she must, as we all must. But she has learned that her power comes from a place outside language. 'I need to know more. About where I come from, about the other slayers', she tells Giles at the beginning of season five (5.1). In a most unlikely move, Buffy becomes a student of history. She studies the ancient stories of the slayer line, seeking the place where it all began, in the time *before* the Symbolic.

Buffy finally finds what she's looking for towards the end of the show's seventh and final season. In 'Get it Done' (7.15), Buffy visits the dreamtime once again. This time she goes all the way back to the beginning, to re-enact the event which created the first Slayer. Here *Buffy* examines its own creation myth. Since the slayers seem to represent the Symbolic order, this also lets the show examine the foundational myth of *our* culture. Buffy meets the Shadow Men, the ancient patriarchs who made the Primal Slayer. They chain Buffy, promising to show her the source of her power. Buffy protests. 'The First Slayer did not talk so much', remarks a Shadow Man. Nor could she, for she had not yet created the Symbolic order. The patriarchs show Buffy the demon energy which gives the slayers their power. She refuses it, but they won't listen. Suddenly she realizes that she is experiencing a rape, a violation. These men forced this demonic essence into a young woman against her will. These ancient fathers raped their daughter; from this violation the Symbolic was born. As Lacan surmised, the Law originates in the crucible of Oedipal desire.

But Buffy's been flirting with the Real for a while now, and she's ready to take back this ancient night. She defeats the Shadow Men, and breaks their staff. 'It's always the staff': Buffy knows a Lacanian phallus when she sees one. For the remainder of the series, Buffy pursues the destruction of this primal, patriarchal Symbolic. And at last she succeeds. At the end of the show,

Buffy and her friends change the world. Buffy rallies her army of potential slayers, and makes her 'Crispin's Day' speech before the big battle: 'In every generation one slayer is born because a bunch of men who died thousands of years ago made up that rule' (7.22). Buffy rejects her own foundational myth. She rejects the Oedipal logic which established the Symbolic. She acknowledges that the ancient patriarchs 'were powerful men'. But she insists that her best friend Willow is 'more powerful than all of them combined'. And indeed, Willow lives up to her press. The young witch works a spell which makes every 'potential' into a full-fledged slayer. In this way Buffy's power is diffused through an entire community. It's a radically democratic move. Buffy is no longer 'Slayer, comma, The'. The Law has been thoroughly fragmented. Indeed, following this rupture in the Symbolic, there is no longer a monolithic Law at all. There is instead a play of forces and flows, a give and take. Buffy has created a community of post-anarchist vampire slayers.

The show's conclusion demonstrates that Buffy is anything but a fascist brownskirt. At the end of season seven, Buffy holds nominal command over an army of slayers. But *Buffy* season eight comic books reveal that this 'army' is really a diverse collection of free-thinking riot grrrls, third-wave feminists and lesbian separatists. They're *all* 'hot chicks with superpowers' (7.21) now, and they're anarchists to boot. They would just as soon kick Buffy's ass as salute her. The slayers are an anarchist army, not unlike those that fought against Franco's fascists during the Spanish civil war. As for Buffy herself, she's a reluctant revolutionary. For most of her career she has been the sheriff of the Symbolic, wielder of the Name, bearer of the Law. But to her credit, when the Real came calling, she answered. By returning to the very moment of the Symbolic's creation, she found a space before language, a space of resistance. She made that space into a weapon and used it to fragment the Symbolic order which had imprisoned the slayers for so long. In this way Buffy modelled an effective, engaged post-anarchist politics. *Buffy* made that politics available to audiences of various ethnicities, genders, sexualities and social classes. Let the Buffy Studies and post-anarchist communities rejoice together at the arrival of Buffy, the post-anarchist vampire slayer.

NOTES

1. Dialogue quotations are taken from the excellent Buffyverse Dialogue Database at <http://vrya.net/bdb/>. I have made minor corrections to some dialogue. Episodes are cited by season number and episode number, e.g. (4.1) for season four, episode one. For a complete episode list, see <http://vrya.net/bdb/ep.php>. Thanks to Peggy Q for loaning me season four DVDs.

2. It turns out that the working-class tavern owner spiked the beer in order to get back at the snotty, elitist upper-class students who frequent his pub. 'Beer Bad' thus enacts a bar-room class struggle between bourgeois students and working-class 'townies'. Mainstream films like *Good Will Hunting* have tried this before, but *Buffy* is able to take it much further by stripping the arrogant intellectual elite of its weapons of rationalism.

3. The narrative structure of season four is unique, for this is the only season of *Buffy* which features a denouement. Every other season concludes with a climactic battle between Buffy and the current 'Big Bad'. But in season four, this battle occurs in the season's penultimate episode, 'Primeval'.

REFERENCES

Adams, J. (2003). 'Postanarchism in a Bombshell'. Retrieved 18 May 2009 from <http://aporiajournal.tripod.com/postanarchism.htm>. Also see <http://theanarchistlibrary.org/HTML/Jason_Adams__Postanarchism_in_a_Nutshell.html >.

Adams, M. (2003). *Slayer Slang: A Buffy the Vampire Slayer Lexicon*. New York: Oxford University Press.

Baudrillard, J. (1976). *Symbolic Exchange and Death* (I.H. Grant, trans.). Thousand Oaks, CA: Sage.

Bey, H. (1985) [1982]. *T.A.Z.: The Temporary Autonomous Zone, Ontological Anarchy, Poetic Terrorism*. Brooklyn, NY: Autonomedia.

Bussolini, J. (2005). 'Los Alamos Is the Hellmouth'. *Slayage: The Online International Journal of Buffy Studies* 5(2). Retrieved 12 May 2009 from <http://slayageonline.com/essays/slayage18/Bussolini.htm>.

Deleuze, G., and Guattari, F. (1983). *Anti-Oedipus: Capitalism and Schizophrenia* (R. Hurley et al., trans.). Minneapolis: University of Minnesota Press.

Foucault, M. (1978). *The History of Sexuality, vol. 1: An Introduction* (R. Hurley, trans.). New York: Vintage Books.

Franks, B. (2007). 'Postanarchism: A Critical Assessment'. *Journal of Political Ideologies* 12(2): 127–45.

Grosz, E. (1990). *Jacques Lacan: A Feminist Introduction*. New York: Routledge.

Hicks, K.S. (2008). 'Lord Acton is Alive and Well in Sunnydale: Politics and Power in *Buffy*'. In E. Dial-Driver et al. (eds). *The Truth of* Buffy: *Essays on Fiction Illuminating Reality*. Jefferson, NC: McFarland.

Irigaray, L. (1985). *This Sex Which Is Not One* (C. Porter, trans.). Ithaca, NY: Cornell University Press.

Jameson, F. (1972). *The Prison-House of Language: A Critical Account of Structuralism and Russian Formalism*. Princeton: Princeton University Press.

King, N. (2003). 'Brownskirts: Fascism, Christianity and the Eternal Demon'. In J.B. South (ed.). *Buffy the Vampire Slayer and Philosophy*. Chicago: Open Court.

Kromer, K. (2006). 'Silence as Symptom: A Psychoanalytic Reading of "Hush"'. *Slayage: The Online International Journal of Buffy Studies* 5(3). Retrieved 12 May 2009 from <http://slayageonline.com/essays/slayage19/Kromer.htm>.

Lavery, D. (2004). '"I Wrote My Thesis on You": *Buffy* Studies as an Academic Cult', *Slayage: The Online International Journal of Buffy Studies* 4(1–2). Retrieved 12 May 2009 from <http://slayageonline.com/essays/slayage13_14/Lavery.htm>.

Marini, M. (1992). *Jacques Lacan: The French Context*. A. Tomiche (trans.). New Brunswick, NJ: Rutgers University Press.

Newman, S. (2008). 'Editorial: Postanarchism'. *Anarchist Studies* 16(2): 101–5.

—— (2001). *From Bakunin to Lacan: Anti-Authoritarianism and the Dislocation of Power*. Lanham, MD: Lexington Books.

Pasley, J.L. (2003). 'Old Familiar Vampires: The Politics of the Buffyverse', in J.B. South (ed.). *Buffy the Vampire Slayer and Philosophy*. Chicago: Open Court.

Richardson, J.M., and Rabb, J.D. (2007). '*The Existential Joss Whedon: Evil and Human Freedom in* Buffy the Vampire Slayer, Angel, Firefly *and* Serenity'. Jefferson, NC: McFarland.

Wall, B., and Zryd, M. (2001). 'Vampire Dialectics: Knowledge, Institutions and Labour'. In R. Kaveney (ed.). *Reading the Vampire Slayer*. New York: Tauris Parke.

13
Sexuality as State Form

Jamie Heckert

In recent years, the collaborative writings of Gilles Deleuze and Félix Guattari have been read as contributing to an anarchist tradition or even constituting, along with other mostly French, mostly male theorists, a new anarchism. In either case, the depth of their opposition to the state and the profundity of their awareness of and desire for other possibilities has obvious affinities with anarchism. At the same time, their writings are also being looked to in order to reinvigorate a queer theory in danger of becoming established (see, for example, O'Rourke, 2006; Nigianni and Storr, 2009). I can see why. Beginning with a deconstruction of Oedipal heteronormativity, their radical two-volume love child, *Capitalism and Schizophrenia*, was born of a love which, in Deleuze's words, was 'nothing to admit' (1977a). He refuses the admission of homosexuality demanded of him; to do so would reduce homosexuality into a state of being. And for Deleuze, being is always becoming (Millett, 2006). It is this refusal to be categorized and judged that inspires both anarchist and queer readings. So too, is their refusal to separate the libidinal from the political, thus affirming the significance of sexuality as well as that of states and markets (see also Bedford and Jakobsen, 2009). For Guattari, 'a transformation of homosexuals cannot come about without simultaneous undoing of state power for which an ongoing experimentation with people, things and machines is tantamount' (Conley, 2009: 33). In this essay, I cannot separate the anarchist from the queer. Their philosophy is anarchist because it is queer, queer because it is anarchist. Or perhaps it would be more consistent to say that their philosophy is a contribution to becoming-anarchist, becoming-queer. In any case, they are neither queer nor anarchist when those words become fixed signs with clear and definite meanings. Deleuze and Guattari are too strange to be normalized.

When I first heard of them, they sounded too strange for me. I have a memory of standing on the doorstep of the tenement building in Edinburgh which housed the postgraduate office I used. Knowing something of my anarchist politics, one member of the department said with what I imagined was derision, you must be interested in Deleuze and Guattari's nomadology. I blushed with shame, wanting to appear academically sensible and found myself agreeing that that sounded crazy – not something I'd be interested in. Later, though, when I read Todd May's *Political Philosophy of Poststructuralist Anarchism* (1994), the state form and the nomad seemed all too familiar. I recognized them from stories I'd been hearing about sexuality.

I've been trying to make sense of sexual orientation for most of my life, it sometimes seems. Supposedly it's simple – just answer two questions: (1) Are you a woman or a man? (2) Do you fancy women, men or both? The thing is, neither of those questions seem all that simple to me. Oh, I've tried and thrown myself into various identities with the expected politics and efforts at community. While I don't want to underestimate the sustenance I received from these efforts, they were ultimately unsustainable. I couldn't keep trying to fit these boxes. I came to feel resentment, that never-quite-satisfying anaesthetic (Nietzsche, 1994), for not experiencing the great gay community advertised in those glossy magazines I nervously bought as a teenager. And so I argued strongly against identity politics, trying to convince LGBT activists that they were doing it wrong and should become anarchists instead (a gentler version of which appears as Heckert, 2004). My resentment faded as I realized my efforts were all too often leading to alienation rather than transformation. I wanted to develop a more compassionate approach to be able to connect with those who value the politics of Pride, not least my younger self. I also wanted inspiration for political alternatives that might inspire others so much more than being told, once again, that what they were doing wasn't good enough.

I tried a new approach to understanding sexual orientation. I asked people how they experienced it and listened to their stories (Heckert, 2005; 2010). I didn't ask just anyone – I imagine blank stares from folk who have no questions about the innateness of their heterosexuality, homosexuality or bisexuality. It has, after all, become 'the truth of the self'. Instead, I invited people in mixed relationships (e.g. lesbian/bi, gay/straight, it's complicated/it's complicated in a different way) because I expected them to have interesting stories about lives lived across the borders of these categories. And they did.

This chapter is a story about how I developed a deeper understanding of sexual orientation through these stories with the help of anarchist/post-structuralist thought and, more specifically, Deleuze and Guattari's concepts of the state form and the nomad. It's a story that has changed and will change again, for understanding, too, is a becoming.

AN ANARCHIST POST-STRUCTURALIST FRAMEWORK

If anarchism is not a fixed ideology, but a continually evolving trend in human history 'to dismantle [...] forms of authority and oppression' (Chomsky, 1970), then it seems clear to me that anarchism can be seen in the queer critiques of any supposed border existing in between heterosexual and homosexual, and the violence that its policing involves. So, in this sense, an anarchist approach to sexual orientation is neither particularly original, nor necessary. Queer theory, and the feminist and other movements from which and with which it evolves, is already doing this work. Saying that, I suggest that an explicitly anarchist critique of sexual orientation is valuable in recontextualizing histories, understanding contemporary experiences, and developing new forms of social relationships and movement.

Even with concerns about May's (and others') arguments for French post-structuralist theory as a *new* anarchism (e.g. Cohn and Wilbur, 2003), I have found the framework he developed under that name to be very valuable for my understanding this concept called 'sexual orientation'. Furthermore, it helps me to address confusions ascribed to post-structuralist and queer theories. Seidman (1997) among others has been concerned by the failure of queer theorists to specify any ethical commitments. May (1994) argues that while post-structuralist theorists may resist spelling out their ethical principles in order to avoid producing a foundation from their anti-foundational critiques, one can nonetheless find an unspoken ethics within this body of work. May's framework entails five conceptual components, including ethical principles: (1) structure and power as decentralized, relational and non-deterministic forces, which are continuously produced by human action; (2) a rejection of essentialist humanism for a performative understanding of human identity; (3) a radical ethical critique of representation; (4) an ethical commitment to difference; and, (5) a multi-value consequentialist understanding of both history and ethics. These components intersect to produce tools not only for understanding social life, but for radical social change.

Structure and Power: The Continuous and Pluralistic Production of Social Reality

May suggests that we can differentiate a 'tactical' politics from those which he terms 'strategic'. The defining characteristic of May's notion of strategic political philosophy is that it 'involves a unitary analysis that aims toward a single goal' (1994: 10). For certain Marxisms this would be centred on economics, or for certain feminist philosophies, on gender relations. In these cases, all forms of oppression and injustice can be reduced to a singular source (e.g. capitalism or patriarchy). This source, then, is the centre from which all power emanates. This conception of centralized power underlies the strategic notion that particular subject positions can be better placed to understand and address the problematic of power. Thus, traditional Marxist groups incorporate a party vanguard who claim power in the name of the proletariat. Certain feminisms have been similar in this respect in the suggestion that women (especially lesbian women), by virtue of their oppressed status, possess particular knowledge of the social world and are placed to produce revolutionary change (e.g. Frye, 1983). Feminist women of colour have responded that their experience cannot be reduced to a singular oppression, nor the sources of their affinity be reduced to one category of people (bell hooks, 1981; Moraga and Anzaldúa 1981).

Like these anti-racist feminisms, some post-structuralist theories define a tradition of tactical political philosophy. A tactical approach, in May's terms, argues that there is no centre of power, that it is irreducible to any particular source (e.g. capitalism, racism or patriarchy). Instead, Deleuze and Guattari, for example, use a metaphor of the rhizome to describe power – neither has a centre, a beginning nor an end; both form complex intersecting patterns. Likewise, Foucault suggests that power is exercised in multiple forms, through diverse social relations and in 'dispersed, heteromorphous, localised procedures' (1980: 142). It was the anti-authoritarian student and worker uprisings of Paris in 1968 that inspired and encouraged Foucault to carry on with his efforts to understand relations of domination outwith those traditionally analysed by Marxism.

Although Foucault had begun to explore the issue of power before 1968, it was his experience of this insurrection that spurred him on. While Guattari had long been politically active, Deleuze was to become deeply politicized by the events of 1968. Only after these revolutionary days did Deleuze become involved with political movement and activism, including the *Groupe d'information sur les prisons* (GIP) initiated by Foucault and others. He also worked in support of the Palestinians and homosexual people and in opposition to the Gulf War and the French nuclear strike force (Patton, 2000). In a sense, then, the suggestion that Foucault and Deleuze invented a new form of anarchism (May, 1994) understates the significance of the activist and anarchist contexts within which their work developed (see also Halperin, 1995: 25–6 on Foucault).

This anarchist approach to social organization might also be understood as recognizing structures as internal to human relations rather than as sources of power outside the social realm. Thus, post-structuralism does not, as some have suggested, deny the reality of either domination and oppression, or the apparent stability of structures of capitalism and government. Rather, theorists such as Foucault and Deleuze argue that structures are not fixed, nor are they historical forces that are simply maintained, but that these apparent structures are continuously produced through social relations. In theory, people could produce very different forms of social organization by changing the nature of their social relationships. This argument is continuous with elements of so-called classical anarchism.

In practice, such activity is difficult but not impossible and benefits from a tactical approach – recognizing the application of power within local and specific contexts. If, as Guattari, Foucault and Deleuze argue, power has no centre, then the vanguardist approach promoted by Leninism–Marxism and certain formulations of lesbian feminism can no longer be justified by claims of subject positions in relation to centres of power. Likewise, Ebert's (1996) criticism of Foucault (and Butler) as anarcho-capitalists who fail to recognize the exploitation of capitalism misinterprets, it seems to me, Foucault's anarchism. It is not simply the state, as a set of juridical and disciplinary apparatuses, that Foucault opposes, but the state-like relationships of power (e.g. disciplinary, penal, psychiatric) whose cumulative effects are the state; simultaneously, the state apparatus depends upon such decentralized relationships of power and obedience in order to exist.

If oppression is experienced in diverse locations and is produced by the intersection of various micropolitical forces, it is difficult to imagine that any one group of people can claim a social position that better enables them to politically address these problems than anyone else. In this respect, the work of Guattari, Foucault and Deleuze is very much anarchist in that it rejects vanguardism and promotes an ethic of decentralized social action. At the same time, in recognizing the multiplicity of the state, post-structuralist theories might offer interesting contributions to anarchist thought on the internal contradictions and complexities of the state as apparatus (e.g. Pringle and Watson, 1992). In other words, can one do unstatelike things within the apparatus of the state? Can one be in the institution but not of the institution (Shukaitis, 2009)?

Importantly, then, power might be understood not simply as suppressive, but is always profoundly productive. Power, in this sense, does not emanate down from the state. Rather the state may be considered that name which we give to the oppressive effects produced through decentralized relations of domination, surveillance, representation and control. According to 'stateless theories of the state', the state is a discursive effect rather than an autonomous agent outside of social relations (see Jessop, 2001 for overview). Likewise, relations of power can also produce more desirable effects, in anarchist terms, such as food cooperatives, workplace resistance, childcare, community gatherings or the production of anarchist theory.

While both vanguardist elements of lesbian feminism and advocates of 'sexual citizenship' (e.g. Plummer, 2003; Weeks, 1998) aim to undermine relations of domination, I'm concerned about the simultaneous relations of domination that remain unspoken, unaddressed. To prioritize, and thus present as discrete, one axis of oppression like sexual orientation is to evade all of the difficult issues that arise when sexuality is acknowledged as raced and classed, as intertwined with states and markets. I mean no disrespect in saying this: I have made such evasions myself when doing so was the only way I can imagine having the energy to focus on understanding sexuality. At the same time, I'm concerned, for example, how to address the homonormativity which arises when gay and lesbian rights claims coincide with the racial politics of state/capital/Empire, for example (Puar, 2008).

An Anti-Representationalist Ethic

In rejecting the notion of a human (or gay, etc.) essence, it is consistent to reject the humanist notion of discovering and cultivating this essence. If indeed the epistemological project of understanding an essence is at the same time a political project of defining and constraining human potential, then we might come to understand representation of a subject or a category of subjects as an act of violence. This violence applies to acts of representation in both senses of the term. To claim the authority to speak for another is a violation of that person's capacity to speak for themselves, to tell their own stories. 'Practices of telling people who they are and what they want erect a barrier between them and who (or what) they can create themselves to be' (May, 1994: 131). This is not to suggest a voluntaristic notion of the self, where one can choose who or what they want to be in the same sense that one can choose one's wardrobe. Identity is produced through numerous relations of power and social practices, over which one can only have limited control. This first sense of representation thus relates to the second: to speak for others depends upon claims to define others, that is to say who they really are or what their interests are, which is in itself an oppressive relationship. A rejection of representation is essential to direct or anarchist democracy as well as to post-structuralist critiques of essentialism. For Deleuze, a critique of representation is 'something absolutely fundamental: the indignity of speaking for others' (Deleuze, 1977b; see also Sullivan, 2005; Tormey, 2006). The critique of representation is, at the same time, an anti-capitalist sentiment. The apparatuses upon which capitalist social relations depend – factories, schools, prisons, hospitals, nuclear families and the military – function through disciplinary techniques, producing docility.

The Value of Difference

In keeping with the principle of anti-representation, the second ethical principle of anarchist post-structuralism is 'that alternative practices, all things being equal, ought to be allowed to flourish and even to be promoted' (May, 1994: 133). This principle, too, is a key commitment of queer theory. The first axiom of Eve Sedgwick's germinal work, *Epistemology of the Closet*, is that 'people are different from each other' (1990: 22). While queer theory, in keeping with its anarchist and post-structuralist roots, advocates a politics of difference, it's refusal to articulate an ethical principle of anti-representation has resulted in a misunderstanding of this commitment to difference. For example, Sheila Jeffreys (1993) has suggested that paedophilia, and Stephen Angelides (1994), rape, might also constitute sexual difference that would then be necessarily promoted by queer politics. However, rape certainly involves representation in the sense of not listening to what someone else wants (or does not want); paedophilia, when referring to childhood sexual abuse, does so as well (see Teixeira, n.d. for a critical anarchist discussion of paedophilia). Thus, in these cases, all things are not equal. So, promoting difference is not to advocate 'anarchy' in the sense of a lack of ethical standards, but anarchy in the sense of people deciding for themselves, in relation with others, how to live their lives without being told (or telling themselves) that they are doing it wrong. Post-structuralist/anarchist thought prioritizes the value and necessity of difference over identity both through a rejection of the coherent, rational, individual self in favour of a fluidity and multiplicity of desires embodied within and between individuals and through a rejection of over-deterministic notions of structure for a decentralized conception of power.

Of Ends and Means

Finally, post-structuralist ethics can be understood in terms of consequentialism: that ends cannot be separated from means. Consequentialism has deep roots within the anarchist tradition, exemplified by Bakunin's debates with Marx over the possibility of a 'workers' state' withering away to result in an egalitarian society. Bakunin's recognition that oppressive power is not centralized within capitalism and that history is a continuous process whereby the ends cannot be separated from the means is decidedly congruent with French post-structuralism. Furthermore, his accurate prediction of a 'red bureaucracy' suggests that history is a continuous process and that the ends are inseparable from, and cannot justify, the means. Consequentialism is still potentially authoritarian, as in the example of utilitarianism, in which the aim must always be the greatest happiness for the greatest number. Rather, May (1994) suggests that post-structuralist anarchism advocates a multi-value consequentialism, in which ends and means are inseparable and in which those ends and means are based on diverse values in particular locations. If societies, relationships and individuals are all continuously produced, if history is a continuous process, how is it possible to separate ends from means? As Giorgio Agamben writes, there are only 'means without end' (2000). Unlike Karl Marx or Francis Fukuyama (1992), post-structuralist theorists argue that there can be no 'end of history', whether communist or capitalist. Nor are consequences either linear or predictable. The future cannot be plotted, planned, forced or demanded – these are the efforts of states (Scott, 1998). All visions of the future are fantasy; it can be predicted no more than it can be controlled. Diverse practices of prefiguration are intertwined in such a way that the consequences cannot be predetermined. Life is always becoming otherwise.

SEXUAL ORIENTATION AS STATE FORM

Just as Foucault, and generations of anarchists before him, look beyond the state as institution to wider, decentralized practices of governmentality, Deleuze and Guattari see the state everywhere: in philosophy as state thought and in everyday life as state form. Fortunately, for those of us looking for anarchist inspiration, they see alternatives everywhere as well. 'The operation', they say, 'that constitutes the essence of the State' is overcoding (1977: 199). To overcode is to attempt to capture the endless creativity of life through the deployment of categories of judgment.

Of course, we all use categories to make sense of the world – coding is crucial in research methodology or other forms of storytelling where communication only happens because we can distinguish between the princess and the pea or the capitalist and the anarchist. Overcoding, on the other hand, is the colonizing strategy of declaring, with authority not to be questioned, both how things are and how they should be, regardless of the local and particular knowledge of those who are always, already living with these questions.

Overcoding is practised by the state as apparatus or institution in the form of law, for example. To limit our perception of the state to institution is to risk missing the manner in which macropolitical practices (that produce the appearance of 'institutions') are themselves products of interwoven micropolitical relationships and practices. Deleuze and Guattari use the notion of state forms to describe micro- and macro-level operations that have a relationship of mutual dependence with the state apparatus and which serve its goals of control, maintaining the illusion of centralized power. 'The purpose of the state-form is to bind all nomadism to certain structures, to make sure that its creativity does not overflow certain boundaries or certain identificatory categories' (May, 1994: 105). Thus, the state form helps to fulfil the essential function of the state, which is to conserve, to control, to capture. The state can be understood as 'a process of capture of flows of all kinds, populations, commodities or commerce, money or capital' (Deleuze and Guattari, 1988: 386). So too, flows of emotion, desire, attraction and kinship. But the state is not able to capture all flows, to control all creativity. Some things escape. These are the creative forces of nomadism: 'not tied to any given social arrangement; they are continuously creative, but their creativity is not naturally bound to any given types or categories of product. Such nomadism is central to Deleuze's thought, because it provides the possibility of conceiving new and different forms of practice, and thus resisting current forms of identification as unwanted constraints' (May, 1994: 104–5). This is creativity which refuses to be contained; it continually escapes, overflows, undermines, transgresses and subverts. It is the queer fecundity of life itself that changes, connects, evolves in ways that cannot be predicted. Reading about the state form and the nomad, the idea of sexual orientation started to make sense to me in a new way. It, too, is a system of categorizing and judging bodies, identities, desires and practices according to certain criteria. Intertwined with the state as apparatus, sexual orientation as state form involves borders and policing, representation and control. This is illustrated in two examples from interviews which were particularly influential in my developing an anarchist/queer framework for understanding sexual orientation.

> I socialise on the gay scene constantly. [...] I had a very good friend who used to walk into every gay bar in [the city] with me and say 'this is my friend and HE'S STRAIGHT, BY THE WAY'. And I got so pissed off with that, that I said to him one day, 'look, I'm not straight. I'm not gay. I'm not bisexual. I'm Mark and if I'm happy to live with that then you've got to accept it'. And my friends have. I mean there are people that [...] because of the [voluntary sector health] work I do, it kind of puts you in [...] a position of power where people snipe at you and they like to throw labels at me but I just refuse to take them up. So I think it kind of leaves them feeling frustrated. That's what labels are about, I think, aren't they? About other people being able to put you in a box and then [...] I don't know, deal with you or not deal with you, as they feel fit. And my experience has been that if you refuse to be pushed into one of their boxes, they're kind of (*shrugging*). I don't know a word [...] it leaves them slightly powerless and confused. ('Mark')

> Well I kind of tried to conform to a heterosexual box because that's pretty much what I thought I should do and then I sort of didn't try to conform to but considered a lesbian box and I thought it didn't really fit. I felt really uncomfortable with that and with all the connotations that I could see around that particular box and with the gay scene and I sort of considered a bisexual box and that didn't feel particularly right either. It felt restrictive and it felt like [...] the most difficult thing for me was that I felt that once I chose a particular thing to call myself, then I'd have to conform to that and I'd have to keep it up like a membership and I couldn't really handle

doing that. So I kind of dropped, not intentionally, but I kind of dropped it all and then, at some stage, I realised that I didn't actually need any of that so I didn't pick it up again. ('Erica')

In these stories, sexual orientation is not the truth of the self but something people do to themselves and to each other. I've come to see orientation less as a compass point where everyone has their own magnetic North and more in the sense used by institutions to orient new students or workers to a particular way of being. Orientation is not a truth, it is a process.

This can be seen, in part, through its historical development. Even before the development of heterosexual and homosexual identities within Western cultures, disciplinary apparatuses, including those of the state and Church, were active in their efforts to define standards for sexual behaviour. The possibility, or rather the perceived possibility, of procreation was sometimes defined as the only justification for sexual pleasure. Indeed, heterosexuality was first defined as a mental illness suffered by those who expressed strong desires for sexual activity with members of 'the other' sex, apart from the respectable necessity of procreation (Katz, 1996). Heterosexuality developed as a new state form, one in which a variety of practices were compressed into a single psychiatric category. This simultaneously placed reproduction as a core element of what a woman should be, to which feminists, anarcha- and otherwise, have long responded by supporting the reproductive freedom of women (see, for example, Passet, 2003). Sexual orientation can be understood as a set of state forms in that a wide variety of practices (including sexual, romantic and gendered) are defined and judged in terms of their capacity to be categorized within, or association with, one of three boxes. Nomadic sexualities are rendered incomprehensible, deviant, dangerous. The maintenance of sexual orientation as a comprehensible social category, in the face of much greater sexual diversity, is linked to the state apparatus through a wide variety of mechanisms. Obvious examples include marriage, sex education and clearly discriminatory laws. Other prime examples are found in sexual-orientation-identity rights movements. Arguments for 'operational essentialism' (Spivak, cited in Butler, 1990), 'strategic essentialism' (Fuss, 1989), or 'necessary fictions' (Weeks 1995), including Gamson's (1996) assertion that sometimes identity politics is the only possible option, come from efforts to be included within the state or to be represented.

At the same time, the character of the dangerous outsider is a necessary figure in state storytelling. What would police, politicians and demagogues do without the promiscuous woman, the queer, the paedophile, the terrorist, the potentially dangerous activist who crosses borders and defies laws? These figures are constructed as monstrous and undeserving of empathy. Empathy for the enemy weakens the soldier and state 'politics is the continuation of war by other means' (Foucault 2003: 15). That which is outside of the state, which is unstatelike, must be rigorously denied, caricatured, attacked, disciplined or subsumed. So, while some LGBT folk who are 'virtually normal' (Sullivan, 1996) in terms of race, class, gender and desire may be offered 'a place at the table' (Bawer, 1994), others continue to be targeted for police violence, bullied, harassed and impoverished. In this respect, I'm in disagreement with those who read nomadology as either celebration of the romantic other (e.g. Alcoff, 2006) or as a mobility privileged by neoliberalism. I see it instead as the flexibility necessary for survival.

The thing is, the state is also a survival strategy. It is, however, a strategy that assumes its survival depends on crushing or containing the Other. This is never the official story – war is presented as exceptional, as justifiable, as necessary. It is always regrettable, yet, too, always the lesser evil in the face of fascism, communism or terrorism. The state as apparatus or state as nation is always a security state, always dependent on fear, on terror, to justify the protection that only it can provide (Brown, 2005; Newman, 2007). The state as micropolitics, as state form, may involve similar emotional patterns. It might also be a way that many of us learned to survive growing up in a culture of domination (Heckert, n.d.).

WHO DO I THINK I AM?

I lie on the sofa and glance down at a draft of this chapter lying on the floor. I find myself asking, Who do I think I am? Imposter syndrome strikes. Am I really clever enough to be writing this? Do I really know what I'm talking about? These are echoes of that question of domination – 'Who do you think you are to question my authority?' Because to have authority is to be someone, not just a nobody *pretending* to be someone.

Later, I sit writing in a garden, breathing in the exhalations of trees and herbs, hedges and grasses while bacteria help the gut to digest a breakfast of grains, nuts, butter and honey. When I pause in writing to lift a cornflower and transplant it, further bacteria, these with anti-depressant properties, pass through skin into blood. Where do I end? Where does garden begin? Where does garden end and the rest of life begin? If these words are mine and you take them in, who are you? And what would it even mean to say these words are *mine?* I rather like being a no body, not enclosed to one singular indivisible and separate body. My flesh is social (Beasley and Bacchi, 2007), my self ecological (Macy, 2007; Tuhkanen, 2009).

In a recent discussion of whether or not I would accept an invitation to visit a university this spring, the woman who invited me said, 'I know – academic time, activist time', acknowledging that I must be very busy. I replied, 'and gardening time', to which she looked stunned and remained speechless. Trying to be an academic or an activist, the state arises within me, enclosing and judging. The role is a rule against which I am measured and eternally found wanting (Anonymous, 2000; Schmidt, 2000). Gardening, I am drawn outside this enclosed self and remember that to be alive is wondrous. This, too, is a form of direct action, of direct relationships with edible and medicinal plants, of skills I learn and share with friends and neighbours.

So when people say that Foucault's turn to the care of the self is a conservative, individualistic, bourgeous or liberal move, I am in disagreement.

For the care of the self, in my experience, is a letting go of the enclosed self, of self-consciousness, of that which is both the effect and the foundation of the state (Foucault, 1982). When I feel less attached to the question of who I really am – activist or scholar, homosexual or bisexual – I find myself experiencing a deeper sense of connection with others. Whether that's through the writing I do, in meetings of shared projects, in talking with friends, family and neighbours or with strangers on trains or in parks, possibilities arise that have been closed off when I want them to know, or want to keep secret, what I might imagine to be the truth of myself.

REFERENCES

Agamben, G. (2000). *Means Without End: Notes on Politics*. Minneapolis: University of Minnesota Press.

Alcoff, L.M. (2006). 'The Unassimilated Theorist'. *Proceedings of the Modern Language Association* 121(1) (January): 255–9.

Angelides, S. (1994). 'The Queer Intervention'. *Melbourne Journal of Politics* 22: 66–88.

Anonymous (2000). 'Give up Activism'. *Do or Die: Voices from the Ecological Resistance* 9: 160–6. Online at <http://www.eco-action.org/dod/no9/activism.htm>.

Bawer, B. (1994). *A Place at the Table: The Gay Individual in American Society*. New York: Simon & Schuster.

Beasley, C., and Bacchi, C. (2007). 'Envisaging a New Politics for an Ethical Future: Beyond Trust, Care and Generosity – Towards an Ethic of "Social Flesh"'. *Feminist Theory* 8(3): 279–98.

Bedford, K., and Jakobsen, J. (2009). *Toward a Vision of Sexual and Economic Justice*. New York: Barnard Center for Research on Women. Retrieved 26 August 2009 from <http://www.barnard.edu/bcrw/newfeministsolutions/reports/NFS4-Sexual_Economic_Justice.pdf>.

bell hooks. (1981). *Ain't I a Woman? Black Women and Feminism*. Boston: South End Press.

Brown, W. (1995). *States of Injury: Power and Freedom in Late Modernity*. Princeton: Princeton University Press.

Butler, J. (1990). *Gender Trouble: Feminism and the Subversion of Identity*. New York: Routledge.

Chomsky, N. (1970). 'Introduction to Daniel Guerin's *Anarchism: From Theory to Practice*'. New York: Monthly Review Press. Online at <http://www.zmag.org/chomsky/other/notes-on-anarchism.html>.

Cohn, J., and Wilbur, S. (2003). 'What's Wrong with Postanarchism?' Institute for Anarchist Studies web site. <http://theanarchistlibrary.org/HTML/Jesse_Cohn_and_Shawn_Wilbur__What_s_Wrong_With_Postanarchism_.html>.

Conley, V.A. (2009). 'Thirty-Six Thousand Forms of Love: The Queering of Deleuze and Guattari'. In Nigianni and Storr (2009).

Deleuze, G. (1977a). 'I Have Nothing to Admit' (J. Forman, trans.). *Semiotexte* 2(3).

—— (1977b). 'Intellectuals and Power: A Conversation Between Michel Foucault and Gilles Deleuze'. In D. Bouchard and S. Simon (eds). *Language, Counter-Memory, Practice* (trans. D Bouchard). Ithaca: Cornell University Press. Online at <http://libcom.org/library/intellectuals-power-a-conversation-between-michel-foucault-and-gilles-deleuze>.

—— and F. Guattari (1988). *A Thousand Plateaus: Capitalism and Schizophrenia* (Brian Massumi, trans.). London: Athlone Press.

—— —— (1977). *Anti-Oedipus: Capitalism and Schizophrenia* (R. Hurley, M. Seem and H. Lane, trans.). New York: Viking Press.

Ebert, T. (1996). *Ludic Feminism and After: Postmodernism, Desire and Labor in Late Capitalism*. Ann Arbor: University of Michigan Press.

Foucault, M. (2003). '*Society Must Be Defended*': Lectures at the Collège de France 1975–1976. New York: Picador.

—— (1982). 'Afterword: The Subject and Power'. In H. Dreyfus and P. Rabinow (eds). *Michel Foucault: Beyond Structuralism and Hermeneutics*. Chicago: University of Chicago Press.

—— (1980). *Power/Knowledge: Selected Interviews and Other Writings* (C. Gordon, ed.; C. Gordon, L. Marshall, J. Mepham and K. Soper, trans.). Brighton: Harvester Press.

Frye, M. (1983). *The Politics of Reality*. Trumansburg, NY: Crossing Press.

Fukuyama, F. (1992). *The End of History and the Last Man*. London: Penguin.

Fuss, D. (1989). *Essentially Speaking: Feminism, Nature and Difference*. London: Routledge.

Gamson, J. (1996). 'Must Identity Movements Self-Destruct? A Queer Dilemma'. In S. Seidman (ed.). *Queer Theory/Sociology*. Oxford: Blackwell.

Halperin, D. (1995). *Saint Foucault: Towards a Gay Hagiography*. New York: Oxford University Press.

Heckert, J. (2010). 'Intimacy with Strangers/Intimacy with Self: Queer Experiences of Social Research'. In K. Browne and C. Nash (eds). *Queer Methodologies in Social and Cultural Research*. Farnham: Ashgate.

—— (2005). 'Resisting Orientation: On the Complexities of Desire and the Limits of Identity Politics' (self-published Ph.D. thesis). University of Edinburgh. <http://sexualorientation.info/>.

—— (2004). 'Sexuality/Identity/Politics'. In J. Purkis and J. Bowen (eds). *Changing Anarchism*. Manchester: Manchester University Press.

—— (n.d.). 'Fantasies of an Anarchist Sex Educator'. In J. Heckert and R. Cleminson (eds). *Dangerous Desires: Essays in Anarchism and Sexuality* (unpublished manuscript).

Jeffreys, S. (1993). *The Lesbian Heresy: A Feminist Perspective on the Lesbian Sexual Revolution*. Melbourne: Spinifex Press.

Jessop, B. (2001). 'Bringing the State Back in (Yet Again): Reviews, Revisions, Rejections and Redirections'. Lancaster: Department of Sociology, Lancaster University. <http://www.comp.lancs.ac.uk/sociology/papers/Jessop-Bringing-the-State-Back-In.pdf>.

Katz, J.N. (1996). *The Invention of Heterosexuality*. London: Plume.

Macy, J. (2007). *World as Lover, World as Self: Courage for Global Justice and Ecological Renewal*. Berkeley, CA: Parallax Press.

May, T. (1994). *The Political Philosophy of Poststructuralist Anarchism*. University Park, PA: Pennsylvania State University Press.

Millet, K. (2006). 'A Thousand Queer Plateaus: Deleuze's "Imperceptibility" as a Liberated Mapping of Desire'. *Rhizomes* 11/12. Online at <http://www.rhizomes.net/issue11/millet.html>.

Moraga, C., and Anzaldúa, G. (eds) (1981). *This Bridge Called My Back: Writings by Radical Women of Color*. Watertown, MA: Persephone Press.

Newman, S. (2007). *Unstable Universalities: Postmodernity and Radical Politics*. Manchester: Manchester University Press.

Nietzsche, F. (1994). *On the Genealogy of Morality* (K. Ansell-Pearson, ed.). Cambridge: Cambridge University Press.

Nigianni, C., and Storr, M. (eds) (2009). *Deleuze and Queer Theory*. Edinburgh: Edinburgh University Press.

O'Rourke, M. (ed.) (2006). 'The Becoming-Deleuzoguattarian of Queer Studies'. *Rhizomes* 11/12 (Fall 2005/Spring 2006). Online at <http://www.rhizomes.net/issue11/>.

Passet, J.E. (2003). *Sex Radicals and the Quest for Women's Equality*. Urbana, IL: University of Illinois Press.

Patton, P. (2000). *Deleuze and the Political*. London: Routledge.

Plummer, K. (2003). *Intimate Citizenship: Private Decisions and Public Dialogues*. London: University of Washington Press.

Pringle, R. and Watson, S. (1992). '"Women's Interests" and the Poststructuralist State'. In M. Barrett and A. Phillips (eds). *Destabilising Theory: Contemporary Feminist Debates*. Cambridge: Polity Press.

Puar, J. (2008). *Terrorist Assemblages: Homonationalism in Queer Times*. Durham, NC and London: Duke University Press.

Schmidt, J. (2000). *Disciplined Minds: A Critical Look at Salaried Professionals and the Soul-Battering System that Shapes their Lives*. Oxford: Rowman & Littlefield.

Scott, J.C. (1998). *Seeing Like a State: How Certain Schemes to Improve the Human Condition Have Failed*. New Haven: Yale University Press.

Sedgwick, E.K. (1990). *Epistemology of the Closet*. Berkeley: University of California Press.

Seidman, S. (1997). *Difference Troubles: Querying Social Theory and Sexual Politics*. Cambridge: Cambridge University Press.

Shukaitis, S. (2009). 'Infrapolitics and the Nomadic Educational Machine'. In R. Amster, A. DeLeon, L. Fernandez, A. Nocella and D. Shannon (eds). *Contemporary Anarchist Studies*. London: Routledge.

Sullivan, A. (1996). *Virtually Normal*. New York: Vintage.

Sullivan, S. (2005). 'An *Other* World Is Possible? On Representation, Rationalism and Romanticism in Social Forums'. *Ephemera* (5)2: 370–92. Online at <http://www.ephemeraweb.org/journal/5-2/5-2ssullivan.pdf>.

Teixeira, R. (n.d.). 'Troubling Subjects: Towards a Poststructuralist Anarchist Understanding of Child and Youth Erotic Autonomy, Paedophilia and Power'. In J. Heckert and R. Cleminson (eds). *Dangerous Desires: Essays in Anarchism and Sexuality* (unpublished manuscript).

Tormey, S. (2006). '"Not in My Name": Deleuze, Zapatismo and the Critique of Representation'. *Parliamentary Affairs* 1: 138–54.

Tuhkanen, M. (2009). 'Queer hybridity'. In Nigianni and Storr (2009).

Weeks, J. (1998). 'The Sexual Citizen'. *Theory, Culture and Society* 15(3/4): 35–52.

—— (1995). *Invented Moralities: Sexual Values in an Age of Uncertainty*. Cambridge, Polity Press.

14
When Theories Meet:
Emma Goldman and 'Post-Anarchism'

Hilton Bertalan

Naturally, life presents itself in different forms to different ages. Between the age of eight and twelve I dreamed of becoming a Judith. I longed to avenge the sufferings of my people, the Jews, to cut off the head of their Holofernos. When I was fourteen I wanted to study medicine, so as to be able to help my fellow-beings. When I was fifteen I suffered from unrequited love, and I wanted to commit suicide in a romantic way by drinking a lot of vinegar. I thought that would make me look ethereal and interesting, very pale and poetic when in my grave, but at sixteen I decided on a more exalted death. I wanted to dance myself to death. (Goldman, 1933: 1)

The spaces in which subjectivities and perspectives are affirmed as non-hegemonic, mobile, and constantly drifting are often associated with post-structuralist thought. Yet this language resonates elsewhere. In fact, it can be located in radical voices and texts often considered out of reach to the theoretical abstractions of post-structuralist thought. Perhaps most surprising is that it can be found in the anarchist–feminist Emma Goldman. Known best for her assiduous political activity, unkillable energy, repeated arrests, remonstrative oratory skills, sardonic wit, and status as the 'most dangerous woman in the world', another reading of Goldman's work reveals a dimension that is often overlooked; that is, one that is connectable to the theoretical and political efforts of several contemporary theorists. To be sure, this initial and modest knotting of voices is only a beginning, an interceding requisition for future analysis, or, put simply, a punctuating of moments in Goldman's work worthy of closer examination. Such work, I would argue, is necessary to avoiding a disavowal of anarchist histories, and to understanding how the traces of certain textual and political histories resonate with, and can work to inform, contemporary conditions. If, in our contemporary condition, we are left without a state of things to be reached or attained – if we have buried pedantic, concretizing thoughts of revolution and subjectivity, and instead found some measure of comfort in contingent, prefigurative, productively failing and always labouring presuppositions – it is important that in asking what it means to articulate futures and measure efficacy under such conditions, we first glean the past for figures who confronted similar dilemmas. I would argue that Goldman is such a figure. In doing so I am suggesting that the manner in which many contemporary activists and social movements conceptualize resistance and organization is not entirely new.

I am not attempting to graft the past onto contemporary theoretical and political conditions, nor suggesting a genealogical line between the two, but rather, locating resonances between fields so as to support still relevant ethico-political projects. What is most important about this task is a regenerative reading of Goldman that draws out her commitment to ceaseless epistemological and political change. This affinity echoes not only with contemporary activists and social movements, but also, in particular for my purposes here, the thought of Friedrich Nietzsche, Gloria Anzaldúa, Judith Butler and Gilles Deleuze. Using these thinkers to facilitate a remembrance of Goldman makes it possible to connect her work with that of post-structuralist anarchism (and post-structuralist thought more generally).

At the outset I should mention feeling some displeasure toward the brevity with which I'm forced speak of those who have written about Goldman. Despite my sense of affinity for this diminutive group, I feel it necessary to offer an accounting, albeit brief, of the ways Goldman has been discussed. Considering the attention Goldman received during and after her life, her emblematic mugshot, and her iconic status within activist culture and anarchist historiography and scholarship, it may appear puzzling to suggest that her work has not been read in the way I am arguing it could. What is of interest to me here is how Goldman *has* been read, and therefore, how it has come to be that certain elements of her work have been given little consideration – how particular dimensions have been overlooked or addressed with only passing, tepid reference.

Collections, historiography and contemporary anarchist theory tend to credit Goldman with introducing feminism to anarchism, and for her tireless and diverse activism, yet fail to take her seriously as a political thinker with an original voice. Anarchist anthologies (Graham, 2005), anarchist historiographies (Avrich, 1994), anarcha-feminist collections (Dark Star Collective, 2002), and anarchist reference websites (anarchyarchives.org) have all dedicated a great deal of attention to Goldman. Despite this, however, they do not discuss theoretical dimensions of her work, but rather, give a broad account of her personal and political life. More recent theoretical discussions of anarchist thought make no mention of Goldman (Day, 2005; Sheehan, 2003), while George Woodcock's important text, *Anarchism: A History of Libertarian Ideas and Movements* (2004), and more contemporary texts from Todd May (1994), Lewis Call (2002), Saul Newman (2001) and Murray Bookchin (1995) make only passing remarks. Although usually credited with providing a 'feminist dimension' (Marshall, 1993: 396) that 'completely changed' (Woodcock, 2004: 399) anarchist thought, subsequent suggestions that she was 'more of an activist than a thinker' (Marshall, 1993: 396) overlook the extent to which she contributed to anarchist theory. Murray Bookchin (1995) similarly praised Goldman yet took her work even less seriously. Bookchin's suggestion that he 'can only applaud Emma Goldman's demand that she does not want a revolution unless she can dance to it' (1995: 2) is followed by a complaint about 'Nietzscheans like Emma Goldman' (8). Bookchin's text *Social Anarchism or Lifestyle Anarchism: An Unbridgeable Chasm* (1995) is dedicated to describing a perceived divide between the 'postmodernist [...] flight from all form of social activism' typified by Michel Foucault and Friedrich Nietzsche ('lifestyle anarchism'), and a commitment to 'serious organizations, a radical politics, a committed social movement, theoretical coherence, and programmatic relevance' (19) typified by 'classical anarchists' such as Michael Bakunin and Peter Kropotkin ('social anarchism'). While it is easy to recognize Bookchin's preference, what is most interesting is that Goldman is the only figure he places on both sides of the chasm. Although he associates Goldman with the postmodernists who, he suggests, 'denigrate responsible social commitment' (10), he commends her dedication to social change. Bookchin never responds to this disjunctive tension or the implications it has for his prescribed schism. Instead, he mentions Goldman only once more, suggesting that she 'was by no means the ablest thinker in the libertarian pantheon' (13). Not only does this provide another example of refusing to take Goldman seriously as a thinker, it also demonstrates how she provided a committed political articulation alongside an affinity for the ceaseless transgressions that Bookchin finds to be such a troubling and apolitical dimension of postmodernist thought.

In his canonical *The Political Philosophy of Poststructuralist Anarchism* (1994), Todd May also makes a quick, albeit important reference to Goldman. In a seminal text dedicated to the intersections of anarchist and post-structuralist thought, Goldman is mentioned only once. By using the work of Bakunin, Kropotkin, and Pierre-Joseph Proudhon to discuss anarchism, May is able to show the similarities between anarchism and post-structuralism yet also sketch a demarcation between the 'essentialism' of the former and 'anti-essentialism' (13) of the latter. A third of the way through, however, May claims that Goldman is one exception to the essentialism of anarchism. 'While anarchists like Emma Goldman resisted the naturalist path (in an echo of Nietzsche, who was founding for poststructuralist thought)', argues May, 'the fundamental drift of anarchism has been toward the assumption of a human essence' (64). Although I am not disputing the decision to focus on the 'fundamental drift' of anarchism, I am suggesting that May's valuable, albeit brief, reading of Goldman inaugurated a new way of reading her work. In his book *Postmodern Anarchism* (2002), Lewis Call also makes a single positive reference to Goldman. According to Call, Goldman 'anticipated' the postmodern 'theory of simulation [and] denial of the real' (93). Similarly here, it is interesting that the anarchist who 'anticipated' a type of thought that Call connects to Nietzsche, Deleuze, Foucault and Butler does not stimulate more interest or enquiry. Further distinguishing between classical anarchism and postmodern anarchism – for the purpose of demonstrating the radical nature of Nietzsche's theoretical project – Call argues that 'previous concepts of subjectivity (and thus previous political theories) focused on being' (50). Call then suggests that Nietzsche has 'shifted our attention to becoming' and further demonstrated that 'our subjectivity is in a constant state of flux' (50). Coincidentally, 'constant state of flux' is the precise wording Goldman used to describe herself. And so while their dealings with Goldman are curiously concise, I am indebted to May and Call for their intimation, and for retrieving Goldman (however measured their glances might be) by recognizing her connection to contemporary thought.

GOLDMANIACS AND GOLDMANOLOGISTS[1]

In a documentary produced for PBS, *Emma Goldman: An Exceedingly Dangerous Woman*, Alice Wexler (2003), one of the most prominent Goldman biographers, suggests that Goldman couldn't bring herself to criticize Leon Czolgosz for his assassination of American President William McKinley because she 'identified him with Berkman' (Goldman's long-time partner). Wexler's view toward sublimation represents the tendency to psychoanalyse Goldman's life while ignoring certain elements of her work. Wexler ignores not only the fact that Berkman himself condemned Czolgosz, but most importantly, Goldman's equable, thoughtful arguments for why she, nearly alone amongst her contemporaries, refused to criticize Czolgosz (despite the fact that he credited her as his inspiration). One way to imagine this more clearly is to think of Deleuze's (2004) discussion of the judge's response in the trial of American activist Angela Davis. Deleuze writes:

> It's like the repressive work by the judge in the Angela Davis case, who assured us: 'Her behavior is explicable only by the fact that she was in love'. But what if, on the contrary, Angela Davis's libido was a revolutionary, social libido? What if she was in love because she was a revolutionary? (273).

The point Deleuze is making is that we should rethink the assumption about the motivating factors in lives of revolutionaries – that they are radical because they are in love. Instead, we can view Davis, and for our purposes here, Goldman, as driven by a broader ethic of love that makes each more radical, open and vulnerable. She is in love, and able to defend Czolgosz, because she is radical, not because of some sense of substitutability. Therefore, it is because of a radical pre-existing imaginary and a co-constitutive commitment that certain kinds of relations are imaginable, that love can be articulated in the ways set out by Goldman (ways that I will explicate below). For Goldman, only when it is always already there can it be unconditionally expressed, rather than something that can be picked up and discarded, manipulated and strategically deployed, or rooted, as in the case of Wexler, in the confused projections of the heart.

In the first biography of Goldman, Richard Drinnon (1961) initiated the aforementioned trend by suggesting Goldman 'was by no means a seminal social or political thinker' (314). In the first biography to focus on Goldman's feminism, Alix Kates Shulman (1971) similarly argued that Goldman was 'more of an activist than a thinker' (37). One year later, Shulman (1972) again emphasized that Goldman 'was more of an activist than a theoretician', stating further that 'her major contribution to anarchist theory was to insist on gender as a primary category of oppression' (36). Goldman is often commended as an indefatigable and inspiring political force, yet one whose only theoretical contribution is the grafting of gender upon a pre-existing anarchist framework. Martha Solomon (1987) continued the theme by suggesting that Goldman was 'not, however, an original theorist', but rather, a 'propagandist of anarchism' (38). According to Solomon (1988), even those who came to see Goldman speak 'came to see her as an eccentric entertainer rather than a serious thinker' (191). Nearly ten years later, Oz Frankel (1996) locates Goldman's 'main strength' not in her theoretical insights, but rather, 'her wizardry on the stump', 'theatrical presentation', and her 'full control of voice modulation' (907). The more recent suggestion that 'Goldman was a person of action, not primarily a thinker and a writer' (Moritz and Moritz, 2001: 6), perfectly demonstrates that more than 40 years of biographies have declined to classify Goldman's life and work as especially relevant to political thought or, for that matter, as particularly radical, but rather, as the interesting work of a vigorous and spirited agitator.

There are, on the other hand, a number of writers who have mined Goldman's work for its theoretical and political merit. Bonni Haaland (1993), Lori Jo Marso (2003), Terence Kissack (2008) and Jody Bart (1995) have each examined Goldman's feminism through a close reading of her views on gender, sexuality, reproduction and the women's suffrage movement. Most important to contemporary Goldman scholarship is the work of Kathy Ferguson (2004), who has examined the connections between Goldman and Foucault's later work on the care of the self. Jim Jose (2005) has also presented a criticism of the limited roles in which Goldman has been cast and how the exclusive focus on her as an interesting diarist and activist has served to overlook her contributions to political thought. Leigh Starcross (2004) offers the lone but important examination of Goldman's connection to Nietzsche. In her short but vital article, Starcross initiates a discussion that takes seriously the 'fundamentality of Nietzsche for Goldman' (29) by pointing out the number of times she lectured on Nietzsche and several of their shared targets (state, religion, morality).

Throughout the rest of this piece, I shall periodically reference Lewis Call's (2002) distinction between postmodern and classical anarchism to explicate Goldman's bridging of the two. According to Call, postmodern anarchism maintains classical anarchism's objection to the state, capitalism and centralized authority, but adds further dimensions by analysing power outside the government and the workplace, and by rejecting humanistic and naturalistic notions of subjectivity. More specifically, Call claims that classical anarchism suffered from three theoretical tendencies that distinguish it from postmodern anarchism, thus 'seriously limiting its radical potential' (22). The three characteristics that Call argues create this incommensurability are: classical anarchism's tendency to carry 'out its revolution under the banner of a problematically universal human subject'; an 'almost exclusive focus on the undeniably repressive power structures characteristic of capitalist economies [thus] overlooking the equally disturbing power relations which are to be found outside the factory and the government ministry: in gender relations, in race relations'; and anarchism's 'rationalist semiotics' and its subsequent application of 'the method of natural sciences' (15–16). Yet much of Goldman's understanding of social change was not prescriptive, nor did it argue for the final liberation of a universal self.[2] Her view of power as present in fields of sexuality, gender, culture, everyday life and internal struggle illustrates that her analysis was not exclusively focused on class or economic systems. And as May (1994) points out, she 'resisted the naturalist path' (64) followed by many of her contemporaries. These distinctions allow us to begin reading Goldman as an important thinker in the trajectory of post-anarchist thought and as a bridge between it and classical anarchism.

NIETZSCHE'S DANCING STAR

I had to do my reading at the expense of much-needed sleep, but what was physical strain in view of my raptures over Nietzsche? (Goldman, 1970a: 172)

I have been told it is impossible to put a book of mine down – I even disturb the night's rest. (Nietzsche, 1992: 43)

Goldman was mostly alone when letting in encounters with particular philosophers, none more so than with her political and textual love of Nietzsche. Most radicals of her era dismissed Nietzsche as a disquieting and depoliticizing aristocrat whose work undermined the unquestionable and fixed liberatory and procedural equation of anarchism. Against this habit, Goldman searched Nietzsche's work for its impulse toward revolt, poring through his texts looking for the undetected spirit of radical incitation. Described by Call (2002) as 'strand one' of the 'postmodern matrix' (2) and by May (1994) as 'founding for poststructuralist thought' (64), Nietzsche helps locate moments in Goldman's work that resonate with certain contemporary fields of theory. Goldman spoke more highly and with greater intensity about Nietzsche than any other thinker (anarchist or otherwise). 'The fire of his soul, the rhythm of his song', said Goldman (1970a), 'made life richer, fuller, and more wonderful for me.' 'The magic of his language, the beauty of his vision', she continued, 'carried me to undreamed-of heights' (172). Nietzsche's influence on Goldman distanced her from most contemporaries, many of whom viewed him with derision, as a 'fool' with a 'diseased mind' (Goldman, 1970a: 193). Reflecting upon a heated exchange with Ed Brady (her partner at the time) about the relevance of Nietzsche's work, Goldman described their relationship as 'a month of joy and abandon [that] suffered a painful awakening [...] caused by Nietzsche' (1970a: 193). On a similar occasion, a friend, bewildered by her commitment, assumed Goldman would be apathetic to Nietzsche due to the lack of a palpably political tone in his work. Goldman, enriched by, and defensive of, his work, argued that such a conclusion stemmed from an intransigent refusal to understand that anarchism, like the work of Nietzsche, 'embraces every phase of life and effort and undermines the old, outlived values' (1970a: 194).[3] For Goldman, anarchism constantly challenged existing values, and should therefore have found its greatest inspiration in the theorist whose work was, according to Deleuze (1983), prefaced upon the belief that 'the destruction of known values makes possible a creation of new values' (193). For Nietzsche (1969), thinking should 'first be a destroyer and break values' (139). Elsewhere, Nietzsche (1989) clarified the affirming character of this destruction as 'saying Yes to and having confidence in all that has hitherto been forbidden, despised, and damned' (291). At times, Goldman's conception of anarchism directly draws from this aspect of Nietzsche's work. Anarchism 'is the destroyer of dominant values', Goldman (1998) argued, and the 'herald of NEW VALUES' (147). In the same essay Goldman used Nietzschean-inspired language by calling anarchism the 'TRANSVALUATOR', what she termed 'the transvaluation of accepted values' (169).[4] Elsewhere, Goldman (1969) explicitly acknowledged that she borrowed this concept from Nietzsche's work: 'I believe, with Nietzsche, that the time has come for a transvaluation of things' (241). Following Nietzsche, Goldman viewed the transformation of values as a constant process – one that created new values while undermining the basis and legitimacy of existing ones. In claiming that 'Nietzsche was an anarchist [...] a poet, a rebel and innovator' (1970a: 194), Goldman saw a political relevance in his work at a time when many radicals perceived Nietzsche as apolitical and irrelevant. At the height of political censorship in the United States (1913–1917) – when Goldman was frequently arrested, refused access to many halls and theatres, and her lectures closely monitored or cancelled by local authorities – she spoke on Nietzsche more than at any other time.[5] From this I conclude two things: one, that Goldman responded to consistent persecution by lecturing on Nietzsche at a time when his work was not considered threatening or radical; and two, that Goldman perceived undetected anarchistic sensibilities in his work and used this to intimate the radicality of her speeches. What local authorities failed to realize was that much of Goldman's anarchism was rooted in Nietzsche, in whose work she saw the greatest potential for radical social and individual transformation.

It is not surprising then that the phrase for which Goldman has come to be known ('If I can't dance I don't want to be part of your revolution') resonates with an analogy that was very important for Nietzsche. Throughout his work, Nietzsche makes use of dance to explain perpetual and creative epistemological shifts. As Deleuze (1983) suggests, for Nietzsche, 'dance affirms becoming and the being of becoming' (194). Nietzsche's (1995) most fervent admiration is reserved for 'books that teach how to dance [and] present the impossible as possible' (139), as well as those that allow its reader 'to be able to dance with one's feet, with concepts, with words' (Nietzsche, 1982: 512). Works of this motif would, according to Nietzsche (1969), ideally 'give birth to a dancing star' (46). This is precisely the effect Nietzsche had on Goldman. Although the famously attributed phrase was never actually spoken by Goldman, the story from which it is taken conveys Goldman's embodiment of Nietzsche's 'dance'.[6] Upon dancing with what was described as 'reckless abandon', Goldman was taken aside and told that 'it did not behoove an agitator to dance', especially someone 'who was on the way to become a force in the anarchist movement' (Goldman, 1970a: 56). Considering her passionate commitment to his work, Goldman's style of dance itself might have been stirred by her attachment to Nietzsche: 'better to dance clumsily than to walk lamely', Nietzsche said (1969: 305).[7] Subjected to governessy reproof and told 'her frivolity would only hurt the Cause', Goldman (1970a) became furious with the austere suggestion that 'a beautiful ideal' such as anarchism 'should demand the denial of life and joy' (56). Not only does this story provide an example of Goldman envisioning social change as taking place in everyday spaces and expressions – challenging Call's reading of 'classical' anarchists as exclusively concerned with politics and the economy – it also suggests that her conception of joy, play, dance and free expression (notions that more generally contributed to her view of social change) were inspired by Nietzsche. More than simply the physical embodiment of creative expression, or the counterpoint to the perceived and sought-after gravitas of classical anarchism, dance describes Goldman's approach to an anarchist life. Goldman's desire to dance herself to death (present in the epigraph of this piece) – that is, to remain in a permanent state of conceptual and political motion – was directly influenced by Nietzsche's work.

Goldman's (1998) view of the state was another aspect of her thought inspired by Nietzsche. Echoing one of Nietzsche's most oft-cited metaphors, she wrote, 'I still hold that the State is a cold monster, and that it devours everyone within its reach' (426).[8] According to Goldman, the state 'always and everywhere has and must stand for supremacy' (1998: 103). Similarly, Nietzsche called for 'as little state as possible' (1982: 82), pointing toward his ideal location outside of its purview: 'there, where the state ceases – look there, my brothers' (Nietzsche, 1969: 78). According to Call (2002), however, Nietzsche's criticism of the state did not result in a rationalist counter-system as it did for many classical anarchists. 'A Nietzschean', according to Call,

> could argue that the anarchists ended up promoting a political theory which would replace the nations of Germany and France with a 'nation' of Bakuninites. The dominant figure in Nietzsche's utopian political imaginary is much more profoundly nonsectarian. She is indeed nomadic in character. (41)

Precisely, *she* is Goldman. Here Call is referring to tendencies amongst classical anarchists to prescriptively construct hegemonically utopian, and often pastoral, imaginings. Goldman, however, problematized this tendency. Goldman did not envision a nation of Goldmanites, nor did she imagine the final eradication of domination brought forth by a new system based on rationalist principles of human nature. Goldman recognized that any conception, however rational it may have seemed, was the product of particular conditions, and that those conditions were always subject to change. As Nietzsche (1968) put it, 'the character of the world in a state of becoming is incapable of formulation' (280). Following Nietzsche, Goldman (1998) argued that the state (and for that matter, any social or economic system) 'is nothing but a name. It is an abstraction. Like other similar conceptions – nation, race, humanity – it has no organic reality' (113).[9] Goldman's willingness to divorce herself from ideas premised upon a move toward rational and natural conditions or social systems does, in fact, separate her work from many classical anarchists. Goldman (1998) suggested that 'the true, real, and just State is like the true, real, just God, who has never yet been discovered' (102). Here again Goldman questioned the desire to formulate a final and ideal social world based on rationalist assumptions. Nietzsche (1968) similarly attacked socialism 'because it dreams quite naively of "the good", true, and beautiful' (398).[10] From Nietzsche, Goldman borrowed a sense of constant change that necessarily undermined notions of a universal and final solution to domination and oppression. Although at times Goldman remains wedded to the dream of many socialists and anarchists, her reading of Nietzsche couples her fantast moments with a commitment to forms of chance and transformation. In fact, despite Nietzsche's lack of interest in politics and his vocal disdain for nineteenth-century socialism and anarchism, Goldman was, in many ways, the type of thinker he foresaw – the proverbial fish he hoped to catch:

> Included here is the slow search for those related to me, for such as out of strength would offer me their hand for *the work of destruction*. – From now on all my writings are fish-hooks: perhaps I understand fishing as well as anyone? [...] If nothing got *caught* I am not to blame. *There were no fish*. (Nietzsche, 1979: 82)[11]

THE PINK PANTHER OF CLASSICAL ANARCHISM

Two themes inform the rest of this piece: the concept of transformation as it relates specifically to social change and political theory, and transformation more generally focused on the self. For Goldman, transformation of the social (organization, resistance, theorizing social change) is equal to transformation of the self (responsibility, care, ethics of relationality, issues of control and domination, notions of subjectivity). I will here continue to make use of Call's distinction between classical and postmodern anarchism to show how the transformative elements in Goldman's work can be viewed as both theoretically anticipatory and as a bridge between two seemingly disparate modes of thought.

According to Call (2002), by 'refusing to claim for itself the mantle of absolute truth', postmodern anarchism 'insists upon its right to remain perpetually fluid, malleable, and provisional' (71). Yet Goldman too voiced this refusal, and similarly viewed anarchism in this light. 'Anarchism', Goldman (1969) argued, 'cannot consistently impose an iron-clad program or method on the future' (43). It 'has no set rules', she proposed, 'and its methods vary according to the age, the temperament, and the surroundings of its followers' (2005a: 276). Nietzsche also refused to offer a blueprint for future (or even present) readers to follow. 'Revolution [...] can be a source of energy', Nietzsche (1995) wrote, 'but never an organizer, architect, artist, perfecter of human nature' (249). Nietzsche's (1982) further claim to 'mistrust all systematizers' (470) not only describes the approach of Call's postmodern anarchism, but is also similar to Goldman's conception of anarchism. As her statement above suggests, Goldman's anarchism was non-prescriptive and contingent. That is, she viewed it not as a closed mapping that sketched forms of resistance or social organization, but rather, as a flexible and open political philosophy in a state of perpetual transformation. May's description of a contemporary politics informed by Deleuze reiterates Goldman's view: 'Our task in politics is not to follow the program. It is not to draft the revolution or to proclaim that it has already happened. It is neither to appease the individual nor to create the classless society [...] Our task is to ask and answer afresh, always once more because it is never concluded' (May, 2005: 153). Deleuze (1983) himself states likewise that 'the question of the revolution's future is a bad one, because, as long as it is posed, there are going to be those who will not become *revolutionaries*' (114). Call (2002) too argues for 'a state of permanent and total revolution, a revolution against being' (51). What this demonstrates is that Goldman's work resonates with the shared affinity of Deleuze, Call, and May for a political philosophy that 'leaves posterity free to develop its own particular systems' (Goldman, 1969: 43). Her work shares with them a desire for struggle, victories, political dissensus and processes, and social change, without an accompanying interest in becoming a totalizing discourse, movement, or political philosophy. As Deleuze is arguing above, the foreclosure of the unknown not only prevents people from becoming revolutionaries, it also serves to stop revolutionaries from becoming. Or, as Goldman (2005a) made clear, 'there is no cut-and-dried political cure' (402).

Goldman's (1998) refusal to 'claim that the triumph of any idea would eliminate all possible problems from the life of man for all time' (440) was met with discontentment. '"Why do you not say how things will be operated under Anarchism?"', Goldman (1969) lamented, 'is a question I have had to meet a thousand times' (43). Deleuze and Guattari (1983) would have supported her reluctance: 'Where are you going? Where are you coming from? What are you driving at? All useless questions [...] all imply a false conception of voyage and movement' (58). Goldman believed that a political philosophy could be radical and emancipatory without tethering itself to anodyne universals or essentialist notions. For Goldman, anarchism was not encoded with a linear progression – it did not have an identifiable beginning, ending or goal. Instead, it was closer to Deleuze and Guattari's (1983) claim that 'there is no general recipe' (108) than the attempts by many of Goldman's contemporaries to locate the most egalitarian and natural forms of social organization. As one of the most tireless and prolific radicals of the twentieth century, Goldman was uniquely clear that her efforts were not focused upon a single, attainable goal. Rather, her anarchism could best be described as based on what Deleuze (2004) called 'ceaseless opposition' (259) – an approach that remains 'open, connectable in all its dimensions [...] capable of being dismantled [...] reversible, and susceptible to constant modification' (Deleuze and Guattari, 1983: 26). What was for Goldman (1969) a political philosophy that had 'vitality enough to leave behind the stagnant waters of the old, and build, as well as sustain, new life' (49) is, for Deleuze and Guattari (1983), 'the furniture we never stop moving around' (47). 'How, then, can anyone assume to map out a line of conduct for those to come?', Goldman wondered (1969: 43). The approach one could instead take, according to Deleuze (2004), is by 'not predicting, but being attentive to the unknown knocking at the door' (346). Goldman would have agreed. 'I hold, with Nietzsche', she argued, 'that we are staggering along with the corpses of dead ages on our backs. Theories do not create life. Life must make its own theories' (2005a: 402). Goldman's anarchism did not predict or initiate a single and dramatic political shift, but rather, was constantly renewed by the context and conditions of resistance and the collectives and individuals taking part in struggles.

Goldman's political activity demonstrates just how radical the concept of constant transformation is. It is not an apathetic, detached, apolitical theoretical exercise lacking a consideration for consequences. Positions *are* taken, identities *are* asserted, injustices *are* addressed, and conceptual and logistical spaces *are* occupied. However, as the above section has shown, contingency and the accompanying refusal to prescribe or locate a static utopian social or personal state are affirming and highly political positions that serve to open up and cultivate possibilities for social change. As Call (2002) states of Nietzsche's 'utopian' thought, 'it develops a devastating critique of the world as it is, and dreams of a better future. But the construction of that future is for those who follow' (55). Deleuze and Guattari (1987) also warned that

> smooth spaces are not in themselves liberatory. But the struggle is changed or displaced in them, and life reconstitutes its stakes, confronts new obstacles, invents new paces, switches adversaries. Never believe that a smooth space will suffice to save us. (500)

Likewise, Goldman can be seen to have searched for smooth spaces while recognizing that this search was constant and contextual. Even the similar phrasing of Nietzsche, Deleuze, Anzaldúa and Goldman is, at times, particularly striking: 'continual transition' (Nietzsche, 1968: 281); 'state of permanent creation' (Deleuze, 2004: 136); 'state of perpetual transition' (Anzaldúa, 1987: 100); 'state of eternal change' (Goldman, 1970b: 524). This similarity stands in contrast to Call's (2002) argument that the 'ongoing, open-ended, fluid anarchist discourse' of postmodern anarchism is categorically distinct from the 'modern anarchist tradition' (65) in which Goldman is most often situated (by Call and others). For example, Goldman did not envision a core human nature that could be set free from political and economic constraints. 'Human nature', Goldman (1998) argued, 'is by no means a fixed quantity. Rather, it is fluid and responsive to new conditions' (438). Engaged in what Butler (1993) would come to term 'resistance to fixing the subject' (ix), Goldman perceived identity as always shifting. In Goldman's (2003) work there is a move away from a fixed being; instead she refers to 'little plastic beings' (270).

Goldman's (1970b) talk of 'life always in flux' and 'new currents flowing from the dried-up spring of the old' (524) introduced a notion of anarchism as 'constantly creating new conditions' (Goldman, 1969: 63). The fact that these statements span 40 years of Goldman's life also demonstrates that this current is present throughout most of her work.

These elements of Goldman's work extended beyond her thoughts on political and state apparatuses, also informing her views of gender and sexuality. In fact, her rejection of the argument that gender is biologically determined anticipated the anti-essentialism of many fields of contemporary feminist thought. Goldman's (1998) understanding of identity as always 'in a state of flux' (443) marks a shift in anarchist notions of gender (and identity more generally). Most of Goldman's contemporaries maintained a gendered binary that perceived women as having biological predispositions that distinguished them from men. If women were considered as deserving of political and economic equality they were, at best, viewed simply as different biological characters, and at worst, undeveloped thinkers. The latter was put forth by Kropotkin (one of the pillars of classical anarchism) during a discussion with Goldman:

> 'The paper is doing splendid work,' he warmly agreed, 'but it would do more if it would not waste so much space discussing sex.' I disagreed, and we became involved in a heated argument about the place of the sex question in anarchist propaganda. Peter's view was that woman's equality with man had nothing to do with sex; it was a matter of brains. 'When she is his equal intellectually and shares in his social ideals,' he said, 'she will be as free as him'. (Goldman, 1970a: 253)

For many of Goldman's contemporaries, 'sex' was either an issue of little or no importance or justified as a category of exclusion. For others, the inequality and oppression that stemmed from dichotomous distinctions based on 'sex' was itself the issue to be opposed, rather than the categories themselves, as well as their accompanying naturalist assumptions. Goldman on the other hand, was not simply engaged in a public discussion of gendered oppression and exclusion – for though she was outspoken on this topic, she was not alone (a big fish in a small bowl perhaps). Rather, what resonates with contemporary discourses is the way Goldman conceptualized 'sex'. Goldman's (1969) demand that we 'do away with the absurd notion of the dualism of the sexes, or that man and woman represent two antagonistic worlds' (225) is a good example of this. Not only is this a unique rejection of the (still standing) biological distinction between men and women, it also pre-dates Simone de Beauvoir's (1989) famous assertion that 'one is not born, but becomes a woman. No biological, psychological, or economic fate determines the figure the human female presents in society: it is civilization as a whole that produces this creature' (267). Gender, like morality and the belief in the necessity of the state, is, for de Beauvoir and others, an inscribed referent. 'This conceptual realization', Monique Wittig (1992) wrote, 'destroys the idea that women are a "natural group"' (9). 'The concept of difference between the sexes', she continued, 'ontologically constitutes women into different/others' (29). For Goldman and those who followed, this divisive binary both failed to understand the historical and cultural specificity of gender and served to limit the diverse ways it could be conceptualized and expressed. What Goldman (1933) called 'the various gradations and variations of gender' (2) abandoned the delimiting belief in a biological predisposition, thus anticipating contemporary articulations of gender and identity as 'shifting and multiple' (Anzaldúa, 1987: 18). Adopting this perspective is, as Anzaldúa suggests, 'like trying to swim in a new element, an "alien" element' (ibid). Like the kind of fish Nietzsche hoped to catch, however, Goldman swam against the conventional current of her day, adopting a unique view of gender that resonates with a contemporary form of thought whose 'energy comes from continual creative motion that keeps breaking down the unitary aspect of each new paradigm' (ibid.: 2).

This nuanced mode of thought came through most in Goldman's criticism of the women's suffrage movement. 'Woman will purify politics, we are assured' Goldman (1969: 198) said with some irony. The essentialist footing of the suffrage movement not only failed to ask who was economically and politically excluded from the category of 'woman', it also assumed that the simple presence of women (privileged white women) would deracinate the workings of chauvinisms, inequities and injustices and initiate democratic, sensitive, convivial and inclusive practices. 'I do not believe that woman will make politics worse', Goldman (1998) argued, 'nor can I believe that she could make it better' (209). Elsewhere, Goldman (1970c) stated, 'I am not opposed to woman suffrage on the conventional ground that she is not equal to it, but that cannot possibly blind me to the absurd notion that woman will accomplish that wherein man has failed' (53). Instead, 'woman' must, according to Goldman (1969), begin 'emancipating herself from emancipation' (215). That is, women, in fact everyone, should cast off the conceptual and personal devotion to a static and universal self that can be liberated through even the most minor participation (voting) in a liberal democracy. As Butler (1993) puts it, the category of gender 'becomes one whose uses are no longer reified as "referents", and which stand a chance of being opened up, indeed, of coming to signify in ways that none of us can predict in advance' (29). Interestingly, Goldman's (2005b) criticism of the suffrage movement and her refusal to adopt its naturalist category of 'woman' was perceived as anti-feminist and injurious to a crucial and unquestionable political cause (two criticisms that Butler has confronted).

Another important dimension of Goldman's work is her prefigurative conception of social change. In rejecting the idea of a natural, universal, permanently liberated self, and by divorcing herself from the dominant yearning for the singular revolutionary event, Goldman envisioned social change as a continuous process that mirrored the sought-after social world. For Goldman (1998), 'the *means* used to *prepare* the future become its *cornerstone*' (403). In this context, democratic forms of interacting and organizing are not deferred, but rather, borne out immediately. 'No revolution can ever succeed as a factor of liberation', Goldman argued, 'unless the MEANS used to further it be identical in spirit and tendency with the PURPOSES to be achieved' (1998: 402). Not only does this indicate a rupture from Marxist and utopian socialist pictorials of a better world to be constructed at a later date, it also differs from several anarchist contemporaries who imagined a revolutionary moment springing from an inborn, natural human condition. Anarchism, according to Goldman (1970b), 'is not a mere theory for a distant future', but rather, 'a living influence' (556). Goldman took this further by also focusing on personal transformation. Rather than paying exclusive attention to the alteration or eradication of external economic and political conditions, Goldman (1998) demanded a struggle against what she called the 'internal tyrants' (221) that, as she further suggests, 'count for almost nothing with our Marxist and do not affect his conception of human history' (122). Goldman's thoughts on tendencies toward the domination of the self and others resonate with thinkers often cast as voices of post-structuralist thought. Foucault (1983), for example, similarly advocated for 'the tracking down of all varieties of fascism, from the enormous ones that surround and crush us to the petty ones that constitute the tyrannical bitterness of our everyday lives' (xiv). For both Goldman and Foucault, there is no pure individual to be left alone or cultivated in the ideal environment. Desire, justice, democracy and revolutionary social change do not appear simply by adjusting external fields or institutions. Rather, they appear when radical visions of social change are immediate aspects of our interactions, language and forms of organization, and when we work to make better versions of ourselves as we do better versions of our social world.[12] Concerned with living their political philosophy, and unwilling to accept the argument that 'better' selves are simply and retrievably stalled or contained by manipulative sources of power, Goldman and Foucault each questioned how a strong allegiance to authority (our desire to dominate and to be dominated) maintained such a strong psychic footing. Foucault's (1983) curiosity toward 'the fascism that causes us to love power, to desire the very thing that dominates and exploits us' (xiii) is similar to Goldman's (1969) position that the individual 'clings to its masters, loves the whip, and is the first to cry Crucify! the moment a protesting voice is raised against the sacredness of capitalistic authority or any other decayed institution' (77).

With yet another allusion to Nietzsche, Goldman (1998) explicates a self animated by perpetual transformation:

> I do not mean the clumsy attempt of democracy to regulate the complexities of human character by means of external equality. The vision of 'beyond good and evil' points to the right to oneself, to one's personality. Such possibilities do not exclude pain over the chaos of life, but they do exclude the puritanic righteousness that sits in judgment on all others except oneself. (215)

In contemporary terms, Goldman's recognition of the political implications of self-reflection can be read as 'staying at the edge of what we know' (Butler,

2004: 228) about both our social world and ourselves – what Butler also calls the 'radical point' (ibid.) or Anzaldúa (1987) termed the 'Coatlicue state' (63–73).[13] The Coatlicue state, according to Anzaldúa, 'can be a way station or it can be a way of life' (68). This way of thinking can stand for immobile darkness and inactivity or it can offer constant introspection that opens new possibilities and refuses a certain amount of ethico-theoretical comfort. For Goldman, self-reflection is a constant process. Thus, she can be connected to Anzaldúa as well as Butler (2004), who argued that the unitary subject

> is the one who knows already what is, who enters the conversation the same way as it exits, who fails to put its own epistemological certainties at risk in the encounter with the other, and so stays in place, guards its place, and becomes an emblem for property and territory. (228)

Or, as Goldman (2005a) put it (with the unfortunate pronoun of course), 'I hold when it is said of a man that he has arrived, it means that he is finished' (153). Goldman was not interested in subjects who sought arrival at a final cognitive–theoretical resting point. Goldman's anarchism was a political philosophy with currents that rejected the desire for foundations, naturalist bases, fixed subjects and prescriptions, instead, in a decidedly Nietzschean move, favouring the unknown. Deleuze and Guattari (1983) express this notion of transformation perfectly:

> Form rhizomes and not roots, never plant! Don't sow, forage! Be neither a One nor a Many, but multiplicities! Form a line, never a point! Speed transforms the point into a line. Be fast, even while standing still! Line of chance, line of hips, line of flight. Don't arouse the General in yourself! Not an exact idea, but just an idea (Godard). Have short-term ideas. Make maps not photographs or drawings. Be the Pink Panther, and let your loves be like the wasp and the orchid, the cat and the baboon. (57)

BEAUTY IN A THOUSAND VARIATIONS

The works of Anzaldúa, Butler and Deleuze are clearly marked with an affinity for multiplicity and interconnectivity – what I would refer to as an ethic of love. Though known primarily for her discussion of love with regard to her personal relationships and struggle for open sexual expression, Goldman used the term to describe more broadly a spirit or ethic that desired meaningful personal and organizational connections on multiple levels. Love, according to Goldman (1970c), was a 'force', providing 'golden rays' and the 'only condition of a beautiful life' (46). Always more at home in promissory love letters than prescriptive texts or travelling along programmatic routes, Goldman understood love as the most important element of life. It was, I would argue, a constant drift through her work that constituted an element of thought and interaction that most assured radical social and personal change. Love as a whirling of possibility, a potentially binding political landscape, as an affinity for the unknown, for futurity, for constant responsibility, open and vulnerable connection, the multiple – this is the guiding spirit of Goldman and the thinkers I have so far discussed. For Goldman, without an ethic of love, social change is meaningless: 'high on a throne, with all the splendor and pomp his gold can command, man is yet poor and desolate, if love passes him by' (Goldman, 1970c: 44). 'Love', continued Goldman, 'is the strongest and deepest element in all life, the harbinger of hope, of joy, of ecstasy; love, the defier of all laws, of all conventions; love, the freest, the most powerful moulder of human destiny' (44). Once again we see the presence of Nietzsche in Goldman's interest in the intractable, what Chela Sandoval (2000), through her concept of 'hermeneutics of love', refers to as 'a state of being not subject to control or governance' (142). Or, as Nietzsche (1989) wrote, 'that which is done out of love always takes place beyond good and evil' (103). In this, a Goldman sense of love, we do not love under certain conditions, or because we understand one another, or because we share a particular vision, or even because we recognize each other as something relatable, translatable or familiar to something in our psychic, preferential, emotional or political sensibilities. It is not because we will be loved or find a desire satisfied, a lack filled, or be offered something absent. Instead, for Goldman, love takes place prefiguratively, before the encounter, before the advance or event that usually marks its beginning or containment in reachable social and political visions. This ethic of love also articulates the desire for a multiplicity of political positions and activities. As Foucault wrote:

> We all melt together. But if we choose to struggle against power, then all those who suffer the abuses of power, all those who recognize power as intolerable, can engage in the struggle wherever they happen to be and according to their own activity or passivity ... provided they are radical, without compromise or reformism, provided they do not attempt to readjust the same power through, at most, a change of leadership. (Foucault and Deleuze, 2004: 213)

What is important for Foucault (and for other thinkers mentioned) is the radical element – the element that does not re-inscribe, reform, or take over existing systems of power. Love does not want power, nor does it want what already exists. Multiplicity and interconnectivity, as important aspects of love, cannot be found in hegemonic spaces of social organization and resistance. Love does not seek to reform, but rather, to transform, over and over, amidst a cluster of identities and tactics. Goldman recognized the radical potential of this multiplicity: 'Pettiness separates; breadth unites. Let us be broad and big. Let us not overlook vital things because of the bulk of trifles confronting us' (Goldman, 1998: 167). Goldman not only saw danger in confrontations that foreclosed multiplicity, she also celebrated multiple tactical and political positions. The solidarity Goldman envisioned was not contingent on a universal notion of social change or identity. Instead, Goldman argued for solidarity for its own sake. As Anzaldúa (1990a) put it, 'unity is another

Anglo invention like their one sole god and the myth of the monopole' (146). Goldman's affinity for constant transformation refused a fixed and stable unity while, paradoxically, her ethic of love demanded interconnectivity and community. What this interconnectivity is based on, however, remains shifting and under review. As Anzaldúa (1987) suggested:

> It is where the possibility of uniting all that is separate occurs. This assembly is not one where severed or separated pieces merely come together. Nor is it a balancing of opposing powers. In attempting to work out a synthesis, the self has added a third element which is greater than the sum of its severed parts. That third element is a new consciousness – a mestiza consciousness – and though it is a source of intense pain, its energy comes from continual creative motion that keeps breaking down the unitary aspect of each new paradigm. (101–2)

Goldman's anarchism cultivated multiplicity rather than attempting to universalize disparate positions under a single theoretical rubric. Goldman (2005a) called for 'diversity [and] variety with the spirit of solidarity in anarchism and non-authoritarian organization' (348). What this meant for Goldman anticipates Foucault's indictment of the idea of reform – an idea that, as Deleuze most clearly suggests (Foucault and Deleuze, 2004), is 'so stupid and hypocritical' (208). Goldman supported those individuals and organizations that neither sought to reinforce existing structures of power, nor refused connection with those whose tactics, organization and political philosophy did not mirror their own. Like Deleuze, Goldman (1970a) saw it as 'ridiculous to expect any redress from the State' (122), following Nietzsche (1995), who argued that the state 'tries to make every human being unfree by always keeping the smallest number of possibilities in front of them' (157). In this regard, appealing to the state for change does not open it up to multiplicity. At best, the state can be asked to include additional elements, as long as those elements do not make certain demands (radical change, uncertainty, revaluation of the legitimacy of the state). In a politics of reform, the state form must remain dominant. However, multiplicity not only demands diversity, but also refuses the domination and centralization of a single form of organization, resistance, interaction or identification. The starting point of such an ethic 'includes instead of excludes' (Anzaldúa, 1990b: 379). The question then becomes, how can things be opened up, expanded, and interrogated, rather than asking how others can be incorporated into an existing paradigm. Goldman's (1998) praise of life as representing 'beauty in a thousand variations' (150) also appears to be drawn from her reading of Nietzsche. She states, 'I venture to suggest that his master idea had nothing to do with the vulgarity of station, caste, or wealth. Rather did it mean the masterful in human possibilities [to] become the creator of new and beautiful things' (ibid.: 232–3). 'Nietzsche's practical teaching', Deleuze (1983) wrote, 'is that difference is happy; that multiplicity, becoming and chance are adequate objects of joy by themselves and that only joy returns'

(190). Deleuze (2004) argued that Nietzsche should be understood as an 'affirmation of the multiple' which lies in 'the practical joy of the diverse' (84). Goldman too understood Nietzsche in this way, and consequently used his work to construct her notion of anarchism as embracing the multiple and the relational. Drawing from Nietzsche's affinity for multiplicity, Goldman's work, like Anzaldúa's (1987) new mestiza, 'operates in a pluralistic mode' (101). 'She [the new mestiza] has discovered that she can't hold concepts or ideas in rigid boundaries', Anzaldúa argued, 'she learns to juggle cultures, she has a plural personality' (1987: 101). Put simply, Goldman imagined the greatest potential for radical social change in the cultivation and interconnection of multiple conceptual and political forms.

And so it was that Goldman was content to occupy an itinerant intellectual and political world without answers – happy to imagine a thousand tactical, personal and political interconnecting variations. Butler (2004) too expresses an affinity for 'an affirmation of life that takes place through the play of multiplicity' (193). This demonstrates that by relying upon Nietzsche and theoretical affinities that would come to be associated with post-structuralist thought (indictment of rationalist and naturalist assumptions, refusal to accept binaries, rejection of fixed notions of revolution, social change and state forms, and an affinity for multiplicity and perpetual transformation), Goldman theorized resistance in a way that was distinct from many of her predecessors and contemporaries. As Call (2002) points out, 'today it may not be enough to speak out only against the armies and the police, as earlier anarchists did' (11). Yet Goldman would have agreed with his suggestion that an anarchist analysis must look further than the usual targets. 'Any solution', Goldman (1969) argued, 'can be brought about only through the consideration of *every phase* of life' (50). Similarly, Foucault (1980) contended that 'we can't defeat the system through isolated actions; we must engage it on all fronts' (230). Anzaldúa (2002) too demanded that we 'make changes on multiple fronts: inner/spiritual/personal, social/collective/material' (561). Goldman did not concern herself with only the most traditional and recognizable sites of power. Power, for Goldman, existed in all institutions and relationships, and therefore the struggle against domination needed to take place constantly and in every aspect of life. As Goldman (1998) suggested with regard to 'sex' and power, 'a true conception of the relation of the sexes will not admit of conqueror and conquered' (167). That is, power is not a force wielded by some and denied others, but rather, is present in all relationships and institutions.

One of the ways Goldman's multiplicity manifested itself was through the practice of solidarity. Goldman's solidarity with anti-colonial struggles in Africa and the Philippines and the participants of the Mexican and Spanish revolutions (as well as countless other groups and struggles) was an important element of her work:

It requires something more than personal experience to gain a philosophy or point of view from any specific event. It is the quality of our response to the event and our capacity to enter into the lives of others that help us to make their lives and experiences our own. (Goldman, 1998: 434)

For Goldman, ethico-political encounters must remain open and democratic. For example, despite being credited as 'the most dangerous woman in the world' for over two decades, Goldman rejected the call from several contemporaries to counsel those fighting in the Spanish revolution. 'We must give our Spanish comrades a chance to find their own bearings through their own experience', Goldman (1998: 424) argued. Her constant displeasure with American workers and their failure to align themselves with struggles taking place elsewhere in the world (1969: 142) anticipated the popularized slogan 'teamsters and turtles', used by many within contemporary anti-globalization struggles to explain a 'new' form of solidarity. However, the example that stands out most among her contemporaries, and the one with which I will conclude, having come full circle, was her defence of Czolgosz. Though she herself disagreed with the tactic, Goldman (1998) made an important distinction in her criticism: 'I do not believe that these acts can, or even have been intended to, bring about the social reconstruction' (60). For Goldman, each act of resistance did not have to be a sanctioned tactic that acted as a component of a fixed trajectory toward the revolution. Dissensus could and should be present (and coupled with democratic forms of decision making) and tactics should be reconsidered, but not at the expense of empathy, connection and a consideration of contexts. We should not 'arrive', as Goldman stated earlier, nor desire that everyone else challenging power reside in the same polit-ico-theoretical space. Goldman's (1970a) insistence that 'behind every political deed of that nature was an impressionable, highly sensitive personality and a gentle spirit' (190) signified a unique and nearly solitary understanding of the event. Goldman not only rejected the prevailing wisdom of distancing oneself from certain people or groups with the hope of avoiding the indictment of power or public opinion, she also refused the dichotomous view of acceptable or unacceptable tactics. Moreover, she located the affirmative element within Czolgosz's action. As Deleuze (1983) suggested, 'destruction becomes active to the extent that the negative is transmuted and converted into affirmative power' (174). By suggesting that Czolgosz's 'act is noble, but it is mistaken' (Goldman, 2003: 427), Goldman was attempting to open an inter-tactical dialogue – one that neither condemns nor endorses, but recognizes the limitations of any one tactic. Goldman's suggestion that political acts need not be stepping stones toward a universal and agreed-upon goal is similar to Michael Hardt and Antonio Negri's reading of Frantz Fanon and Malcolm X in *Empire* (2000). Hardt and Negri defend what might be framed as an unpopular tactic by arguing that the 'negative moment' articulated and supported by Fanon and Malcolm X 'does not lead to any dialectical synthesis' nor act as 'the upbeat that will be resolved in a future harmony' (132). As such, the dialectic is no longer a necessary political framework through which activists make tactical decisions. In Czolgosz's case, Goldman understood that his act was not the dialectical 'upbeat that will be resolved in a future harmony'.

Under the wrinkling labour of contemporary political and theoretical debates several questions have been asked. Among them: How is it possible to maintain attachments to others, to subjectivities, to futurity and imaginings, and to forms of organizing that remain contingent? What does it mean to occupy the shaky scaffolding of unstable and contradictory identities? What can be made of a theoretical turn that involves the loosening of a commitment to a final revolutionary moment? Prior still is the question about the consequence of this shift and the coming to terms with certain losses? If radical social change is perceived and articulated as an unrealizable fiction that maintains a utopian imaginary without being wedded to its actual realization, what becomes of political futures? Finally, are the political protests, forums and ethico-political practices that have captured the imagination of a wide range of theorists and been cast as constitutive of a palpably euphoric and near utopian shift in social and political possibility, and further, described as perpetually changing and unique aggregates of previously conflicting groups and ideologies now communicating and working across geographical and political lines, entirely new? My argument here is simply that each of these questions requires a dimension of remembrance, one that draws from the impetuses, imaginings, political practices and failures of the past. To this end, Emma Goldman offers one important and inheritable moment to which we can look back as we move forward.

NOTES

1. Candace Falk (1984) (curator and director of the Emma Goldman Papers Project) uses the term 'Goldmaniacs' to describe those with a passionate interest in Goldman (xviii). The term 'Goldmanologists' was used to describe those who may object to the historically inaccurate Broadway musical portrayal of Goldman's involvement in the assassination of McKinley (June Abernathy 'On Directing Assassins', <www.sondheim.com/shows/essay/assassin-direct.html>).

2. Although Goldman, like many others (including Nietzsche) sometimes spoke in terms of an imagined utopian space, this does not undermine the argument I am making, for three reasons: One, my intention is to make suggestions for further readings by locating certain elements of Goldman's work. Two, I would argue that although Goldman did sometimes speak in this way, she maintained the demand that utopian visions remain open to constant modification and criticism. Three, I would further argue that Goldman's vision of a democratic, creative and open world is the expected result of political activity. That is, this vision does not undermine one's ability to embrace uncertainty and multiplicity. Rather, being inflexibly wedded to a very particular vision is what results in the exclusion and lack of open-mindedness that Goldman problematized in her work.

3. The resistance Goldman experienced with respect to her attachment to Nietzsche shows that what would otherwise be insignificant anecdotes from her autobiography in fact represent important sources for understanding her notion of anarchism.

4. This clearly draws from Nietzsche's notion of a 'revaluation of all values' (Nietzsche, 1979: 96; 1982: 579). The different terms 'revaluation' and 'transvaluation' hold the same meaning for Goldman and Nietzsche. In fact, Goldman's use of the term 'transvaluation' seems to be drawn directly from her German reading of Nietzsche, rather than a new term inspired by him.

5. Unfortunately, federal authorities confiscated the notes from Goldman's lectures (including those on Nietzsche) during a raid at the New York office of her anarchist journal, *Mother Earth*. They have since been destroyed or have not been released.

6. Considered an authority on Goldman, Shulman (1991) was asked to provide a friend with a photo of Goldman and an accompanying phrase to be embossed on T-shirts and sold at an anti-Vietnam protest in the early 1970s. Shulman provided a number of passages from which quotes could be drawn, with particular emphasis on one from Goldman's autobiography. In this passage, Goldman describes a party at which another anarchist confronted her about her style of dance. What resulted was a paraphrasing of this confrontation: 'If I can't dance I don't want to be part of your revolution'.

7. It is worth noting that this arguably ableist, albeit analogous, comment not only predates disability studies, but is also connected to Nietzsche's general contempt for physical 'sickness'/'imperfection' – something he himself was for most of his life.

8. In an earlier essay, Goldman credited Nietzsche with first calling the state a 'cold monster' (1998: 117).

9. This comment also demonstrates Goldman's prescience and anticipation of the contemporary (and arguably postmodernist) denial of organic reality (the socially constructed 'nature') of categories such as race.

10. Nietzsche viewed socialism *and* anarchism as an arrogant and prescriptive 'will to negate life' (1968: 77), desirous of homogeneity.

11. Despite Nietzsche's suspicion of activists, he did periodically expose a certain appreciation: '[T]here is nothing contemptible in a revolt as such [...] there are even cases in which one might have to honor a rebel, because he finds something in our society against which war ought to be waged – he awakens us from our slumber' (Nietzsche, 1968: 391).

12. I am indebted to Mark Lance for this phrasing.

13. Anzaldúa describes the Coatlicue state as 'a rupture in our everyday world. As the Earth, she opens and swallows us, plunging us into the underworld where the soul resides, allowing us to dwell in darkness' (1987: 68).

REFERENCES

Anzaldúa, Gloria (2002). 'Now Let Us Shift ... the Path of Conocimiento ... Inner Work, Public Acts'. In *This Bridge We Call Home: Radical Visions for Transformation* (G. Anzaldúa and A. Keating, eds). New York: Routledge.

—— (1990a). 'En rapport, in Opposition: Cobrando cuentas a las nuesrats'. In *Making Face, Making Soul/Haciendo caras: Creative and Critical Perspectives by Feminists of Color* (G. Anzaldúa, ed.). San Francisco: Aunt Lute Books.

—— (1990b). 'La conciencia de la mestiza: Towards a New Consciousness'. In *Making Face, Making Soul/Haciendo caras: Creative and Critical Perspectives by Feminists of Color* (G. Anzaldúa, ed.). San Francisco: Aunt Lute Books.

—— (1987). *Borderlands/La frontera: The New Mestiza* (2nd edn). San Francisco: Aunt Lute Books.

Avrich, Paul (1994) [1988]. *Anarchist Portraits*. Princeton, NJ: Princeton University Press.

Bart, Jody (1995). '"If I Can't Dance": The Political Philosophy of Emma Goldman'. *DAI* 55(9) (March).

Beauvoir, Simone de (1989) [1949]. *The Second Sex* (H.M. Parshley, ed. and trans.). New York: Vintage Books.

Bookchin, Murray (1995). *Social Anarchism or Lifestyle Anarchism: An Unbridgeable Chasm*. San Francisco: AK Press.

Butler, Judith (2004). *Undoing Gender*. New York: Routledge.

—— (1993). *Bodies that Matter: On the Discursive Limits of 'Sex'*. New York: Routledge.

Call, Lewis (2002). *Postmodern Anarchism*. New York: Lexington Books.

Dark Star Collective (2002). 'Foreword'. In *Quiet Rumours: An Anarcha-Feminist Reader* (Dark Star Collective, eds). San Francisco, CA: AK Press.

Day, Richard (2005). *Gramsci Is Dead: Anarchist Currents in the Newest Social Movements*. Toronto: Between the Lines.

Deleuze, Gilles (2004). *Desert Islands and Other Texts, 1953–1974* (D. Lapoujade, ed.; M. Taormina, trans.). Los Angeles: Semiotext(e).

—— (1983). *Nietzsche and Philosophy* (H. Tomlinson, trans.). New York: Columbia University Press.

—— and Félix Guattari (1987). *A Thousand Plateaus: Capitalism and Schizophrenia* (B. Massumi, trans.). Minneapolis: University of Minnesota Press.

—— —— (1983). *On the Line* (J. Johnston, trans.). New York: Semiotext(e).

Drinnon, Richard (1961). *Rebel in Paradise: A Biography of Emma Goldman*. Chicago: University of Chicago Press.

Falk, Candace (1984). *Love, Anarchy and Emma Goldman*. London: Rutgers University Press.

Ferguson, Kathy E. (2004). 'E.G.: Emma Goldman'. In *Feminism and the Final Foucault* (D. Taylor and K. Vintges, eds). Chicago: University of Illinois Press.

Foucault, Michel (1983). 'Preface'. In Gilles Deleuze and Félix Guattari (1983). *Anti-Oedipus: Capitalism and Schizophrenia* (R. Hurley, H.R. Lane and M. Seem, trans.). Minneapolis: University of Minnesota Press.

—— (1980). *Power/Knowledge: Selected Interviews and Other Writings, 1972–1977* (Colin Gordon, ed.). New York: Pantheon Books.

—— and Deleuze, Gilles (2004) [1972]. 'Intellectuals and Power'. In Deleuze (2004).

Frankel, Oz (1996). 'Whatever Happened to "Red Emma"?: Emma Goldman, from Alien Rebel to American Icon'. *Journal of American History* 83(3): 903–42.

Goldman, Emma (2005a). *Emma Goldman: A Documentary History of the American Years, vol.2. Making Speech Free, 1902–1909* (C. Falk, B. Pateman and J. Moran, eds). Berkeley: University of California Press.

—— (2005b). *The Social Significance of Modern Drama*. New York: Cosimo Classics.

—— (2003). *Emma Goldman: A Documentary History of the American Years, vol.1. Made for America*. (C. Falk and B. Pateman, eds). Berkeley: University of California Press.

—— (1998). *Red Emma Speaks: An Emma Goldman Reader* (3rd edn; A.K. Shulman, ed.). New York: Humanity Books.

—— (1970a). *Living My Life, vol.1*. New York: Dover Publications.

—— (1970b). *Living My Life, vol.2*. New York: Dover Publications.

—— (1970c). *The Traffic in Women and other Essays on Feminism*. Ojai, CA: Times Change Press.

—— (1969). *Anarchism and Other Essays*. New York: Dover Publications.

—— (1933). 'An Anarchist Looks at Life'. Retrieved in March 2004 from <http://sunsite3.berkely.edu/Goldman/Writingsw/Speeches/foyles.html>.

Graham, Robert (ed.) (2005). *Anarchism: A Documentary History of Libertarian Ideas*. Montreal: Black Rose Books.

Haaland, Bonnie (1993). *Emma Goldman: Sexuality and the Impurity of the State*. Montreal: Black Rose Books.

Hardt, Michael, and Negri, Antonio (2000). *Empire*. Cambridge, MA: Harvard University Press.

Jose, Jim (2005). '"Nowhere at Home": Not Even in Theory'. *Anarchist Studies* 13(1): 10–20.

Kissack, Terence (2008). *Free Comrades: Anarchism and Homosexuality in the United States, 1895–1917*. Oakland, CA: AK Press.

Marshall, Peter (1993). *Demanding the Impossible: A History of Anarchism*. London: Fontana Press.

Marso, L.J. (2003). 'A Feminist Search for Love: Emma Goldman on the Politics of Marriage, Love, Sexuality and the Feminine'. *Feminist Theory* 4(3) (December): 305–20.

May, Todd (2005). *Gilles Deleuze: An Introduction*. Cambridge: Cambridge University Press.

—— (1994). *The Political Philosophy of Anarchism*. Pennsylvania: Pennsylvania State University Press.

Moritz, Theresa, and Moritz, Albert (2001). *The World's Most Dangerous Woman: A New Biography of Emma Goldman*. Vancouver: Subway Books.

Newman, Saul (2001). *From Bakunin to Lacan: Anti-Authoritarianism and the Dislocation of Power*. London: Lexington Books.

Nietzsche, Friedrich (1995). *Human, All Too Human* (G. Handwerk, trans.). Stanford, CA: Stanford University Press.

—— (1989). *Beyond Good and Evil: Prelude to a Philosophy of the Future*. New York: Vintage Books

—— (1982). *The Portable Nietzsche* (W. Kaufmann, trans.). London: Penguin Books.

—— (1979). *Ecce Homo: How One Becomes What One Is* (R.J. Hollingdale, trans.). London: Penguin Books.

—— (1969). *Thus Spoke Zarathustra: A Book for Everyone and No One* (R.J. Hollingdale, trans.). London: Penguin Books.

—— (1968). *The Will to Power* (W. Kaufmann, trans.). New York: Vintage Books.

Sandoval, Chela (2000). *Methodology of the Oppressed*. Minneapolis: University of Minnesota Press.

Sheehan, Sean M. (2003). *Anarchism*. London: Reaktion Books.

Shulman, Alix Kates (1991). 'Dances with Feminists'. *Women's Review of Books* 9(3): 1–3.

—— (1972). 'Dancing in the Revolution: Emma Goldman's Feminism'. *Socialist Review* 61(12): 31–44.

—— (1971). *To the Barricades: The Anarchist Life of Emma Goldman*. New York: Crowell Press.

Solomon, Martha (1988). 'Ideology as Rhetorical Constraint: The Anarchist Agitation of "Red Emma" Goldman'. *Quarterly Journal of Speech* 74: 184–200.

—— (1987). *Emma Goldman*. Boston: Twayne Publishers.

Starcross, Leigh (2004). '"Nietzsche was an anarchist": Reconstructing Emma Goldman's Nietzsche Lectures'. In *I Am Not a Man, I Am Dynamite: Friedrich Nietzsche and the Anarchist Tradition* (J. Moore and S. Sunshine, eds). Brooklyn, NY: Autonomedia.

Wexler, Alice (2003). *American Experience: Emma Goldman* (PBS transcript). Retrieved from <http://www.pbs.org/wgbh/amex/goldman/filmmore/pt.html>.

Wittig, Monique (1992). *The Straight Mind and Other Essays* (M. Wildeman, trans.). Boston: Beacon Press.

Woodcock, George (2004) [1962]. *Anarchism: A History of Libertarian Ideas and Movements*. Peterborough, ON: Broadview Press.

15
Reconsidering Post-Structuralism and Anarchism

Nathan Jun

I

The concept of representation looms large in post-structuralist philosophy. For Derrida, Foucault and Deleuze representation is arguably the principal vehicle by which relational concepts are subordinated to totalizing concepts: difference to identity, play to presence, multiplicity to singularity, immanence to transcendence, discourse to knowledge, power to sovereignty, subjectivation to subjectivity, and so on. Representation plays a similar role in anarchist critique, which is one reason that Lewis Call (2003) counts 'classical anarchism' among the historical precursors of post-structuralism. Call was not, however, the first scholar to make this association. Gayatry Spivak and Michael Ryan (1978), 24 years earlier, published a groundbreaking analysis of the connections between post-structuralist philosophy (including that of Derrida, Deleuze and Guattari) and the *nouvel anarchisme* of 1968. This was followed 14 years later by Todd May's seminal work *The Political Philosophy of Poststructuralist Anarchism* (1994), which presented the first book-length argument that the political philosophy of Deleuze, Foucault and Lyotard represents a new kind of anarchism.[1] May was followed by Saul Newman (2001) (who refers to 'post-anarchism') as well as Lewis Call (who refers to 'postmodern anarchism'). The common theme of these and related works is that post-structuralist political philosophy is an anarchism, one that consciously or unconsciously borrows several key ideas from 'classical anarchism' and proceeds to reaffirm, elaborate and ultimately 'improve' these ideas.

My own position is that (a) the so-called 'classical anarchists' had already discovered several of the insights attributed to post-structuralists more than a century before the latter appeared on the scene; (b) that anarchism, consequently, is a postmodern political philosophy and not (or not *just*) the other way around; (c) that post-structuralist political philosophy, particularly as developed by Deleuze and Foucault, indeed elaborates, expands, and even (to a certain extent) 'improves' upon 'classical' anarchist ideas, but not in the way, or for the reasons, that May and others suggest; and (d) that rather than regard post-structuralist political philosophy as a totally new and ready-made form of anarchism, it is better to view post-structuralist ideas as potential ingredients for the development of new anarchist recipes. As I have already offered considerable support for (a) and (b) elsewhere, I will mostly focus in what follows on defending the other claims. In order to do so, however, we ought briefly to consider the political context within which post-structuralism emerged.

II

Although the revolutionary events of May 1968 were short-lived, the major uprisings having been quelled after only six weeks, they nonetheless had far-reaching and lasting effects. Among other things, they marked the end of the Stalinist PCF's long-standing dominance over the French left (cf. Hamon, 1989: 10–22, 17), laid the foundation for the German and Italian *Autonomia* movements of the 1970s and 1980s, and would eventually exert a profound influence on various anti-globalization movements of the 1990s. They also radicalized a whole new generation of intellectuals, including Michel Foucault and Gilles Deleuze. Unlike his long-time friend and collaborator Félix Guattari, who had been involved in radical activism since the early 1960s, Deleuze did not become politically active until after 1968 (Patton, 2000: 4; cf. Deleuze and Guattari, 1972: 15; cf. Feenberg and Freedman, 2001: xviii). 'From this period onward', writes Paul Patton, 'he became involved with a variety of groups and causes, including the *Groupe d'Information sur les Prisons* (GIP) begun by Foucault and others in 1972' (ibid.: 4). More importantly, Deleuze's prior commitment to speculative metaphysics gave way to a deep interest in political philosophy as he attempted to make sense of the political practices he encountered in 1968. Four years later, in 1972, Deleuze and Guattari published *Anti-Oedipus: Capitalism and Schizophrenia* (1977), the first of a two-volume work on political philosophy.[2] The second volume, entitled *A Thousand Plateaus* (1987), followed ten years later.

As mentioned above, Todd May has argued at great length that the political theories of Foucault, Deleuze and Lyotard were deeply influenced by the Paris Spring and the anarchists and anti-authoritarians who helped foment it. May thinks this explains, at least in part, why the political philosophy of post-structuralism developed into a kind of anarchism. At the same time, he acknowledges that Foucault and Deleuze were in all likelihood completely unfamiliar with the so-called 'classical anarchists', which suggests that anarchism came to them second hand, by way of the *Enragés* and the Situationists. This strikes me as plausible enough, but it is not the only possible explanation. Many of Nietzsche's ideas are remarkably similar to those of Proudhon, Bakunin and other anarchists even though it is certain that Nietzsche was unfamiliar with their writings (and vice versa, at least until after Nieztsche's death). Given the enormous influence of Nietzsche upon both Foucault and Deleuze, it is also possible that they inherited a portion of Nietzsche's unconscious anarchism (or the anarchists' unconscious Nietzscheanism, depending upon how one looks at it).

Either way, May successfully demonstrates that Deleuze has considerable philosophical affinity with the classical anarchists. To begin with, he rejects the so-called repressive thesis – the idea that power is by definition repressive and for this reason ought to be abolished. For Deleuze, as May notes, 'power does not suppress desire; rather it is implicated in every assemblage of desire' (1994: 71). Given the ubiquitous and ontologically constitutive nature of power, it goes without saying that power *simpliciter* cannot be 'abolished' or even 'resisted'. This does not mean that repressive social forces cannot be opposed. It does imply, however, that for Deleuze, as for Spinoza, the crucial question is not whether and how resistance is possible, but how and why desire comes to repress and ultimately destroy itself in the first place (Deleuze and Guattari, 1977: xiii). Answering this question requires, among other things, theoretical analyses of the various assemblages that come into being over time (*vis-à-vis* their affects, their lines of flight, etc.) as well as experimentation at the level of praxis. We shall say more about this below, but for the time being it is enough to note that Deleuze, like Bakunin, Kropotkin and other classical anarchists, agrees that power can be active or reactive, creative or destructive, repressive or liberatory.[3] More importantly, both are agreed that power is ontologically constitutive (i.e. that it produces reality) and that it is immanent to individuals and society as opposed to an external or transcendent entity (Kropotkin, 1970: 104–6; Lunn, 1973: 220–7).

Like the anarchists, Deleuze also rejects the concentration thesis – that is, the idea that repressive forces emanate from a unitary source rather than multiple sites (see Marx and Engels, 1974: 544; Bakunin, 1972: 89; Bakunin, 1953: 224). In Deleuze's philosophy, the interplay of multiple forces within and among multiple nodes, which are themselves interconnected via complex networks, is precisely what gives rise to the social world (this is what he means when he suggests that power is 'rhizomatic' as opposed to 'arboreal'). This is not to say that power does not become concentrated within certain sites; indeed, much of *Capitalism and Schizophrenia* is given over to an analysis of how such concentrations express themselves in particular political and economic forms, how these forms operate, and so forth. These analyses are similar to Foucault's genealogies insofar as they seek to unearth how power (or force or desire) as manifested in concrete assemblages *works*. For Foucault, a genealogy of actuality is simultaneously a cartography of possibility: forms of power always produce forms of resistance; thus in analysing how power operates one also analyses how power is or can be resisted. Similarly, for Deleuze, 'to analyze a social formation is to unravel the variable lines and singular *processes* that constitute it as a multiplicity: their connections and disjunctions, their circuits and short-circuits and, above all, their possible transformations' (Smith, 2003: 307). A social formation is not just defined by its actual operation, but also by its 'lines of flight', the internal conditions of possibility for movement, transformation, 'deterritorialization' (Deleuze and Guattari, 1987: 216; cf. Deleuze and Parnet, 1987: 135). Although the rejection of the concentration thesis entails a greater number of *explananda*, which in turn require a greater number of *explanantia*, different and multiple forms of domination ensure that different and multiple forms of resistance are possible.

Even a cursory summary of the complicated political ontology outlined in *Capitalism and Schizophrenia* would well exceed the scope of this work. Fortunately, such a summary is unnecessary. For our purposes, it is enough to note that Deleuze ontologizes politics much more vividly than the classical anarchists even though both deny the existence of Kantian pure reason or any other model of universal, transcendent rationality (Deleuze, 1995: 145–6) as well as the existence of a universal, transcendent subject (Deleuze, 1992: 162). As Smith writes:

> What one finds in any given socio-political assemblage is not a universal 'Reason', but variable processes of rationalization; not universalizable 'subjects', but variable processes of subjectivation; not the 'whole', the 'one' or 'objects', but rather knots of totalization, focuses of unification, and processes of objectification. (2003: 307)

Generally speaking, Deleuze takes the idea of social physics in a radically literal direction by shifting political analysis to the level of pre-social, pre-subjective processes, operations and relations of force. This shift requires, among other things, the invention of new concepts as well as the redefinition of extant concepts using complex, technical and highly idiosyncratic terminology.

We need not go into exhaustive detail about 'machines', 'becomings', 'molar lines', and the like to note (a) that Deleuze disdains 'abstractions', which he typically regards as 'anti-life' (Deleuze and Guattari, 1994: 47; Deleuze, 1995: 85; Deleuze and Guattari, 1988: 23); (b) that the most objectionable form of abstraction for Deleuze, as for the anarchists, is representation (Deleuze, n.d.: 206–7; cf. Patton, 2000: 47–8; May, 2005: 127); and (c) that Deleuze believes that representation at the macropolitical level arises from representation at the micropolitical level (Deleuze and Parnet, 1987: 146; cf. May, 2005 :142). As Todd May notes regarding (b):

> The power to represent people to themselves is oppressive in itself: practices of telling people who they are and what they want erect a barrier between them and who (or what) they can create themselves to be. *Anti-Oedipus* can be read in this light as a work whose project is to demolish current representational barriers between people and who they can become, and in that sense Foucault states its point exactly when he calls it a 'book of ethics'. (1994: 131)

As for (c), Deleuze locates the origin of representational practices in micropolitical orders, identities and regulatory practices (what he calls 'molar lines') and in the 'overcoding' of these 'molar lines' by more complicated power mechanisms (what he calls 'abstract machines'). A particular society may represent individuals in terms of a variety of constructed identities – for example, familial identities ('son'), educational identities ('school child'), occupational identities ('professional') racial identities ('Caucasian') and so on.

That same society may also represent individuals via a system of normalized ordering – for example, from 'son' to 'school child' to 'professional', etc.

Alongside systems of ordering and identifying, there may be other distinct regulatory practices such as 'the minute observation and intervention into the behavior of bodies, a distinction between the abnormal and the normal in regard to human desire and behavior, and a constant surveillance of individuals' (May, 2005: 140). For Foucault, discipline is nothing more than the collocation of these practices, the concrete manifestation of which is the prison (Foucault, 1978: 184). Discipline itself 'does not exist as a concrete reality one could point to or isolate from the various forms it takes' (May, 2005: 141). Instead, Deleuze describes discipline as an 'abstract machine' that collocates diverse representational practices (i.e. 'overcodes molar lines') into a single regime of power.

For Deleuze, the state does not create representations of its own. Rather, 'it makes points *resonate* together, points that are not necessarily already town-poles but very diverse points of order, geographic, ethnic, linguistic, moral, economic, technological particularities' (Deleuze and Guattari, 1987: 433). More specifically, the state helps to actualize a variety of abstract machines (e.g. discipline), to bring them into a relationship of interdependence with itself and with each other, to expand and maintain them (ibid.: 223–4; Deleuze and Parnet, 1987: 130). At the same time, the state 'territorializes' – that is, it marshals these machines against the various micropolitical forces, identities, multiplicities, relations, etc. that threaten or oppose it ('molecular lines' or 'lines of flight', as well as the various abstract machines which could bring these lines together – e.g. radical political movements). Capitalism, on the other hand, is an axiomatic 'defined not solely by decoded flows, but by the generalized decoding of flows, the new massive deterritorialization, the conjunction of deterritorialized flows' (Deleuze and Guattari, 1977: 224).

A given social formation is a dynamic system comprised of various 'flows' – of matter, people, commodities, money, labour, and so on. Whereas the medieval state, for example, 'overcoded' flows of people, land, labour, etc. by subordinating them to the abstract machine of serfdom, capitalism liberated ('decoded') these flows by wresting control of labour and property from the state ('deterritorialization'). The decoded flows initially escape along a line of flight – workers are free to sell their labour, inventors can create and sell products, entrepreneurs can buy patent rights to these products and invest in their manufacture, etc. Capitalism does not establish codes – i.e. rules that govern relationships among specific people or between specific people and things – but establishes a generic ('axiomatic') framework for governing relationships among diverse people and things. It accomplishes the latter by reterritorializing the lines of flight it frees from codes, subordinating decoded flows to exchange value, and bounding the circulation of flows within the orbit of the capitalist axiomatic. This is what the anarchists referred to as 'appropriation' – the seemingly magic ability of capitalism to transform the fruits of freedom and creativity ('decoded flows') into commodities to be bought and sold (Kropotkin, 2002: 137–9). (Early capitalism transformed labour into a commodity; late capitalism does the same thing with lifestyles, modes of subjectivity and even 'radical' ideologies.)

The latter point underscores an important feature of social formations more generally, one that was recognized as well by the anarchists. Social existence writ large, no less than the macropolitical institutions or micropolitical practices that comprise it, is a battlefield of forces, none of which has an 'intrinsic' or 'essential' nature (Kropotkin, 2002: 109–11; Kropotkin, 1970: 117–18). As the classical anarchists and post-structuralists both realize, one and the same force can be at odds with itself – for example, within a single human being, or a group, or a federation of groups. The tension produced by a force simultaneously seeking to escape and re-conquer itself is precisely what allows ostensibly 'revolutionary' or 'liberatory' movements (e.g. Bolshevism) to occasionally metamorphose into totalitarian regimes (e.g. Stalinist Russia). For the anarchists, the prefigurative ethic is intended in part to maintain, as much as possible, a balance or equilibrium among forces or within a single force.

III

Such are the various parallels and points of intersection that have led Todd May and others to conclude that there is a strong affinity between classical anarchism and the post-structuralist philosophies of Foucault and Deleuze. As I noted earlier, however, much of *The Political Philosophy of Poststructuralist Anarchism* is devoted to showing that there are irreconcilable differences between the two. For example, May repeatedly alleges that classical anarchism depends upon an essentialistic conception of human nature (1994: 63–4), that the classical anarchists endorse the repressive thesis (ibid.: 61), etc. Although I do not address these charges here, I mention them because they constitute a major weakness of *Poststructuralist Anarchism* and related texts. In my view, the works of many self-identified 'post-anarchists' have been characterized by insufficient scholarly engagement with – and, by extension, inaccurate interpretation of – classical anarchist texts. (In fact, the very idea of 'classical anarchism' or a 'classical anarchist tradition' is deeply problematic, but I shall not discuss this here.)

There can be no doubt that post-structuralist political philosophy elaborates, expands and even improves upon 'classical' anarchist ideas. Deleuze cuts a much wider and more incisive swathe, which makes sense given the mid-twentieth-century context in which he thought and wrote. Nor can anyone reasonably deny that his political critique is much more sophisticated than that of Proudhon or Kropotkin, even if it is not quite as novel as some have claimed. Indeed, it is simply wrong to assert that post-structuralist political philosophy represents a totally 'new' form of anarchism that was 'discovered', complete and intact, by otherwise admirable scholars like Todd May and Saul Newman. This has to do not only with the foregoing evidence, nor with some post-anarchists' tendency to misinterpret that evidence, but also with their habit of misconstruing important aspects of post-structuralist philosophy, chief among them the status of normativity.

In the final chapter of *The Political Philosophy of Poststructuralist Anarchism*, for example, May rehearses the oft-repeated accusation that post-structuralism engenders a kind of moral nihilism (1994: 121–7). Such an accusation is a product, he thinks, of the post-structuralists' general unwillingness to 'refer existence to transcendent values' (ibid.: 127), which is surely the dominant strategy of much traditional moral philosophy in the West. Strangely, May goes to great lengths to explain why Deleuze rejects classical 'ethics', only to argue that certain of Deleuze's other commitments implicitly contradict this rejection. As he notes:

> [Deleuze] praises Spinoza's *Ethics*, for instance, because it 'replaces Morality ...' For Deleuze, as for Nietzsche, the project of measuring life against external standards constitutes a betrayal rather than an affirmation of life. Alternatively, an ethics of the kind Spinoza has offered ... seeks out the possibilities life offers rather than denigrating life by appeal to 'transcendent values.' Casting the matter in more purely Nietzschean terms, the project of evaluating a life by reference to external standards is one of allowing reactive forces to dominate active ones, where reactive forces are those which 'separate active force from what it can do'. (Ibid.)

In the same breath, however, May argues that Deleuze provides no explicit means by which to distinguish active forces from reactive ones beyond a vague appeal to 'experimentation' (ibid.: 128). Such a means, he thinks, can only be discovered by extracting 'several intertwined and not very controversial ethical principles' from the hidden nooks of the Deleuzean corpus.

The first such principle, which May terms the 'anti-representationalist principle', holds that 'practices of representing others to themselves – either in who they are or in what they want – ought, as much as possible to be avoided' (ibid.: 130). The second, which he calls the 'principle of difference', holds that 'alternative practices, all things being equal, ought to be allowed to flourish and even to be promoted' (ibid.: 133). In both cases, May provides ample textual evidence to demonstrate that Deleuze (*inter alia*) is implicitly committed to the values underlying these principles. This claim, which we ourselves have already made, is surely correct. It is very clear from the foregoing that 'Gilles Deleuze's commitment to promoting different ways of thinking and acting is a central aspect of his thought' (ibid.: 134). What I take issue with is the idea that the avowal of such values, implicit or otherwise, is *a fortiori* an avowal of *specific normative principles*.

As May himself notes, the defining characteristics of traditional normativity are precisely abstraction, universality and exteriority to life, all of which, as we have seen, Deleuze rejects. Incredibly, May goes on to argue that Deleuze's unwillingness to prescribe universalizable norms is itself motivated by a commitment to the aforesaid principles. Such an argument, however, amounts to claiming that Deleuze is self-referentially inconsistent; it does not lead, as May thinks, to a general acquittal on the charge of moral nihilism. If it is true that Deleuze scorns representation and affirms difference – and I think that it is – then surely the operative values cannot be articulated and justified by means of representation or the suppression of difference except on pain of dire contradiction. Of course this is precisely the opposite of what May wishes to argue.

The normative principles which May attributes to Deleuze are problematic not because they are categorical but because they are transcendent; they stand outside of any and all particular assemblages and so cannot be self-reflexive. It is easy to see how such principles, however radical they may seem on the surface, can become totalitarian. To take a somewhat far-fetched but relevant example, the principle of anti-representationalism would effectively outlaw *any* processes of majoritarian representation, even in banal contexts such as homecoming competitions or bowling leagues. Likewise, the principle of difference permits, or at least does not obviously prohibit, morally suspect 'alternative practices' such as thrill-killing or rape. A year after the publication of *Poststructuralist Anarchism*, May (1995) amended his views somewhat, expanding them into a comprehensive moral theory. The foundation of this theory is a revised version of the anti-representationalist principle, according to which 'people ought not, other things being equal, to engage in practices whose effect, among others, is the representation of certain intentional lives as either intrinsically superior or intrinsically inferior to others' (ibid.: 48). The principle of difference drops out of the picture altogether.

May buttresses the revised anti-representationalist principle with what he calls a 'multi-value consequentialism' (ibid.). After suggesting that 'moral values' are 'goods to which people ought to have access' (ibid.: 87), he proceeds to argue that the 'values' entailed by the anti-representationalist principle include 'rights, just distributions, and other goods' (ibid.: 88). May's theory judges actions as 'right' to the extent that (a) they do not violate the anti-representationalist principle nor (b) result in denying people goods to which they ought to have access. Whatever substantive objections one might raise against this theory would be quite beside the point. The problem, as we have already noted, is that the very idea of a 'moral theory of poststructuralism' based on universalizable normative principles is oxymoronic. What distinguishes normativity from conventional modes of practical reasoning is the universalizable or categorical nature of the rational reason in question – i.e. the fact that in all relevantly similar circumstances it applies equally to all moral agents at all times. Typically this rational reason has taken the form of a universal moral principle, and to this extent, May's 'principle of anti-representationalism' is no different from Kant's categorical imperative or Bentham's principle of utility. It is precisely this universal and abstract character that makes normativity 'transcendent' in the sense outlined earlier, and post-structuralism is nothing if not a systematic repudiation of transcendence.

Some would suggest that normativity is attractive precisely because it provides us with a clear and unambiguous methodology by which to guide our actions. It is not at all obvious, however, that this requires *transcendent moral principles*, especially if ordinary practical reasoning will suffice. The prefigurative principle, which demands that the means employed be consistent with the desired ends, is a practical principle or hypothetical imperative of the form 'if you want X you ought to do Y'. Anarchists have long argued that incongruity between the means and the end is not pragmatically conducive to the achievement of the end. As such, it is not the case that one ought to do Y because it is the 'morally right' thing to do, but because it is the most sensible course of action given one's desire to achieve X. A principle of this sort can be regarded as categorical or even universalizable, but it is scarcely 'transcendent'. Its justification is immanent to its purpose, just as the means are immanent to the desired end. It provides us with a viable categorical norm without any concept of transcendence.

It may be possible to preserve some semblance of normativity in Deleuze. Paul Patton, for example, has suggested that the 'the overriding norm [for Deleuze] is that of deterritorialization' (2000: 9). In shifting the focus of political philosophy from static, transcendent concepts like 'the subject' and 'rationality' to dynamic, immanent concepts such as 'machinic processes', 'processes of subjectivication', etc., Deleuze also shifts the focus of normativity from extensive to intensive criteria of normative judgment. As Patton notes, 'What a given assemblage is capable of doing or becoming is determined by the lines of flight or deterritorialization it can sustain' (ibid.: 106). Thus normative criteria will not only demarcate the application of power by a given assemblage but 'will also find the means for the critique and modification of those norms' (Smith, 2003: 308). Put another way, political normativity must be capable not only of judging the activity of assemblages, but also of judging the norms to which said assemblages gives rise. Such normativity is precisely what prevents the latent 'micro-fascism of the avant-garde' from blossoming into full-blown totalitarianism.

Transcendent normativity generates norms that do not and cannot take account of their own deterritorialization or lines of flight. Because the norms follow from, and so are justified by, the transcendent ground, they cannot provide self-reflexive criteria by which to question, critique, or otherwise act upon themselves. The concept of normativity as deterritorialization, on the contrary, does not generate norms. Rather, it stipulates that

> what 'must' always remain normative is the ability to critique and transform existing norms, that is, to create something new [...] One cannot have preexisting norms or criteria for the new; otherwise it would not be new, but already foreseen. (Smith, 2003)

Absolute deterritorialization is therefore categorical, insofar as it applies to every possible norm as such, but it is not transcendent; rather, it is immanent to whatever norms (and, by extension, assemblages) constitute it. (There can be no deterritorialization without a specific assemblage; thus normativity of deterritorialization both constitutes and is constituted by the particular norms/assemblages to which it applies.)

Considered as such, normativity as deterritorialization is ultimately a kind of 'pragmatic' normativity. It determines what norms ought or ought not to be adopted in concrete social formations according to a pragmatic consideration – namely, whether the norm adopted is capable of being critiqued and transformed. This further entails that a norm cannot be adopted if it prevents other norms from being critiqued and transformed. We might say, then, that a norm must (a) be self-reflexive and (b) its adoption must not inhibit the self-reflexivity of norms. Because normativity is a process that constitutes and is constituted by other processes, it is dynamic, and to this extent we should occasionally expect norms to become perverted or otherwise outlive their usefulness. Pragmatic normativity provides a meta-norm that is produced by the adoption of contingent norms but stands above them as a kind of sentinel; to this extent it is categorical without being transcendent.

Such a view of normativity, while interesting and promising, is not without its problems. Among other things, it does not specify when it is advisable or acceptable to critique or transform particular norms; rather, it only stipulates that any norm must in principle be open to critique and transformation. For example, suppose I belong to a society that adopts vegetarianism as a norm. The adoption of this norm obviously precludes other norms, such as carnophagy. Is this a reason to reject it? Not necessarily. As long as we remain open to other possibilities, the norm is at least *prima facie* justified. But this by itself does not explain (a) what reasons we may have to adopt a vegetarian rather than a carnivorous norm in the first place; and (b) what reasons we may have to ultimately reject a vegetarian norm in favour of some other norm. Such an explanation would require a theory of value – that is, an axiological criterion that determines what things are worth promoting/discouraging *vis-à-vis* the adoption of normative principles.

Whether or not we ought to have done with normativity, we cannot simply ignore the charge of moral nihilism. The problem with May is that he cannot see a way around this charge without normativity – that is, without some reference to laws, norms, imperatives, duties, obligations, permissions and principles that determine how human beings ought and ought not to act (May, 1994); that do not just describe the way the world is, but rather prescribe the way it ought to be (Korsgaard, 1996: 8–9).[4] As we have already had occasion to mention, however, ethics is not concerned merely with expressing what is *right* (i.e. what ought to be done); it is also concerned with determining what is *good* (i.e. what is worth being valued, promoted, protected, pursued, etc.). The latter is the purview of *axiology*, the study of what is good or valuable for human beings and, by extension, what constitutes a good life (ibid.: 1–4).[5]

The *ethical* question of 'how one should live' (i.e. what constitutes a good life) is of primary importance and 'involves a particular way of approaching life [...] It views life as having a shape: a life – a human life – is a whole that might be approached by way of asking how it should unfold' (May, 2005: 4). For the ancients, a life is judged *vis-à-vis* its relationship to the cosmological order – the 'great chain of being' – in which it is situated. At the summit of this order is the Form of the Good (for Plato) or the specifically human *telos* known as *eudaimonia* (for Aristotle) 'which ought to be mirrored or conformed to by the lives of human beings' (ibid.). The good or the valuable is 'above' the realm of human experience because it is, in some sense, *more real*. Consequently, the things of this world not only strive to become *better* but to *be* – that is, to exist in the fullest and most real sense (Korsgaard, 1996: 2). In the case of human beings, success in this striving is manifested in *arete* – that is, excellence or virtue. The question *How should one live?* was gradually replaced by another one – viz. *How should one act?* (May, 2005: 4). Enlightenment philosophers such as Kant and Bentham were no longer concerned with what constitutes a good life (the ethical question) but with how one ought or ought not to act (the normative or moral question). In rejecting the idea of a 'great chain of being' – i.e. a qualitative ontological hierarchy with God (or the Forms) at the top and brute matter at the bottom (ibid.: 5)[6] – modern moral philosophy shifted the focus of moral judgment to individual subjects, as opposed to the relation of human life in general to a larger cosmological whole. Consequently, morality is no longer concerned with the shape lives take; rather, it establishes the moral boundaries or limits of human action. As long as one acts within said boundaries, the direction one's life as a whole takes is entirely up to oneself; it is, in a word, a 'private concern' (ibid.).

Morality, as opposed to ethics, is not 'integrated into our lives'; rather, it exists outside of and exterior to human beings (ibid.). Whether the ultimate foundation of said morality is the divine commandments of God or the dictates of an abstract moral law (e.g. Kant's categorical imperative or Bentham's principle of utility), it is no longer situated in our world or woven into the fabric of our experiences. It is exterior, transcendent, *other*. All of this changes in the nineteenth century with Nietzsche, whose most radical moves are without question his announcement of the death of God[7] and his systematic critique of traditional morality.[8] In one fell swoop, Nietzsche not only destroys the idea of 'theological existence', but with it 'the transcendence in which our morality is grounded' (May, 2005: 6–7). This gives rise to a new question: not *How should one live?* or *How should one act?* but rather *How might one live?* In lieu of any transcendent 'outside' to constrain our actions or establish what sorts of lives are worthwhile for us to pursue, we are free to pursue new ambitions and projects, to explore new ways of being – in short, to discover with Spinoza 'what a body is capable of' (Deleuze, 1990: 226).

As with Nietzsche, the question of *How might one live?* is the cornerstone of both classical and post-structuralist anarchism (May, 2005: 3). Rather than attempting to refine either so as to make them conform to the commonplaces of post-Kantian moral philosophy, critics should instead recognize and celebrate the radical alternative that they propose. That alternative is precisely a turn to *ethics* of the sort Deleuze associates with Nietzsche and Spinoza. It is the ethical, after all, which underlies the anarchist concept of self-creation, the Deleuzean concept of experimentation, and Foucault's 'care of the self'. The question, of course, is what such an ethics would entail.

Ever since Kant, moral philosophers have tended to regard rationality as the foundation of normativity. As Christine Korsgaard puts it:

Strictly speaking, we do not disapprove the action because it is vicious; instead, it is vicious because we disapprove it. Since morality is grounded in human sentiments, the normative question cannot be whether its dictates are true. Instead, it is whether we have reason to be glad that we have such sentiments, and to allow ourselves to be governed by them. (1996: 50)

The point here is that an immoral action – one which we *ought not* to perform – is one which we have a *rational reason* not to perform. We already know that ethics is to be distinguished from morality on the basis of its concreteness, particularity and interiority to life itself. Rather than posing universal codes of conduct grounded in abstract concepts like 'rationality', ethics is instead concerned with the myriad ways in which lives can be led. To this extent, the traditional notion that ethics is concerned with *values* rather than *norms* is not entirely unfitting. Clearly values can be and often are universalized and rendered transcendent, as in the case of natural law theory. Even the Greeks, for whom value was a function of particular standards of excellence proper to particular things, believed that such standards were uniform for all human beings.

For the classical anarchists, every human being is the product of a unique and complicated multiplicity of forces, including the inward-directed forces of self-creation (Bakunin, 1972: 89, 239–41; Goldman, 1998: 67–8, 439; Kropotkin, 1924: 16–26; Kropotkin, 2002: 119–29; Kropotkin, 1970: 136–7, 203). Thus their highest value is life – the capacity of the social individual (and the society of freely associated individuals) to be *different*, to change, move, transform and create (Proudhon, 1989; Goldman, 1998: 118); Malatesta, 2001: 29–36; Malatesta, 1995: 90–100). To value something, to treat it as good, is to treat it as something

we ought to welcome, [to] rejoice in if it exists, [to] seek to produce if does not exist [...] to approve its attainment, count its loss a deprivation, hope for and not dread its coming if this is likely, [and] avoid what hinders its production. (Ewing, 1947: 149)

There is no doubt that the anarchists value life in this way. On the other hand, I am not sure whether they would regard it as 'intrinsically valuable', if by this is meant that the value of life obtains independently of its relations to other things, or that life is somehow worthy of being valued on its own account. For the anarchists, it makes no sense to speak of life in this way, since by its very nature life is relational and dynamic (Malatesta, 1965: 21–2). There is no doubt, however, that anarchists believe that life is *worthy* of being protected, pursued, promoted. As for the question of *why* this is so, Bakunin's response is that 'only an academician would be so dull as to ask it' (Bakunin, 1953: 265; cf. Proudhon, 1989: 115–16). At the risk of being dull, and in the interest of being brief, I shall leave it to one side for now.

IV

Near the end of his life, Foucault sought to address the following problem: given that power is pervasive, and given that power shapes, moulds and constitutes both knowledge and subjects, how is it possible to resist power? More importantly, when and why is it appropriate to resist power?[9] Though recast in Foucaldian parlance, this is the traditional problematic of classical anarchism and, indeed, of all radical philosophy. (That Foucault raises this question, that he calls it an *ethical* question, is perhaps evidence enough that he was neither a nihilist nor a quietist, but rather a new and very different sort of radical.) For Foucault, power is pervasive; it is neither concentrated in a single juridical entity (such as the state) nor exerted upon subjects from somewhere outside themselves:

> If it is true that the juridical system was useful for representing, albeit in a nonexhaustive way, a power that was centred primarily around deduction and death, it is utterly incongruous with the new methods of power whose operation is not ensured by right but by technique, not by law but by normalization, not by punishment but by control, methods that are employed at all levels and in forms that go beyond the state and its apparatus. (Foucault, 1978: 89)

Thus resistance necessarily emerges *within* power relations and is primary to them. To resist power as though it were somehow *elsewhere* or *outside* is merely to react against power. And as radicals of all stripes have witnessed time and again, such reactive resistance is either quickly defeated by extant power structures or else ends up replicating these power structures at the micropolitical level. In the place of reactive resistance, Foucault recommends an active form of resistance in which power is directed against itself rather than against another form of power (such as the state). To actively resist is to enter into a relation with oneself, to reconstitute oneself, to create oneself anew. Through this process, extant power relations are challenged and new forms of knowledge emerge. Bakunin and Kropotkin could not possibly have put the point better.

For Foucault, the relation of the self to itself forms the basis of ethics or 'modes of subjectivation'. In 'Technologies of the Self' (2003: 145–69), he formulates a history of the various ways that human beings 'develop knowledge about themselves' *vis-à-vis* a host of 'specific techniques'. These techniques, which Foucault calls *technologies of the self,*

> permit individuals to effect by their own means or with the help of others a certain number of operations on their own bodies and souls, thoughts, conduct, and way of being, so as to transform themselves in order to attain a certain state of happiness, purity, wisdom, perfection, or immortality. (Ibid.: 146)

Technologies of the self are to be distinguished as such from three other types of technology (or 'matrices of practical reason'): (1) technologies of production (labour power), by which we 'produce, transform, or manipulate' objects in the world; (2) technologies of signs systems, which includes human languages specifically as well as the use of 'signs, meanings, symbols, or signification' more generally; and (3) technologies of power, by which human behaviour is directed, coordinated, compelled, engineered, etc., in 'an objectivizing of the subject' (ibid.).

In Greco-Roman civilization, Foucault claims, there were initially two major ethical principles – 'know yourself' (the Delphic or Socratic principle) and 'take care of yourself'. To illustrate the idea of care for the self, Foucault examines the 'first' Platonic dialogue, *Alcibiades I*, and extracts from it four conflicts, viz. (1) between political activity and self-care; (2) between pedagogy and self-care; (3) between self-knowledge and self-care; and (4) between philosophical love and self-care. The principle of self-knowledge (or self-examination) emerges as victor in the third conflict and gives way both to the Stoicism of the Hellenistic/imperial periods as well as Christian penitential practices in the early Middle Ages. For the Stoics, the importance of self-knowledge is manifested in the practices of quotidinal examinations of conscience; the writing of epistles, treatises and journals; meditations on the future; and the interpretation of dreams. Foucault summarizes:

> In the philosophical tradition dominated by Stoicism, *askesis* means not renunciation but the progressive consideration of self, or mastery over oneself, obtained not through the renunciation of reality but through the acquisition and assimilation of truth. It has as its final aim not preparation for another reality but access to the reality of this world. The Greek word for this is *paraskeuazō* ('to get prepared'). It is a set of practices by which one can acquire, assimilate, and transform truth into a permanent principle of action. *Alethia* becomes *ethos*. It is a process of becoming more subjective. (Ibid.: 158)

For the early Christians, in contrast, self-examination involves not self-mastery but rather self-denial: the repudiation of the flesh, the renunciation of *mundum*, the purification of the soul as a way of preparing for death. This emphasis on self-denial, in turn, gives rise to the absolute obedience of monasticism as well as the entire *dispositif* of the confessional (both in early, public forms (*exomologesis*) and later, private forms (*exagouresis*)). Whereas the Stoic seeks to know himself in order to become a vehicle for the 'acquisition and assimilation [read: mastery] of truth', the Christian seeks to know himself in order to become a vehicle for transcendence. Self-knowledge and disclosure involve a renunciation of the body – the locus of sin and fallen-ness – and a purification of the soul.

In the modern era, the principal technology of self is *self-expression* – that is, the process of expressing those thoughts, beliefs, feelings and desires that are constitutive of one's 'true self'. On my reading, the 'true self' here is neither an immortal soul nor a transcendental subject but rather that aspect of one's subjectivity which one has affected oneself. Modern consciousness takes for granted that there is an inner life that we are constantly forced to suppress in our myriad roles within the capitalist machine. Underneath one's roles as student, son, tax-paying American, etc. – all of which are constructed from without by power relations – there is a self that one does not discover but rather *fashions*. The potential for such self-construction is not necessarily radical in and of itself, since self-construction can and often does merely replicate extant power relations that lie 'outside' or 'on top of' the self. But it is precisely through self-construction that radical political resistance becomes possible.

It is clear that for Foucault, as for the anarchists, power is or ought to be directed toward the creation of *possibilities* – the possibility of new forms of knowledge, new ways of experiencing the world, new ways for individuals to relate to themselves and others – whereas under our present circumstances power is directed toward crystallizing and maintaining institutions of repression, circumscribing knowledge, severely delimiting modes of subjectivity and representing individuals to themselves through various mechanisms of totalization (e.g. religion, patriotism, psychology, etc.) (Malatesta, 1965: 49; cf. Bakunin, 1974: 172). I do not think it is outlandish to claim that the later Foucault, the *ethical* Foucault, cherished life in the same way the anarchists did. Life, after all, is not only a condition of possibility for the 'care of the self' but also *is* the 'care of the self'.

Much of what we have said here about Deleuze applies to Foucault. Deleuze's valorization of 'difference' and scorn of 'representation' surely hint at, if they do not reveal, a similarly vitalistic theory of value. Time and again Deleuze, like Nietzsche, like the anarchists, emphasizes the importance of *Leben-liebe* – the love and affirmation of life. Likewise it is clear that *Leben-liebe* is both a condition and a consequence of creativity, experimentation, the pursuit of the new and the different. To the extent that representation and its social incarnations are opposed to life, they are condemnable, marked by 'indignity'. This strongly suggests that for Deleuze, life is loveable, valuable and good; that it is worthy of being protected and promoted; that whatever is contrary to it is worthy of disapprobation and opposition. At the same time, however, we must recall that the life of which the anarchists speak is something virtual, and there is no guarantee that its actualizations will be affirmative and active. Of course, this is simply one more reason why Deleuze, like Foucault, like the anarchists, emphasizes experimentation on the one hand and eternal vigilance on the other (Malatesta, 1995: 121). 'We do not know of what a body is capable.' Our experiments may lead to positive transformations, they may lead to madness, they may lead to death. What starts out as a reckless and beautiful affirmation of life can become a death camp. It is not enough, therefore, to experiment and create; one must be mindful of, and responsible for, one's creations. The process requires an eternal revolution against domination wherever and however it arises – eternal because *atelos* (without *telos*), and *atelos* because domination cannot be killed. It can only be contained or, better, outrun. Whatever goodness is created along the way will always be provisional, tentative and contingent, but this is hardly a reason not to create it. Anarchism is nothing if not the demand that we keep living.

Political postmodernity, then, is coextensive with anarchy, an eternal revolution against representation which is itself an eternal process of creation and transformation, an eternal practice of freedom. Anarchy is both the goal of political postmodernity as well as the infinite network of possibilities we travel in its pursuit. In other words, political postmodernity just is the blurring or overlapping or intersection of means and ends, the multiple sites at which our desires become immanent to their concrete actualization, the multiple spaces within which the concrete realizations of our desire become immanent to those desires. Such sites and spaces are constantly shifting into and out of focus, moving into and out of existence like rooms in a fun house. In producing them we occupy them; in occupying them we produce them. The freedom we seek as an end is created by our seeking. It is a process of eternal movement, change, becoming, possibility and novelty which simultane-ously demands eternal vigilance, eternal endurance, an eternal commitment to keeping going, whatever the dangers or costs. To stop, even for a moment, is to court domination and representation – in short, death. The forces of death and reaction, no less than the forces of life and revolution, are always and already with us awaiting actualization. There is neither certainty nor respite at any point. There are no stable identities, no transcendent truths, no representations or images. There are only the variable and reciprocal and immanent processes of creation and possibility themselves.

Like Bakunin (1974), all anarchists are 'true seekers'. They seek nothing in particular save greater and more expansive frontiers to explore. Such frontiers, moreover, promise nothing save the possibility of further exploration. Freedom is the practice of opening up new spaces for the practice of freedom. We might call these practices 'life-possibilities' and say that political postmodernity, that *anarchy*, is nothing more than a 'life-creation process'. However, if all life is an indeterminate flow, we can never know in advance what forms lives can or will take. 'There is a bit of death in everything', wrote Rilke. Thus to be revolutionary is to be on guard against death, to prepare oneself not to flee death, nor even to fight it, but simply to change the subject, to do and think otherwise, to seek what is new and vital – all in the hope that some life can and will come from that death, that there is a 'bit of life' in everything, too.

There is a book that will demonstrate that all of this is already happening, that it has been happening for a long time, and that it will continue to happen. When France erupted in revolution, 30 years ago, a small window of anarchy, of postmodernity, opened up and quickly closed. Within the space of that window, paradoxical slogans such as '*soyez réalistes, demandez l'impossible!*' ('be realistic, demand the impossible!') became logical and real. For what were the *Enragés* doing if not making possible what was represented to them as impossible? Nearly ten years ago, when Seattle was shrouded in tear gas and tens of thousands of labourers, students, environmentalists, peace activists and anarchists successfully shut down the World Trade Organization ministerial, I watched another window open up. Just as before, it was quickly closed.

Still, there was a space within that brief aperture within which the cry of the Zapatistas – *'otro mundo es posible!'* ('another world is possible!') – took on the appearance of an axiom, of a self-evident and unquestionable truth. For what were we doing in Seattle if not showing an alternative to a world that has been represented to us as lacking alternatives? There are many other examples, but each would belie a common theme: that the unjust, inequitable and violent limitations that are placed upon the many for the benefit of the few – the forces that separate us from our active power, from what we can do – are not unshakeable, immutable realities, but representations. When people begin to think and act otherwise, these representations begin to crack and splinter; when and if people ever grow tired of death, when and if they refuse death and come together as a massive tidal wave of *life*, these representations will be obliterated. Everything we have been told is real and unchangeable will be revealed as lies, and in refusing them we will make them change. Into what? No one knows, but that is not important. What is important is the change itself.

Politics is about power and political philosophy is a negotiation between power and images of power, between actual power relations and their capacity to become otherwise. So, too, political modernity, in both its liberal and socialist forms, is predicated precisely on the theoretical denial and practical suppression of possibilities. What it offers instead is a series of representations – of who we are as individuals and groups, of what we should and should not want, of what we can and cannot do or think or become. The anarchists of the nineteenth and early twentieth centuries were the first to launch a systematic attack on political modernity – not only by challenging its system of representational thoughts, practices and institutions, but by offering alternative ways of thinking and acting. In this they were followed by Nietzsche, Foucault, Deleuze, and countless others, all of whom, in his or her own way, have contributed to an ongoing struggle to move beyond modernity into postmodernity and anarchy, the process of thinking, acting and being otherwise. Much, much more needs to be said and written and *done* on this subject, but for the time being, I hope I have given us some sense of where we have been, where we are now, and where – with sufficient resolve and creativity and above all, *lebens-lieben* – we might go.

NOTES

1. May's book is based on an earlier piece entitled 'Is Post-Structuralist Political Theory Anarchist?' (1989). Similar works include Amster (1998), Carter and Morland (2004), Dempsey and Rowe (2004) and Sheehan (2003).
2. Though we ought not to underestimate Guattari's contributions to this and later works in political philosophy, I will only refer to Deleuze in the present chapter for purposes of clarity and convenience.
3. Consider Bakunin's famous aphorism, 'The destructive passion is also a creative passion.'
4. For further reading on normativity in general see Sosa and Villanueva (2005); Gert (2004); Dancy (2000); Kagan (1997).
5. For more on this distinction see especially Hursthouse (2002); McIntyre (1984); Slote and Crisp (1997).

6. As May notes, both developments pave the way for modern liberal democratic theory.
7. Cf. Nietzsche (1988; prologue, s.2); Nietzsche (1974: s.125).
8. See for example Nietzsche (1991; esp. s.3); Nietzsche (1988; esp. 'On the Old and New Tablets' and 'On Self Overcoming'); Nietzsche, 1969; esp. essay 2, ss.11–20).
9. See Foucault (1985; 1986).

REFERENCES

Amster, R. (1998). 'Anarchism as Moral Theory: Praxis, Property and the Postmodern'. *Anarchist Studies* 6(2): 97–112.
Bakunin, M. (1974). *Selected Writings* (A. Lehning, ed.; S. Cox and O. Stephens, trans.). New York: Grove Press.
—— (1972). *Bakunin on Anarchy* (S. Dolgoff, ed. and trans.). New York: Knopf.
—— (1953). *The Political Philosophy of Bakunin* (G.P. Maximoff, ed.). Glencoe, IL: Free Press.
Call, Lewis (2003). *Postmodern Anarchism*. Lanham, MD: Lexington Books.
Carter, J., and Morland, D. (2004). 'Anti-Capitalism: Are We All Anarchists Now?' In *Anti-Capitalist Britain* (J. Carter and D. Morland, eds). Gretton, Cheltenham: New Clarion Press.
Dancy, J. (2000). *Normativity*. London: Blackwell.
Deleuze, G. (1995). *Negotiations* (M. Joughin, trans.). New York: Columbia University Press.
—— (1992). 'What Is a "Dispositif"?' In *Michel Foucault: Philosopher* (T. Armstrong, trans.). New York: Routledge.
—— (1990). *Expressionism in Philosophy: Spinoza* (M. Joughin, trans.). New York: Zone Books.
—— (n.d.). 'Intellectuals and Power: A Conversation between Michel Foucault and Gilles Deleuze'. Retrieved 15 April 2010 from <http://libcom.org/library/intellectuals-power-a-conversation-between-michel-foucault-and-gilles-deleuze>.
—— and Guattari, F. (1994). *What is Philosophy?* (H. Tomlinson and G. Burchell, trans.). New York: Columbia University Press.
—— —— (1988). *Spinoza: Practical Philosophy* (R. Hurley, trans.). San Francisco: City Lights Books.
—— —— (1987). *A Thousand Plateaus* (B. Massumi, trans.). Minneapolis: University of Minnesota Press.
—— —— (1977). *Anti-Oedipus: Capitalism and Schizophrenia* (R. Hurley, M. Seem, and H.R. Lane, trans.). New York: Viking Press.
—— —— (1972). 'Deleuze et Guattari s'expliquent ...', *La Quinzaine Littéraire* 143 (June):16–30.
—— and Parnet, C. (1987). *Dialogues* (H. Tomlinson and B. Haberjam, trans.). New York: Columbia University Press.
Dempsey, J., and Rowe, J. (2004). 'Why Poststructuralism Is a Live Wire for the Left'. *Radical Theory/Critical Praxis: Making a Difference beyond the Academy?* (D. Fuller and R. Kitchin, eds). Praxis.
Ewing, A.C. (1947). *The Definition of Good*. London: Macmillan.
Feenberg, A., and Freedman, J. (2001). *When Poetry Ruled the Streets: The French May Events of 1968*. Albany, NY: SUNY Press.
Foucault, M. (2003). 'Technologies of the Self'. In *The Essential Foucault* (P. Rabinow and N. Rose, eds). New York: The New Press.
—— (1986). *The History of Sexuality, vol.3: The Care of the Self* (R. Hurley, trans.). New York: Random House.
—— (1985). *The History of Sexuality, vol.2: The Uses of Pleasure* (R. Hurley, trans.). New York: Random House.
—— (1978). *Discipline and Punish* (A. Sheridan, trans.). New York: Pantheon.
Gert, J. (2004). *Brute Rationality: Normativity and Human Action*. Cambridge: Cambridge University Press.
Goldman, Emma (1998). *Red Emma Speaks* (A.K. Shulman, ed.). New York: Humanity Books.
Hamon, H. (1989). ''68: The Rise and Fall of a Generation?' In *May '68* (D.L. Hanley and A.P. Kerr, eds). London: Macmillan Press.

Hursthouse, R. (2002). *On Virtue Ethics*. New York: Oxford University Press.

Kagan, S. (1997). *Normative Ethics*. Westview Press.

Korsgaard, C. (1996). *Sources of Normativity*. Cambridge: Cambridge University Press.

Kropotkin, Peter (2002). *Anarchism: A Collection of Revolutionary Writings* (R. Baldwin, ed.). New York: Dover.

—— (1970). *Kropotkin's Revolutionary Pamphlets* (R. Baldwin, ed.). New York: Dover.

—— (1924). *Ethics: Origins and Developments* (L. Friedland and J. Piroshnikoff, trans.). Dorset: Prism Press.

Lunn, E. (1973). *The Romantic Socialism of Gustav Landauer*. Berkeley: University of California Press.

Malatesta, Errico (2001). *Anarchy*. London: Freedom Press.

—— (1995). *The Anarchist Revolution*. London: Freedom Press.

—— (1965). *Life and Ideas* (V. Richards, ed.). London: Freedom Press.

McIntyre, A. (1984). *After Virtue*. Notre Dame, IN: University of Notre Dame Press.

Marx, K., and Engels, F. (1974). *The Marx–Engels Reader* (R. Tucker, ed.). New York: Norton.

May, Todd (2005). *Gilles Deleuze*. Cambridge: Cambridge University Press.

—— (1995). *The Moral Theory of Poststructuralism*. University Park, PA: Pennsylvania State University Press.

—— (1994). *The Political Philosophy of Poststructuralist Anarchism*. University Park, PA: Pennsylvania State University Press.

Nietzsche, F. (1991). *Daybreak* (R.J. Hollingdale, trans.). New York: Cambridge University Press.

—— (1988). *Thus Spake Zarathustra* (W. Kaufmann, trans.). New York: Penguin.

—— (1974). *The Gay Science* (W. Kaufmann, trans.). New York: Vintage Books.

—— (1969). *On the Genealogy of Morals* (W. Kaufmann and R.J. Hollingdale, trans.). New York: Vintage Books.

Newman, Saul (2001). *From Bakunin to Lacan: Anti-Authoritarianism and the Dislocation of Power*. Lanham, MD: Lexington Books.

Patton, P. (2000). *Deleuze and the Political*. New York: Routledge.

Proudhon, P.J. (1989). *Systems of Economical Contradictions*. London: Pluto Press.

Sheehan, S. (2003). *Anarchism*. London: Reaktion Books.

Slote, M., and Crisp, R. (1997). *Virtue Ethics*. New York: Oxford University Press.

Smith, D. (2003). 'Deleuze and the Liberal Tradition: Normativity, Freedom, and Judgment'. *Economy and Society* 32(2) (May): 299–324.

Sosa, E., and Villanueva, E. (2005). *Normativity*. London: Blackwell.

Spivak, G., and Ryan, M. (1978). 'Anarchism Revisited: A New Philosophy'. *Diacritics* (June): 66–79.

16
Imperfect Necessity and the Mechanical Continuation of Everyday Life: A Post-Anarchist Politics of Technology

Michael Truscello

In his recent book *Anarchy Alive! Anti-Authoritarian Politics from Practice to Theory*, Uri Gordon describes the 'curious ambivalence in contemporary anarchists' relationship with technology' (Gordon, 2008: 109).[1] On the one hand, contemporary anarchism has utilized global information communication technologies (ICT) to promote anti-authoritarian politics and to organize direct action against state-sponsored repression, also contributing various forms of hacktivism, electronic civil disobedience and culture jamming (Juris, 2008); on the other hand, anarcho-primitivism, a summary rejection of technology and the 'megamachine', remains a prominent expression of contemporary anarchism (for example, Jensen, 2006a, 2006b; Zerzan, 1994, 2002, 2005, 2008; Watson, 1997, 1998). Classical anarchism exhibited a similar ambivalence, 'oscillating between a bitter critique driven by the experiences of industrialism, and an almost naive optimism around scientific development and its enabling role in a post-capitalist society' (Gordon, 2008: 113). The question of technology in anarchism remains a pervasive but under-theorized topic. While the entire history of this ambivalence deserves a book-length study, in the limited space here I propose only to sketch elements of the contemporary ambivalence based on the prominence of anarcho-primitivism, and how that divide might be bridged by the concept of 'imperfect necessity' (Oleson, 2007).

On 11 September 2008, a jury in Britain decided that Greenpeace activists who damaged a coal-fired power station in Kent had a 'lawful excuse' to damage property to prevent the greater harm of global warming. In the United States and Canada, this defence is known as the 'doctrine of necessity'. J.C. Oleson says 'the radical potential of the [necessity] defence remains unrealized' (Oleson, 2007: 20); he calls necessity 'populist lightning in a jar, a fundamentally transformative legal force, a doctrine that casts a revolutionary shadow' (2007: 29–30). Necessity in the legal sense also has a potentially revolutionary *communicative* function:

> inasmuch as the necessity defence serves a communicative function – providing the defendant a solemn forum in which to espouse his views,

forcing a formal response from the government, and involving jurors and officers of the court in the debate over the legitimacy of the violated law – widespread availability of the imperfect necessity defence would also facilitate public dialogue of this kind. (Oleson, 2007: 39)

A derivation of the necessity defence, imperfect necessity, offers anarchists what I believe is a generative theoretical and pragmatic post-anarchist form of insurrection. Imperfect necessity frames agency in the post-structuralist sense of being distributed, through its graduation of culpability: 'Unlike a defense of perfect necessity, in which jurors must agree that the disobedient is either entirely guilty or altogether blameless, the defense of imperfect necessity admits the possibility of graduated culpability' (Oleson, 2007: 39). 'Imperfect necessity' and its correlative 'graduated culpability' offer anarchists epistemological and pragmatic possibilities for describing and overcoming the ambivalence towards technology in a decidedly post-anarchist social assemblage.

The concept of necessity in this discussion also refers to the means by which revolutionaries could survive in the context of continuing revolution. This meaning of necessity divided the earliest socialists and anarchists. Marxists proposed the state as the means by which necessity could be administered and revolution could persist, and anarchists offered the solution of free communities (Bookchin, 2004: 46). 'The problem of want and work', writes Bookchin, 'was never satisfactorily resolved by either body of doctrine in the last century' (2004: 47). Bookchin's own solution was 'social ecology', which required technology to 'replace the realm of necessity by the realm of freedom' (2004: 48), a proposal justifiably met with derision by anarcho-primitivists. The problem of necessity in the period of late capitalism is intimately bound to the problem of technology, since most people who live in industrial societies depend on massive technological systems for sustenance, and since the current population of the planet greatly surpasses the number that could be supported by living as hunter–gatherer societies, the primitivist ideal. To revolt against these technological systems from within industrial societies would seem to be an act of self-destruction; to preserve these systems would be equal folly. For anarchists, the problem of the technological society therefore necessitates a paradoxical solution.

'Imperfect necessity', one such paradoxical solution, guides this chapter in at least three significant ways: first, the phrase recognizes that life in industrial societies is so profoundly mediated by technology, or what Jacques Ellul called the 'total phenomenon' of *la technique*, that the existence of most individuals depends on it, and as a result, to oppose the total phenomenon, as anarcho-primitivists do, carries with it an almost suicidal or genocidal tendency (simultaneously, to endorse the total phenomenon without qualification is equally insane); therefore, despite the toxicity of modern technology, it may be *necessary* to embrace *some* technology while simultaneously opposing authoritarianism and promoting deindustrialization; second, 'imperfect necessity' signifies an epistemological condition in which socio-technical structures are contingent and path-dependent, and therefore the liminal spaces of anarchist resistance must adapt to indeterminate but historical and ideological forms of oppression; this *necessity* refers to the shifting but essential conditions that enable continuous insurrection; and finally, the phrase 'imperfect necessity' has a legalistic reality that presents an opportunity for opposition through constructs of the law, not to reinforce the statist hegemony of the law but rather to enact discursive stresses within the state and its hegemonic apparatus. Ultimately, the technological society must be contested paradoxically, through the limited use of technology in a pluralistic insurrection that advocates deindustrialization.

As Uri Gordon notes, 'Where mainstream critics ultimately fail [...] is in their respective agendas of technological democratization, and their ultimate reconciliation to technological modernity as a process that can be managed and controlled, but not fundamentally contested' (Gordon, 2008: 111). Below, I consider critics of technology who, while not always endorsing anarcho-primitivism, nonetheless show sympathy for the general programme of deindustrialization; these critics include David Watson, Bob Black, Langdon Winner and Uri Gordon.

The anarcho-primitivist movement – which contains within it a variety of anarchisms, such as anti-civilizationists, deep ecologists, revolutionary environmentalists and New Age mystics – is for some simply the most recent manifestation of Romanticism in the West; however, such a delimitation ignores the specificity of the contemporary milieu, especially the catastrophic forms of environmental degradation that are now well documented, and against which primitivists are unanimously aligned; and so a purely dismissive reading of anarcho-primitivism is imprudent. The contemporary expression of anarcho-primitivism can be traced to early twentieth-century thinkers such as Ellul and Lewis Mumford; however, its most visible dialogues emerged in the 1980s, with publications such as *Fifth Estate* (Millett, 2004). The movement promotes several basic premises: the 'reform' agenda of the left does not address the root problem of injustice, civilization itself, variously defined; the alienating features of civilization can be located in the advent of agriculture/domestication (or, for John Zerzan, in the emergence of symbolic culture); agricultural civilization enabled the division of labour and the rise of hierarchical political structures; a form of 'natural anarchy' existed when humans lived in hunter–gatherer societies, the 'original affluent societies', as described in the work of anthropologists Marshall Sahlins and Richard B. Lee. For most anarcho-primitivists, the technological society in which we now live in the West must be destroyed before it destroys us. Not all anarcho-primitivists advocate such an immediate and violent solution, however, and the latter part of this chapter will examine some of the more nuanced theories. A post-anarchist politics of technology should be open to multiple practices.

Anarcho-primitivists focused much of their critiques in the late 1990s on the social ecology of Murray Bookchin. Bookchin, a staunch critic of Ellul, Ernst Juenger, deep ecology and primitivism – what he famously described as 'lifestyle anarchism' (Bookchin, 1995) – saw technology as 'the basic structural support of a society' (ibid.: 43), and advocated for the embrace of technology to 'reawaken man's sense of dependence upon the environment' (ibid.: 64) by freeing humans from menial labour. Computer technology, he believed, 'is capable of taking over all the onerous and distinctly uncreative mental tasks of man in industry, science, engineering, information retrieval and transportation' (ibid.: 54). This decentralized technology would also be capable of satisfying a form of what Bookchin called libertarian municipalism. 'A technology for life', Bookchin wrote, 'would be *based* on the community; it must be tailored to the community and the regional level' (ibid.: 81; italics in original). Bookchin's social ecology was influential in environmentalist circles; it seemed to recognize and respond to the environmental crisis unfolding globally. However, his programme for social revolution through ecology smacked of techno-utopian delusion – dotting the countryside with more technology would somehow bring humans closer to nature? – and primitivists were quick to recognize Bookchin's problematic understanding of technology.

In *Beyond Bookchin: Preface for a Future Social Ecology*, neo-tribalist David Watson questioned the soundness of Bookchin's belief that the conditions for a free society could arise from 'technics created by modern industrial capitalism itself' (Watson, 1997: 119):

> It's simply confused to see a liberatory society as the unintended result of technics produced under capitalism, as Bookchin has done from the beginning, and then to paint technics as little more than the passive recipient of human intentions and interactions. (Ibid.: 120)

Bookchin places too much emphasis on the society in which technologies emerge (ibid.: 122), and a 'notion of a distinct realm of social relations that determines [this] technology is not only ahistorical and undialectical, it reflects a kind of simplistic base/superstructure schema' (ibid.: 124). Bookchin's view of progress 'proves indistinguishable from the familiar Marxist version' (ibid.: 129), and his depiction of labour-saving technology would be at home in the pages of Wired magazine.

Labour abolitionist Bob Black attacked Bookchin's reverence for work and demolished Bookchin's arguments for social ecology in his seminal post-left text, *Anarchy after Leftism* (1997). Black, who does not identify as a primitivist but believes there is much to learn from them (ibid.: 107), noted that the advance of technology tends to increase the quantity of work while decreasing the quality of the work experience: 'The higher the tech, the lower the wages and the smaller the work force' (ibid.: 134). Post-leftist anarchy is, unlike Bookchinism, if not necessarily rejective, then at least suspicious of 'the chronically unfulfilled liberatory promise of high technology' (ibid.:143–4).[2]

Murray Bookchin's faith in technology reflects a naive understanding of technology, one that foregrounds the society in which technology emerges over the ideologically productive capacity of technological systems; or, as David Watson writes, 'Reducing the problem to who will "use" technology is patently a version of the ideology of technological neutrality' (1997: 125);

one must recognize 'the social organization and dependencies generated by mass technics' (ibid.: 144). The 'neutrality' thesis was discredited by Langdon Winner, among others, in his classic work *Autonomous Technology: Technics-out-of-Control as a Theme in Political Thought* (1978). Winner recognized, following Ellul, that technology is a 'vast, diverse, ubiquitous totality that stands at the center of modern culture' (ibid.: 9), and, again following Ellul, that we must recognize the 'self-augmentation of technique', the 'elements of dynamism, necessity, and ineluctability built into the *origins* of the process' of technological rationality (ibid.: 65; italics in original).

The system of mass technics tends to drift in the direction of self-reinforcing development, a form of positive feedback. As Uri Gordon writes, 'The neutrality thesis has been rejected since it disregards how the technical or from-design structure of people's surroundings delimits their forms of conduct and relation' (2008: 115). In other words, 'There are times when a choice [concerning technological development] cannot be made and when the drift of events cannot be halted' (Winner, 1978: 71); at the same time, self-augmentation is not a process of absolute inevitability. The problem with contemporary studies of technology is that they too often place too much faith in the ability of individuals or groups to intervene and control technological systems.

Winner sees a paradox in the way technology evolves, a paradox he calls 'voluntary determinism' (1978: 99). This paradox describes the choices we make within a context of 'technological drift' (ibid.: 88). Technology heavily influences the constraints of our choices, it 'enforces limits upon the possible and the necessary' (ibid.: 81). Such constraints on our necessities and desires become 'highly specific' once a 'particular technical form' is adopted (ibid.: 84), which produces a condition of 'necessity through aimless drift' (ibid.: 89); ubiquitous computing in the West is an example of a specific technical form often dictating necessities and delimiting desires. Technology is never neutral; instead, it is 'an environment – a totality of means enclosing us in its automatism of need, production and exponential development' (Watson, 1998: 121). A post-anarchist politics of technology must theorize its limits – its necessities and desires – as inherently imperfect, discursively constructed within the flow of technological drift, never to be perfected in some utopian state of fixity. Winner recognized that the most powerful decisions in the technological society 'cope with necessities arising from an existing configuration of technical affairs' (1978: 258), in particular if those technical affairs affect the survival of individuals within the system (ibid.: 273).

Winner's sense of the futility of contemporary reforms to the technological society 30 years ago may also explain why 30 years after his classic text some anarchists have turned for answers, perhaps out of desperation, to primitivism. Winner suggested a form of 'epistemological Luddism', or a 'method of carefully and deliberately dismantling technologies', as 'one way of recovering the buried substance upon which our civilization rests' (ibid.: 330). David Watson suggests that Winner's Luddism could help us to break up the structures of daily life, and to take meaning back from the meaning-manufacturing apparatus of the mass media, renew a human discourse based on community, solidarity and reciprocity, and destroy the universal deference to machines, experts and information. (Watson, 1998: 145)

In a pedestrian sense, 'abolishing mass technics means *learning to live in a different way* – something societies have done in the past, and which they can learn to do again' (ibid.: 144; italics in original). To succeed, Watson argues, we need not attempt a literal return to past models such as the ancient Greeks or Native Americans; rather, we need to model our response to mass technics on 'the Greek emphasis on harmony, balance and moderation, and Indians' stubborn desire to resist dependence' (ibid.: 140).

Uri Gordon's position on technology is similarly 'very sympathetic' to the primitivist orientation, though he does not believe primitivism can be 'a basis for a broad-based approach' (2008: 110). His astute commentary on technology and anarchism is prefaced by an awkward navigation of the for-or-against-primitivism question, which concludes by 'remaining largely neutral towards' primitivism (ibid.: 110), an unsatisfying provision that appears largely because of the divisive quality of 'primitivism' within anarchist circles and not because of the primitivist ideas themselves. Gordon's excellent summary of anarchism and technology, which uses Winner as the foundation for contemporary anarchist ideas about technology, builds an anarchist politics of technology on the distinction between *technique*, defined here as a particular application of knowledge, and *technology*, defined as the recursive application of techniques (ibid.: 120). From the idea that technique must be extracted 'from its sublimation in progress' as a 'social project of rationalised surplus- and capacity-building', Gordon concludes that anarchists are 'going to have to bite the bullet' and embrace a 'retro-fitting process of decentralization that amounts to quite a significant roll-back of technology' (2008: 127). So, while Gordon prefaces his remarks on technology with a gesture of neutrality on primitivism, he nonetheless concludes that 'at least some measure of technological abolitionism must be brought into the horizon of anarchist politics' (ibid.: 128). Like Watson, Gordon also advocates the 'revival of traditional knowledge' (ibid.: 137).

The collective wisdom of Watson, Black, Winner and Gordon suggests a post-anarchist politics of technology based on imperfect necessity, based, that is, on the necessary programme of deindustrialization and decentralization combined with a 'disillusioned' use of some technology, as anti-authoritarian movements attempt to dissociate themselves from technological dependence and provide sustenance with as little connection as possible to the necessities produced by 'aimless [technological] drift'. (Philosopher John Clark provides a more detailed list of the qualities of potential anarchist technologies; see Clark, 1985: 197.)

Naturally, this is not the first time activists and scholars have promoted the concept of technology in harmony with nature. Clark, for example, checklists a host of famous theories that demand consonance between human beings and nature: 'what Illich calls "convivial tools", Schumacher labels "intermediate technology", and Bookchin (perhaps most adequately) describes as "liberatory technology", or "ecotechnology"' (ibid.: 196). The primary difference between these theories and a post-anarchist politics of technology is the anti-humanist and anti-foundationalist suppositions of post-anarchism, important distinctions at least for the ways in which they make possible an affinity between post-anarchist technologies and the biocentricity of revolutionary environmentalism (Best and Nocella, 2006).

While Bookchin's understanding of technology foregrounds the society in which it emerges, and posits an essentially humanist teleology as the end point of progress – 'the real issue we face today is [...] whether [technology] can help to *humanize* society' (Bookchin, 2004: 48; italics in original) – a post-anarchist politics of technology, with elements of the anarcho-primitivist critique, would correct these oversights by articulating a distinctly historical, socio-technical and anti-humanist model of technological development. The post-structuralist approach of most post-anarchism provides a sound theoretical foundation for exploring technology in a global context. Like contemporary post-structuralist understandings of technology, post-anarchism maintains that there is no centre of power, only intersecting practices of power (May, 1994: 11). But there are also radical potentialities in a post-anarchist reading of technology based on its anti-foundationalism and anti-humanism. The principal feature I wish to add to these theorizations is what might be called *the neo-primitivist tactic*, the possibility that one reason to engage technology is to be better able to abolish or destroy it. This, of course, is just a short-term tactic, not a long-term strategy, which should include, I believe, characteristics of what Michael Schmidt and Lucien van der Walt call 'mass anarchism' (2009: 20).

In the primitivist ethos of John Zerzan, postmodern/post-structuralist thought, such as that of Fuller, Wark and Guattari, is antithetical to all that is natural, ethical and intimate. His distaste for postmodern culture occasionally leads to caricature, and often produces selective readings. For Zerzan,

postmodernism [...] bears the imprint of a period of conservatism and lowered expectations [...] Postmodernism tells us that we can't grasp the whole, indeed that the desire for an overview of what's going on out there is unhealthy and suspect, even totalitarian [...] Skeptical about the claims and results of previous systems of thought, postmodernism has in fact jettisoned pretty nearly all desire or hope of making sense of reality as we experience it. PM abandons the 'arrogance' of trying to figure out the origins, logic, causality, or structure of the world we live in [...] Postmodernism celebrates evanescent flows, a state of no boundaries, the transgressive. In the actual world, however, this translates as an embrace of the unimpeded movement of capital, the experience of consumer novelty [...] The political counterpart of postmodernism is pragmatism, the tired liberalism that accommodates itself to the debased norm. (2002: 165–7)

While it is true that postmodernism is sceptical of metanarratives (Lyotard, 1984), often associating epistemological totality with totalitarianism, it is absurd to equate all forms of scepticism, even philosophical relativism, with complete detachment from any kind of material reality or application. Zerzan reduces an extensive philosophical tradition, which can be traced to the ancient Sophists or Hume or Nietzsche, to a pithy insult. For example, Zerzan claims, 'Postmodernism is predicated on the thesis that the all-enveloping symbolic atmosphere, foundationless and inescapable, is made up of shifting, indeterminate signifiers that can never establish firm meaning' (2008: 73). Contrary to Zerzan's central contention about postmodernism, it is not a defeatist ethos that unravels meaning into nihilism; instead, as arch-deconstructionist Jacques Derrida wrote, '[r]ather than destroying, it was also necessary to understand how an "ensemble" was constituted and to reconstruct it to this end' (Derrida, 1988: 2). In some ways the anarcho-primitivist dispute over technology and postmodernism shares the same dynamics as the so-called Science Wars of the 1990s, a battle of the books which culminated in Alan Sokal's hoax (Truscello, 2001). Ultimately, for Zerzan, there is only one meaningful question: Are you on the side of Nature? For post-anarchism, there is more than one answer.

A German journalist frustrated by the inability of conscientious Germans to stop Nazism in the 1930s attributed this inability to the 'mechanical continuation of normal daily life' (quoted in Scott, 2007: 243–4). I hope this phrase resonates for anarchists and their ambivalence over technology in at least two ways: first, mechanical can mean 'routine' or 'unreflexive', and a post-anarchist politics of technology should be disruptive, creative and reflexive; second, 'mechanical continuation' can refer to the pervasive reach of massive complex technological systems in industrial societies, and this situation appears to be the primary, though not singular, barrier to real anti-authoritarian opposition in the West. The technicity of everyday life, the naturalization of complex technological systems, the *total phenomenon* of the technological society, cannot be critiqued and dismantled from a single position of insurrection, but must instead be confronted from multiple, disparate nodes in a network of communicative and strategic orientation. In industrial societies, only a multiplicity of mechanical discontinuities in everyday life can foster conditions consonant with anarchist politics. The phrase with which I introduced this topic and guided this chapter – imperfect necessity – encapsulates an orientation toward socio-technical authoritarian discourse and design; 'imperfect necessity' is a paradoxical totalizing *tendency* rather than a categorical fixity; in this sense, imperfect necessity may have much in common with Saul Newman's concept of 'unstable universalities', which he sees as the indicative logic of the anti-corporate globalization movement (Newman, 2007: 181). Keeping in mind this tendency, the inclination of a post-anarchist trajectory should converge with at least two essential but neglected discourses: the congruence of anarchism, anti-corporate globalization and environmentalism (Curran, 2006); and Third World environmentalism (Peritore, 1999; Guha, 2000). The anarcho-primitivist orientation is a flawed but important component of contemporary anarchist discourses on technology; but its suppositions suffer from a preponderance of Western white privilege, an idealization of hunter–gatherer societies (Bird-David, 1992; Kaplan, 2000), and a deficit of pragmatic thought.

NOTES

1. I wish to thank Rob Glover, who introduced me to the writings of John Zerzan; Karl Wierzbicki, who introduced me to the writings of Hakim Bey; and Duane Rousselle, whose comments enriched the content of this article.
2. Black's post-left anarchism converges with post-anarchism in at least one broad sense, the belief that the tactics and ideas of the left have demonstrably failed and are inadequate to contemporary forms of oppression. At times primitivists seem to echo the failures of the left, rather than transcend them. For example, post-anarchists recommend multiple points of insurrection, rather than traditional single-issue opposition. In the anarcho-primitivist camp, conversely, one finds unsettling examples of this critique of identity politics taken too far.

REFERENCES

Best, Steven, and Nocella, Anthony J. II (2006). 'A Fire in the Belly of the Beast: The Emergence of Revolutionary Environmentalism'. In Steven Best and Anthony J. Nocella II (eds). *Igniting a Revolution: Voices in Defense of the Earth*. Oakland, CA: AK Press.
Bird-David, N. (1992). 'Beyond the "Original Affluent Society": A Culturalist Reformation'. *Current Anthropology* 33(1): 25–47.
Black, Bob (1997). *Anarchy after Leftism*. Columbia, MO: Columbia Alternative Library.
Bookchin, Murray (2004). *Post-Scarcity Anarchism*. Oakland, CA: AK Press.
—— (1995). *Social Anarchism or Lifestyle Anarchism: An Unbridgeable Chasm*. Oakland, CA: AK Press.
Clark, John (1985). *The Anarchist Moment: Reflections on Culture, Nature and Power*. Montreal: Black Rose Books.
Curran, G. (2006). *21st Century Dissent: Anarchism, Anti-Globalization and Environmentalism*. Houndmills: Palgrave Macmillan.
Derrida, Jacques (1988). 'Letter to a Japanese Friend'. In D. Wood and R. Bernasconi (eds). *Derrida and Difference*. Evanston IL: Northwestern University Press.
Gordon, Uri (2008). *Anarchy Alive! Anti-Authoritarian Politics from Practice to Theory*. Ann Arbor, MI: Pluto Press.
Guha, Ramachandra (2000). *Environmentalism: A Global History*. New York: Longman.
Jensen, Derrick (2006a). *Endgame, vol.1: The Problem of Civilization*. New York: Seven Stories Press.
—— (2006b). *Endgame, vol.2: Resistance*. New York: Seven Stories Press.
Juris, Jeffery S. (2008). *Networking Futures: The Movements against Corporate Globalization*. Durham, NC: Duke University Press.
Kaplan, D. (2000). 'The Darker Side of the "Original Affluent Society"'. *Journal of Anthropological Research* 56(3): 301–24.
Lyotard, Jean-Francois (1984). *The Postmodern Condition: A Report on Knowledge*. Manchester: Manchester University Press.
May, Todd (1994). *The Political Philosophy of Poststructuralist Anarchism*. University Park, PA: Pennsylvania State University Press.
Millett, Steve (2004). 'Technology is Capital: *Fifth Estate*'s Critique of the Megamachine'. In J. Purkis and J. Bowen (eds). *Changing Anarchism: Anarchist Theory and Practice in a Global Age*. Manchester: Manchester University Press.
Newman, Saul (2007). *Unstable Universalities: Poststructuralism and Radical Politics*. Manchester, UK: Manchester University Press.

Oleson, J.C. (2007). 'Drown the World: Imperfect Necessity and Total Cultural Revolution', *Unbound* 3(19): 20–104.

Peritore, N. Patrick (1999). *Third World Environmentalism: Case Studies from the Global South*. Gainesville, FL: University Press of Florida.

Schmidt, Michael, and Walt, Lucien van der (2009). *Black Flame: The Revolutionary Class Politics of Anarchism and Syndicalism*. Oakland, CA: AK Press.

Scott, Peter Dale (2007). *The Road to 9/11: Wealth, Empire and the Future of America*. Berkeley: University of California Press.

Truscello, Michael (2001). 'The Clothing of the American Mind: The Rhetorical Construction of Scientific Ethos in the Science Wars'. *Rhetoric Review* 20(3/4): 329–50.

Watson, David (1998). *Against The Megamachine*. Brooklyn, NY: Autonomedia.

—— (1997). *Beyond Bookchin: Preface for a Future Social Ecology*. Brooklyn, NY: Autonomedia.

Winner, Langdon (1978). *Autonomous Technology: Technics-out-of-Control as a Theme in Political Thought*. Cambridge, MA: MIT Press.

Zerzan, John (2008). *Twilight of the Machines*. Los Angeles: Feral House.

—— (2005). *Against Civilization: Readings and Reflections*. Los Angeles: Feral House.

—— (2002). *Running on Emptiness: The Pathology of Civilization*. Los Angeles: Feral House.

Contributors

Jason Adams is a Ph.D. candidate in political science at the University of Hawaii and in media and communications at the European Graduate School. He hosts the post-anarchism listserv, home to some of today's most influential anarchist and post-structuralist thinkers. He also created and hosts the Postanarchism Clearinghouse web site. Two of his pieces will also be published in the German and Spanish post-anarchism anthologies.

Alan Antliff, Canada Research Chair in art history at the University of Victoria, is author of *Anarchist Modernism: Art, Politics, and the First American Avant-Garde* (2001) and *Art and Anarchy: From the Paris Commune to the Fall of the Berlin Wall* (2007), and editor of *Only a Beginning* (2004), which is a documentary anthology of anarchist writings and activism in Canada.

Hilton Bertalan is a doctoral candidate in sociology at York University. His interests include sexuality, queer theory, global justice movements, post-structuralist theory, love, and the connections these areas have with, and may 'learn' from, anarchism.

Hakim Bey has written histories of piracy, Sufism, the 'Assassins', and spiritual anarchism in colonial America, including *Pirate Utopias* (Autonomedia, 1997), *Sacred Drift: Essays on the Margins of Islam* (City Lights, 1993) and *Scandal: Essays in Islamic Heresy* (Autonomedia, 1993).

Lewis Call is assistant professor of history at California Polytechnic State University, San Luis Obispo. He is an associate editor for the journal *Anarchist Studies*. He is the author of *Postmodern Anarchism* (Lexington Books, 2002). He has written extensively about post-anarchist science fiction, exploring post-anarchist themes in the novels of Ursula K. Le Guin, the film *V for Vendetta*, and the television series *Battlestar Galactica*. He received the 2007 Mr Pointy Award for best article in the field of Buffy Studies.

Richard J.F. Day is an associate professor at Queen's University (Canada). Richard's Ph.D. thesis was published by the University of Toronto Press as *Multiculturalism and the History of Canadian Diversity* (2000). His subsequent work focuses on the broader question of the articulation of social subjects with group identities, such as those offered up by nations, states and capitalist corporations. One of his latest and most critically received books was *Gramsci Is Dead: Anarchist Currents in the Newest Social Movements* (Between the Lines, 2005). He maintains a commitment to strengthening cooperative forms of social organization wherever and whenever possible.

Süreyyya Evren is a writer working on literature, contemporary art and radical politics, with a particular focus on Turkish post-structuralist anarchism. He is a postgraduate researcher at Loughborough University and contributes to such journals as *New Formulations, Anarchist Studies, Framework, Springerin* and, more recently, *Fifth Estate*. He is currently editor-in-chief of *Siyahi*, a magazine which acts as a platform for contemporary theory, culture, art and politics.

Antón Fernández de Rota is a researcher in anthropology and sociology at the Universidade da Coruña. He is interested in the study of subjectivity, identity, post-structuralism and social movements.

Benjamin Franks is a lecturer in political and social philosophy at the University of Glasgow, where his lecture themes include 'Imagined Futures', exploring the relation between science fiction and utopian thought. One of his most popular books has been *Rebel Alliances: The Means and Ends of Contemporary British Anarchisms* (AK Press, 2006).

Jamie Heckert is a political activist and author of various works on anarchism and sexuality. He is involved in a number of projects including the Knowledge Labs, a series of research events based around 'open source' principles. He received his Ph.D. from the University of Edinburgh in 2005 for his research into an anarchist critique of sexual orientation as the continuous effect of everyday state-like relationships of representation.

Sandra Jeppesen is a Toronto-based anarchist activist and writer. She received her Ph.D. in English language and literature in 2005 from York University and is currently a professor at Concordia University.

Nathan Jun is assistant professor of philosophy and coordinator of the philosophy programme at Midwestern State University in Wichita Falls, Texas. He is co-editor of *New Perspectives on Anarchism* (with Shane Wahl, 2009) and *Deleuze and Ethics* (with Daniel Smith, 2010).

Andrew M. Koch is currently an associate professor of political philosophy at Appalachian State University in Boone, North Carolina. He is the author of a number of works on anarchism, post-structuralism, and the links between epistemology and political ideas. One of his more recent contributions appeared in the widely discussed Autonomedia publication *I Am Not a Man, I Am Dynamite!* (2005). Another recent work is *Knowledge and Social Construction* (Lexington Books, 2005).

Todd May obtained his Ph.D. from Penn State University in 1989 and has since been Lemon professor of philosophy at Clemson University. He is best known for his role in developing the political philosophy of post-anarchism, alongside Saul Newman. His 1994 book *The Political Philosophy of Poststructuralist Anarchism* (Penn State Press) was the first work, since his 1989 submission to *Philosophy and Social Criticism* 'Is poststructuralist political theory anarchist?', to explicitly combine post-structuralist and anarchist theory. His other acclaimed philosophical books focus on the work of Michel Foucault, Gilles Deleuze and, more recently, Jacques Rancière. His work is said to seek a connection between the Anglo-American and continental styles of philosophy that developed in the early twentieth century.

Tadzio Mueller is a lecturer in political science, international relations and international political economy in the social sciences department at the University of Kassel. He holds a D.Phil. in international relations from the University of Sussex, Brighton (2007); his thesis *Other Worlds, Other Values: Alternative Practices in the European Anticapitalist Movement* was supported by the British Economic and Social Research Council. Alongside his scholarly work, he also maintains an active commitment within the alter-globalization movement.

Saul Newman is a research associate in politics at the University of Western Australia. His research is in the area of radical political and social theory, particularly that which is informed by perspectives such as post-structuralism, discourse analysis and psychoanalytic theory. He has written such books as *From Bakunin to Lacan: Anti-Authoritarianism and the Dislocation of Power* (Lexington, 2001), *Power and Politics in Poststructuralist Thought: New Theories of the Political* (Routledge, 2005) and *Unstable Universalities: Postmodernity and Radical Politics* (Manchester University Press, 2007). He has also written about Stirner, Foucault, Nietzsche and Deleuze. His newest book, from Edinburgh University Press, is entitled *The Politics of Postanarchism*.

Duane Rousselle is the founder and editor of the journal *Anarchist Developments in Cultural Studies* and a librarian for 'The Anarchist Library' project. He has published in the *International Journal of Žižek Studies*.

Michael Truscello is an assistant professor of English at Mount Royal University in Calgary. His publications appear in journals such as *Postmodern Culture*, *Technical Communication Quarterly*, *Rhetoric Review*, *TEXT Technology*, and *Cultural Critique*. He is currently at work on a book-length study of the role of technology in the anarchist tradition.

Index

Printed and bound by CPI Group (UK) Ltd, Croydon, CR0 4YY

16/04/2025

14658482-0004